W9-AZK-006

INFANCY

LINDA SMOLAK

Kenyon College

Prentice-Hall, Englewood Cliffs, New Jersey 07632

Library of Congress Cataloging-in-Publication Data

Smolak, Linda, (date)
    Infancy.

    Bibliography: p. 261
    Incudes index.
    1. Infants—Development.   I. Title.
RJ134.M87 1986   612'.654   85-21757
ISBN   0-13-464322-4

Editorial/production supervision and
    interior design: Marianne Peters
Cover design: Wanda Lubelska Design
Cover photo: Teri Stratford
Manufacturing buyer: Barbara Kelly Kittle

© 1986 by Prentice-Hall
A Division of Simon & Schuster, Inc.
Englewood Cliffs, New Jersey 07632

All rights reserved. No part of this book may be
reproduced, in any form or by any means,
without permission in writing from the publisher.

Printed in the United States of America

10   9   8   7   6   5   4   3   2

ISBN   0-13-464322-4   01

Prentice-Hall International (UK) Limited, *London*
Prentice-Hall of Australia Pty. Limited, *Sydney*
Prentice-Hall Canada Inc., *Toronto*
Prentice-Hall Hispanoamerican, S.A., *Mexico*
Prentice-Hall of India Private Limited, *New Delhi*
Prentice-Hall of Japan, Inc., *Tokyo*
Prentice-Hall of Southeast Asia Pte. Ltd., *Singapore*
Editora Prentice-Hall do Brasil, Ltda., *Rio de Janeiro*
Whitehall Books Limited, *Wellington, New Zealand*

To Marsha Weinraub
who initiated my professional interest in infancy
and to Marlyce Lagalo
who showed me the practical side of infant development.

Contents

Preface

Few things in life are more exciting than having a baby. Yet few things are also more challenging than raising a baby. The demands of parenting a young child are tremendous. The pressure has only intensified in recent years as we become increasingly convinced that infancy is a "special time" that influences, if not determines, future development.

Yet, few, if any, of us have a good understanding of infants and their development. We often underestimate or overestimate their capabilities. These errors influence our parenting, teaching, and care of babies. Similarly, our treatment of babies may be influenced by our misperceptions of our own effects upon their development.

My goal in writing this book was to clear up some of those misperceptions. Although we have a long way to go before we truly "understand" infants, we have accumulated a substantial amount of information about their abilities and development. We know how well they see and hear, how their development is influenced by prenatal development, the path of their language development, and so on. This book catalogues such information.

A listing alone would be of very limited value, however. The book therefore also includes considerable information about the whys and hows of development. This information is much less definitive than our knowledge of the actual behaviors. So, we have to be careful how we interpret these explanations. With this in mind, I have tried to present critical evaluations of the major theories of infant development. These critiques include, of course, some consideration of methodological issues.

As you read this book, you will encounter numerous boxes and tables intended to clarify some of these methodological issues. You will also find boxes and tables (as well as sections of the text) that are meant to demonstrate how our knowledge of infant development can be applied at home, in day-care centers, and so on. Again, these are included to try to counteract many of our misconceptions about infancy and infant development.

Gathering the information for and writing this book has, of course, been a large undertaking. It could not have been completed without the encouragement and support of many people. Thanks are due first to the people at Prentice-Hall. Bob Thorensen first suggested that I write this book and has provided continued interest throughout the project. John Isley and Susan Willig served as patient, helpful editors throughout.

My colleagues at Kenyon College have also been supportive, particularly Michael Levine, Mary Suydam, and Judy Smith, who never allowed me to give up hope that this manuscript would someday be completed. My mentor, Marsha Weinraub of Temple University, also provided practical, as well as emotional, support.

As the work progressed, my reviewers provided helpful, insightful comments. The following people substantially influenced the final product and deserve special thanks: Jay Belsky of Pennsylvania State University, Belinda Blevins of the University of Arkansas at Little Rock, John R. Cryan of the University of Toledo, Carol Gray of the University of Washington, Bryan Robinson of the University of North Carolina at Charlotte, Barbara Rogoff of the University of Utah, and Marguerite Stevenson of the University of Wisconsin.

Finally, I want to thank my daughter, Marlyce. She tolerated having to explain why there were always books all over the floor. And she heard "wait one more minute" more times than she thought was possible. Her humor and patience were continual sources of inspiration and served as quiet testimony to the adaptability of young children.

1

Issues in the Study of Infancy

When a baby is born, her parents often have a lot of questions. What can my baby do right now? Can she see or hear? When will she walk and talk? How should I treat her? Should I let her cry or should I run to her when she's upset? Should I follow my mother's advice and put the baby on a feeding schedule or should I take my La Leche advisor's recommendation and let the baby nurse whenever she wants to? How much does it matter what I do? After all, at least some of the baby's talents and characteristics are inborn, aren't they? When should I start teaching my baby the alphabet? The questions are almost endless.

Many of these questions will be addressed in this book. The more specific questions—those on visual functioning and no language development, for example—will be considered in later chapters. But, in general, these questions really reflect the four broad issues in infant development to be examined in this introductory chapter.

The first issue is how our conceptualization of infancy has changed in recent years. This is important because many new parents are confused by conflicting advice given by their own parents and by their friends. The second issue concerns the importance of infancy as a foundation for later development. Increasingly, the popular press seems to be suggesting that infancy is a particularly ripe time for learning (for example, *Time*, 1983). New parents need to know whether infancy truly presents a unique opportunity for learning. They also need to know whether negative effects occurring during infancy are irreversible.

The third issue is the question of whether a child's characteristics are inborn or acquired. This is the core question of the nature-nurture controversy. Parents want to know what aspects of their children's development they can influence. They also want to know how to "make the best" of their children's inborn talents and characteristics.

The final issue concerns the concept of the "average child." Despite our best intentions, we all compare our children's development to that of other children. How do we know what "average" is? And what deviations from "average" are acceptable? This is the question of normative data vs. individual differences.

These four issues are the focus of this chapter. As will be the case throughout the book, the emphasis is on the infancy period, the first 2 years of life. Let's begin by examining how our conceptualization of those first 2 years has changed during the twentieth century.

CONCEPTUALIZATIONS OF INFANCY:
PAST AND PRESENT

In 1928, John Watson became the first psychologist to publish a parenting manual for the mothers of infants. Watson told mothers that infants were "made, not born." He believed that all infants were essentially the same at birth. His instructions to mothers were strict and, by today's standards, rigid. He said, for example, that mothers should not kiss their babies too much, nor rock them, or in any other way "spoil" them with affection. Serious toilet training was to start at age 8 months. Thumbsucking was to be discouraged right from the start. If your child was still doing any thumbsucking (even in his sleep) at 12 months, Watson suggested keeping his hands in fingerless mittens continuously (even at night) for 2 weeks.

How times have changed! In his opening chapter, Benjamin Spock (1977) tells parents that "some children are more difficult" than others. He suggests rocking the baby. Toilet training is to be delayed until the child shows signs of "readiness," usually somewhere between 18 and 24 months. Dr. Spock interprets thumbsucking as a sign that the baby needs more "sucking" (feeding) time. He specifically advises against the use of hand restraints (such as Watson's mittens), for he thinks they frustrate the baby in her attempts to explore the world.

The differences between Watson and Spock exemplify our changing view of infancy. Let us examine four specific ways our conceptualization of infants and infancy has changed during this century. These four issues form the core of our current view of infancy (Yarrow, 1979).

Infant Competence.   First, our view of infant abilities, or *infant competence*, has changed dramatically. As recently as the 1960s, people thought of infants as being minimally aware of their surroundings. In fact, when a friend of mine had a baby in 1975, she asked me when he would be able to hear her voice.

We now know that babies not only can hear when they are born but also can see, smell, and in fact, use all their senses. More importantly, the baby's senses work to organize the world in a sensible, meaningful way. Even young babies, for example, can recognize their mother's voices (DeCasper & Fifer, 1980). They also seem to process language differently than other sounds, such as music (for example, Molfese, Freeman & Palermo, 1975). As we shall see throughout this book, newborns and infants possess an often surprising range of abilities.

The ability to respond to and engage in social interaction is another area of infant competence. We used to think of infants as almost less than human because of their apparently limited social competence. In fact, the term *infant* comes from a Latin root and means "without language." In other words, the word *infant* itself seems to emphasize babies' limited interactional capabilities.

In recent years, however, it has become clear that infants can and do possess social skills. Four-month-olds can distinguish sad faces from surprised expressions. Young infants show facial expressions and gestures that are remarkably adultlike when they are engaged in "conversation" (Trevarthen, 1979). In addition, babies will work hard to reinstate an interrupted interaction. These examples represent only a fraction of the infant's abilities in the social realm.

Early Experience. Our impression of the competence of the infant is not the only way our image of infants has changed. We have now given a special importance to infant experiences. Many people believe that early experience can shape all of our life. We probably owe our view about the importance of childhood to Freud. However, the work of many other developmental researchers has cemented this view. Harry Harlow's (for example, 1959) work with monkeys demonstrated that the lack of a mother during infancy could have long-term effects. Monkeys raised without their mothers had such poor social skills as adults that they were virtually nonfunctional. The work of Rene Spitz (for example, 1945/1973) and John Bowlby (1951) with infants deprived of mothering seemed to confirm these findings. This emphasis on *early experience* is not restricted to social or emotional functioning. Many theorists, including Jean Piaget, view the first 2 years as crucial for mental development.

We need to be careful not to overstate the case here. As Michael Rutter (1979) has noted, early experience is not necessarily a determinant of all future development. Certainly part of its power lies in the fact that most of us continue to develop in the same environment we started out in. So, if we are "neglected" as infants we are also likely to be neglected as toddlers, preschoolers, children, and adolescents. As we shall see when we discuss the nature-nurture controversy, even the most severe deprivation can be at least partially reversed with a dramatic change in environment.

Parent-Infant Interaction. The third area in which our perception of the infant has changed is in terms of the parent-infant relationship. There are several ways in which this has changed. We have come increasingly to emphasize the psychological care of the infant. Many communities now have "infant stimulation" programs, where new parents can learn how to encourage their child's development in such diverse areas as language, self-esteem, and intellectual functioning. Jerome Kagan (1979) has pointed out that this is partially because parents need to spend less time worrying about their children's physical well-being than did previous generations.

Another change in our understanding of the parent-infant relationship is indicated by our choice of terminology. Notice that we are using the term *parent-infant* rather than *mother-infant*. Numerous researchers, especially Michael Lamb (for example, 1978) and Ross Parke (for example, 1979), have demonstrated that not only are fathers adequate caregivers but they make a unique contribution to child development as well.

Ecological Validity.   Finally, there is increasing emphasis on how babies react in real-world situations with real caregivers (for example, Bronfenbrenner, 1977). It is not enough to know how babies behave in laboratories. This doesn't mean that laboratory data are useless. It means that if we are to understand infant behavior and development, we need to know how it is affected by its environmental context. The more "real" the context within which a behavior is examined, the more *ecologically valid* we say the research is.

So, our current view differs in many ways from that of Watson and his contemporaries. We now view the infant as a complex, interactive, competent being. Every infant is unique and is growing up in a unique environment. This environment includes both mother and father. Examining the total ecology of the child is now viewed as crucial to understanding infant development. As our knowledge of infant behavior accumulates, this view may change. However, it is certainly a sophisticated, complex model which should serve us well for many years.

THE ROLE OF INFANCY IN DEVELOPMENT

Many major theorists view infancy as a unique stage of development. Jean Piaget (1954), for example, believed that infant thought was qualitatively different from thought at any other stage. This means, he argued, that infants do not simply know less than older people. Instead, they know it differently. According to Piaget, infants organize and interpret the world in an action-oriented, here-and-now fashion. They do not have the ability to picture objects mentally the way children and adults do. Their knowledge of objects is "sensorimotor." It is limited to their immediate sensory and motoric interaction with the objects.

Erik Erikson (1959/1980) also views infancy as different from other periods of development. He proposed an eight stage theory of personality development. At each stage, the person faces a different crisis that must be resolved. In infancy, the crisis is trust vs. mistrust. Erikson argues that the infant must develop a sense of trust in the world: The baby must come to believe that the world is a safe and interesting place. Without such trust, the child's development will be permanently impaired. When this crisis is resolved, the child then moves on to the next crisis. There is, in other words, a shift in focus from one stage of development to the next.

Both Piaget and Erikson are *stage theorists*. They believe that development can be demarcated into distinct periods. Distinctions among th stages do not simply rest on age differences. Rather, though each stage has its own unique characteristics, each stage builds upon the preceding stages. So, for example, one cannot reach Piaget's final stage of formal operations without first passing through three other stages. This implies that for Piaget and Erikson (as well as for other stage theorists) the first stage is the foundation for all later development. The infancy period is therefore of great importance. If development during infancy is abnormal, the child's future development will be impaired unless the "damage" is corrected later.

Not all theorists believe in stages. Some, like B.F. Skinner, argue that the infant learns in the same way as all other humans. Even in these theories, however, infancy is important. The infant's experiences still provide the first building blocks of development. The difference here lies in terms of the nature of the foundation rather than in the importance of infancy.

Having established a sense of what we believe infancy is and why it is important, let's now consider what might "cause" infant behavior and development.

THE NATURE-NURTURE CONTROVERSY

Whenever people read about a mass murderer like Charles Manson, they always wonder whether he was born that way or whether "something happened" to make him that way. We are often curious about the roots of a person's behavior. Even when we describe ourselves, we say things like "My dad had trouble with math too" or "I have my mom's sense of humor." The question is, were we born with the behavior or did we learn it?

Nature or Nurture?   This question of whether a behavior is inborn or learned is often referred to as *the nature-nurture controversy*. Traditionally, the *nature theorists* argue that behaviors are innate, that is, inborn. These theorists, who are also known as maturationalists, believe that the bases for behavior are present at birth. As development proceeds, the behaviors simply unfold. The behaviors may be due to genetic, evolutionary, or prenatal (prebirth) influences. A baby may be irritable, for example, because she inherited the trait from her parents or because her mother was under a good deal of stress during pregnancy. The point is that the characteristic is present when the child is born.

Noam Chomsky's (1957) theory of language-development exemplifies the nature position. He believes we are born with a structure called the Language Acquisition Device (LAD), which is present in all human beings. Its role is to enable us to learn grammar. According to Chomsky, simply hearing language "triggers" the LAD. Thus, in Chomsky's theory the environment does have to stimulate the LAD.

Indeed, in most maturational theories the environment has a small role. The most important components of the behavior, however, are considered to be innate.

Nurture theorists, on the other hand, minimize the role of innate structures. They emphasize the importance of the environment in determining behaviors. Parents, siblings, social class, schools, and television are all examples of environmental influences. They are all things external to the child that may shape her behavior. The child is viewed as a *tabula rasa*, or blank slate, waiting to be written upon. At birth, she has few, if any, characteristics seen as being important to her individual development. This view is sometimes referred to as the environmental-learning model.

B.F. Skinner is a well-known proponent of this model. Skinner (1974) believes that almost all behaviors are learned through reinforcement. If we are rewarded ("positive reinforcement") for a behavior, we are more likely to perform that behavior again. For example, if you give your child a cookie when he uses the potty chair, he should want to use the potty chair again. Punishment should reduce the chance that a behavior will recur. These principles are used everyday by parents in teaching and disciplining their children. Skinner believes that these principles can explain the development of language, sex-role concepts, perception, and virtually any other behavior.

Interactionism.   Noam Chomsky and B.F. Skinner represent the extremes in the nature-nurture debate. In a way, they are trying to answer the question of whether behavior is innate *or* learned. Most modern developmentalists are no longer trying to answer that question. They believe that behavior is too complex to be completely inborn or completely a result of environmental influences. Rather, they believe that nature and nurture *interact* to produce behavior. Many prominent developmental theorists, including Jean Piaget and Erik Erikson, are *interactionists*. They believe that the characteristics of the child work together with the environment to determine the rate and final outcome of the child's development.

A specific example might help us to understand how the characteristics of the child might interact with the environment to determine a child's development. Jarmila Koluchova (1976) described a case of twin boys in Czechoslovakia whose mother died shortly after they were born. For the first 11 months of their lives they lived in a children's home. At that time, their overall development appeared normal. When their father remarried, the boys went to live with him and his "new family." For about 5½ years the boys lived in deplorable conditions: They lived in a closet with only a few building bricks for toys. The only furniture in the closet was a small table. They slept on the floor. They were severely beaten regularly, sometimes to the point of unconsciousness. The boys were malnourished. They had virtually no contact with people.

When they were found at age 8, they seemed to be mentally retarded. They functioned at a level comparable to that of most 3-year-olds. They were taken from their parents and placed in a special children's home. Eventually, they were adopted. By the time they were 11 years of age, they were scoring as "normal" on IQ tests.

The twins had not been able to demonstrate their intellectual potential in their original home environment. When the environment became more favorable, their development improved dramatically. Neither a strict nature explanation nor a strict nurture perspective can explain this. From the nature perspective, the boys were intellectually normal at birth and should have continued to function as more or less normal. A nurture position would seem to suggest that the boys should not have developed at all in their father's home. After all, there was virtually no reward for any behavior. An interactionist explanation does seem to work. It appears that native potential and environment interacted to produce intellectual functioning. Their harsh first environment did not completely prevent development. It also did not make them permanently retarded. On the other hand, their "native" ability could not overcome that environment while they were in it. Similarly, their better second home did not "make" them normal. Even the best environment can not reverse biologically based mental retardation (such as Downs syndrome). Instead, the special home and their adoptive family facilitated their individual development so that their "innate" potential was better expressed.

The interactionist position suggests one way that nature and nurture might work together to determine development. Basically, the interactionist model argues that nature and nurture are "additive." A "healthy" child in a "healthy" environment has the best chance for normal development. A "healthy" child in an "unhealthy" environment has less of a chance, and so on. The *transactional model*, proposed by people such as Arnold Sameroff (1975), presents a somewhat different view of how the child and the environment might work together to produce a specific developmental pattern.

Transactions. The transactional model might best be introduced with a hypothetical example. Imagine a new mother. This particular woman is concerned about her ability to care for a child. She is worried that she won't be able to make her baby comfortable and happy. When the baby is born, he cries a great deal of the time. He isn't easy to soothe. He doesn't sleep very well. His behaviors make the mother feel like a failure. All of her fears about her mothering abilities are being confirmed. Her baby doesn't seem to be comfortable and happy. She doesn't know what to do. She becomes more and more anxious when interacting with the baby. She starts to withdraw from him. He cries more and more and, in her opinion, becomes more difficult every day.

What has happened here? The baby was irritable and cranky. The mother interpreted his behavior as being due to her own inadequacy as a mother. This interpretation strengthened her belief that she could not properly care for a baby. So, her mothering ability got worse and worse as did the baby's behavior.

What if she had interpreted the baby's behavior as being attributable to a physical illness such as colic or a milk allergy? She might have handled the situation very differently. She might have been increasingly sympathetic to the baby. She might have held him more and more. He might have reacted positively and become less irritable.

The crucial component in this example is the mother's appraisal of the baby's behavior. On some level, the baby was probably interpreting the mother's behavior, too. Such interpretations form the core of the transactional model. This model suggests that the environment and the child are not "separate" components in the developmental process. Instead, the environment "defines" the child and the child "defines" the environment. It is this mutual influence, or transaction, that determines developmental outcome.

There are, then, four general models of "causality" for understanding infant development. These are the nativist (nature) approach, the environmental learning (nurture) approach, the interactionist approach, and the transactional model. These perspectives are summarized in Figure 1-1.

Throughout this book, you will see how these models are used to explain a wide variety of infant behaviors. Typically, the behaviors to be explained represent the "average" or normal behavior of a group of children. Let's now examine the validity of the assumption that there is such a thing as average or normal development.

NORMATIVE DATA AND INDIVIDUAL DIFFERENCES

Most parents believe in normal development. They want to know if their babies are "fast," "slow," or "on time." So, they often ask when their baby will sit up, walk, and talk. Typically, someone tells them that the baby will sit up around 6 months and will begin to walk and talk around 12 months. In fact, many pediatricians and infant stimulation classes provide new parents with charts outlining such developmental "milestones." Where do they get this information?

Such information is based upon research. Usually, research data are reported in terms of group performance. The researchers provide group averages and then compare these averages to see if there are any important age differences. If enough children are tested (and especially if children of various social classes and races are included), we say that such data are *normative*. In other words, the data indicate what the average child is capable of doing at any given age.

Normative data are useful in many ways. They help us set realistic expectations of children. The importance of realistic expectations is underscored by the child-abuse literature. Abusive parents often seem unaware of what babies are like in terms of amounts of crying, sleeping, and so forth (Kempe & Kempe, 1978). Normative data also help us to identify children who seem to be developing extremely slowly or extremely quickly.

However, normative data are also potentially dangerous. They leave us with the impression that all children develop at the same rate. For example, Shirley's (1933) data suggested that on the average children begin to walk at 13 months. Does this mean that a child who walks at 9 months is "gifted"? Conversely, is the

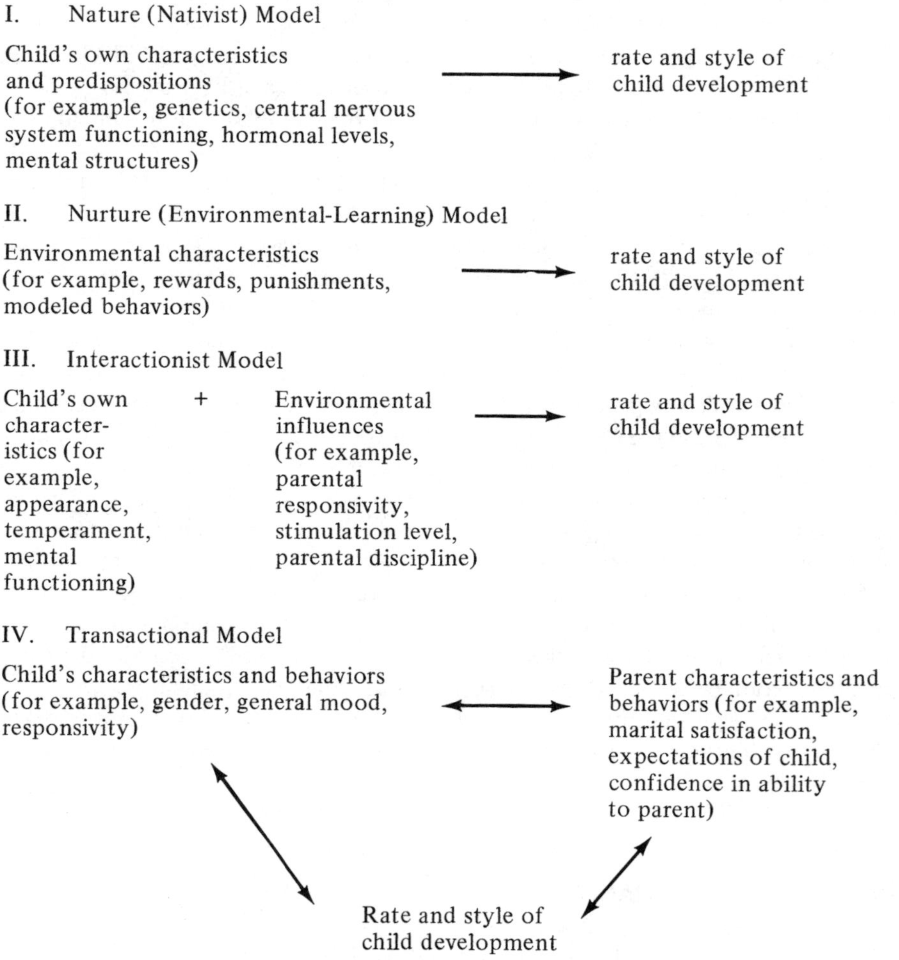

I.   Nature (Nativist) Model

Child's own characteristics
and predispositions   ⟶   rate and style of
(for example, genetics, central nervous   child development
system functioning, hormonal levels,
mental structures)

II.   Nurture (Environmental-Learning) Model

Environmental characteristics   rate and style of
(for example, rewards, punishments,   ⟶   child development
modeled behaviors)

III.   Interactionist Model

Child's own   +   Environmental   ⟶   rate and style of
character-   influences   child development
istics (for   (for example,
example,   parental
appearance,   responsivity,
temperament,   stimulation level,
mental   parental discipline)
functioning)

IV.   Transactional Model

Child's characteristics and behaviors   Parent characteristics and
(for example, gender, general mood,   ⟷   behaviors (for example,
responsivity)   marital satisfaction,
                                                expectations of child,
                                                confidence in ability
                                                to parent)

                          Rate and style of
                          child development

FIGURE 1-1   Diagrams Depicting the Four Major Models of Development.

child who does not walk until 17 months retarded? Not necessarily. There is no single "correct" age to begin to walk. There is instead an age *range* during which walking ought to start. That range may encompass several months and, perhaps, even a full year. We should not take "norms" as absolutes.

Normative data also give the impression that all children follow the same pattern of development. A child sits, then crawls (pulls himself by his arms), then creeps (on all fours), then walks with help, and finally walks alone. This is the most common pattern of motor development. But not all children follow it. Some children never creep or crawl. Yet, they are still normal. Language development provides another example: The vocabulary of most beginning talkers is dominated by nouns. For many years, theorists suggested that all children began this way (for example, McNeill, 1970). However, Katherine Nelson (1973a) and others have demonstrated that some children begin by trying to say short phrases (for example, "I want that" or "give me some") that are run together so that they sound like one word. Such children are difficult to understand initially and have smaller vocabularies than the children who say nouns first; but by age 3, both groups of children show comparable language development (Nelson, 1981).

These examples point out that there are *individual differences* in development. Children develop at different rates and, in some areas of behavior, with different styles. Why is it important to understand individual differences? For one thing, they are crucial to our understanding of the complex interaction between the infant and her environment. They are also important in our ability to identify children with special needs. Recall the example of children who never crawl. We would not want to erroneously label them as abnormal. After all, some people believe that the labeling itself could lead to abnormal development (for example, Rosenthal & Jacobson, 1968). If one adopts a transactional model, then the implications of such an erroneous appraisal could clearly be devastating.

As with normative data, too much emphasis on individual differences is potentially dangerous. The goal of infancy research, as in any scientific endeavor, is to discover general principles that guide development. The study of individual differences does not preclude the existence of such principles. Rather, it suggests that there may be more than one path (but not an infinite number of paths) to normal development. It also suggests, once again, that we need to consider the complex interaction between the characteristics of the child and her environment.

We have consistently referred to the development of the infant, but we have not carefully defined what we mean by development. Let's now turn our attention to that issue.

DEVELOPMENTAL CHANGE

The most common mistake that most people make in defining development is to equate development with age. They talk as if age caused a behavior to appear. They say things such as "He's throwing tantrums because he's two." Age in and of itself causes nothing. Age is simply a marker, a unit of measurement. It is no more a cause of development than inches are a cause of height.

What is development? It is a change in an individual's behavior that is age related. The change is more or less a permanent rather than a temporary reaction to external or internal stimuli. The roots of the change may lie in maturation, environmental contingencies (such as rewards and punishments), or both (see the preceding discussion of models of development).

Developmental change is not random. Throughout development, we move toward increasing levels of differentiation and integration (Werner, 1967). This means that behavior becomes increasingly skilled and specific. We move, for example, from trying to pick up small objects using our entire hand to using the thumb and forefinger in opposition ("pincer"). At the same time, however, behaviors become more intercoordinated. Walking, for example, involves coordinating the movement of both feet with arm movements as well as with sensory information about balance and the presence of obstacles.

Does saying that development is not random mean that it is directed toward a specific endpoint? Stage theorists, such as Piaget and Erikson, argue that it is. They postulate final stages that represent "maturity" in thought and personality functioning. Other theorists, such as Skinner or Albert Bandura, suggest that there is no final goal. They believe that people simply continue to accumulate information. In their opinion, there is no universal form of "maturity."

Whether or not developmental change is goal directed, it is assumed to be orderly. There are identifiable patterns of development. How do we identify these patterns? Let's now look briefly at two common research designs to examine what each can contribute to our understanding of infant development.

DEVELOPMENTAL RESEARCH

Two major types of research design are used in studying infant behavior. These are the cross-sectional and longitudinal studies.

The cross-sectional approach is the more common. In a cross-sectional study, behavior is assessed in two or more different age groups of children. So, a group of 6-month-olds might be tested. A group of 10-month-olds would also be tested. Then the average score of the 6-month group would be compared to that of the 10-month group. If the difference between the averages is large enough, we say it is a statistically significant difference. This means that the difference is too large and too consistent, within each group, to have occurred by chance.

Only one group of children is observed in a longitudinal study. These children are tested repeatedly. So, they might be tested once at 6 months and again at 10 months. Longitudinal studies may last for a few weeks or they may go on for many years. The Berkeley Growth Study, for example, began in 1928 and still continues its work.

Advantages and disadvantages to both types of designs exist (see Table 1-1). The cross-sectional study is faster and less expensive than a longitudinal study.

TABLE 1-1   Advantages of Cross-sectional vs. Longitudinal Research Designs.

ADVANTAGES OF CROSS-SECTIONAL DESIGNS

1. Quicker and less expensive.
2. Little likelihood that measures will become outdated during the study.
3. Easier to obtain a representative sample.
4. Less staff turnover means greater likelihood that measures will be administered and scored in a consistent manner.

ADVANTAGES OF LONGITUDINAL DESIGNS

1. Individual differences in rate and style of development can be examined.
2. Greater certainty that you are seeing developmental change rather than group differences (group differences could be due to differences in IQ, gender, parental attitudes, and so on).

Because it requires less commitment from the participants, the cross-sectional study is also likely to attract a wider range of people. The sample (that is, the participants) in a cross-sectional study is, therefore, more likely to truly represent the broader population of infants. This is important because we want to be able to draw generalizations from our research to the broadest possible group of infants.

On the other hand, the cross-sectional design has two very serious drawbacks. First, since each infant is tested only once, we cannot really look at individual differences in development or behavior. Thus, cross-sectional research can provide only normative data (the disadvantages of which were discussed earlier). Individual differences can be examined in longitudinal research. Second, we cannot be certain that any group differences observed in cross-sectional research are attributable to development. They could be due to other group differences such as gender, family factors (for example, sibling status on patterns of mother-infant interaction), social class, or exposure to specific experiences (for example, watching "Sesame Street" or being read to). In longitudinal studies, we are more certain that the changes are indeed developmental. After all, the same children are being observed and we are seeing change within the children. That is development.

THE APPROACH OF THIS BOOK

Our current view is that infants enter the world as complex, organized beings. One of the goals of this book is to describe the abilities of newborns (and even fetuses!). Of course, there are dramatic changes in behavior during the first 2 years of life. These changes are also described.

Descriptions of infant behavior and development are interesting. However, we also want to understand *why* the changes occur. The four broad models of development introduced in this chapter are frequently cited to help us understand why. More specific theoretical approaches are also discussed.

Like virtually every developmental researcher, I have a model preference and it is reflected here. The dominant model is the interactional model. Where the data permit, the more complex transactional model is applied. Thus, throughout the book we examine both the child's and the environment's contributions to development.

One final note about the assumptions of this book is needed. Traditionally many of our beliefs about children and parents were subtly influenced by the language we used to describe them. The term *mother* (or the feminine pronoun) was in the past frequently treated as synonymous with *parent*. The infant was frequently referred to as *he*. I have made a conscious attempt here to avoid these linguistic pitfalls. Both male and female pronouns are used in exemplifying parents and infants throughout the book. So, use of the term *mother* or *father*, rather than *parents*, in describing research findings implies that only maternal or paternal behavior was examined.

SUMMARY

We have defined infancy as the first 2 years of life. Current views of infants stress the competence of infants and the complexity of their interactions with the environment. Although it is clear that there are dramatic changes during these 2 years, the roots of such changes remain unclear. Most theorists believe that both innate characteristics and environmental factors play a role in infant development. How these affect one another remains an area of some debate.

The implications of infancy for later development also are debated. Most theorists see infancy as the foundation for later development. Few believe, though, that characteristics and behaviors that develop during infancy are by definition permanent. Rather, the early characteristics and behaviors tend to seem permanent because the infant usually remains in the same situation throughout his childhood and adolescence. Dramatic changes in setting can, however, produce major changes in functioning.

In order to understand infant development, it is important to keep in mind that the infant is an individual growing up in a complex environment. We need to be careful not to be bound by "average ages" and sweeping generalizations about the environment. Not all babies are the same. Nor are all mothers or fathers. The scope of the baby's experiences, including her impact on her family, needs to be taken into account.

2
Prenatal Heritage

Even as a newborn, every person is a unique individual. Some newborns are more active than others; some prefer auditory stimulation while others prefer visual stimulation; some cry a great deal, others only when they are uncomfortable (for example, Escalona, 1963; Osofsky & Danzger, 1974). While the specific roots of these differences remain a mystery, we can consider the two general mechanisms most likely to be responsible. These are genetic differences and prenatal and peri-natal influences.

GENETICS

Genetic determinism of physical characteristics is widely accepted. We expect Kareem Abdul-Jabbar's children to be taller than Mickey Rooney's children. We often seem to believe that environment usually has only a negligible effect on physical traits. However, our primary interest here is in the effects of genetics on individual differences in behavior. Modern theorists have often minimized the role of genetics in behavior, seeing the environment as a more important determinant of most behaviors. Indeed, genetic influences on development have received only limited attention until recently.

One reason that genetic influences have frequently been ignored is that most people do not think of genetic phenomena as truly developmental (Plomin, 1983). As noted in Chapter 1, development implies change, specifically, age-related change. To most people, saying a behavior is genetically determined means that it is permanently fixed before birth. Yet recent research suggests that genes themselves change (for example, are turned on and off) at various times. Also, the expression of genetic material can be influenced by environmental conditions.

The interplay of the environment and genetics is clear even in physical characteristics. For example, monozygotic twins raised in significantly different environments will be of different heights and weights despite their identical genetic makeup (Tanner, 1978). In fact, in certain environments, Mickey Rooney's children might be taller than Kareem Abdul-Jabbar's children. The impact of environmental influences on the expression of genetically encoded information is so widespread that it is necessary to distinguish between genotypes and phenotypes when discussing genetics. *Genotype* refers to the information actually encoded in the DNA (the material of which genes are made). *Phenotype* refers to the physical expression of those genetic codes. Phenotype and genotype may or may not be identical (see Figure 2-1).

This interplay of genetics and environment is also evident in behavior. Let's take an example from intellectual functioning, since more work has been done concerning the effect of genetics on intelligence than on all other behaviors combined (Plomin, 1983). It has long been clear that genetics has played a role in intellectual functioning at least in cases of severe mental retardation. Down's syndrome and PKU (phenylketonuria) are two forms of genetically caused mental retardation. PKU is a recessive gene disorder which results in the inability to metabolize the enzyme phenylalanine. This, in turn, causes a build-up of substances which are toxic to the devloping central nervous system. The result is mental retardation. However, an early dietary regimen can "reverse" the genetically encoded path. The child with PKU who is given a low phenylalanine diet will show normal blood bio-

FIGURE 2-1   Exemplifying the Comparability of Genotype vs. Phenotype

DIFFERENT GENOTYPE, SAME PHENOTYPE

Genotype:		Phenotype:
Two genes for brown eyes	⟶	Brown-eyed child
One gene for brown and one for blue eyes	⟶	Brown-eyed child

SAME GENOTYPE, DIFFERENT PHENOTYPE

| Down's syndrome (three chromosomes at twenty-first pair) | + High-stimulation environment | ⟶ | Mild or borderline retardation |
| Down's syndrome | + Low-stimulation environment | ⟶ | Profound to moderate retardation |

chemistry and normal intellectual development. This works only if the diet is begun when the child is very young, prior to serious damage to the central nervous system (McClearn & DeFries, 1973). So we see that even in a behavioral realm, *genetic* does not mean "immutable."

If genetics can contribute to mental retardation, then it seems sensible to assume that it also contributes to individual differences in intelligence across all levels of functioning. This, however, has not been a popular view among developmentalists (see, for example, Kamin, 1974). If one believes *genetic* means "immutable," then the presence of genetic differences could be used to discriminate against individuals and groups. This is what happened when Arthur Jensen (1969) argued that blacks were genetically inferior to whites. However, if we understand that genetics and environment work together, then this fallacy is avoided. We have already seen how the environment can alter the expression of genetic predispositions. It is also true that genetics can influence our environment. Genetic predispositions may affect the type of activities and situations we choose. These choices will influence our development (Scarr & McCartney, 1983; Scarr & Weinberg, 1983).

With this in mind, we can understand the potential value of behavioral genetics in helping us to understand individual differences in behavior. Genetic effects have been documented in intelligence (Scarr & Weinberg, 1983), personality and temperament (Goldsmith, 1983), learning disabilities (Pennington & Smith, 1983), language development (Hardy-Brown, Plomin & Defries, 1981), and other behaviors. The precise nature of the genetic input remains undefined for most of these behaviors. However, the genetic-behavior link frequently is known for behavior disorders. Table 2-1 provides several examples of these relationships.

It seems likely, then, that some of the individual differences observed among newborns are attributable to genetic differences. However, the prenatal environment may also influence both physical and behavioral development. Let us now look at some possible relationships between prenatal environment and neonatal functioning.

PRENATAL DEVELOPMENT

Before we can fully understand influences on prenatal development, we need to have some conceptualization of prenatal development itself. What do we mean by *prenatal*? The term *natal* means birth. Therefore, *prenatal* means "before birth," *perinatal* means "during birth," and *postnatal* means "after birth." Although the development of all major organs and organ systems is reviewed here, we emphasize the two physiological systems of greatest interest to developmentalists: the central nervous system and sexual differentiation.

Prenatal development unfolds in a fixed sequence. Because the sequence is predictable, physicians are able to monitor fetal development (see Box 2-1). This sequence is encoded in the ovum, or egg. When the egg is fertilized by a sperm, the

TABLE 2-1 Some Genetically Based Disorders

DISORDER	DESCRIPTION OF BEHAVIOR	GENETIC ROOT
Phenylketonuria (PKU)	Mental retardation, developmental delay, behavioral problems	Recessive gene
Lesch-Nyhan syndrome	Cerebral palsy, mental retardation, involuntary movements of facial muscles and limbs, aggression, compulsive self-biting.	Sex-linked (males only), recessive gene
Tay-Sachs disease	Normal at birth; soon after, nystagmus and paralysis followed by retardation, blindness, and death (usually by 2 years of age)	Recessive gene
Speilmeyer-Vogt disease	Similar to Tay-Sachs disease but degeneration does not typically begin until after 6 years of age, with the average age at death being 16 years	Recessive gene
Huntington's Chorea	Does not onset until 25-55 years. Disorganized muscular movements, progressive mental deterioration, death	Dominant gene
Maple syrup urine disease	Mental retardation, feeding problems, persistent vomiting	Recessive gene
Early menopause syndrome	Mental retardation, menstrual irregularities, and early menopause	Sex chromosome anomaly (XXX)
Turner's syndrome	Cognitive deficits (perceptual organization), infantile sexual development	Sex chromosome anomaly (X)
Down's syndrome	Mental retardation (often severe)	Third chromosome at twenty-first pair
Edward's syndrome	Hypertonicity of skeletal muscles, severe retardation, death during early infancy	Third chromosome at eighteenth pair
Cri du chat syndrome	Weak cry that sounds like cat mewing, severe retardation	Deletion of part of fifth chromosome
Klinefelter's syndrome	Mental retardation in about half of individuals, various personality and psychiatric problems	Sex chromosome anomaly (XXY)

(Information from Gardner, 1982; Previte, 1983.)

pattern is triggered. Within this sequence, each organ and organ system has periods during which certain developments must occur. Fingers and toes, for example, are formed from 6 to 8 weeks of pregnancy. If anything, for example, drugs or radiation, interferes with digit development, the damage will be permanent. The fingers and toes cannot develop or "self-correct" later on in pregnancy. These periods of rapid growth and differentiation are *critical periods*. In human beings, most of the critical periods for organ development occur within the first 12 weeks, that is, the first trimester, of pregnancy. So, the developing embryo is most susceptible to toxins and trauma during the first trimester.

BOX 2-1 *IS THE FETUS HEALTHY?*

Not so many years ago, parents had to wait until their child was born to find out whether the baby was healthy. For parents who were carriers of genetic disorders, this meant a tortuous 9 months. In fact, many of them simply decided not to have children. This was also true of older women, since women over 40 have a much greater chance of giving birth to a child with Downs syndrome or other problems.

In recent years, however, this has changed. There are now available several methods of fetal diagnosis that enable physicians to ascertain the status of the developing fetus. These methods include amniocentesis, fetoscopy, and sonograms.

In amniocentesis, a needle is inserted through the woman's abdomen into the amniotic sac, the "bag of waters" surrounding the fetus. A small amount of amniotic fluid is withdrawn. The fluid contains cells that the fetus has shed. These cells contain information about the genetic constellation of the fetus. Thus, chromosomal anomalies (for example, Down's syndrome) can be detected. The biochemical composition of the fluid can also be analyzed. This allows the diagnosis of various metabolic disorders such as Tay-Sachs disease (Annis, 1978; Previte, 1983).

A second diagnostic technique is fetoscopy. In this method, an instrument called a fetoscope (or endoscope) is used to look directly at portions of the developing fetus. This enables the physician to confirm the presence of malformations. The fetoscope can also be used to draw fetal blood, permitting the diagnosis of sickle-cell anemia and other blood disorders (Annis, 1978).

Finally, sonograms (ultrasound) allow parents to see a "picture" of the fetus. Sound waves, transmitted through the woman's abdomen, are "bounced off" the fetus. Depending on the age and position of the fetus, these are sometimes detailed enough to ascertain the fetus's sex. Medically, they are useful in exploring the fetus's position. If the fetus is not in proper position, that is, with head down, birth complications such as anoxia (oxygen deprivation which can result in mental retardation or death) may occur. Sonograms are also used to gauge the maturity of the fetus (Birnholz & Farrell, 1984). The availability of such information allows the physician to decide the safest way, and time, to deliver the baby. Sonograms can also be used to diagnose many neurological, cardiac, and limb deformities (Birnholz & Farrell, 1984).

None of these methods is without risk. About 3% of the women who undergo amniocentesis, for example, develop infections and 1-2% miscarry (Annis, 1978). Such risks are relatively small and are well balanced when the medical information to be gained is needed. The use of such methods for more frivolous reasons (for example, to find out the sex of the baby) is not justifiable.

What can the parents do if the tests indicate the fetus is not healthy? One option is to terminate the pregnancy. This decision is made more difficult by the fact that the determination of fetal status sometimes is not made until the second trimester. Amniocentesis cannot be performed until at least 14 weeks of pregnancy. Before then, the fetus does not have enough amniotic fluid for the physician to safely draw a sample. After the sample has been drawn, it takes about a month to complete the tests. Thus, the woman has frequently felt movement and her pregnancy is obvious to everyone at the time the decision must be made.

Not all parents, however, are faced with this decision. The defect may simply require special care when the birth occurs. Prenatal diagnosis facilitates such care. Prenatal intervention is also sometimes possible. For example, doctors have successfully performed in-utero surgery on hydrocephalic (fluid on the brain causing severe brain injury) fetuses. They insert a shunt into the fetus's head to drain some of the fluid, resulting in the birth of a healthy child (Birnholz & Farrell, 1984). In the future, such procedures will become more common and may be extended to include other disorders.

The second and third trimesters are basically periods of refinement and growth. Especially during the third trimester, the fetus shows dramatic gains in weight and height. At the end of the first trimester, the fetus is 3-4 inches long and weighs about .5 ounces. By the end of the second trimester, it is 8-10 inches long and weighs about 1.5 pounds. When the baby is born at the end of the third trimester, it is about 20 inches long and weighs about 7 pounds.

Table 2-2 summarizes the milestones of prenatal development. It is important to note that although the fetus looks human at 12 weeks of pregnancy, it is not yet viable. In other words, it could not yet survive outside the uterus. The minimum gestational age of a viable fetus is currently set at 24 weeks. Even at this age, chances of survival are slim.

TABLE 2-2 Timetable of Prenatal Development

AGE	WHAT TAKES PLACE
1 day	The union of egg and sperm forms the zygote, the beginning of the new individual. The first cell division of the zygote, the first step in its growth, is completed within 36 h. By future cell divisions (mitosis) all the cells and tissues of the new individual will arise from the zygote.
4 days	Motula stage—special techniques can tell the sex of the new individual at this early stage.
7 to 9 days	Blastocyst stage—embryo reaches cavity of uterus and attaches to the lining of the uterine wall, burying itself in its glands.
2.5 to 4 weeks	Neurula stage—by three weeks the foundations for brain, spinal cord, and entire nervous system are established. Blood vessels start forming at 2.5 weeks, the heart a day later. At 3.5 weeks, the heart, a simple tube, starts to pulsate. From 3 weeks, the primitive digestive system and the forerunner of the kidney form.
4.5 weeks	The three main parts of the brain are present. Eyes, ears, nasal organs, digestive tract, liver, gallbladder, and arm and leg buds are forming.
5 weeks	Embryo is 1/3 in. long and weighs 1/1000 oz. The early differentiation of the cerebral cortex is seen. Pituitary gland begins to form.

TABLE 2-2 (continued)

AGE	WHAT TAKES PLACE
5.5 weeks	All muscle blocks present. Embryo may begin to move, but mother does not feel this for another 6 to 10 weeks. The heart begins to subdivide into its four chambers.
6 weeks	Embryo is 1/2 in. long. Earliest reflexes can be elicited. Electro-cardiogram (ECG) and electroencephalogram (EEG) can be recorded. Fingers, then toes, begin to form. Especially during the first 6 to 8 weeks of embryonic life, the embryo is most vulnerable to the effects of drugs, radiation, infections (particularly viral), noxious substances (such as alcohol and nicotine), and nutritional deficiencies of the mother.
8 weeks	Embryo is 1.5 in. long and weighs 1/30 oz. The face appears quite human. Heart completes the formation of its four chambers. Hands and feet are well-formed and distinctly human. Cerebral cortex begins to acquire typical cells. At the end of 8 weeks all organs, facial features, and limb structures have begun to form. Everything is present that will be found in the newborn baby. The fundamental plan of the human body is completely mapped out by the end of the second month. During the remainder of pregnancy the various organs will mature in structure and function.
9 weeks	The growing child is now called a fetus. When the eyelids or palms of the hands are touched, they both respond by closing; this indicates that both nerves and muscles are functioning.
10 weeks	Except for refinements, the brain is much as it will be at birth. If the forehead is touched, the fetus turns the head away.
12 weeks (3 months)	Fetus is 3–4 in. crown-rump length, and weighs about 1/2 oz. The thumb can now be opposed to the forefinger (a characteristic of all the primates). Fetuses of this age begin to show individual variations, probably based on behavioral patterns inherited from the parents. By the end of the twelfth week, the fetus has developed all organ systems and is virtually a functioning organism. The fetal organs become more and more like what they will be in the newborn infant.
4 months	Fingerprints, unique to the individual, are formed. The fetus responds to touch and spontaneously stretches and exercises both arms and legs.
5 months	Fetus measures 8 in. crown-rump length, and weighs 8 to 10 oz. The fetus exhibits a firm hand grip, good muscular strength, coordination and reflex action, and kicks, moves, turns in the womb, hiccups, develops patterns of sleep and wakefulness, and reacts in an individual way to loud noise, music, or jarring or tapping the abdomen.
6 months	During this month, the eyes become sensitive to varying intensities of light and darkness but not to objects.
7 months	Fetus measures 12 in. crown-rump length and weighs 2 to 3 lb. The fetus (now called a premature baby if born) continues growing and maturing. Every added day spent in the uterus until birth prepares the baby all the better to assume an independent role.

(Physician members of the Value of Life Committee, Inc. *Timetable of a human individual's development before birth.* Copyright © 1980, Value of Life Committee, Brighton, Mass.)

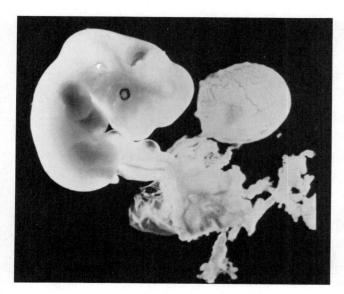

A 5.5-week-old embryo. It is about 1 cm long. (Courtesy of Lennart Nilsson in *A Child Is Born* (1977), Dell Publishing Co., New York.)

One reason the fetus is not viable at 12 weeks is because of the immaturity of the brain. Let's now examine the structural and functional development of the brain.

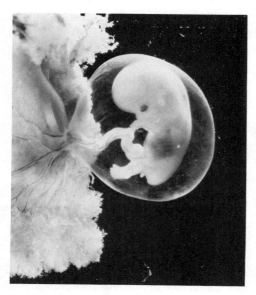

A fetus at two months, 1 week. It is about 1.5 inches long. (Courtesy of Lennart Nilsson in *A Child is Born* (1977), Dell Publishing Co., New York.)

A 4.5-months-old fetus demonstrating the sucking reflex. It is just over 7 inches long. (Courtesy of Lennart Nilsson in *A Child Is Born* (1977), Dell Publishing Co., New York.)

The Brain

Structural Development.   In the first few days after conception, brain development begins with the formation of the neural plate. This plate is composed of columns of cells that can still reproduce themselves. By about 23 days gestational age (that is, 23 days of pregnancy), the neural plate has folded, forming a partially fused neural groove. By 28 days gestational age, the fusion is complete and the neural tube has been formed. This process of *neurulation* is apparently guided by forces within the neural plate itself. Even before it is completed, though, there is evidence of enlargements which will become the brain and spinal cord. By the end of the fourth week of pregnancy, the neural tube is bent into a C-shape and has three distinct regions: the forebrain, the midbrain, and the hindbrain. The hindbrain eventually becomes the brainstem, including the pons, the medulla, and the cerebellum. The midbrain will eventually house centers for hearing and vision—the superior and inferior colliculli, for example. The forebrain has already divided into two sections by now. One of the sections, the telencephalon, will become the cerebral cortex. The other, the diencephalon, will become the eyes, the thalamus, and the hypothalamus (see Table 2-3). The remainder of the neural tube retains a smaller diameter and eventually becomes the spinal cord. Although the gray and white matter of the spinal cord has achieved an adultlike configuration by the middle of pregnancy, development of the spinal chord is not fully completed until adolescence (Previte, 1983; Timeras, 1972).

The cerebral cortex, believed to be the center of the higher-order human functions such as language and problem solving, is of special interest. It begins to

TABLE 2-3   Summary of Brain Structures and Their Functions

EARLY PRENATAL STRUCTURE	BRAIN STRUCTURE	"MATURE" FUNCTION
FOREBRAIN		
Diencephalon	Eyes	
	Thalamus	Receives and relays sensory information to the cortex
	Hypothalamus	Regulation of basic motivation (for example, hunger and thirst), basic emotions (for example, flight or fight), physical homeostasis
Telencephalon	Cerebral cortex	Higher-order functioning including voluntary behavior, language, and interpretation of sensory information
MIDBRAIN	Midbrain	Controls eye movements, origin of nerve cells that produce dopamine
HINDBRAIN	Medulla	Controls involuntary functions (for example, heartrate and breathing)
	Pons	A "bridge" carrying messages to other parts of the brain
	Cerebellum	Controls balance, equilibrium, and muscle coordination

take form by 6 weeks' gestational age. At this time, the division of the cerebral hemispheres is evident. The corpus callosum, the bundle of nerve fibers connecting the two hemispheres, has attained adult shape and structure by the end of the fifth fetal month. The layers of the cerebral cortex are evident by 24 weeks' gestational age.

The cerebral cortex does not mature uniformly. The "primary" areas (as opposed to the "association" areas) develop first in the following order: primary motor, primary somatosensory, primary visual, and primary auditory. Development of the motor and sensory areas exemplifies the principle of cephalocaudal development. This principle states that development begins in the head and proceeds downward through the trunk and arms and finally into the legs. So, in the primary motor and sensory areas, the nerve cells controlling the head area (for example, the tongue and the lips) develop first, followed by the trunk and finally the legs. In fact, the leg areas are not completely developed until at least 2 years postnatally. This sequence is reflected in behavioral functioning. The infant's mouth is functional at birth; neck muscles become operative at 8-10 weeks, enabling the baby to hold his head up steadily; reaching and grasping appear at 3-4 months; and walking begins at 12-14 months.

So, by the end of 6 months of pregnancy the fetal brain is quite similar to the adult brain. At birth, the brain will be closer to adult size than any other organ except the eye. The newborn's brain is approximately 25% of its adult weight. By age 10, the brain will have attained 95% of its adult weight. Compare this to overall body weight. At birth the child's weight is roughly 5% of adult weight, and by age 10 roughly 50% of adult body weight has been achieved (Timeras, 1972). No wonder babies' heads appear disproportionately large!

Still, the brain is far from completely developed at birth. Interconnections among the nerve cells, for example, must still be made (Parmelee & Sigman, 1983). In addition, the myelin sheath, which enables the nerves to carry messages more quickly and efficiently, must still be formed around most nerve cells (Timeras, 1972). In fact, central nervous system development may not be complete until early adulthood. Because brain functioning is not completely "wired in" at birth, infants and young children can make better recoveries from brain injury than can adults. For example, when an adult's brain is injured, any skills that were "housed" in the injured area of the brain must be relearned and "rewired." Old habits often interfere with such relearning. In the young children, the brain is much more flexible. There are fewer "old wirings" to interfere with "relearning." We say that the brain of the young child has greater *plasticity* than the brain of the adult. Given these structural differences, it is not surprising to find that the brain of the newborn does not function exactly like an adult's.

Functional Development.   Research concerning reflexes has provided some information about prenatal brain functioning. The basic reflex arc—the input stimulating the central nervous system and thus resulting in behavior—appears in the spinal cord by 8 weeks' gestational age. Some "protective" reflexes, involving muscle contraction when touched, have been observed in 9-10 week fetuses. By 11 weeks, the rudiments of the grasping and plantar reflexes are evident. The true Babinski reflex is seen by 14 weeks, the hand grasp by 15-18.5 weeks, and suckling reflexes by 22 weeks of pregnancy (Carmichael, 1970; Timeras, 1972). (These reflexes are described in Chapter 3.)

Reflexes are so fully developed by birth that they are often used to measure the functioning and integrity of the newborn's central nervous system. We discuss the importance of the newborn's reflexes in more detail in the next chapter.

Reflexes, however, are mediated through the spinal cord and hindbrain. They do not tell us anything about cerebral cortex development. EEG (electroencephalogram) readings can provide such information. EEGs measure brain electrical activity. Although spontaneous EEG readings can be obtained as early as 43 days of pregnancy, such activity is believed to be subcortical, that is, from the spinal chord or brainstem, until at least 6 months of pregnancy. Clear signs of cortical maturation appear at 7-8 months' gestational age. Now there is continuous electrical activity from the brain. Sleep-waking cycles, marked by different rates of brain activity, appear; and the EEG shows that the brain now reacts to sensory stimuli (Eichorn, 1970).

The EEG is not mature at birth. In fact, it has been suggested, based on EEG research, that the cerebral cortex is not truly functional at birth. Alpha rhythms, which signal that the brain is in an alert and aware state, are not evident until about 3 months after birth. Even at this time, the alpha rhythms are slower than in the adult brain. Adultlike EEG readings are not obtained until approximately age 13 (Parmelee & Sigman, 1983).

Sexual Differentiation

Both structurally and functionally, brain development is a lengthy process. It is easy to understand why so many factors (for example, drugs and diseases) can negatively affect its development. This is not true with sex differentiation. Sex differentiation occurs quite early in pregnancy and is highly susceptible to trauma or toxins only then.

You might ask why we are so interested in sex differentiation. The answer is that many investigators believe that prenatally formed sex differences are not restricted to the reproductive system. For example, Money and Ehrhardt (1972) have suggested that many play and social behaviors are influenced by prenatal hormonal levels. So, understanding the process of prenatal sex differentiation becomes potentially important in understanding sex differences in behavior.

For about the first 7 weeks of pregnancy, all embryos have identical reproductive "apparatus." These structures include the following:

1. Undifferentiated gonad
2. Wolffian (tubular) structure
3. Mullerian (tubular) structure
4. Genital tubercle
5. Single external opening

If the XY chromosome constellation is present, that is, if the child is genetically a male, the HY antigen is produced. The HY antigen causes the undifferentiated gonad to become a testis. This occurs at 7 weeks' gestational age. It is the only known effect of the XY constellation. From here on, sexual differentiation relies on hormonal, rather than genetic, action. The fetal testes produce testosterone and Mullerian inhibitor. The testosterone causes the Wolffian system to develop into the male reproductive system, that is, the vas deferens, the seminal vesicles, and the ejaculatory ducts. The Mullerian inhibitor stops the development of the internal female reproductive system (from the Mullerian system). Testosterone also mediates the development of external male genitalia, which appear by 12 weeks of pregnancy. If the testosterone is not present, the child will develop female genitalia despite the presence of the XY chromosomes (Money & Ehrhardt, 1972; Wachtel, 1983) (see Figure 2-2).

Female development is less well understood. It is not clear why the undifferentiated gonad becomes an ovary in the presence of the XX chromosome. No equi-

FIGURE 2-2 Prenatal Sexual Differentiation.

SEXUAL DIFFERENTIATION IN THE HUMAN FETUS

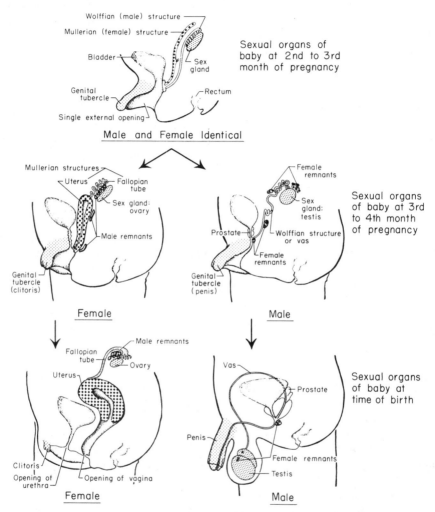

(From J. Money & A. Ehrhardt (1972) *Man & Woman, Boy & Girl.* Reprinted by permission of Johns Hopkins University Press.)

valent of the HY antigen has been found. In fact, it has been hypothesized that the absence of the HY antigen results in an ovary. Similarly, the fetal ovary does not produce any known substance that results in the development of internal or external female physiology. In other words, the development of the female system does not appear to require the presence of a particular hormone the way that the male system depends on testosterone. All that is known is that around 12 weeks' gestational age, the ovary develops from the undifferentiated gonad. Then, the

Mullerian system develops into a uterus, oviducts, and vagina. The Wolffian system becomes vestigial. By 14 weeks, female external genitalia are evident. If testosterone is introduced, as in adrenogenital syndrome, the child will develop male genitalia even without the Y chromosome (Money & Ehrhardt, 1972).

The common beginnings of male and female, as well as the vestigial remains of the opposite gender's reproductive system, underscores the fact that gender is not truly a dichotomy. This will be clear when we discuss gender differences. There is always a continuum of "masculine-feminine" with representatives of both genders at all points on the scale.

As we have seen, the timing of prenatal development is rigidly fixed. Knowing this will help us to understand why the timing of a toxin or trauma determines its effects on the developing embryo and fetus. For example, if a woman contracts rubella (German measles) during the first trimester of pregnancy, the results can be devastating. Depending upon the precise timing of the disease, the child may be born blind, deaf, mentally retarded, or with any number of other birth defects because the organ systems are developing at this time and the virus interferes with their development. If a woman contracts rubella during her last trimester, the results will be much less marked, perhaps nonexistent, because the organ systems are basically developed and so are much less susceptible to severe damage.

With this issue of timing in mind, let us now turn our attention to some of the drugs, diseases, and environmental situations that may adversely affect prenatal development.

INFLUENCES ON PRENATAL DEVELOPMENT

We must be cautious in interpreting much of the existing information about prenatal influences. There are several reasons for this. First, much of the data involves retrospective report. This means that sometime after delivery, women are asked about their pregnancies. They are frequently asked to focus on the first trimester. Often this is difficult, not only because of the normal shortcomings of human memory but also because many women do not know exactly when they got pregnant. They may not have been aware of their pregnancy for several weeks. So, their reports may not be reliable.

Another problem is that because of ethical considerations, virtually all the controlled experimental research is done with animals. Although this research provides valuable information, it typically fails to capture the complexity of the comparable human situation. For example, a good deal of research has been done with rats concerning drinking during pregnancy. This research generally indicates severe effects which are in some ways comparable to the effects observed in humans (see, for example, Abel, 1981). Although the alcohol appears to cause the effects seen in rats, we cannot make a comparable statement about humans. Why? Human alcoholics may have biochemical disorders that predispose them to drinking problems. They are probably stressed. They tend to smoke more than nonalcoholics.

They may have poorer diets. Any or all of these other factors may be at least as influential as the alcohol itself in the effects seen in humans.

Drinking during pregnancy is one of the issues we will be examining in some detail in this next section, after we look closely at malnutrition and cigarette smoking. The effects of several other factors on prenatal development are summarized in Table 2-4.

Malnutrition

The animal data (mainly with rats and pigs) indicate that malnutrition adversely affects cognitive, emotional, and neurological development. This is particularly true in the case of protein deprivation. Generally, the earlier the malnutrition starts and the longer it lasts, the more severe the effects. The animal research also suggests that the effects of malnutrition may be cumulative over generations. In other words, the effects on the second malnourished generation are more severe than on the first, the effects on the third generation more marked than on the second, and so on (example, Cowley & Giesel, 1963; Osofsky, 1975).

Human studies are somewhat less clear. Several researchers (for example, Osofsky, 1975; Jeans, Smith & Stearns, 1955) have failed to find severe effects of prenatal malnutrition. Howard Osofsky has suggested that this may be due to sample characteristics. He has argued that many of the women seen in clinics in the United States are not severely malnourished. Indeed, in his own group of mothers, protein intake exceeded the recommended daily allowance and calorie intake was only slightly below the RDA even though these women were very poor. Furthermore, Osofsky has noted, these women were voluntarily seeking prenatal care.

It appears that Osofsky may have been right. When women are severely malnourished, the effects on their children parallel the animal data (for example, Bhatia, Katiyar & Agarwal, 1979; Winick, 1971). This is particularly true in terms of brain damage (for example, brain protein, DNA, and brain-weight losses) and mortality rates. The behavioral effects of prenatal malnutrition are more difficult to evaluate, since malnutrition often continues after birth. If the baby is lethargic or cranky, it may be due to either prenatal or postnatal influences (or, most likely, both).

Several researchers have altered the postnatal environment in order to understand more fully the effects of prenatal malnutrition. Supplementing the children's diets postnatally appears to result in improvements in their intellectual development. Dietary supplements alone, however, do not seem to eliminate the lag attributable to the prenatal malnutrition (for example, Cravioto, DeLicardie & Birch, 1966). When the dietary supplements are combined with special high-stimulation day care, however, the effects are more dramatic. The prenatally malnourished children appear to catch up to normal children (for example, Zeskind & Ramey, 1978). This, again, underscores the complexity of evaluating prenatal influences on human development.

TABLE 2-4 Some Potential Influences on Prenatal Development

INFLUENCE	POTENTIAL EFFECTS
DRUGS	
Heroin and Methadone	Retarded growth; withdrawal symptoms such as tremors, irritability, hyperactivity, shrill cry; SIDS (crib death)
Aspirin (large doses, last trimester)	Blood clotting problems for both mother and newborn
DES (a synthetic hormone frequently used between 1945 and 1970 to prevent miscarriage)	Abnormalities in reproductive system, including pregnancy complications and cervical cancer
Caffeine	Unclear; probably minimal unless combined with cigarette smoking or in very high doses
Streptomycin	Hearing loss
Tetracycline	Dental malformations
DISEASES	
Rubella	Congenital cataracts, deafness, heart disease, microcephaly, stunted growth
Syphilis	Spontaneous abortion common; deafness, blindness, various malformations, mental retardation; syphillis
Herpes II	Life threatening if it infects the central nervous system during first 4 weeks postnatally; transmitted during or after birth only
Diabetes	Abnormally large babies, frequently resulting in delivery complications; higher rate of fetal and neonatal mortality
ENVIRONMENT	
Stress	Unclear but perhaps Downs syndrome, pyloric stenosis, various behavior problems
Radiation (large doses)	Fetal death, microcephaly, mental retardation, various malformations, possibly delayed cancers and leukemia
Mercury (ingested by eating contaminated meat or fish)	Central nervous system damage manifested postnatally by tremors, convulsions, irritability, and abnormal EEG
Hot saunas (especially at 3-4 weeks of pregnancy)	Anencephaly (no cortex)
Hexochlorophene (frequent exposure)	Various severe malformations

(Information from Annis, 1978; Clarke-Stewart, Friedman & Koch, 1985; Hamilton, 1980; Quilligan, 1980; Stechler & Halton, 1982).

Cigarettes

Most of us would recognize that women should not use drugs extensively during pregnancy. But most of us do not think of cigarettes as a drug. Oh, we realize they present a health risk—but to our lungs, not to a developing fetus.

A substantial amount of research indicates the deleterious effects of maternal smoking on fetal development. In fact, this link was noted as early as 1868 when Kostial reported a high rate of spontaneous abortion among female tobacco workers. By 1940, there were fairly strong animal data indicating that exposure to nicotine adversely affected fetal functioning and development. Thus, the argument that smoking is "bad for babies" is not a new one. Let us look at some of the documented effects of cigarette smoking during pregnancy in humans.

The clearest effect is that the newborns of smoking women are an average of 200 grams lighter than the neonates of nonsmokers. This finding was first reported by Simpson in 1957 (cited in USDHEW, 1979). It has since been corroborated by over 45 studies examining more than 500,000 births. What is particularly impressive about this finding, aside from its consistency, is that the relationship between smoking and birth weight appears to be independent of all other known factors that influence birth weight. This includes race, maternal size, parity (that is, number of pregnancies the woman has had), a socioeconomic status, sex of the child, and gestational age. Other measures of growth—such as shoulder circumference, head circumference, and length—have also been found to be negatively correlated with maternal smoking (USDHEW, 1979).

The long-term effects of maternal smoking on the child's growth have received less attention. At least three studies (Dunn et al., 1976; Hardy & Mellits, 1972; Wingerd & Schoen, 1974), have found significant size differences between the children of smoking and nonsmoking mothers. Wingerd and Schoen reported size differences as late as 11 years of age. However, Hardy and Mellits found differences at 1 year but not at 4 and 7 years. A recent study by Lefkowitz (1981) found no differences at age 11. Thus, the question of long-term effects on physical growth remains a fruitful area for research.

Cigarette smoking also seems to increase the likelihood of fetal and infant death. This is particularly true in the cases of women whose pregnancies are already "at risk." This includes women who are poor, younger (under 20), older (over 35), small (under 5 feet), or have had more than 4 children. The major differential cause of prenatal death is hemorrhage. The major causes of infant death are immaturity, respiratory distress syndrome, pneumonia, and asphyxia (USDHEW, 1979).

Alcohol

Alcohol and cigarette use have much in common. First, alcohol is a drug that most people don't think of as a drug. We talk about drug and alcohol abuse as though the two were distinct categories. Second, it is a widely used, socially acceptable drug. Third, it has deleterious effects on the developing fetus.

As with cigarettes, the relationship between alcohol and pregnancy was noted many years ago. There are warnings concerning drinking during pregnancy even in the Bible! Physicians observed the link between chronic maternal alcoholism and birth defects as early as 1726 (Rosett & Sander, 1979). However, the Food and Drug Administration did not officially warn pregnant women about the potentially negative effects of alcohol until 1977. This warning followed a still-continuing surge of research in response to the description of Fetal Alcohol Syndrome (FAS) by Seattle researchers in 1970.

FAS is a relatively rare disorder (estimates vary from 0.4 to 3.1 per 1,000 live births) that has been observed only in children born to alcoholic mothers. Even among such women, FAS babies are relatively rare (probably about 25 per 1,000 live births) (Abel, 1981). The major symptoms include the following:

1. Prenatal and postnatal growth deficiencies. These include "small for date" babies who weigh less than expected given their gestational age and "failure to thrive" babies who for no known medical reason fail to grow at normal rate.
2. Microcephaly (an undersized head, resulting in mental retardation).
3. Fine motor dysfunction.
4. Facial abnormalities, especially cleft palate and epicanthic folds (skin around the inner eye that gives the eye a slanted appearance).
5. Often mentally retarded, especially in cases where the features of FAS are clearest; sometimes hyperactive.

Notice that in the fifth symptom we implied that not all cases of FAS are equally clear. There are a variety of Fetal Alcohol Effects (FAE) also associated with maternal drinking. These fall short of the full-blown FAS but are related to it. It appears there is a continuum of FAE ranging from miscarriage, stillbirth, and FAS at the one end to the less obvious (but still damaging) neurological disorders in the absence of physical anomalies. The incidence of FAE is higher than that of FAS. Estimates vary, but somewhere between 78 and 690 per 1,000 babies born to alcoholics suffer from FAE (Abel, 1981).

An interesting effect of maternal drinking is that it seems to adversely affect the infant's sleep patterns (Havlicek, Childiaeva & Chernick, 1977; Rosett et al., 1979). Babies born to alcoholics seem to be more restless and to interrupt their sleep more frequently than do other babies. This may have serious implications for the mother-infant relationship. Chances are, the mother is still drinking. This in combination with the baby's sleep problems may increase the likelihood of abuse, neglect, or simply poor mothering.

However, third-trimester abstinence may alleviate some of the effects of maternal drinking (Rosett & Sander, 1979; Rosett et al., 1979). This is true in terms of growth as well as sleep disturbances. If you think back to the description of prenatal development, this finding is not surprising. Recall that the third trimester is the period of greatest growth. Also, it is during the third trimester that sleep-waking patterns first appear in the EEG readings.

The effects of alcohol, like those of cigarettes, are dose related. In other words, the more a mother drinks, the more likely it is that her infant will be negatively affected. However, ascertaining which effects are due to the alcohol itself remains difficult. There are many confounding factors in studying alcohol's effects on the human fetus. For example, FAS children may have alcoholic fathers in addition to alcoholic mothers. This is interesting because sperm samples of alcoholics have been found to be grossly abnormal. These abnormalities may contribute to the children's problems. Another example of a confounding variable is birth complications. Obstetrical complications occur much more frequently in the delivery of children of alcoholic mothers than in the general population. These complications may contribute to some of the effects (especially mental retardation and hyperactivity) often seen in the children of alcoholics (Abel, 1981). So, there remain many unanswered questions about alcohol and birth defects. Nonetheless, the general finding that alcohol can negatively affect fetal development is quite well established.

It is important to note that in the majority of cases, prenatal development proceeds smoothly. Only certain substances (and very few events) can alter this positive outcome. Those substances typically have to occur in very high dosages for clearly negative outcomes. The human organism, even in its most immature form, appears to be resilient and adaptable.

LABOR AND DELIVERY

Before we can discuss newborn functioning, one more developmental "event" must be considered: labor and delivery. We will focus on the effects of drugs given during labor and delivery on the functioning of the newborn.

Labor proceeds through three stages. The first, effacement and dilatation, involves the flattening and opening of the cervix. In first-time mothers, this takes place in two separate steps. In multiparous women, effacement and dilatation occur simultaneously. That is why first labors are typically longer than later ones. During this portion of labor a variety of drugs may be given. These include uterine stimulants such as oxytocin to speed up labor; tranquilizers such as sparine vesprin; and narcotic and nonarcotic analgesics.

The second phase is the birth of the baby. If anesthesia is to be given, it will be administered just before the baby is born. Anesthesia may be general or local. However, local anesthesia is much more commonly used, even in cesarean-section (C-section) births.

The final phase is the birth of the placenta. Typically, no drugs are administered at this time.

Many people seem to think that most babies today are born without drugs. The popularity of Lamaze and Leboyer births (see Box 2-2) is assumed to indicate a decline in obstetrical drug usage. Although it is true that anesthesia, especially general anesthesia, is used less commonly, other drugs are gaining in popularity. In fact, some studies indicate that as many as 95% of all deliveries involve drugs. Some of this drug usage is due to the rapid increase in the number of C-sections being performed (Brackbill, 1979).

Virtually all obstetrical medications cross the placental barrier. In other words, they reach the about-to-be-born baby. This is worrisome because the human newborn is ill prepared to deal with drugs. First, the central nervous system is relatively immature. Compared to adult absorption of drugs, higher levels of the drug will enter the newborn's brain and will lodge in the still-developing areas. Second, the baby's liver and kidneys are immature. Therefore, the drug cannot be cleared from the infant's system as quickly as from the mother's (Brackbill, 1979).

BOX 2-2   *THE EFFECTS OF BIRTH TECHNIQUES*

Many parents now opt for a form of "natural childbirth" (for example, Lamaze or Leboyer) with the father attending the birth. The Lamaze method (for example, Karmel, 1959) involves training in breathing and concentrating techniques. These techniques minimize the mother's perception of pain so that she can avoid anesthesia. The Leboyer technique (Leboyer, 1975) adds to this a child focus. The lights in the delivery room are lowered and sounds are reduced. The newborn is placed first on his mother's stomach where his back is gently massaged. Then, the baby is placed in a warm bath. This "gentle birth" supposedly "eases" the baby into the world. Without the shock of a typical birth, the baby should be more contented and better ready to use her inherent abilities.

The use of these techniques is so common that people studying the effects of father presence at birth have difficulty finding a comparison group of fathers who were not present at the birth of their children (Palkovitz, 1985). The popular press has led us to believe that natural childbirth is preferable. What do the data suggest?

From the baby's perspective, the biggest advantage to natural childbirth is that no anesthesia is used. We have already seen that anesthetized births result in a variety of behavioral deficiencies. In addition, babies born using the Leboyer technique appear to be more calm and relaxed than those born using other procedures (even if the other babies were not born under anesthesia). They also are more alert (for example, Salter, 1978; Sorrell-Jones, 1983. Both cited in Clarke-Stewart, Friedman & Koch, 1985).

When the Leboyer technique was first introduced, many obstetricians were concerned that it was risky. A friend of mine approached her physician about using Leboyer in the late 1970s and was told "We're delivering a baby, not a fish." Doctors were concerned that delaying a physical examination, turning down the lights, and so forth, endangered the child's well-being. These fears apparently were not well founded. There have not been reports of greater birth or health complications using these techniques. Indeed, as noted earlier, the babies do seem more content and alert.

Obviously, the positive effects of these techniques can affect parent-newborn interaction. But how wide-ranging are the effects? And are the parents' own attitudes and behaviors affected? As is discussed in Chaper 3, the effects of early contact between parents and infants is not clear. Probably the effects vary greatly from family to family depending on the couples' needs and values (Palkovitz, 1985).

There is, though, one other birth method that may affect the parents themselves. This is the cesaerean birth. Different researchers have reported different effects, however. One study, for example, found that mothers played less intensely and were less positive with C-section babies (Pedersen et al., 1981, cited in Clarke-Stewart et al., 1985). This same study found that fathers of C-section babies were less comfortable about their babies' well-being. These findings may reflect continued concern about the baby's health. After all, a C-section is often an "emergency" procedure, precipitated by signs of fetal distress.

On the other hand, Palkovitz (1982) found that fathers who did not attend their child's birth were more involved with their babies when the mother was also present. This may be because the fathers are trying to "make up" for "missing" the birth. Again, most C-sections are emergencies and the parents find out at the last minute that the father will not be present. This may leave both parents feeling disappointed, angry, and generally negative about the birth experience (Hedahl, 1980, cited in Palkovitz, 1985).

Several of the commonly used obstetrical drugs are known to negatively affect newborn functioning. Demerol, frequently used as an analgesic, depresses EEG activity and alertness. Oxytocin, a uterine stimulant, may decrease motor functioning. Anesthesia depresses motor functioning and increases irritability. Infants born under anesthesia also show poor state regulation in that they do not "self-quiet" well when crying. Some studies have shown effects of anesthesia continuing into early childhood (see Brackbill, 1979).

Noted pediatrician T. Berry Brazelton (1981) has suggested that the most negative effects of anesthesia may actually be the indirect ones. He argues that the first hours after birth may be particularly meaningful and important in establishing a good mother-infant relationship. The anesthetic's effects on the mother and infant may result in less than ideal interactions. A baby may be labeled cranky or a poor eater because of these effects. This label may stick, influencing the mother's perception of the baby and herself.

REVIEW AND PREVIEW

Every adult we know is truly an individual with his or her own personality, interests, and so forth. We have seen that these differences begin before birth. Some of them are genetically rooted. This may explain part of the reason that certain behavioral characteristics "run in families." Of course, genetic differences are not the whole story. Some behaviors "run in families" because they are learned by one generation from another. (We discuss in Chapters 3 and 8 how early such learning can begin.) In addition, the environment can influence the expression of genetic material.

Genetic effects do not even account for all the individual differences seen among newborns. Many factors, such as poor diet, smoking, and drinking, can influence prenatal development. Pregnant women need to monitor their eating and drug habits carefully, particularly during the first trimester of pregnancy, to maximize the likelihood of optimal development. As with the genetic realm, some of these effects are reversible.

Genetics and prenatal influences explain some of the differences among people. There are, of course, also commonalities. We have seen that the sequence of prenatal development is the same for everyone. We have also seen that male and female children are identical for the first few weeks of pregnancy. Let's now see how these similarities and differences are reflected in newborn behavior.

3

The Newborn

The day after I brought my daughter home from the hospital, a friend came to visit us. She immediately asked to see my baby. I replied, "Sure, but wouldn't you rather wait 'til she wakes up?" My friend, looking puzzled, asked, "Why? What difference does it make whether she's awake or asleep?" Now, I was confused. "Because she looks cuter awake," I said. "What do you mean? Her eyes are closed all the time, aren't they?" "That," I said with astonishment, "is puppies. Humans are born with their eyes open!"

My friend was not alone in being misinformed about the capabilities of newborns. Many people have mistaken ideas. One of the purposes of this chapter is to clear up some of those misconceptions. This is important because our beliefs about newborns may well affect our treatment of and interactions with them. Imagine, for example, the way you might play with your new baby if you thought your baby couldn't see. You might not show her toys. You might not hang up a mobile. You even might not bother to spend much time looking directly into her face. Now imagine how your behavior might be different if you believed your baby could see fairly well. The effects of parental expectations on parent-newborn interaction are also considered in this chapter.

Of course, not just the expectations about the baby herself influence parental behavior. The parents' experience and the baby's own characteristics play a role, too. Understanding these factors facilitates our understanding of parent-newborn interaction and, therefore, our understanding of infant development. Let us begin our exploration of the newborn period by looking at the baby herself.

CHARACTERISTICS OF THE NEWBORN

Physical Appearance

An average full-term baby weighs about 7 pounds and is about 21 inches long. Of course, there are wide individual differences here. Any baby that weighs over 5.5 pounds is considered to be within the normal range; the largest baby ever born weighed over 20 pounds.

Newborns' heads look disproportionately large. As noted in Chapter 2, this is due to the relatively rapid development of the brain compared to other parts of the body. Also, the baby's head typically appears misshapen. This is because the baby's head assumes the shape of the birth canal during delivery. This is made possible by the fontanel, or "soft spot," where the skull has not yet joined. The size of the fontanel varies at birth and is not indicative of anything. Similarly, the fontanel closes at different ages in different babies (somewhere between 9 and 24 months).

A one-minute-old newborn. (Courtesy of Lennart Nilsson in *A Child Is Born* (1977), Dell Publishing Co., New York.)

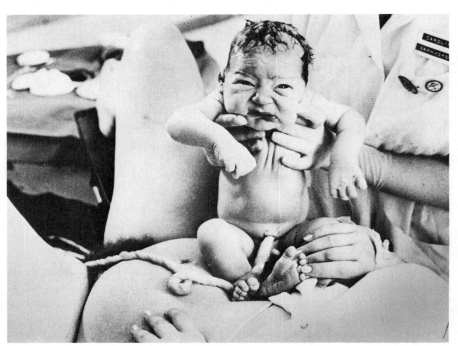

Again, the age of closing is not usually important. Contrary to popular belief, the baby cannot be easily injured if the fontanel is touched (Spock, 1977).

Beyond these characteristics, the variability in infant appearance is too great to catalogue. Newborns have differing amounts and color of hair (which usually falls out, often to reappear in a different color) and different skin tones and textures (many still have fetal body hair, or *lanugo*). A few even have teeth.

Such differences in appearance may affect the way adults interact with their babies. It is possible that a newborn who doesn't live up to his parents' expectations of attractiveness may receive less attention than a "cuter" baby would. The effects of neonatal attractiveness on mothers and fathers has not received research attention. However, nurses tend to pay more attention to newborns with more hair and with "cuter" features (Corter et al., 1978), and college students rate "cuter" newborns as probably being easier and more rewarding to care for (Stephan & Langlois, 1984). These differences in expectations and treatment may be related to later behavioral differences in more vs. less attractive children (for example, Langlois & Stephan, 1981).

Another aspect of physical functioning that needs to be mentioned is the greater susceptibility of some newborns to illness. Of particular interest is that boys seem to be more vulnerable than girls. This is true from the moment of conception (more male fetuses are miscarried). The longer life expectancy of women indicates that it continues to be true throughout life. The reasons for this difference are not known. It may be due to the greater physiological maturity of girl newborns, to hormonal differences, to the slightly greater amount of genetic material in girls, or to some unknown factor (Williams, 1979).

Sensory and Perceptual Functioning

All senses are functional at birth. Furthermore, sensory information is integrated and interpreted in a meaningful way. This does not mean that the neonate sees, hears, or tastes exactly as does an adult. It does mean that the baby's world is orderly and interpretable rather than chaotic and confusing.

Touch, Taste, and Smell.   The newborn has more skin receptors per square inch than she will have at any other time in her life. So, she is extremely responsive to touch. She also has more tastebuds than she will ever have again. This makes her very sensitive to tastes and may explain young babies' preference for bland foods. While most taste preferences will have to be acquired, newborns do seem to prefer sweet-tasting food. This may be why breast milk, which is sweeter than cow's milk or formula, is so appealing to infants.

Smell is also operative at birth. As anyone who has ever had a cold knows, the ability to smell relies on the amount of air moving through the nose. Since babies' noses are small, smell is probably not well differentiated. Babies do react negatively to pungent odors, though whether this is attributable to the bad smell or simply to irritation of the nasal membranes is not clear. The sense of smell does operate well enough to allow a breast-fed baby to recognize the odor of his mother's milk within the first few days (Russell, 1976).

Since the infant cannot move well enough to stay physically close to his parents, he must rely on vision and audition for much of this contact. Visual abilities have received particular attention from researchers.

Vision.   Newborns can see, but not very well. The eye is not fully developed at birth. The retina, where the light receptor cells are located, does not achieve adultlike structure until abut 11 months of age. Neonatal visual acuity is estimated to be about 20/600 (compared to 20/20 in normal adults) or about 30 times lower than adult acuity (Banks & Salapatek, 1983). While this seems like extremely poor vision, it is actually comparable to that of a house cat (Allik & Valsiner, 1980). This low level of acuity led early researchers to believe that newborns could not focus their eyes. They can, although, again, their ability to focus is severely limited compared to older infants and adults (von Hofsten, 1983). They see best at distances of about 8-10 inches, which means they can see mother's face while nursing.

Newborns can follow the movement of objects with their eyes, but the eye motion is not smooth. Instead, it is marked by rapid, jerky refixations, or *saccades*, on the observed object (von Hofsten, 1983).

We don't know if newborns can perceive color. Research does suggest they can distinguish red from green or blue (Jones-Molfese, 1977). Whether this is done on the basis of color or brightness differences is not known (Jones-Molfese, 1977). They cannot, however, distinguish blue from green (Jones-Molfese, 1977). In fact, the ability to perceive blue may not be available even at two months (Banks & Salapatek, 1983).

So, the visual system is functional but hardly mature at birth. How organized is the neonate's visual world, then? While many questions remain unanswered, evidence suggests that newborns have viewing preferences that enable them to adapt to and explore the world.

First, newborns prefer to look at complex rather than simple visual stimuli. This means that much of the time they will prefer to look at a human face because it is the most interesting pattern available. Several theorists and researchers, including John Bowlby (1958), have gone so far as to argue that there is an innate preference for faces. Generally, research has not supported this notion. Numerous studies have failed to find a clear preference for the human face over other complex visual stimuli in infants less than 2 months of age (for example, Fantz, 1965; Haaf, 1974; Watson, 1966). In fact, only one study (Goren, 1975) has presented evidence that newborns prefer the human face over other complex stimuli. However, since the study was plagued by a variety of methodological problems, these results must be interpreted cautiously (Cohen, DeLoache & Strauss, 1979).

Once infants are looking at a face, they seem incredibly well equipped to discriminate what the face is doing and to react to it. For example, Andrew Meltzoff and M. Keith Moore (1983a) have shown that infants who are less than 72 hours old can imitate adult mouth movements. Tiffany Field (1983) reports similar findings. She found that neonates were able to discriminate among happy, sad, and surprised faces. The newborns also showed some imitation of these different expressions. They were, for example, more likely to widen their own eyes when viewing the wide-eyed surprised expression than when watching the sad or happy face. Thus, newborns seem able to discern and react to movements of the human face.

Another sign of organization in the neonate's visual system was provided by Claus von Hofsten (1982). He found that newborns were able to exercise some control over arm movements on the basis of visual information. The babies came closer to reaching an object when they were looking at it than when they were not. They also opened their hands more frequently as they got closer to the object when they were staring at the object. Of course, eye-hand coordination is far from mature at birth. It will be many weeks before the infant is regularly successful in grasping an object she is looking at. However, von Hofsten's work does suggest that the visual system is innately designed to facilitate the exploration of objects.

Finally, other studies indicate that babies can coordinate visual information with other sensory information. For example, newborns will turn their heads to search for the source of a sound (for example, Field et al., 1980). They also turn their heads to search for the source of a touch (Humphrey, Muir & Dodwell, 1981, cited in von Hofsten, 1983). This evidence indicates that the visual system does not function in isolation. Instead, sensory and motor systems are intercoordinated. These connections may also facilitate environmental exploration.

Audition.   Since the auditory system is functionally connected to the visual system at birth, newborns must be able to hear. The question is, how well can they hear?

As with other senses, hearing is far from mature at birth. The threshold, that is, the minimum level of stimulation needed, for hearing a sound is at least 10-20 decibels higher for newborns than for adults. Also, newborns may be particularly poorly equipped to hear very high pitched sounds (Aslin, Pisoni & Jusczyk, 1983), but they can localize sounds (for example, Muir & Field, 1979). This is even true of premature infants (Muir et al., 1978, cited in Aslin, Pisoni & Jusczyk, 1983).

In a fascinating demonstration of the organized nature of early hearing, DeCasper and Fifer (1980) found that 3-day-olds preferred their mothers' voices over a stranger's. This may be due to in-utero experience, since it has been demonstrated that the mother's voice can reach the fetus (Querleu & Renard, 1981). However, this does not imply in any way that the newborn understands anything that the mother is saying (see Chapter 9).

Summary.   Human beings at birth are able to process all sorts of sensory information. Equally as important is the evidence that suggests that the sensory-perceptual system is designed to allow the child to explore the environment. As we shall see in later chapters, such capabilities may be instrumental in the development of more complex social and cognitive skills.

Reflexes

Newborns are equipped with a variety of *reflexes*–specific involuntary reactions to specific forms of stimulation. In fact, reflexes become operative early in fetal development (see Chapter 2). Table 3-1 includes names and descriptions of several reflexes.

TABLE 3-1 Neonatal Reflexes

REFLEX	DESCRIPTION
Plantar grasp	The toes curl under when pressure is applied to the ball of the baby's foot.
Hand grasp	When a stick is placed in their hands, newborns can hold on so tightly that the stick can be lifted and the baby can support her own weight.
Babinski	The toes spread out when the sole of the foot is stimulated.
Automatic walking	When supported, the newborn makes small stepping movements.
Crawling	When pulled up onto all fours, the newborn makes crawling motions.
Moro	When head position changes, arms fly out to the side and the fingers extend. To test for this reflex, the infant is placed in an infant seat that is lifted a few inches and then dropped.
Rooting	When the newborn's cheek is touched, she turns her head in the direction of the stimulus.
Sucking	When the newborn's lips are touched, he sucks.
Babkin	When the baby is lying on her back, pressure is applied to both palms. The baby's mouth opens, her eyes close, and she brings her head back to midline.

This table represents only a partial listing of the reflexes observed in normal newborns. The Brazelton scale assesses twenty reflexes.

(Information from Als et al., 1979; Gardner, 1982; Hetherington & Parke, 1979.)

Reflexes are important for several reasons. First, they reflect how well the central nervous system is functioning. Virtually every neonatal assessment scale, including the APGAR, which is routinely administered in most hospitals, examines the strength of the reflexes. Inadequate, or nonexistent, reflexes are often the first indicator of severe brain injury.

Reflexes are also important to the newborn's survival. This is obvious in the case of the "feeding" reflexes (rooting, sucking, swallowing). However, keep in mind that any behavior that draws or keeps adults near the infant also increases the baby's chances for survival. Smiling and grasping are examples of reflexive behaviors that may serve this purpose.

Finally, theorists such as Piaget (1954) have suggested that reflexes form the basis for later, more sophisticated behaviors. Piaget points out that even during the first few days of life, sucking is generalized to nonnutritive objects. Eventually, sucking becomes an important way of exploring and organizing the world. Many infants seem to put almost anything in their mouths. This enables babies to learn about taste, texture, size, shape, and hardness. Thus, what started as a reflex may evolve into a behavior that provides the information used in early concepts and categories.

Crying

Crying, like reflexes, is crucial to the baby's survival. This is because crying serves a communicative function (Wolff, 1973). Even the first cry, as the baby is being born, has communicative value. It signals to the parents that the baby is alive and is doing what she is expected to do (Osofsky & Connors, 1979). Yet cries communicate more than life even in newborns. Newborns have at least three types of cries: the basic cry, the mad cry, and the pain cry (Wolff, 1973). Each type may communicate different "needs" to the parents.

Each cry has distinctive physical characteristics (for example, the amount of "build-up" to the cry or how much air is forced through the vocal cords). The pain cry is particularly distinguishable. It is subjectively different from the basic and mad cries in three ways. First, it starts suddenly, with little or no moaning or whimpering. Second, the initial cry in the sequence of crying and "resting" is longer than in the basic and mad cries. Finally, this first long cry is followed by a relatively lengthy breath-holding period.

The communicative value of crying relies heavily, if not exclusively, on the parents' interpretation. Most early mother-infant interactions are initiated by crying. The importance of this finding is increased when you realize that some babies cry more frequently than others. In fact, there are considerable individual differences in both the frequency and length of crying episodes. Babies who cry a great deal are more likely to receive maternal attention than those who are passive (Korner, 1971). Of course, not all mothers respond quickly or consistently. First-time mothers are more likely to respond immediately to crying than are other mothers (Wolff, 1973). But, the pain cry brings mothers running regardless of their mothering experience (Wolff, 1973). Fathers, by the way, are just as able to read newborn cues as mothers and are equally responsive (Parke & Sawin, 1981). Crying, then, provides an example of how even a newborn can affect her parents and their caregiving style.

Another similarity between crying and reflexes is that crying indicates how well the central nervous system is functioning. The cry of premature infants, for example, sounds different than that of full-term infants, even to the untrained ear. Adults find the premature's cry more "grating" (Zeskind & Lester, 1978). This may make the "preemie" less appealing and may be one of the contributing factors in the premature's increased risk for abuse. Cri du chat syndrome provides another example of how crying can be indicative of nervous system functioning. Cri du chat is a genetically based form of mental retardation. One symptom of the disorder is that the newborn's cry resembles a cat meowing. In fact, the cry of brain-damaged infants is generally different from that of normal newborns. It is usually more shrill and piercing. Such cries seem to be particularly aversive to adults (Wolff, 1973).

States and Habituation

Crying is one of the states an infant can be in at any given moment. The term *state* refers to level of consciousness or awareness. Peter Wolff (1966) has identified six states that are displayed by the typical newborn. These include regular sleep, irregular sleep, periodic sleep, alert inactivity, waking activity, and crying vocalizations. Infant state is important for several reasons. The state of the infant influences his responses to stimulation. A baby who is just waking up, for instance, will respond differently than one who is wide awake and alert. This is important to consider when testing a newborn (see Box 3-1). As we shall see shortly, the baby's state and ability to respond is also important in parent-newborn interaction.

BOX 3-1　*NEONATAL ASSESSMENT WITH THE BRAZELTON SCALE*

As researchers have become increasingly aware of the behavioral capacities of the newborn, there has been a burgeoning interest in the relationship of neonatal behaviors to later behaviors. Of course, there are also always new questions about the newborn himself. Several measures have been developed to investigate newborn behavior and its relationship to later functioning. Perhaps the best known and most widely used of these scales is the Brazelton Neonatal Behavioral Assessment Scale (BNBAS) developed by T. Berry Brazelton (1973). The popularity of the BNBAS is not the only reason it is of interest to us. The strengths and weaknesses of the BNBAS underscore many of the difficulties encountered in trying to assess newborn functioning in general.

The BNBAS consists of three sections. First, there are twenty reflexes that are examined to ascertain the intactness of the baby's nervous system. Then there are broad behavioral ratings of the newborn's social attractiveness and need for stimulation as an organizing force in his behavior. These ratings yield global information about how organized and integrated the baby's behaviors are. The third, and largest, section involves the assessment of twenty-seven behaviors. These behaviors tap the neonate's (1) ability to interact with the environment, (2) ability to control and integrate motor behaviors, (3) state-regulation capabilities, and (4) ability to cope with stress. The scale is supposed to be administered at least twice (at about 3-4 days and 9-10 days) in order to see how well the baby is "recovering" from the birth process (Brazelton, 1978). In fact, Brazelton believes that the difference in these two scores (which he calls the "recovery curve") may be the single most important indicator of the baby's present and future functioning.

Since the purpose of any test is to summarize an individual's behavior, the usefulness of the BNBAS relies heavily on its relationship to nontest-situation behaviors. This is true for any neonatal assessment scale. We might ask, for example, whether a baby who is alert and responsive during testing is more likely to be alert and responsive during feeding or other social interactions.

There are studies which report modest relationships between neonatal behaviors in the testing situation and during mother-infant interaction (for example, Osofsky & Danzger, 1974; Osofsky, 1976). For example, visual behavior during assessment (such as looking at a ball, rattle, and face) was correlated with the amount of eye contact the infant had with his mother during interaction (Osofsky, 1976).

However, we cannot simply assume that such findings conclusively demonstrate that behaviors measured on the BNBAS are unchanging. In Osofsky's studies, the BNBAS items were given only a few hours after the interactional observations were made. What would have happened if the assessment and observational had been separated by several days or weeks? Another way of phrasing this question is to ask, what is the predictive validity of the BNBAS?

Before we can examine predictive validity, though, we need to consider stability. In measuring the stability of the BNBAS we are simply asking whether children typically get the same scores on multiple administrations of the test. In other words, if you test a baby when she is 2 days old and when she is 14 days old, will the scores be comparable?

Kenneth Kaye (1978) has done just this kind of study. He found that scores on day 2 did not predict well to scores at 2 weeks. Other researchers (for example, Horowitz, Sullivan & Linn, 1978) have reported similar results. This is why Brazelton himself argues that it is the overall picture of the neonate gained from multiple testings that is important (Brazelton, 1978; Als et al., 1979). The baby's performance on any given day is too easily influenced by extraneous variables (such as obstetrical medication). Furthermore, the newborn period is one of rapid developmental change. Therefore when Brazelton (and others) use the scale in clinical situations, they use that overall impression rather than a single day's score.

We are still left with the question of whether this overall impression has any predictive validity. The answer seems to be yes. For example, Edward Tronick and Brazelton (1975) tried to predict the developmental outcome of fifty-three "neurologically suspect" newborns on the basis of multiple BNBAS assessments during the first 6 days of life. The validity of these predictions was compared to the validity of predictions based upon a standard neurological examination during the same period. The children were followed for 7 years. The BNBAS and neurological examinations were about equally good at identifying neurologically disordered children. However, the BNBAS was better than the neurological examination in distinguishing healthy from disordered children. Specifically, healthy children were less likely to be mislabeled as abnormal on the basis of the BNBAS. This is important because early labeling might affect parent-infant interaction. We need to be able to identify abnormal infants if we are to maximize their chances developmentally. This cannot be done at the cost of labeling normal children as abnormal.

Other studies have also found evidence of the predictive validity of the BNBAS (see Als et al., 1979, for a summary).

Overall, we can conclude that the BNBAS is useful in identifying problem infants. This seems to be true only if the test is given several times so that an overall impression of the newborn can be formed. Thus, the BNBAS does have a clinical use. In situations where only one BNBAS is administered, as would often be the case in research, its stability problems make it somewhat less useful (Kaye, 1978), although modifications are being made to improve its heuristic value. The stability and validity problems faced, and in some cases solved, by the BNBAS are the same as are faced by other scales, such as the Graham/Rosenblith (Rosenblith, 1979). Many of the problems will remain unsolved until we better understand the relationship of neonatal behavior to later behavior. Without those links, we cannot realistically expect to see stability in early assessments.

Another aspect of state important to parent-neonate interaction is state regulation. The parents' ability to alter the newborn's state (for example, to get the baby to sleep or to make the baby stop crying) affects their self-esteem and, therefore, behavior toward the baby. It is also important that the newborn be able to regulate her own state. Most newborns can, for example, calm themselves if the "startling" stimulation is not too great. Such self-regulation provides the parents with cues about the baby's need for caretaking attention (Brazelton, 1979).

Habituation is a skill related to state regulation. Habituation means that, after a brief reaction, the baby is able to "shut out" extraneous stimuli (such as a noise or a light). This enables the baby to sleep when there is not total silence or darkness or even when the baby is being moved. This ability also allows the baby to maintain her focus during social interactions. She can, for example, continue to attend to her father's vocalizations while her siblings are playing nearby. As with crying and reflexes, habituation can also serve as an indicator of nervous system integrity.

Temperament

Crying is not the only behavior in which we find individual differences among newborns. There are also differences in neonatal temperament. What is temperament? Unfortunately, the term has not always been carefully defined. In fact, it often seems as though temperament is simply defined as what temperament scales measure (Campos et al., 1983). This means that different investigators use different definitions, an obviously confusing state of affairs. In recent years, however, theorists and researchers have tried to arrive at a consensus definition.

Temperament is a person's characteristic style of behavior. Notice that we are not referring to emotional responses that all of us have at some time or another, such as fear or sadness. Instead, we are focusing on questions such as, How quickly does the person show an emotional reaction to a situation? How long does it take for him to "calm down"? How intense is the reaction? Individual differences in these dimensions affect the baby's behavior (for example, amount of crying and how easy it is to soothe the baby) as well as the parent's behavior toward the child. Several examples of temperament dimensions are defined in Table 3-2.

TABLE 3-2 Commonly Measured Temperament Dimensions

DIMENSION	DESCRIPTION
Activity level	Amount of motor behavior apparently attributable to general arousal.
Adaptability	Ability to change initial affective reaction to stimuli. In some studies, only soothability (the ability to modify negative affective reactions) is measured.
Impulsivity (Threshold)	Speed of affective or motoric reaction.
Distractibility	How quickly the newborn reacts to a new stimulus when she/he is already involved in an activity.
Affect	May involve measuring the balance of positive and negative affect or it may be the assessment of specific emotional reactions such as anger.

(Adapted from Campos et al., *Handbook of Child Psychology* (1983) New York. John Wiley & Sons, Inc.)

Because babies can differ from one another on any of these dimensions, a listing of all of the possible individual differences in temperament is impossible. However, we can make a few general points (keeping in mind our earlier warnings about group data!). Boy newborns, for example, appear to be more active than girls (for example, Korner, 1974) though not all studies report this (for example, Korner et al., 1985). Activity levels also may vary with ethnicity. Freedman (1974) has presented evidence that Chinese-American and Navajo neonates are more passive than Caucasian babies. Although Freedman's data have not gone unchallenged, there do appear to be some temperament differences between Oriental and Caucasian babies that deserve further investigation (Super, 1981).

Newborn illness also seems to affect temperament. Jamie Greene (Greene, Fox & Lewis, 1983) found that both preterm and full-term sick newborns were less likely to attend to stimuli and were more irritable than healthy babies. Other researchers (for example, Goldberg, 1981) have suggested that premature infants are generally less responsive to stimuli and less able to stop themselves from crying. Some of these differences are probably attributable to the increased rate of illness among preterms. Others are probably due to the relative immaturity of the premature infant's central nervous system (Parmelee & Sigman, 1983).

What causes individual differences in temperament? There is a temptation to attribute them to genetic influences. Indeed, there may be a genetic component in some temperament differences. Some research suggests, for example, that irritable babies may have abnormally low levels of monoamine oxidase (MAO), a substance that breaks down neurochemical transmitters in the brain. If you have too little MAO, you will also have excessive levels of neurotransmitters. In a sense, your brain will "overstimulate" itself. This might make you more easily irritated by stimuli. Genetics seem to affect MAO levels (Sostek & Wyatt, 1982).

It would be simplistic to suggest that all temperament differences are genetically determined, however. Recall, for example, our discussion of prenatal influences: Maternal alcohol consumption affects sleep patterns and reactivity. We have also just seen that neonatal illness and prematurity affect temperament. So, individual differences may have different causes. Even in an individual baby, multiple causes may be at work.

We have examined some of the characteristics of the newborn and seen how these behaviors might affect the parents. The effects of the newborn on her interaction with her parents is greater than implied here. Before we do greater justice to the complexity of newborn-parent interaction, we need to see what the parents bring to the process.

PARENT CHARACTERISTICS

Parents, too, influence the nature of their interaction with their baby. Their personal characteristics (for example, gender, social class, and parenting experience) affect their expectations of the newborn's behavior and, therefore, their behaviors toward their babies. These characteristics also influence the parents' definitions of their own parenting roles. A second factor in parental behavior is their reaction to the birth itself. This includes postpartum depression as well as the perceived stressfulness of the postpartum period. Such factors may affect the parents' ability or, at least, readiness to interact with their neonates. They may also influence the parents' perceptions of their own ability to parent.

Personal Characteristics

Several writers (for example, Klaus & Kennell, 1976) have suggested that the earliest maternal behaviors are *species-specific* behavior. This means that all (normal) mothers should touch, hold, or look at their babies in similar, if not identical, manners. However, research indicates that cultural background influences mother-newborn interactions. For example, Wenda Trevathan (1983) found that Hispanic lower-class women handled their newborns differently than white middle-class mothers. The English-speaking mothers seemed to be more active in their exploration of their newborns.

Maternal experience also influences very early interaction. Observations suggest that first-time mothers are more persistent, but less effective, in feeding their newborns (Thoman et al., 1970). First-time mothers also seem more reserved in their exploration of their babies (Trevathan, 1983). Thoman (Thoman et al., 1970) points out that these interactional patterns may be the early precursors of birth-order effects. Many studies have reported that parents are less relaxed and more "pushy" with first-borns than with later-borns. This, in turn, has been related to the higher levels of achievement motivation and dependency on parents often observed in first-borns (for example, Sutton-Smith, 1982). The hypothesis that such effects may begin during the neonatal period underscores the potential importance of early parent-child interactions.

Gender also affects parental expectations and behaviors. Fathers seem to have somewhat different beliefs about how to treat a newborn than do mothers (Parke &

Sawin, 1980). For example, compared to maternal attitudes, fathers seem to believe that newborns need more affection (holding, verbal stimulation, and so on). Fathers also find more pleasure in their newborns. They also were prone to attribute greater visual competence to their newborns. Interestingly, the relationships between maternal and paternal perceptions change. By the time the infants are 3 months old, mothers' beliefs about both affectional needs and pleasure and visual competence surpass fathers'.

You might think that the mother-father differences are at least partially attributable to the discrepant levels of experience and knowledge that men and women bring to parenting. Men do usually have less experience with infants. They also have less "rehearsal" for the parenting role both in terms of play (dolls) and real-life situations (babysitting). Men with more experience seem to adjust better following the birth (Wente & Crockenberg, 1976). How this affects actual interaction with the newborn is not known. However, research with older infants suggests that fathers with extra "experience" are more like fathers with less experience than they are like mothers (for example, Lamb et al., 1982). Thus, experience alone cannot account for the differences between mothers and fathers.

Interaction between husband and wife also influences parenting behavior. This is true on a number of levels. First, the quality of the marriage seems to be important. Men in good marriages seem more satisfied with their fathering role and may be more likely to participate in the care of the infant (Feldman, Nash & Aschenbrenner, 1983). Second, attitudes of one parent may influence the behavior of the other. The wife's satisfaction within the marriage predicts the likelihood of the father's involvement with the infant. The happier the wife, the more likely the father is to participate in and be satisfied with parenting (Feldman, Nash & Aschenbrenner, 1983). We need to emphasize that these measures of marital satisfaction were taken before the baby was born. We will see shortly that marital satisfaction may be influenced by the birth of a baby, but it also seems that marital satisfaction prior to the birth influences the care and interaction the baby receives.

Parental Reactions to the Birth

The birth of a baby is often thought of as a stressful experience for a number of reasons. First, if we think of the family as a small social system of interrelated roles, the addition of a new person may be seen as having a potentially dramatic effect. Consider for a moment the birth of the first baby. Prior to this time, the husband and wife had relative freedom socially and sexually. They did not have to think about getting up with a baby after an evening out. They did not even have to make extensive plans to spend an evening out. Timing of sexual relations was simply a matter of choice. In other words, they were responsible primarily for and to themselves. Obviously, a baby alters this situation.

Second, think about the situation surrounding the birth. The mother has just been through a tiring labor and delivery process. Increasing numbers of husbands are now also actively involved. First-time labors average about 12 hours. The parents, then, greet their newborn in a mixed state of exhaustion and elation. Immediately, they are faced with making or implementing a variety of decisions such as how to feed the baby (breast or bottle), rooming-in, medical treatments for the baby, and so on. Most of these decisions fall on the mother, since mothers are still typically the primary caregivers for newborns and young infants.

Of course, these changes and responsibilities are not totally unexpected. The parents have had time to prepare and adjust during the pregnancy. Women's maternal feelings, for example, increase over the course of the pregnancy. Women also begin to view themselves, their husbands, and their own mothers differently (Alpert & Richardson, 1980). They do not, however, seem to spend much time thinking about all of the role changes the baby will bring. Fathers do (Chester, 1979; Fein, 1976). These differences in concerns during pregnancy may account for the differences in husband vs. wife adjustment during the postpartum period.

How stressful is the postpartum period for new mothers and fathers? Early research (for example, Dyer, 1963; LeMasters, 1957) indicated that the postpartum period was a time of "crisis." A majority of the couples in both studies reported "severe" adjustment difficulties. In addition, the arrival of children has been associated with a decline in marital satisfaction (Glick, 1977). Several other studies, however, found the time following the birth to be one of transition rather than crisis (for example, Hobbs, 1965; Hobbs & Cole, 1976; Russell, 1974). In fact, Fein (1976) actually reported a decrease in paternal anxiety from the prenatal to the postpartum period. While such mixed results do not permit us to draw a clear conclusion, there does seem to be some consensus that the birth of a baby typically requires, at most, moderate adjustment.

This view is supported by the available research on postpartum depression. Since fathers and mothers differ in both the frequency and severity of postpartum depressions, we will consider them separately.

Contrary to popular belief, not all mothers experience postpartum depression. It is unusual for any depression that does occur to be severe enough to require treatment. About 10-20% of all new mothers experience no depressive reaction. A comparable percentage experience moderate to severe depression. The majority of mothers (55-60%) experience only a temporary case of "the blues." New mothers with the blues are usually teary, despondent, and anxious. They have trouble concentrating. This problem usually begins 2-4 days after the birth. In the majority of cases, the blues last only 2 or 3 days (Pitt, 1982).

Fathers also get the "baby blues." As you might expect, this has received less research attention than maternal depression. However, Martha Zaslow (Zaslow et al., 1981) reported that about two-thirds of the fathers she studied suffered mild to moderate postpartum blues. None suffered true depression. So, both the rate (about 67% for men and 80-90% for women) and the severity of postpartum blues is less for men than for women.

Some men do, though, have more negative reactions to the birth than other men. About one-third of the men in the Zaslow study had the blues for more than eight days. The men experiencing the more extended blues reported problems in relation to their wives and in their new role as fathers. They seemed to be uncertain as to what to do or how to help their wives. This is consistent with Fein's (1976) report that fathers with a well-defined role in relation to newborn care were more likely to adjust well during the postpartum period. Notice that the nature of the father's role is less important than the existence of a role for him. Fein found that it didn't matter whether the father assumed a traditional "breadwinner" role or became an active "participant" in parenting. He simply needed a defined role.

Zaslow's study included only thirty-seven couples, so it can only be viewed as suggestive. However, it is generally accepted that new fathers have fewer and less serious adjustment difficulties than new mothers. Why might this be the case? As mentioned earlier, men might be more "prepared" for the role changes accompanying a birth than women (for example, Chester, 1979). However, the mother also typically assumes much greater responsibility for the physical care of the newborn. Not only is this a strain on her physically but it also puts her in a position of relative social isolation. She may find it difficult to go out of the house regularly, much less resume her normal social or work life. In other words, the mother may experience more extensive role changes than the father and be psychologically less prepared for them. Of course, we cannot overlook the possibility that hormonal fluctuations of pregnancy and childbirth may contribute to the greater vulnerability of the other (Pitt, 1982).

We do not want to leave the impression that reactions to birth are strictly negative. Indeed, most parents are elated immediately following delivery and report very little stress during the hospitalization period itself (Parke & Sawin, 1980). Both mother and father are usually "engrossed" with their new baby. For example, 97% of the fathers in one study said they were "very glad" right after the birth (Greenberg & Morris, 1974). Of course, parental reaction can be affected by factors such as anxiety, birth complications, and so on. However, most parents come to their first interactions with their babies with excitement and enthusiasm.

PARENT-NEWBORN INTERACTION

It is clear, then, that newborns bring a variety of skills and characteristics to their first interactions with their parents. Parents come to the interactions with varying levels of skills and expectations about their new baby and her abilities and needs. These early parent-child interactions are more important than you might think. Mothers tend to interpret even the smallest behaviors of their newborns (Brazelton, Koslowski & Main, 1974). By the time the baby is 2 weeks old, the mother has developed ideas about her baby's "personality" based on neonatal behaviors such as alertness and activity level (Bennett, 1971). Some studies have found that these impressions are not permanent (for example, Broussard & Hartner, 1970, 1971) and are not predictive of later behavior (for example, Palisin, 1980), but others have found that they do continue to exert an influence even when they are no longer appropriate (Greene, Fox & Lewis, 1983). For example, mothers seem to react to the higher levels of irritability and inattentiveness of sick newborns with more physical caretaking and less emotional expressiveness than mothers of healthy newborns. These differences in mothering style were still evident 3 months later even though the sick baby's irritability and inattentiveness that had "triggered" the maternal behavioral differences had disappeared. This underscores the importance of the mother's "definition" of the baby's status in her maternal behavior (Greene, Fox & Lewis, 1983).

The Effects of Parental Interpretation of Neonatal Characteristics

How much of the mother's behavior is based upon realistic appraisal of the newborn and how much upon her own beliefs and experience? Tiffany Field (Field et al., 1978) has found that mothers' evaluations of their newborns are quite accurate. She found maternal appraisals were highly correlated with evaluations by professionals using the Brazelton scale (see Box 3-1). This was not true of all mothers, though. Middle-class white mothers seemed more accurate in their assessments than lower-class black mothers. The lower-class mothers, for example, tended to overestimate their newborn's motoric functioning. This belief guided the mother's stimulation of her newborn, so that these mothers gave their babies much more motoric stimulation than did the middle-class mothers.

The middle-class mothers in Field's study also acted in a manner consistent with their appraisals. Similarly, Joy Osofsky (Osofsky & Danzger, 1974; Osofsky, 1976) found that lower-class black mothers acted in a manner that seemed "tuned in" to their babies' abilities. She found, for example, that some newborns were more sensitive to auditory stimulation while others were more responsive to visual stimulation. Mothers in her study tended to stimulate their baby's "preferred" sense.

Another finding in Field's study suggests that mothers react to the baby rather than exclusively to their own belief system. When questioned, mothers often expressed the belief that their newborns could neither hear nor see. Yet, these same mothers constantly talked to their babies and provided them with visual stimulation. As we know, the newborns can see and hear. Perhaps the neonates' responses to the mother's stimulation "encouraged" the mothers to keep talking to the babies and showing them objects. Expectations can play some role here, however. Fathers, for example, tend to rate their newborns as having greater visual abilities than mothers rate them as having. Fathers visually stimulate their babies more than mothers do (Parke & Sawin, 1980).

Maternal behaviors are also influenced by neonatal temperament. The irritability and soothability of the baby, for example, both influence the mother's own self-esteem (Korner, 1979). You can well imagine that a mother of a baby who cries easily and is difficult to comfort might doubt her mothering abilities. Such mothers may withdraw from their infants. They may even become abusive (Sameroff & Chandler, 1975). We should emphasize here that not all mothers of these "difficult" babies will react this way. Some mothers may become more attentive. The mother's appraisal of herself and her baby as well as her behavioral reactions seem to be heavily related to the child's eventual outcome. Mothers of difficult children who make negative appraisals have children who are more likely to develop behavioral disorders (Sameroff & Chandler, 1975). Again, then, we see support for the transactional model of parent-child relationships. This transaction is depicted in Figure 3-1.

The mother's ability to alter the state of the newborn also has an effect. As just noted, some babies are easier to soothe than others. Even more dramatically, some babies do not even display the full range of states. This usually bodes poorly for their future development. T. Berry Brazelton (1979) described one very extreme case of this. One of the babies he observed seemed to have only two states—deep sleep and crying. His mother never had the opportunity to have a pleasant, calm interaction with him. Right from the beginning, his mother felt "rejected." She was overwhelmed by the job of caring for him.

Clearly, maternal behaviors are influenced by neonatal characteristics. This implies that it may be helpful to educate new mothers so that their expectations and interpretations of their baby's behavior is as realistic as possible. This may be particularly important in cases where the child is "difficult" or ill. Mothers need to be given support and advice about coping with such a child rather than being left to feel incompetent (see Box 3-2).

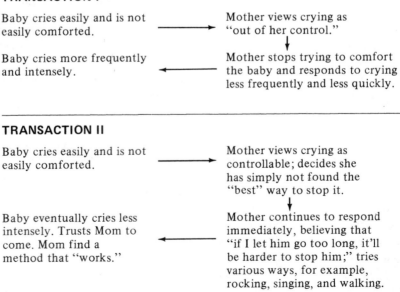

TRANSACTION I

| Baby cries easily and is not easily comforted. | ⟶ | Mother views crying as "out of her control." |

Baby cries more frequently and intensely. ⟵ Mother stops trying to comfort the baby and responds to crying less frequently and less quickly.

TRANSACTION II

Baby cries easily and is not easily comforted. ⟶ Mother views crying as controllable; decides she has simply not found the "best" way to stop it.

Baby eventually cries less intensely. Trusts Mom to come. Mom find a method that "works." ⟵ Mother continues to respond immediately, believing that "if I let him go too long, it'll be harder to stop him;" tries various ways, for example, rocking, singing, and walking.

FIGURE 3-1   Exemplification of Two Possible Transactions between a Mother and a Difficult Baby.

BOX 3-2 *EASING THE TRANSITION TO PARENTHOOD*

While becoming a parent does not seem to be a crisis for most adults, it is a time of considerable transition. This transition can be stressful, especially if the newborn is "difficult." The research on the transition into parenthood does, though, suggest some ways to ease the stress.

First, parents need to be educated about differences among newborns. Their expectations of having a "Gerber baby" need not be dashed. It should be pointed out to them, however, that some babies cry more than others, sleep less, have irregular schedules, and so forth. Parents need to understand that such problems are not *really* problems. They are simply differences. More importantly, they need to understand that the differences are not their fault. Such education can help to prevent the negative transaction depicted in the first example in Figure 3-1.

Second, parents need to be reminded that while child rearing is a huge responsibility, they still have some responsibility to themselves. Recall that the data suggest that the extent of role changes, fatigue, and the sense of social isolation may contribute to negative adjustments. Parents need to define what role each will take in the family after the child is born. This seems especially important for fathers (for example, Fein, 1976). Mothers need to be encouraged to let the father help, if he wants to (Barnett & Baruch, 1983). This may be particularly important in terms of the mother's fatigue and sense of isolation. She too needs some time for herself.

Of course, the parents also need time for each other. One reason that marital satisfaction often declines after the first baby is born is because the parents have less time for each other. This lack of time also influences the father's adjustment to and interaction with the baby (Alpert & Richardson, 1980; Feldman, Nash & Aschenbrenner, 1983). While it is important that both parents spend time with the baby, it is also important that they find some time for each other.

Each family must define its own needs, roles, and interactional patterns. The job of professionals (such as nurses, doctors, social workers), friends, and family is to support and encourage the parents in this definitional process.

Father-Newborn Interaction

We do not yet know whether all these newborn characteristics affect fathers in the same way they do mothers. However, Ross Parke has reported a series of studies (summarized in Parke, 1979) that suggest that father-newborn interaction is very similar to mother-newborn interaction. He found that, given the opportunity, fathers interacted with their newborns as much as mothers did. The fathers also showed behaviors (smiling, looking, vocalizing, and so on) at rates similar to the mothers. This was true for both lower- and middle-class fathers.

Yet, there are some differences between the mothers and fathers. Fathers are significantly less likely than mothers to engage in the physical care of the infants

(Parke, 1979). This is true even when the father is taking care of the baby by himself. Surveys of mothers suggest that they are still responsible for the majority of child care in the family, even if they work outside the home (Barnett & Baruch, 1983). This assignment of duties seems to begin in the first few days of the baby's life. Add to this the finding that fathers are more likely to stimulate the newborn socially (especially visually), and we see that the pattern of mother as caretaker and father as playmate emerges very early in child development (Parke & Sawin, 1980).

The Effects of Infant Gender

Another difference noted by Parke (for example, Parke & Sawin, 1980) is the way fathers and mothers react to sons as opposed to daughters. Fathers were more likely to be affectionate toward their daughters (for example, holding them close) than they were toward their sons. The reverse was true for mothers. On the other hand, parents were more likely to attend to and stimulate same-sex newborns. Mothers, for example, showed toys to their daughters more often than to sons. Fathers, again, did the reverse.

These effects of infant gender on parental behaviors have some important implications. First, they underscore the fact that mothers and fathers play different roles in child development. Their roles are complementary rather than simply redundant. This suggests that the absence of one parent at any period during development may have detrimental effects on the child.

A second issue has to do with sex-role development. The finding that gender influences how the baby is treated even as a newborn has powerful implications. It suggests, for example, that the differential training that many theorists (for example, Mischel, 1970) believe determines sex-role development begins very early in life. We used to believe that sex differences in children's behavior that appeared at age 1 or 2 needed an explanation that at least included biological factors. The argument was that social training could not have been going on long enough to account for behavioral differences. In light of findings of differential treatment in the neonatal period, though, such arguments need to be reconsidered. We will return to this issue in Chapter 9.

The Effect of the Parents
on Newborn Behavior

We have seen that newborn characteristics influence the way parents behave. The opposite side of this question is, how do parents affect newborns? In terms of immediate effects, the more sensitive the parent to the newborn, the more likely he or she is to get a positive response from the baby (for example, Korner, 1979; Osofsky, 1976). In other words, babies with sensitive parents will have more positive interactions than other babies. This is a self-perpetuating cycle. The newborns with more positive interactions have parents who will have stronger self-esteem and confidence in their parenting ability. All this should increase the likelihood that the child will develop normally. What we are seeing here is the reciprocity of the parent-child relationship. One influences the other to form the patterns that will determine developmental outcome.

In terms of specific, long-term outcomes, there seem to be few, if any, parental behaviors toward the newborn that permanently alter behavior. For example, factors such as breast vs. bottle feeding, schedule vs. demand feeding, and so on, seem to have little impact on the child's future development. This does not mean that the newborn period is not important for development. Rather, the effects of the neonatal period are general rather than specific. The greatest effects seem to be on parent-child interaction cycles. General feelings of parental competence, impressions of the baby's personality, and sensitive parenting techniques can be rooted in the parent-newborn interaction. These are hardly negligible effects.

The Nature of Parent-Newborn Interaction

The parent-newborn interactions, then, are extremely important. They are also extremely difficult to describe and understand. Our discussion so far exemplifies this problem. We have discussed many ways in which the newborn may influence the parents' behavior. We have also noted ways in which the parents' behaviors might influence the newborn. What we have not done is capture the interactional process. In other words, we do not yet have a sense of the ongoing interchange between parent and newborn.

Although we cannot hope to list all the possible "communications" between parent and infant, we can at least get a sense of how such communication proceeds. T. Berry Brazelton (1979) has provided an example. When a mother speaks to her newborn, he becomes alert. He gradually turns his head to the source of the sound. His movements are slow and relatively smooth rather than "jerky." When the baby finds his mother's face (the sound "source"), his face and eyes widen and soften. He looks eager. He may even lift his chin toward his mother. His muscles tense, but he is quiet and inactive. This wide-eyed attention is almost irresistible. Most moms will feel "impelled" to pick up the baby and cuddle him. The baby will mold to the mother's body, perhaps reinforcing her sense of her mothering ability, and the interaction will continue.

What we see here is that a maternal behavior elicits an infant behavior which in turn elicits a maternal behavior which in turn elicits an infant behavior, and so on. The mother and baby are influencing each other. They are, in some sense, communicating. It doesn't matter which one of them starts the interaction. The important point is that it is an *interaction*. The mother is not simply stimulating the baby, nor is the baby simply eliciting behavior from the mother. There is a mutual, reciprocal regulation of behavior.

Brazelton (1979) has argued that such early parent-infant interactions are extremely important. He notes a parent who "fails" with one child—as in child abuse or neglect for example—is often successful with another child. The parents in these cases often mention their inability to communicate with the "failed" child, even as a newborn. They feel that the child was different from the beginning and that they were never able to "get in touch" with the child. This, in combination with the factors we discussed earlier (for example, difficult temperament or poor health) may contribute to poor parent-infant relationships and, ultimately, to poor child development.

How early must effective parent-child interactions begin if the child is to have the best possible chance at "normal" development? There is an ongoing debate in the field of infant development concerning this question. The debate centers on the importance of bonding during the newborn period.

Bonding

Defining Bonding.   The term *bonding* is typically used in a very specific manner. It refers to the facilitation of parent- (especially mother-) to -infant attachment during a period of heightened parental sensitivity immediately after birth. This definition has several implications. First, the attachment of parent to infant is different from the attachment of infant to parent. For one thing, the parent is capable of becoming attached to the infant long before the infant attaches to the parent (see Chapter 4). Second, the attachment of the parent to the infant is not a "given"; it is not automatic. The parent needs time to get to know the infant. Of course, it is assumed that the parent-to-infant attachment continues to develop well beyond the neonatal period. Few would debate either of these issues. It is the third assumption that fuels the debate.

The third assumption is that the period immediately following birth is especially important to the development of parent-to-infant attachment. This is partially due to the excitement the parents feel. The infant is also more alert and able to respond immediately following birth than she will be for the next several days (Brazelton, 1981). This time is seen as optimal for laying the foundation of parent-to-infant attachment. In fact, some people believe that failure to bond during the neonatal period may permanently impair the parent-child relationship (for example, Klaus & Kennell, 1976).

Rationale for the Importance of Bonding.   Why would anyone believe that bonding is so important? Data from several sources contributed to the development of this concept. Animal data (summarized in Kennell, Voos & Klaus, 1979) suggested that there was a sensitive period for mother-to-infant attachment. If, for example, a mother goat is separated from her kid for just over an hour immediately following its birth, she may refuse to "mother" it when it is returned. She may refuse to nurse the kid. She may even butt and kick it. Obviously, the kid could die without intervention.

We need to emphasize that we are talking about a *sensitive period* here rather than a critical period. A sensitive period means that conditions for the mother-to-infant attachment are optimal. In other words, the attachment can be formed more easily now than during some other period of development. Although the failure to bond may have permanent effects, those effects are not necessarily irreversible.

With goats, for example, if the kid is left with the mother in close quarters during the first 12 hours postpartum, attachment may still occur. However, what would have taken a few minutes of contact after birth now takes 10 days to achieve (Kennell, Voos & Klaus, 1979). If those first few minutes had been a critical period, the effects would be irreversible.

The other sort of data that contributed to the hypotheses about bonding comes from studies of abused and failure-to-thrive infants (infants who do not grow despite physical normalcy). Margaret Lynch (1975) found that a disproportionate number of the abused children in her study had been separated from their mothers during the neonatal period. The fact that premature infants, who are often separated from their parents during the newborn period, are particularly likely to be abused seemed to support Lynch's conclusion (see Kennell, Voos & Klaus, 1979, for a summary of these and related findings).

Mother-Infant Bonding Research. These findings, coupled with their own clinical experience, led John Kennell and Marshall Klaus to the hypothesis that the first few hours after birth might be a sensitive period for the formation of the parent-to-infant bond. They began a series of studies concerning the effects of contact during the first few hours after birth on the mother's behavior with her infant (for example, Klaus et al., 1972). Prior to this time, routine obstetrical care permitted only limited interaction between the mother and her newborn. Typically, mothers got a glimpse of the baby when he was born, then saw the baby for identification purposes when he was about 6 hours old, and then saw the baby every 4 hours for 20-30 minute feedings (Kennell, Voos & Klaus, 1979). The situation was even worse for fathers. Often, their only interaction with their newborns came through the nursery window.

Klaus and Kennell wanted to see what would happen if the mothers were allowed more contact with their newborns. This involved both earlier and more prolonged contact during the hospital stay. Their results indicated that high-contact mothers showed more positive maternal behaviors toward their babies than did the mothers who had experienced the hospital "routine." Even when the babies were 2 years old, the extended-contact mothers could be distinguished from the hospital-routine mothers (Ringler et al., 1975). In fact, indirect effects of the differential early exposure appeared at age 5 (Ringler et al., 1978).

Klaus and Kennell's work generated clinical and empirical interest. The clinical effects—rooming-in, bonding time, and so on—are obvious. Numerous researchers have attempted to replicate, refine, and extend Klaus and Kennell's findings. In some ways, there has been success. Of the almost thirty studies reviewed by Susan Goldberg (1983), only one (Svedja, Campos & Emde, 1980) failed to find any effects of bonding. However, most studies find the effects to be less widespread and of much shorter duration than Klaus and Kennell reported. In fact, some researchers (for example, Grossman, Thane & Grossman, 1981) have found that differences between high-contact and hospital-routine mothers are not discernible after 10 days.

The weakness of these findings has led many reviewers to conclude that there is no sensitive period for mother-infant bonding (for example, Lamb & Hwang, 1982; Svedja, Pannabecker & Emde, 1982). These arguments are bolstered by reference to the positive attachment of adoptive mothers to their babies (with whom, of course, they did not have early contact). Additionally, the data concerning premature infants that we mentioned earlier is challenged because of the complex network of factors (for example, the health of mother and infant, the appearance of the infant, and the ability of the infant to respond to stimulation) that might affect the formation of a proper mother-to-premature bond.

Toward Resolving the Debate.   Two reviewers—Herbert Leiderman (1983) and Susan Goldberg (1983)—caution against dismissing the concept of a sensitive period. Leiderman notes that the discrepancies between Klaus and Kennell and some later researchers may be attributable to sampling differences. The mothers selected for the Klaus and Kennell study were lower class. The mothers in most other studies were middle class. He suggests that bonding might be more important for some mothers (or types of mothers) than for others. This issue requires more attention before the bonding debate can be resolved.

Goldberg also brings up several questions that need to be answered before we can evaluate the importance of early contact. Many of these are methodological issues which we cannot examine here. However, one is of particular interest. Goldberg suggests that we need a model of how mother-to-infant attachment occurs in the neonatal period and throughout the child's life. Without such a model, she argues, we might not be looking at the behaviors crucial for understanding the process. Most studies have looked, for example, at behaviors such as maternal smiling or vocalizing. Are these behaviors indicative of mother-to-infant attachment? Are they better indices than any other behaviors? How are they related to later maternal behaviors? For example, does smiling at the child have the same meaning when the child is 5 years old in terms of strength of attachment? Without a model of the underlying mechanisms of mother-to-infant attachment, we are in many ways floundering in trying to understand existing data and in trying to generate future research.

Probably the safest conclusion at this point is that bonding may or may not be an important phenomenon. Neonatal contact seems to have some effect on mothering, but neither the scope nor the duration of those effects is clear. The only thing that does seem clear is that early contact is not crucial for the development of a good mother-to-infant attachment. At most, bonding makes the achievement of a strong mother-to-infant attachment easier.

Father-to-Infant Bonding.   There are studies of father-to-infant bonding, but they are plagued by methodological problems. These include frequent failures to measure preexisting attitudes toward fathering, experience with children, and maternal attitudes toward the father's role. Many studies have also failed to observe a *noncontact* group of fathers (Palkovitz, 1985). As with the mother-to-infant bonding literature, there is no model guiding the choice of observed behaviors (Goldberg, 1983; Palkovitz, 1985). These problems have resulted in very inconsistent results. Some evidence suggests that early contact improves fathering behavior (for example, Keller, Hildebrandt & Richards, 1981; Lind, Vuorenkoski & Wasz-Hockert, 1973, cited in Kennell, Voos & Klaus, 1979; Rodholm, 1981). Others have found no effects (Pannabecker, Emde & Austin, 1982).

Given these problems, it is difficult to draw any firm conclusions about father-to-infant bonding (Palkovitz, 1985). One interesting finding has emerged, however. It appears that the effects of attending the birth and early contact with the baby may affect father-infant interaction *indirectly* at least as much as directly. This means that these early experiences with the birth process and with their babies may affect the father-mother relationship which may, in turn, affect the father-infant interactions (Palkovitz, 1985). This is consistent with findings presented earlier that maternal attitudes and behaviors influence father-newborn interactions.

As with mother-infant bonding, the safest conclusion seems to be that early or extended contact with the newborn is not necessary for a normal father-infant relationship to develop. In fact, one study has found that fathers who were suddenly unable to be present at the birth (due to a C-section, paternal illness, and so on) were actually more interactive with their babies (in the mother's presence) (Palkovitz, 1982). This seemed to be due to the father's desire to "make up" to the mothers for their absence at the birth. Overall, it appears that the needs of the *couple* for the father's involvement in the birth may determine the importance of early father-newborn contact. So, for some fathers, it will be helpful and for others it will not (Palkovitz, 1985). Once again, then, we see the importance of evaluating the entire familial context in trying to understand influences on infant development.

SUMMARY

It is obvious that the newborn comes to the world equipped for both exploration and interaction. She is able to both respond to and influence her environment. All normal newborns share certain behavioral capabilities. Their senses are functional, they have reflexes, they can communicate, and so on. Newborns are not, however, all identical. There are wide individual differences in temperament, the ability to self-regulate state, and frequency of crying. Some of the individual differences probably have genetic origins while others are probably rooted in prenatal influences.

One of the most important issues during the newborn period is the establishment of parent-child interaction. These early interactions are influenced by child and parent characteristics. It is important to recognize that patterns of interaction established during these first few days may persist indefinitely. However, that does not mean the interactional patterns are by definition immutable.

Our understanding of the importance of these interactions, including the timing of the first ones, is limited. Similarly, we are only beginning to understand the capabilities of the newborn. It is still difficult to link neonatal behaviors and interactions to later ones. Nonetheless, the conceptualization of the neonate as a passive, reactive, empty being seems to be outdated. Rather, the newborn is a complex, integrated being who from the start engages in complex, reciprocal interactions with the environment.

4

Attachment

In discussing bonding, we made a distinction between parent-to-infant and infant-to-parent attachment. Among other things, infant-to-parent attachment is a longer process. This chapter focuses on the process of infant-to-parent attachment and on the importance of that process.

Attachment is of tremendous interest to child development theorists. As we shall see, many theorists see it as the cornerstone of development. Attachment is also of great interest to health professionals, who may wonder if separating the newborn from his parents will negatively affect his development. Parents and day-care workers might worry that putting a child in day care (or with a sitter) will interfere with the parent-child relationship. They are also often concerned about "separation distress." They may wonder if separating a baby from her mother (even for a few hours a day) might be traumatic for the baby. These are some of the issues addressed in this chapter.

DEFINITION AND HISTORY
OF THE ATTACHMENT CONSTRUCT

Attachment is an affectional tie of one person to a specific other person. The tie is enduring and persists even during separations (Ainsworth, 1973; Bowlby, 1977). Note first in this definition that the attachment is specific. John Bowlby (1969), who might be considered the "father"of attachment theory, argued that this is true in all species. Specifically, consider the tie of the infant to her parent(s): The infant does not treat everyone equally. Rather, she develops this special relationship with at most a few people. Some theorists, including Bowlby, go so far as to suggest that there is but one primary attachment; all other relationships are secondary. For most babies, this primary attachment figure is the mother.

Another component of this definition is its emphasis on affect. Here, we mean an emotional bond—love. Since the baby must have some concept and memory of the attachment figure, there is a cognitive component. However, the focus is on affective development in terms of the "causes" of attachment, the behaviors involved in attachment, and the importance of attachment.

Interest in infant-to-mother attachment was sparked by the findings of several researchers during the 1940s and 1950s. The most important research focused on what happened to the child when no attachment relationship existed. The work of Harry Harlow, Rene Spitz, and Bowlby himself seems to have been particularly influential.

In a series of studies with rhesus monkeys, Harlow found that monkeys raised without mothers showed a variety of behavioral problems (for example, Harlow, 1959). These included self-mutilation, lack of exploratory behavior, excessive aggressiveness, and the inability to function in heterosexual or parenting roles. Virtually all socially oriented behaviors were disrupted. In addition, Harlow found that the monkeys seemed particularly to miss the affectional contact ("contact-comfort") of the mother-infant relationship. This finding underscores the emotional aspect of attachment.

Spitz and Bowlby observed similar effects in humans. Spitz (1945/1973; 1946/1973) studied babies in a foundling home. These babies had no consistent caregiver providing the warm, supportive interactions associated with mothers. All of the children examined showed ill effects. The effects ranged from failure to attain appropriate height and weight (now termed failure to thrive) to retarded language development. There was almost nothing normal about any of the children. Spitz concluded that such effects were due to lack of mothering ("maternal deprivation").

Bowlby (1951) reported similar negative effects of maternal deprivation. In fact, he argued that long-term separation would permanently impair the child's development. Even in less dramatic situations, where the child simply formed an inadequate attachment, Bowlby saw the likelihood of long-term problems. He argued, for example, that most psychological disorders are rooted in poor infant attachment (for example, Bowlby, 1977). He traced a variety of disorders such as depression, anorexia nervosa, school phobia, and agoraphobia to poor infant-mother relationships.

We need to emphasize that the lack of a healthy infant-to-mother attachment affects more than just the baby's social and emotional development. Cognitive development may also be negatively affected. For example, infants without attachments seem reluctant to explore their environments (Ainsworth et al., 1978). If

Piaget's (1954) claim that active exploration of and interaction with the environment forms the basis for all cognitive development, the effects of such timidity may be wide reaching.

THEORIES OF ATTACHMENT

Freud

Importance of Attachment. Although Bowlby was the first to develop a full-scale theory of the development of attachment, he was not the first to recognize the significance of the infant-mother relationship. In fact, Bowlby's theory is rooted in the psychoanalytic (Freudian) tradition. Freud was not as specific as Bowlby about either the meaning or the development of attachment, but he did present some seminal ideas about its meaning.

Freud believed that the first attachment to the mother was crucial for several reasons. He saw it as a "prototype" for later attachment relationships. In other words, later attachment relationships (for example, between spouses) would be modeled after the infant-mother relationship. He also argued that attachment was necessary for the development of two of the structures of personality, the ego and the superego.

In Freudian theory, the ego is the structure of personality that deals with reality, with the environment. At birth, no functional ego exists. Instead, the newborn is guided solely by the id's instincts to avoid pain and maximize pleasure. Of course, no environment can completely meet these demands. So, the ego develops to serve as a "moderator" between the id and the environment. However, if the ego is to deal with the environment, the child must be able to distinguish himself and his needs from the rest of the world. This distinction begins to be made through his interactions with his mother.

Superego development also relies on infant-to-mother attachment. The superego is the moral guardian of personality. It actually starts to develop during the Oedipal conflict of the preschool years. However, the Oedipal conflict could not occur in either boys or girls if the child was not first attached to the mother. It is in this sense that superego development relies on attachment.

We see, then, that Freud viewed attachment as important for both personality development and the development of social relationships. He also felt that he had not discovered the full force of their importance. He seemed particularly baffled by the strength of girls' attachment to their mothers (Freud, 1931). So, although Freud acknowledged the importance of infant-to-mother attachment, even he believed he had not dealt with the issues adequately.

Sequence. Freud did propose a developmental progression for attachment. At first, the newborn does not distinguish between himself and the environment. His primary sources of need gratification and pleasure come from his own body (for example, his hands or thumb). An external object becomes important only if it somehow fulfills a need for the baby. In such instances, the infant imbues the object with his own psychic energy. In other words, the object (in this case, the mother) actually becomes part of the infant's psychic system. For the infant, the mother has no independent existence. She exists only in relation to him and his needs.

As their relationship continues, the infant gradually begins to recognize the separateness of the mother. The sheer presence of the mother eventually becomes pleasurable. For example, initially the mother is of interest only when the baby is hungry. Later, as the baby delineates the boundaries between himself and his mother, the mother becomes psychologically important on a continuing basis, not just when the baby is hungry.

Freud argued that infant-to-mother attachment is rooted in the fulfillment of physiological or instinctual needs. This argument has not been supported by empirical work. Harry Harlow's work with monkeys, for example, suggests that warm contact ("contact-comfort") is a more powerful force in attachment formation than feeding. Research with humans indicates that infants are most likely to attach to responsive adults who actively interact with them (for example, Ainsworth et al., 1978). In fact, such interaction appears to be the basis of infant-to-father attachment, since fathers provide little physical care (for example, Lamb, 1978).

Erikson

Erik Erikson (1963) based his theory of personality development on Freud's work. Erikson proposed an eight-stage theory of development. In each stage, there is a psychosocial crisis to be resolved. The resolution of each crisis is influenced by the outcome of the preceding crises. Each stage thus builds upon the previous stages. Therefore, the first stage is the foundation of development.

The psychosocial crisis of the first stage, occurring during the first year of life, is trust vs. mistrust. Ideally, the child emerges from this stage with a sense of trust in the world. She will believe that the world is a safe and interesting place full of people concerned with her well-being. This attitude gives her the freedom to explore and interact with her environment. The infant's interactions with adults form the core of trust. If the mother (or other attachment figure) fails to provide a safe, supportive environment, the child will view the world as a hostile place.

Erikson's view of attachment is in many ways similar to Freud's. For example, he does not provide much specific information about how the attachment is formed. Rather, he is interested in the outcome of the attachment (or lack of attachment). There is, however, one major difference between Erikson and Freud: Erikson believed that warm, positive, and stimulating interactions, as opposed to physical need fulfillment, formed the basis of attachment. As we have just seen, research supports this argument.

Though neither Freud nor Erikson provided a truly complete model of attachment, they both contributed to our understanding of attachment and its importance. John Bowlby's theory shows this influence.

Bowlby

Basic Principles. John Bowlby's theory of attachment continues to be the most influential model in this area. Bowlby's model began with Freud's writings. However, Bowlby (1969) believed that Freud's failure to observe the actual development of attachment in infancy was a major shortcoming. Freud's own theory, of course, was derived mainly from clinical evaluations of his adult patients. Bowlby added an ethological perspective to Freudian psychoanalysis by adopting the ethological emphasis on naturalistic observation of the actual attachment process. He also considered animal data, thereby adding an evolutionary perspective to attachment.

The impact of the ethological perspective is evident in Bowlby's understanding of the goal of attachment. He argued that attachment can be understood only within an evolutionary framework. According to evolutionary theory, a species is designed to optimize its likelihood of survival. The higher species, such as humans, have more flexible (and fewer instinctual or reflexive) behaviors than do lower species. This makes the higher species more adaptable, giving them a better chance at survival. Yet this also means that fewer behaviors are "fixed" at birth. Higher animals need more time to develop. Compared to the lower species, they have a relatively long period of infantile helplessness. The young need to be protected and cared for by adults during this period. It is to the benefit of the species in general and the infant in particular to encourage and sustain adult contact with the baby. This, then, is the goal of attachment behavior, for attachment behavior represents the infant's way of getting an adult to provide care and protection. Thus, for Bowlby, attachment is rooted not in the fulfillment of needs or in interaction patterns, but in the biological, evolutionary history of the species.

Roots of Attachment. Bowlby hypothesized that infants have five innate behaviors that encourage parenting. Crying and smiling serve as signaling behaviors. They activate maternal behavior, bringing the mother near. Sucking, following, and clinging, on the other hand, show the child's active role in seeking and maintaining proximity with the mother. Of course, these five behaviors do not appear simultaneously. Initially, they seem to be relatively independent of one another. Eventually, though, they are organized into an integrated behavioral set focused on the primary attachment figure, usually the mother. These behaviors, then, form the basis of attachment. The mother is a particularly likely focus of these behaviors. Bowlby suggested that this is because the mother is most likely to be caring for the infant and because the mother may in some way be biologically primed to respond to the infant in ways that encourage attachment. We should emphasize, however, that Bowlby did not claim that only the mother could be the primary attachment figure. A child can develop normally with someone other than the mother serving as the primary attachment figure. The important point is that for Bowlby there is but one dominant attachment figure.

Biological and environmental factors are probably involved in the activation of the infant's attachment behavior. When the infant's attachment behaviors are "activated," full-blown attachment does not appear immediately. Bowlby proposed four sequential stages in the development of infant-to-mother attachment. These stages cover approximately the first 3 years of life.

Sequence. The first phase, "undiscriminating social responsiveness," lasts for the first 2 or 3 months. The baby does not seem to show differential interaction patterns with adults. He does, however, have a variety of behaviors (such as crying, visual following, and grasping) that encourage and maintain interaction with adults.

The second phase, "discriminating social responsiveness," lasts until the baby is about 6 months of age. Now the baby not only distinguishes familiar people from unfamiliar people but also reacts to them differently. Initially, the differential response (in smiling, vocalizing, and so on) is evident only when the adult is close by. Eventually, it is also evident when the person is some distance away. The baby may cry, for example, when the mother leaves the room but not when a stranger leaves. Usually, the baby's "special" responsiveness is directed toward the mother and one or two others.

Starting at about 7 months of age, the baby begins the third phase—"active initiative in seeking proximity and contact." Now, in addition to differential responding, the baby actively works to gain and keep closeness ("proximity") with the attachment figure. Motor development, including crawling and increasing control over arm and hand movements, plays an important role here. Behaviors such as following, approaching, and clinging become evident. At this point, the baby is truly "attached" to another person. This is indicated when the infant changes his own behavior to "match" maternal behavior. He will change speed or direction, for example, in response to maternal movement.

The fourth phase, "goal-corrected partnership," is an elaboration of these behavioral sequences. It probably does not begin until about age 3. Instead of simply being guided by immediate feedback, the child can anticipate, and correct for, maternal behavior. He increasingly understands the mother's goals and plans. He knows, for example, when bedtime is approaching. Bedtime represents a separation that he wants to avoid, and so he does things that (he hopes) thwart his mother's plans and serve his own desire to stay close to her. He may ask for a drink or insist that he needs to use the bathroom or claim that there is something important that he forgot to do earlier. Of course, the child will have only limited success in anticipating maternal behavior. His success will rely, at least in part, on his mother's willingness to let him perceive her goals.

Bowlby's theory has generated considerable research. It has been the dominant theory of attachment for several years. It is not without its critics though. Before we consider the research based on Bowlby's work, let's first examine an alternative model of attachment.

Gewirtz

Jacob Gewirtz (1976) approached attachment in a manner very different from Freud, Erikson, and Bowlby. He argued that the term *attachment* is much too vaguely defined. He suggested that we do not need to talk about some kind of emotional bond. Instead, what we are really talking about is that one person's behavior or presence has come to control another person's behavior. The mother has become a positive reinforcer through her association with fulfillment of physical needs, interesting stimulation, and so on. People always want to maximize positive reinforcement. So, the baby tries to keep the mother near. Gewirtz does not argue that anything is "special" about the mother per se; anyone could potentially become the "attachment figure." Also, emphasis on infancy is not inherent in Gewirtz's model. The general model could apply to attachment at any point during the life span. This certainly is not the case with Bowlby's model.

Gewirtz provided an example of how reinforcement might come to control attachment behaviors. He chose crying to exemplify the process because crying during or after separation from the mother has often been used as a measure of attachment (see Box 4-1). First, crying comes under the control of "positive" maternal responding. When the baby cries, her mother comes and provides positive reinforcement such as food, warmth, comfort, or playful stimulation. The baby then cries more when her mother is not near in order to get her to come. The baby cries less when her mother is present. Next, the baby learns to discriminate her mother from other people and cries for her presence even when another adult is available to provide food, comfort, and so on. The baby also learns to discriminate cues and situations signaling that the mother is about to leave. The baby thus learns, for instance, that when a babysitter arrives or when mother puts on her coat, separation is imminent. The baby will cry in these situations; if her mother responds to the crying by staying, the baby will learn to cry more vehemently and more frequently when separation is about to occur.

BOX 4-1 *MEASURING ATTACHMENT: THE STRANGE SITUATION*

Mary Ainsworth's "Strange Situation" (Ainsworth & Wittig, 1969; Ainsworth et al., 1978) is the most frequently used index of infant attachment. The Strange Situation most commonly takes place in a laboratory playroom. It consists of a series of eight episodes increasingly stressful to the infant:

1. A warm-up time during which the mother and infant are "introduced" to the room.

2. A 3-minute free-play period. Only the mother and infant are in the room. The mother does not initiate play but does respond naturally to the child.

3. The stranger enters the room. For the first minute she does nothing; then she talks to the mother and then to the baby. After 3 minutes of her presence, the mother leaves the room.

4. The first separation period. The mother is gone; the stranger tries to interact with the baby. This lasts a maximum of 3 minutes. The time is cut short if the infant becomes very distressed.

5. The first reunion. The stranger leaves and the mother reenters the room. If necessary, she comforts the baby. Otherwise, she sits quietly and does not initiate interaction, though she does respond naturally to the baby. This lasts at least 3 minutes. More time is allowed if the baby is not yet reinvolved in play.

6. The second separation. The mother leaves the baby alone in the room for 3 minutes (less if the baby becomes distressed).

7. The second separation continues. The stranger enters the room and tries to interact with the baby.

8. Second reunion. The mother reenters the room. She greets and picks up the baby. The stranger leaves quietly.

The reunion episodes are particularly crucial. Bowlby argues that an unwanted separation "activates" attachment behavior. So, attachment behavior is most likely to be directed toward the mother when she returns. A number of infant behaviors are rated during the reunion. These "attachment" behaviors include proximity seeking and maintenance, resistance to maternal overtures, avoidance behaviors, and distal interaction (for example, looking at the mother but not approaching her). Crying, smiling, vocalizing, and exploratory behavior are also rated. The child's behavior prior to, during, and after separation can be compared. The child's reaction to the mother and the stranger can also be compared. Through these comparisons, the researcher can categorize the baby's attachment as avoidant, secure, or ambivalent.

Gewirtz is thus claiming that maternal and infant behaviors control each other: The baby's crying affects the mother, and the mother's behavior affects the baby's crying. However, conflicting evidence exists over whether maternal behavior affects crying in the way outlined by Gewirtz. Some research, for example, suggests that mothers who responded promptly to crying did not have infants who cried more than those whose mothers did not respond immediately (Bell & Ainsworth, 1972). However, the methodology and the findings of this particular research have been criticized (for example, Gewirtz & Boyd, 1977). So, the question of the relationship between maternal responsiveness and infant crying remains unresolved. At the same time, evidence does suggest that other infant behaviors, such as smiling and vocalizations, that are commonly included in measuring attachment are affected by positive reinforcement (for example, Rheingold, Gewirtz & Ross, 1959).

Notice that Gewirtz seemed willing to consider each behavior (crying, smiling, and so on) individually. This differs from Bowlby's view in that Bowlby argued that the individual behaviors became organized into an emotional attachment. Gewirtz argued that it is not necessary to postulate such organization. He was not talking about a constellation of behaviors that make up "attachment" the way Bowlby was. Instead, Gewirtz wanted us to focus on the actual behaviors of the mother and infant without resorting to vague hypothetical constructs such as attachment.

Evaluation of the Theories

We have already noted that, contrary to Freud's arguments, feeding does not seem to play an important role in the development of attachment. The minimal importance of feeding also undermines Gewirtz's theory, since feeding would seem to be an easily discernable reinforcer. Because Gewirtz never argued that feeding is the sole or even the primary reinforcement provided by the mother, however, these findings do not completely refute his theory.

Research concerning abused infants might be more difficult for Gewirtz's theory to explain. Widespread evidence suggests that infants may even become attached to people who abuse them (for example, Bowlby, 1977; Rosenblum & Harlow, 1963). Why abuse would not cause the child to perceive the parent as a negative reinforcer is unclear.

Finally, in opposition to Gewirtz's theory, attachment behaviors do seem to be interrelated. Numerous studies report high correlations among behaviors such as crying, smiling, and vocalizing directed toward the mother (for example, Ainsworth, Bell & Stayton, 1971; Ainsworth et al., 1978; Weinraub & Lewis, 1977). At this point, the burden of proof is on those who argue that there is not an organized construct identifiable as attachment.

Bowlby's theory appears to be the strongest. The baby does indeed come equipped with behaviors that might encourage interaction with adults. Mothers (and fathers) seem particularly responsive to these behaviors, especially crying. By not relying on the concept that need fulfillment is a basis of attachment, Bowlby avoids Freud's problems. Finally, Bowlby's argument that attachment is rooted in survival contingencies may help us understand why an abused baby still attaches to his mother. Even an abusive mother is better than no mother as a means to survival.

This does not mean that Bowlby's theory is problem-free. For example, even newborns seem to be able to distinguish their mothers from other people on the basis of smell and voice. This is contrary to Bowlby's portrayal of young infants as undiscriminating in their social responses. The gap between the development of discriminatory abilities and the formation of attachment needs to be explained. Also, Bowlby seems to suggest that the mother is particularly likely to be the attachment figure because of her predisposition to respond sensitively to the baby. Given the evidence of the father's responsivity (for example, Parke & Swain, 1980) this claim seems questionable. Finally, it is not at all clear that there is always (or even usually) a hierarchy of attachment figures. Many infants seem to attach to their mothers and fathers simultaneously (Campos et al., 1983).

COGNITIVE FACTORS IN ATTACHMENT

One of the questions left unanswered by these theories is why there is a gap between the perceptual discrimination of the mother from others and discriminating attachments. Cognitive development may help us to understand this gap.

Jean Piaget (1954) has argued that very young infants do not understand that objects have a permanent existence. They only know that the object exists when it is present, that is, visible, touchable, and so on. Eventually, they come to understand that the object continues to exist even when it is not perceptually available (see Chapter 8). How might this be related to attachment?

Young babies might react differently to people when they are present without understanding that the person always exists. The mother's presence, for example, might be more interesting or satisfying than the presence of the baby-sitter. The baby does not know that he could potentially have the mother all of the time; he does not realize that she exists when he cannot see her. In other words, the baby is reacting to immediate stimuli or behaviors. Once object permanence develops, though, he begins to realize that he could have her near all the time, since she exists all of the time. He might therefore start to direct proximity-seeking and maintaining behaviors toward his mother. This, of course, is the beginning of discriminative attachment. Researchers have found support for this link between cognitive development and attachment (for example, Lester et al., 1974).

INDIVIDUAL DIFFERENCES IN ATTACHMENT

Types of Attachment

Mary Ainsworth (Ainsworth & Wittig, 1969; Ainsworth, Bell & Stayton, 1971; Ainsworth et al., 1978) has identified three broad categories of infant-parent attachment. These categories are primarily based upon the infant's reunion behaviors during the Strange Situation (see Box 4-1).

The first group (group A) is the "anxious-avoidant" attachment group. In most studies, this classification is given to 15-20% of the infants (for example, Ainsworth et al., 1978; Thompson, Lamb & Estes, 1983; Waters, 1978). These babies do not seek proximity, contact, or interaction with their mothers when they are reunited following a brief separation. In fact, they struggle to avoid interaction. They are likely to turn or move away from their mothers upon reunion. Strangers are not treated very differently from the mother.

The second group (group B) is the "modal" group, constituting about 65% of the sample in most studies. These are the "secure" attachment babies. They actively seek proximity and contact with the mother upon reunion, especially if they became very distressed during the separation. The mother's return is met with more than a casual greeting. There is a marked preference for the mother over a stranger.

The third group (group C) usually accounts for 15-20% of the infants, though it is often a bit smaller than group A. These infants demonstrate "anxious-ambivalent" attachments. Their "ambivalence" is evident in that they seek contact and proximity with the mother yet then resist the contact once it is made, especially following the separation. The babies may show "maladaptive" behavior throughout the situation. They are often reluctant to explore the environment. The infants do not seem able to use the mother as a secure base for exploration. Of the three categories, this one is the most difficult to distinguish behaviorally (Ainsworth, Bell & Stayton, 1971; Ainsworth et al., 1978).

These categories have enormous potential value. They could provide a link between early interaction patterns and later behavior. Imagine, for example, the implications of finding that failure to bond during the neonatal period was related to the development of anxious-avoidant attachment and that such attachments predicted poor kindergarten adjustment. Such relationships can be investigated only if we know that infant-parent attachment ratings are stable (Waters, 1983). If the categorizations are easily altered by external factors (such as moving or the mother's return to work) or by developmental phenomena (for example, cognitive development), then the usefulness of the categories becomes much more limited.

Stability of Categorization

Stability over Time.   Mary Ainsworth (Ainsworth et al., 1978, p. 290) concluded that attachment categorization was "strikingly stable over a relatively long period of time" during the second year of life, specifically 12-18 months. This conclusion was based mainly on the research of Connell (1976, described in Ainsworth et al., 1978) and Waters (1978). For example, Waters, studying a group of relatively stable middle-class families, found that 96% of the infant-mother attachment categorizations were the same at 12 and 18 months. A less dramatic, but still significant, percentage of about 60% categorization stability was reported for infants in lower-class, stressed families (Egeland & Farber, 1984; Vaughn et al., 1979). These findings seemed to indicate considerable stability in the nature of infant-mother attachment during the second year, but such attachment could be affected by stressful life circumstances.

The life stresses experienced by lower-class families are not necessarily comparable to those routinely experienced by middle-class families. Such stresses were not measured in Waters's (1978) middle-class families. In fact, he chose families that were particularly unstressed (Vaughn et al., 1979). What would happen in a more representative sample of middle-class families, those who experienced some stress during the 6-months' testing interval? According to Ross Thompson (Thompson, Lamb & Estes, 1983), considerably less stability in the attachment categorizations would be evident. Only 53% of the infants in this study received the same attachment classification at 12 and 19 months. Such stability is no more than is expected by chance. In other words, significant stability was not evident. Changes in caregiving arrangements (for example, the mother's return to work) were particularly likely to affect the attachment pattern. The effects could be either positive (a change from insecure to secure attachment) or negative (from secure to insecure).

However, it is possible that such changes are temporary (Owen et al., 1984). In the Thompson, Lamb, and Estes (1983) study, the length of time between change in caregiving status and the measurement of attachment was not carefully controlled. When Margaret Owen and her associates (1984) allowed at least a 3-

month "adjustment" period, they found no changes in infant-to-mother attachment. Neither returning to work nor quitting work during the second year seemed to affect attachment permanently (Owen et al., 1984). Other questions have also been raised about the Thompson, Lamb, and Estes (1982) study (see Waters, 1983, and the response by Thompson, Lamb & Estes, 1983). Still, it is possible that changes in family situation have at least temporary effects on attachment. Researchers need to keep this in mind when studying attachment.

These effects of life stress are not necessarily incompatible with attachment theory (Egeland & Farber, 1984). After all, if attachment is rooted in maternal behavior (as discussed later in this chapter), then any factors affecting that behavior would, in turn, influence attachment. Indeed, returning to work does seem at least to temporarily alter parent-child interaction (for example, Blanchard & Main, 1979).

Stability across People.   If changes in parent-infant interaction can affect attachment, then differences in adult-child interaction might be expected to result in differing attachments to mother and father. Is a baby who is securely attached to one parent also securely attached to the other? Not necessarily. An infant may demonstrate an anxious attachment to one parent and a secure attachment to the other (Waters, 1983). Only 27 of the 61 infants in one study, for example, received the same attachment categorization with both the mother and father (Main & Weston, 1981). Similarly, "stressors" may affect infant-father and infant-mother attachment differently. Thus, for example, changes in maternal work status may not permanently affect infant-to-mother attachment but they do frequently seem to affect infant-to-father attachment (Owen et al., 1984).

These findings make two interesting points. First, attachment behavior is not an infant "trait." There are not "secure" babies who are securely attached to every one of their attachment figures. Instead, attachment relationships are determined by the interaction of the baby and the attachment figure. We cannot assume stability in the nature of attachment independent of the attachment figure. Second, we need to consider the relationships within the entire family if we are to understand the relationship of attachment to other behaviors.

Although stability has not been conclusively demonstrated, researchers still have some interest in understanding the roots and implications of an attachment relationship as it exists at a certain point in time. The attachment relationship at 12 months might predict later behavior because of its impact on other developing behaviors, even if that attachment later changes. For example, an insecure attachment might impede exploration and therefore cognitive development. Even if the attachment eventually becomes "secure," the effects on cognitive development might continue to be discernable. We examine the roots and implications of various attachment patterns in the next sections. Keep in mind, though, that neither the stability nor the effects of instability of attachment are currently understood.

ROOTS OF ATTACHMENT STYLES

Maternal Characteristics

In her discussions of antecedents of attachment, Ainsworth focused mainly on mothering styles (for example, Ainsworth, Bell & Stayton, 1971; Ainsworth et al., 1978). Relying primarily on Rosenberg's data (1975, cited in Ainsworth et al., 1978) and her own work, Ainsworth concluded that maternal sensitivity is especially important in determining the nature of infant-mother attachment. The mother who is responsive and engages in truly reciprocal interactions with her baby is most likely to have a securely attached infant. Mothers of securely attached infants seem to respond more consistently and appropriately to the baby's "requests" (by crying, smiling, or vocalizing) for social interaction (for example, Blehar, Lieberman & Ainsworth, 1977). When the mother rejects the baby's social overtures, the result is likely to be an avoidant attachment. The anxious-ambivalent infant is likely to have a mother who is less openly rejecting than the avoidant-infant's mother but less accepting than the securely attached infant's mother. These mothers are typically inconsistent in the way they respond to their babies' cues: Sometimes they may respond immediately to the baby's cooing, but they are just as likely to ignore the baby's sounds at other times. They respond in no predictable pattern (see Table 4-1).

TABLE 4-1   Categories of Attachment Status.

CATEGORY	STRANGE SITUATION BEHAVIORS	ASSOCIATED MATERNAL BEHAVIORS	ASSOCIATED INFANT CHARACTER-ISTICS
Group A *ANXIOUS-* *AVOIDANT*	Avoid contact with mother upon reunion	Fails to respond appropriately to baby's "requests." May ignore or overstimulate.	Neonatal irritability.
Group B *SECURE*	Seek contact with mother upon reunion	Responsive, sensitive parenting.	Normal Brazelton scores.
Group C *ANXIOUS-* *AMBIVALENT*	Seek contact with mother upon reunion but then resist the contact	Inconsistent responding to baby. Pattern of response is unpredictable.	Poor 7-day Brazelton scores. Neonatal irritability.

Research has generally supported Ainsworth's conclusion that sensitive mothering is at the root of secure attachment (for example, Belsky, Rovine & Taylor, 1984; Egeland & Farber, 1984). Severely negligent or abusive mothering does increase the likelihood of an insecure attachment (Egeland & Sroufe, 1981), but simply categorizing the mothers of avoidant and resistant babies as "insensitive" is a bit misleading. These two groups of mothers seem to differ from each other in significant ways, though researchers do not agree as to how they differ. Jay Belsky and his associates (1984), for example, reported that mothers of avoidant infants may overstimulate their babies. Byron Egeland and Ellen Farber (1984), on the other hand, found that the avoidant infants' mothers were less interested in mothering than resistant infants' mothers. Clearly, more research is needed to define the nature of the mothering style that contributes to each attachment pattern.

Infant Characteristics

While mothering style clearly contributes to the development of attachment, infant characteristics may also be important. Although Ainsworth (Ainsworth et al., 1978) did acknowledge that the infant may influence the likelihood of maternal responsivity, she focused on the mother. She did not discuss any specific or potential contributions of infant temperament, constitution, and so on, to the nature of the attachment bond. Given our earlier discussions of the capabilities of and individual differences among even newborns, this seems a serious oversight. Certainly the dominant models of child development, the interactional and transactional models, would predict that the child plays a substantial role in determining the nature of his attachment to his mother.

Several studies have found that neonatal characteristics predict attachment classification. Low Apgar scores have been related to the development of ambivalent attachment (Connell, 1975, cited in Campos et al., 1983; Waters, Vaughn & Egeland, 1980). The speed with which the newborn adapts to the outside world also seems to be related to ambivalent attachment. Even though all healthy babies ultimately become adequately oriented to the world, some do it more quickly than others. The slower-adapting babies may have longer periods of impaired mother-infant interactions. In line with this argument, newborns with poor 7-day Brazelton scores (but improved 10-day scores) were more likely to be classified as ambivalently attached at age 1 (Waters, Vaughn & Egeland, 1980). Similarly, infants who are categorized as resistant in their attachment are more likely to show slow development throughout the first year (Egeland & Farber, 1984). Neonatal irritability has also been related to attachment. Highly irritable infants were more likely to display insecure attachments, particularly if their mothers had poorly developed social support systems (Belsky, Rovine & Taylor, 1984; Crockenberg, 1981).

These findings could be interpreted as suggesting that some babies are born to be insecurely attached. The baby may have some temperament trait that determines or at least heavily influences his attachment relationships. This interpretation is supported by the finding that avoidant babies have lower levels of cortisol (a hormone secreted by the adrenal cortex) than babies who are responsive to their mothers following separation (Tennes, 1982). This suggests a biological basis for differences in attachment behaviors.

However, we must be cautious about saying that the baby "determines" the attachment. After all, babies do not necessarily form the same type of attachment to both mother and father. Furthermore, attachment classification may change even when the attachment figure remains the same. These findings suggest that at best infant, or neonatal, characteristics influence parent-child interaction so as to affect attachment. At most, certain infants may be predisposed to develop certain types of attachments. Indeed, boys may be more susceptible to the negative effects of insensitive mothering than are girls (Egeland & Farber, 1984). Again, this interpretation is consistent with the interactional and transactional models of child development.

Timing and Amount of Contact

Although both parent and infant behaviors affect attachment, they are not the sole determinants. The extent of the interactions may also be important.

As noted in Chapter 3, several theorists have argued that neonatal separation might permanently adversely affect the mother-infant relationship. Yet even the prolonged separation of premature infants from their mothers does not seem to affect infant-to-mother attachment negatively (Hock, Coady & Cordero, 1973, cited in Ainsworth et al., 1978; Rode et al., 1981). This suggests that attachment is based on a lengthy pattern of interaction rather than interaction during a short sensitive period.

Another "timing" issue concerns the effects of daily separations from the mother. Specifically, what happens to an infant who is in day care? The baby might not have the opportunity to form a primary attachment to either his mother or his alternate caregiver. Given Bowlby's arguments concerning the importance of a single attachment figure for normal development, it seems that day care might have devastating effects on the child's development.

Day Care

With more and more mothers of young children deciding to work (twice as many as in 1965), the effects of day care has become a crucial issue. Nearly half of married women with children under the age of 3 years now work outside the home (Owen et al., 1984). Assume for a moment that Bowlby was right and that these daily separations would impede attachment. We could potentially be looking at a huge number of children who are at risk for developing abnormal behavior because of their impaired attachment.

In 1978, Jay Belsky and Laurence Steinberg published a critical review of the existing research on day care. In this exhaustive, definitive review, Belsky and Steinberg concluded that day care did not appear to be detrimental to the development of infant-mother attachment. A sizable number of studies supported this argument. The sole exception to this trend was a study by Margaret Blehar (1974) in which she reported a disproportionate number of day-care infants were insecurely attached. This study was plagued by methodological shortcomings and could not be replicated (for example, Moskowitz, Schwartz & Corsini, 1977; Portnoy & Simmons, 1978).

Blehar's was not the only study with methodological problems. In fact, Belsky and Steinberg noted that the entire day-care literature was fraught with serious problems. Much of the early research, for example, was done in high-quality, university-affiliated day-care centers. These centers had fewer children per teacher, better-trained teachers, and better curriculums than did most day-care centers. Furthermore, most children of working mothers are with babysitters or in day-care homes rather than in centers (Belsky & Steinberg, 1978). Since the Belsky and Steinberg review, additional problems in the day-care literature have been noted (see, for example, Schwartz, 1983; Vaughn, Gove & Egeland, 1980). Many of the day-care studies that employed the Strange Situation, for example, focused on children over 3 years of age; this measure of attachment, however, has little established validity with children over 18 months of age (Schwartz, 1983).

Studies by Brian Vaughn (Vaughn, Gove & Egeland, 1980), Ellen Hock (1980), and Pamela Schwartz (1983) have tried to correct some of these problems. In the Vaughn and Schwartz studies, the researchers concluded that day-care experiences beginning prior to age 1 have deleterious effects on infant-mother attachment. More specifically, both studies reported that a disproportionate number of day-care infants displayed anxious-avoidant attachments. Hock, in contrast, found few differences between the attachment behaviors of infants cared for by babysitters and infants who were "home reared." The mothering styles of both groups were also very similar.

These studies point out the need for additional research before any conclusions can be drawn concerning the effect of day-care on attachment. In the first place, simply correcting some of the methodological problems of past research does not seem to result in an absolutely clear picture of day-care effects. Even the more recent studies do not reach a consensus on the effects of daily nonmaternal care. In the second place, both Vaughn and Schwartz found a disproportionate number of avoidant, but not ambivalent, attachments in day-care children. Joseph Campos and Michael Lamb have suggested that avoidant attachments may be more indicative of independence than of poor attachments (Campos et al., 1983). Again, we see debate over whether the effects of day-care are truly deleterious.

RELATIONSHIP OF ATTACHMENT TO OTHER BEHAVIORS

Concurrent Relationships

How are other behaviors related to an infant's current level of attachment? Research has shown that exploratory behavior, cognitive development, and sociability are all related to attachment.

Exploration.   Some tension exists between exploration and attachment by their very nature. Exploratory behaviors take the child away from the mother and out into the world. Attachment behaviors keep the child close to the mother. Exploratory behavior must occur because of its essential role in cognitive development (for example, Piaget, 1952). On the other hand, normal development would be seriously threatened by a lack of attachment. So, the child must achieve a balance between attachment and exploration.

Mary Main (1981) found that securely attached 20-month-olds engaged in more exploration than insecurely attached toddlers. Ainsworth (Ainsworth, Bell & Stayton 1971; Ainsworth et al., 1978) has reported similar relationships. Securely attached infants showed a better balance between attachment and exploration than ambivalently attached babies. The securely attached babies were better able to use their mothers as a "secure base" for explorations. They would explore the environment quite freely but would keep track of the mother and would occasionally briefly return to her. Ambivalently attached babies were more passive. They did less exploring and proximity seeking. Some of them performed repetitive or stereotypic behavior (for example, rocking or hand movements). These findings were reported during Strange Situation assessments and observations of home behaviors.

Cognition and Language.   We saw earlier that cognitive development might be related to the onset of attachment. Specifically, the infant may need to understand object permanence at least partially before attachment behavior can begin.

It is also possible that the nature of the attachment affects cognitive development. This could happen in two ways. First, attachment is related to exploratory behavior. The amount and type of exploratory behavior may be related to cognitive development. Second, the interaction style of the mother and infant, which may contribute to the nature of attachment, may also affect cognition. Mothers who are responsive and stimulating may increase the infant's opportunities for cognitive development. Early language development may also be affected by the infant-mother interactive style (Bretherton et al., 1979).

A number of researchers have reported that cognitive development and attachment are related. Securely attached babies, for example, score higher on "infant intelligence tests" (for example, Bell & Ainsworth, 1972; Main, 1973). Measures of intelligence based on Piaget's theory have shown similar relationships to attachment (for example, Bretherton et al., 1979; Matas, Arend & Sroufe, 1978). Securely attached infants also seem to have more advanced language development (for example, Bretherton et al., 1979; Connell, 1975, cited in Bretherton et al., 1979; Main, 1973).

Unfortunately, we cannot draw the simple conclusion that attachment and cognition are related. Several studies have failed to find such relationships (for example, Clarke-Stewart, 1973). Even the studies that did find relationships (such as Bretherton et al., 1979) did not find them for all cognitive measures. However, no one has yet reported a negative relationship between cognition and attachment. In other words, no one has found that anxiously attached infants have higher levels of cognitive development than securely attached infants. Similar patterns of relationships have emerged for language and attachment, but fewer relationships have been reported for language measures than for cognitive measures.

Another issue complicates cognition-attachment relationships. Securely attached infants may be more comfortable and outgoing in social interactions. This may contribute to their better performance on cognitive measures because they would be more comfortable in a testing situation. Indeed, sociable infants have been found to score better on various measures of intelligence (for example, Stevenson & Lamb, 1979). In addition, securely attached infants seem to approach problem solving with less frustration and more persistence. This, too, may contribute to their better performance on cognitive tests. It may be that securely attached infants are not truly more competent cognitively. Instead, they may be better able to display that competence (Bretherton et al., 1979; Matas, Arend & Sroufe, 1978).

Sociability.   The relationship between attachment status and sociability toward adult strangers is unclear. Such relationships emerge only when subcategories of the attachment classifications are used (for example, Thompson & Lamb, 1983). We cannot simply say that securely attached babies are more sociable.

Studies of peer sociability are a bit clearer. Securely attached infants show greater competence interacting with peers than anxiously attached children (Pastor, 1981; Easterbrooks & Lamb, 1979).

Predictive Relationships

Does the security of attachment predict later behavior? As we noted earlier, this is a tricky question. Stability of attachment has not been conclusively established. Yet, many of the studies investigating the predictive value of attachment assume stability. For example, attachment might be measured at 12 months and cognitive development at 20 months (for example, Main, 1973, cited in Ainsworth et al., 1978). In such a study, the failure to reassess attachment at 20 months makes results difficult to interpret. We therefore need to be cautious in drawing any conclusions about attachment as a predictor of later behavior.

Cognition.   Researchers have reported that security of attachment affects later cognitive functioning. Mary Main (1973), for example, reported that infants who were securely attached at 12 months scored higher on an infant intelligence test at 20 months than anxiously attached infants. Cognitive measures based on Piaget's theory have also been "predicted" by attachment security. Both pretend play and the use of tools to obtain a goal are more sophisticated in toddlers who were securely attached as infants (for example, Bretherton et al., 1979; Matas, Arend & Sroufe, 1978).

Social and Personality Development.   Later social and personality development have also been predicted from infant attachment. Donald Pastor (1981) found that 18-month-olds who were securely attached were more sociable with both peers and their mothers at 20-23 months of age. These securely attached infants were more cooperative, friendlier, and more interested in interaction than the anxiously attached children. Personality variables that have been successfully predicted include amount of positive affect, independence, empathy, and competence in social situations. In all of these, securely attached children obtained higher scores than anxiously attached children (for example, Arend, Gove & Sroufe, 1979; Waters, Wippman & Sroufe, 1979).

These findings seem to suggest that attachment relationships form an important base for later behavior. Again, we need to be cautious because many of these studies assumed stability that might not be there. Ross Thompson and Michael Lamb (1983) did consider the stability issue. They found that attachment at 12.5 months predicted sociability with peers at 18.5 months only when the child's attachment classification was the same at both ages. If the attachment classification was different at 12.5 and 18.5 months, the 12.5 categorization did not predict later sociability.

SEPARATION DISTRESS AND STRANGER ANXIETY

Separation distress, evident as negative reactions to separation from the parents, and *stranger anxiety,* evident as fearful reactions to strangers, are topics of great interest to parents, day-care workers, and health professionals. All these people have to deal with infant-parent separations. They need to know what these behaviors mean and how to deal with them.

Many parents think that separation distress and stranger anxiety indicate something about attachment. If their baby doesn't cry when they leave, they may think that their baby doesn't "like" them. Early researchers (for example, Schaffer & Emerson, 1964) also thought that separation distress and stranger anxiety were related to attachment. However, more recent researchers have argued that these relationships are limited. For example, Mary Ainsworth (Ainsworth et al., 1978) has suggested that the baby's reactions upon reunion with the mother are better indicators of attachment than reactions to her departure. She has also suggested that stranger anxiety is not an adequate indicator of attachment (Ainsworth, Bell & Stayton 1971). Although researchers still assume that some relationship exists, they see other major factors in determining separation distress and stranger anxiety.

Separation Distress

Separation distress refers to the baby's immediate reaction to separation from his mother (or other attachment figure). This reaction may include crying, calling for the mother, or searching for the mother. In other words, "attachment behavior" is "activated" by the separation. Obviously, attachment is involved in the distress reaction, for a child would be much more likely to become distressed if his mother left the room than if a stranger left. But attachment is not the only factor involved in the reaction.

Why do some "attached" babies cry and search frantically while others seem to tolerate the separation quite well? Cognitive development seems to play a role. Children with higher levels of cognitive development are less distressed (for example, Weinraub & Lewis, 1977). Marsha Weinraub (Weinraub & Lewis, 1977) also found that the mother's structuring of the separation event was an important factor. Children whose mothers left the room without saying anything were most likely to become distressed. Those whose mothers told them they would be back were less distressed. The least distress occurred when the mothers not only promised to return quickly but also suggested what the children might do (for example, look at books or build with the blocks) during the separation. This finding provides one hint on how to handle separation distress. Box 4-2 contains others.

BOX 4-2   *HANDLING SEPARATION DISTRESS*

For some families, separation distress becomes a major problem. The mother may come to fear leaving her baby because he gets so upset. This can interfere with her taking a job. It may also reduce the amount of time she and her husband can spend alone, away from the children. In some cases, it may make it virtually impossible for her to spend any time away from her baby. This situation has the potential to cause problems in the mother-infant relationship because she may resent how little time she gets to herself; or, she may identify the baby as "difficult" and start treating him that way. Problems between husband and wife may also develop.

Separation distress can also be a serious problem for day-care workers and hospital staff. These people must deal with children who are being "left," albeit temporarily, by their parents. Although they are typically accustomed to dealing with separation distress, they still find the distressed child disruptive to the day-care center or the hospital. In order to do their jobs well, these professionals need to reduce the child's distress. Also, the child can gain the maximal benefit from the program only if the separation distress is alleviated.

These scenarios demonstrate the importance, and sometimes urgency, of knowing how to reduce separation distress. Research has provided several clues as to how this may be accomplished.

First, a child is less likely to become distressed if she is being left in a familiar situation with a familiar person (for example, Ricciuti, 1974). Attempts should be made to familiarize the child with the people who will be caring for her. This familiarization should be done in the presence of the mother or father. Ideally, parent and child should visit the day-care center at least once before the child is left there. During this time, the child should be encouraged to play with the caregiver(s) who will later be responsible for her. Notice that I said "encouraged." Some children will need some time to warm up to the new situation and people. Indeed, some children may need two or more visits accompanied by their parents in order to make the adjustment.

Familiar objects may also reduce distress (Passman, 1976). More specifically, many children develop a special attachment to a toy or blanket. These "security blankets" should not be viewed as a sign of poor adjustment. Indeed, they allow the child to function well when the "real" attachment figure (for example, the mother) is not present (for example, Winnicott, 1964). Though his mother cannot always be there, the blanket can. So, the child should be allowed, perhaps even encouraged, to take his "special" blanket or toy with him, and day-care workers should be sensitive to the importance of the toy. Other children should not be permitted to play with the toy or to ridicule its owner.

One reason children react negatively to new situations may be that they do not know what is going to happen. This is why familiarization with the setting is so helpful. There is also another way to reduce the child's concern, however. You can "structure" the separation for her. You can tell her that you are leaving and that you will return; you can also tell her what she should do in the meantime (for example, "why don't you play with the blocks while Daddy's gone?"). This approach leads to much less distress than "sneaking out" (for example, Weinraub & Lewis, 1977). Try to put yourself in the baby's position for a moment. How would you feel if your spouse "snuck out" when you weren't looking? Don't you want to know when he (or she) is leaving and will return?

Of course, it is possible to say too much to the baby when you are leaving (for example, Adams & Passman, 1981). When a parent rambles on and on before leaving, she conveys her own nervousness about going. Her distress, subtle though it may be, provides cues to the child and upsets him. Simply tell the child you are going. Then go.

These practices will help to reduce separation distress. They are not guaranteed to eliminate it. Many children will cry anyway. The parent should then go anyway. Assuming you have left your child with a sensitive, responsive caregiver, he will be all right. If he learns that you won't go if he cries, he may only cry more (for example, Gewirtz, 1976).

Some children may take more time than others to get over an episode of separation distress. Some will only cry for a minute or two when left; others for an hour. Similarly, some children will cry only the first day; others will cry for several. This will depend on previous experience with separation, the age of the child, and the child's general temperament. Some children just adapt more quickly to new situations than others. Parents and caregivers need to be patient. If patience is coupled with these suggestions, you can be assured that the separation distress will dissipate relatively soon with no permanent ill effects on the child.

Stranger Anxiety

Stranger anxiety refers to a fearful or distressed response to the presence or the interactive overtures of an unfamiliar person. In order to react negatively to a stranger, you have to recognize that he is unfamiliar. In other words, you need to discriminate unfamiliar from familiar people. If you look back at Bowlby's stages, you will find that he agrees with this perspective. This reasoning led early researchers to believe there was a relationship between stranger anxiety and attachment (for example, Schaffer, 1966). Yet attachment alone does not explain stranger anxiety. Infants' reactions to strangers are mediated by such diverse factors as the height of the stranger, the age and gender of the stranger, and the infant's temperament (Brooks & Lewis, 1976; Weinraub & Putney, 1978). For example, babies are not as distressed by strange infants as by strange adults, and they are more afraid of male than female adult strangers.

The potential relationship between attachment and stranger anxiety can also be questioned on another level. The importance of stranger anxiety as a developmental phenomenon rests on the assumption that it is a reaction more or less restricted to infancy. If stranger anxiety occurs at all (or several) points in development, it has to be more than a reflection of infant attachment. In fact, evidence shows that stranger anxiety may be a situational rather than a developmental phenomenon. Mothers actually show more wariness of strangers, especially as they move closer, than do infants (Kaltenback, Weinraub & Fullard, 1980). What we may be seeing in infant stranger anxiety is the beginning of a pattern of social interaction rather than an extension of attachment.

In sum, separation distress and stranger anxiety are both probably related to attachment, but neither is exclusively determined by attachment. Numerous factors can influence the developmental pattern and the intensity of both. Neither one can therefore be considered a very good indicator of the attachment relationship.

NONMATERNAL ATTACHMENT

Fathers

As more mothers work outside the home, fathers are more pressured to actively participate in child rearing. We have already seen (Chapter 3) that they are capable of caring for young infants. Our concern here is, how do the infants feel about their fathers? Are they as attached to them as they are to their mothers? Does the attachment to the mother form first? Several theorists (for example, Freud, 1948) have suggested that the mother-infant relationship is "unique." If this is true, then the father may not be an adequate replacement for the mother, at least from the child's perspective. Resolving this issue is important for day-to-day infant care and for child-custody cases.

Strength and Timing of Attachment. In the first observational study of father-infant interaction, Milton Kotelchuck (1972) found no marked preference for the mother over the father in home or laboratory settings. However, the youngest infants in the study were 12 months. So, the question of whether attachment to the mother predates attachment to the father was unresolved.

Another problem in Kotelchuck's study was that the observation situations were relatively stress-free. Presumably, attachment behaviors are more likely to be activated in stress than in nonstress settings. Perhaps preferential attachment for the mother would be evident only in stressful situations. Cohen and Campos (1974) found this to be the case. The children in their study sought the mother more than the father in stressful situations, but attachment to the father was also evident. Children clearly preferred their fathers to a stranger. Again, the question of whether the attachment to mother predated that to father was unanswered because the youngest children in the study were 10 months old.

Michael Lamb, in a series of studies, found that even at 7 months of age, infants seemed to be equally attached to their mothers and fathers in relatively stress-free settings. It seems, then, that the attachments begin at the same time. However, Lamb also found that infants preferred their mothers to their fathers during stressful situations. This was true only for infants between about 12 and 18 months of age. So, if the attachment to mother is stronger, it is so only during a limited period of development. In fact, Lamb reported that boys typically preferred their fathers during the second year (in low-stress settings). Girls are less consistent, with some preferring mother, others father, and still others exhibiting no prefer-ence. The sons' preference for their fathers may be at least partially attributable to the fathers' high level of interaction with their sons. Fathers are twice as inter-active with their sons as mothers are but are not nearly as interactive with daughters as with sons (see, for example, Lamb, 1978, 1980, 1981; Campos et al., 1983).

Fathers are capable of sensitive parenting, too.
Courtesy of Mary Suydam.

Basis of Attachment.   Is the basis for infant-to-father attachment the same as for infant-to-mother attachment? No definitive answer can be given to this question, but fathers do spend less time with their infants than do mothers. Kotelchuck (1976) reported that, on the average, mothers were available to their infants 9.0 hours per day of infant waking time. The comparable figure for fathers was only 3.2 hours per day. We have already mentioned that fathers spend less time in physical caretaking activities. What makes fathers so appealing that they can "overcome" the relative lack of time they spend with their infants? The answer is probably "play." Fathers spend a greater percentage of their time with their babies playing (37.5% vs. 25.8% for mothers according to Kotelchuck, 1976). Also, fathers play more physical and unpredictable "games" with their babies than do mothers (Lamb, 1978). In some sense, fathers may be more interesting than mothers. The high interest for fathers may be reinforced by mothers' emphasis on the excitement of father's arrival and presence (Weinraub, 1978).

If these findings concerning infant-father attachment are correct, they have important implications for theories of attachment. Once again, we see that fulfillment of physical needs does not seem important in the formation of attachment bonds. Also, mothers do not seem to hold any special "advantage" as attachment figures. Rather, the nature of adult-child interaction seems important. Specifically, interesting and stimulating interactions may be particularly important in the development of attachment.

Siblings

Another important member of any infant's family is her sibling or siblings. Infants are interested in their older brothers and sisters and spend a substantial amount of time interacting with them. In fact, some researchers have found that by 1 year of age, infants spend more time interacting with their siblings than with their mothers or fathers (for example, Lawson & Ingleby, 1974). Infants frequently imitate their older siblings (for example, Dunn & Kendrick, 1982a). Younger siblings are also quite likely to direct warm, friendly behaviors toward their older brothers and sisters (for example, Dunn & Kendrick, 1982a). Older siblings are clearly concerned when their infant brothers and sisters are distressed and often try to comfort them (for example, Stewart, 1983).

So the relationship between siblings is generally of a positive nature. Research suggests that the relationship appears, from the infant's perspective, late in the first year or early in the second year. However, none of this proves that the infant is "attached" to his sibling. Evidence indicates, though, that infants do become attached to older siblings. They use the older sibling as a base for exploration of a new person or environment. They may become distressed when the older sibling leaves the room. They may even seek comfort or assistance from their older brothers and sisters (Dunn & Kendrick, 1982a; Stewart, 1983).

Typically, these infant-sibling attachments develop after the infant-parent attachments, although some infants do show attachment to their siblings at about the same time as to their mothers (Schaffer & Emerson, 1964; Dunn & Kendrick,

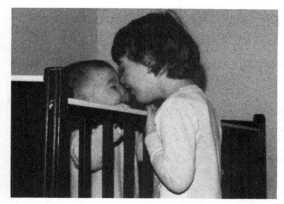

An older sibling can be a source of comfort and entertainment.
Courtesy of Mary Suydam.

1982a). This, again, suggests that mothers are not necessarily the first and, temporarily, only attachment figure. It is likely that the attachment to the sibling is not usually as strong as that to the mother or father. In other words, we would expect that, given a choice, most infants would direct attachment behaviors toward their parents rather than their siblings. This is certainly the case with toddlers (for example, Corter, Abramovitch & Pepler, 1983).

Day Care Workers

We have already discussed one concern about putting an infant in day care, namely, the day-care would interfere with the infant-mother attachment. Another fear is that the infant would spend substantial time every day without an available attachment figure. The lack of an available attachment figure might negatively affect sociability, exploration, and a host of other behaviors.

Both these concerns involve the infant-caregiver relationship. On the one hand, if the infant is too strongly attached to her day-care caregiver, her attachment to her mother might be impeded. On the other, if she is not at all attached to her caregiver, her overall development could be impaired. Research suggests that both these fears are unjustified. Infants do become attached to their caregivers. They prefer the caregivers to strangers. The departure of a caregiver causes distress, and the infant is comforted by the caregiver's return. Yet infants also prefer their mothers to their caregivers (Farran & Ramey, 1977; Fox, 1977).

Maternal Deprivation Reconsidered

Several studies suggesting dramatic negative effects of the lack or loss of an attachment figure were mentioned at the beginning of this chapter. These researchers argued that a child needed a primary attachment relationship for normal development to proceed. They also argued that such a relationship required intensive, continuous interaction in order to develop.

Although research lends some support to these arguments, it also shows that these views are a bit extreme. Infants can develop important attachments without the continuous mothering requirement suggested by Bowlby and others. This is clear from the data concerning fathers and the children of working mothers. The data also indicate that infants often form multiple attachments right from the beginning. If a hierarchy of these attachments exists, it is short lived. Michael Lamb (1978), for example, found that infants' preference for their mothers over their fathers in a stressful situation was limited to a brief age range (12-18 months).

How permanent the negative effects of inadequate attachment are is also in question. Skeels (1966) reported that the effects of maternal deprivation could be significantly reduced by a program of high stimulation. Michael Rutter (1979) also presents evidence of the reversibility of such effects. Of course, the effects can be reversed only if the infant's environment is altered dramatically. This often does not happen, so the effects become more or less permanent.

Finally, we need to reiterate that the mother is not the only person who can serve as an attachment figure. Fathers, particularly, seem capable of sensitive interaction with their children. They often become primary attachment figures, especially for their sons.

All this implies that mothers ought to be able to work without fear that their infants' development will automatically be damaged. Indeed, research has demonstrated that working per se does not negatively affect attachment (for example, Owen et al., 1984). As the old adage goes, it is the quality of time, not the quantity, that determines mother-infant relationships. As long as the mother is able to provide stimulating experiences for her baby and responds sensitively to him, development should not be hampered by daily separations.

OTHER SOCIAL RELATIONSHIPS

In reading this chapter, you could get the impression that attachment relationships are the only relationships infants have. This is not necessarily the case. As the discussions of sibling attachment and stranger anxiety implied, the baby is building a variety of social skills. Let us briefly examine another indicator of the infant's nonattachment social functioning, namely, peer interaction.

Research indicates that even very young infants (those less than 4 months old) are interested in their peers. They will gaze intently at their peers and seem to be physiologically aroused by a peer's presence (for example, Fogel, 1980; Field, 1979a). They seem to react somewhat differently to their peers than to their mothers. Infants may, for example, direct fewer limb and body movements toward their peers than toward their mothers (Fogel, 1980). However, it is not until infants are about 6 months of age that peers really begin to "interact."

Between 6 and 12 months, babies begin to vocalize to, to smile at, and to touch each other. They even offer each other toys. Some reciprocity is evident among even 6-month-olds in that the behavior of one infant affects the subsequent behavior of the other (Field, 1979b; Hay, Nash & Pedersen, 1981; Vandell, Wilson & Buchanan, 1980).

There may also be a form of "empathy" among young peers. Newborns cry when they hear other newborns cry (for example, Sagi & Hoffman, 1976). Six-month-olds may or may not become distressed when a peer cries. It seems to depend on how long the peer cries and how many children are crying. Even when the "listener" doesn't cry, though, he still reacts. He may reach toward or touch the crying peer or look at the distressed peer's mother (for example, Hay, Nash & Pedersen, 1981).

Of course, a variety of factors influence the likelihood and extent of peer interaction between infants. The interaction is affected by the presence of mother or toys, the location of the observations (home vs. laboratory), and the freedom of movement the infants are permitted (playpen vs. "open-field"). In addition, infants are more likely to interact with familiar peers (Field & Roopnarine, 1982).

SUMMARY

Attachment has long been considered the cornerstone of development. Infants without adequate attachments were seen as very likely to suffer cognitively, socially, and emotionally. John Bowlby, whose theory combines psychoanalytic and ethological perspectives, has been a particularly influential proponent of this view.

Certainly this view has been supported by studies of children who completely lack an attachment figure. Institutionalized children or children suffering lengthy separations from their attachment figures often appear retarded in a vast array of behaviors. The data for insecurely attached children are less dramatic but also frequently support this view.

Some researchers disagree with the traditional view of attachment or, at least, raise questions about it. Michael Rutter (1979), for example, has argued that the effects of "maternal deprivation" are neither as dramatic nor as irreversible as Bowlby thought. Bowlby's argument that even short-term separations, such as a day-care experience, would negatively affect attachment has also met with mixed support. Finally, Bowlby's argument that there is but one primary attachment figure has not been clearly supported. Many children appear to be about equally attached to their mothers and their fathers for much of infancy.

Attachment relationships during infancy often dominate discussions of infant social development. However, other indicators of the infant's increasing social abilities abound. The child develops a wariness of strangers, not unlike that frequently seen in adults. She also begins to interact with peers. Once again, we see that infants are sophisticated beings who interact with, and help shape, their environments.

5

Motor Development

A baby's first steps are often one of the most treasured moments of infancy. Yet motor development is much more than a source of parental pride. It has been used to gauge infant intelligence. It plays a substantial role in cognitive and personality development. In addition, of course, it represents a fundamental behavioral skill in its own right.

DEFINING MOTOR DEVELOPMENT

Motor development is the acquisition of skills that involve the voluntary (as opposed to reflexive) control and coordination of muscle movements. These movements involve temporal and spatial patterning. The more accurately and rapidly the movements are made, the more skilled the individual.

There are two broad categories of motor development. The first, *gross motor development,* refers to the control and intercoordination of large muscle groups. Gross motor behaviors include sitting, crawling, and walking. The second category is *fine motor development.* This category focuses on the use of small muscles, particularly the use of the hands and fingers.

THE IMPORTANCE OF MOTOR DEVELOPMENT

In describing development, we "compartmentalize" behaviors. We talk about language or personality development as though it was the only behavior developing at the time. This approach is useful for organizing material on development. However, in real life all these behaviors are developing simultaneously. Further, there are documented interrelationships among these behaviors. Researchers and theorists have linked motor development to cognitive, emotional, personality, and social development. Examining motor development gives us the opportunity to see some of the interrelationships among these various behavioral realms.

Motor Development and Cognition

The term *cognition* refers to a variety of intellectual skills including concepts of objects and events, understanding relationships among objects and events, and memory. Piaget (1954) argued that such skills are rooted in the child's active exploration of the environment. Motor development seems to facilitate exploration. The ability to move makes previously inaccessible objects available (Gustafson, 1984). Also, familiar objects look different when you are crawling or walking than when you are being carried (for example, Mahler, Pine & Bergman, 1975). This may explain why newly mobile children will spend considerable amounts of time exploring empty rooms (for example, Rheingold & Eckerman, 1970).

In short, mobility increases opportunities for exploration that may encourage cognitive development. Indeed, some researchers have reported direct links between mobility and cognitive skills such as those involving the understanding of spatial relations (that is, where things—including the child herself—are in a room) (for example, Acredolo, 1978; but see also Butterworth, 1983). Gross motor development has also been related to the development of fear of falling (Campos et al., 1978). Infants can see "drop-offs" as newborns; yet they will often roll off couches, beds, and so on. This is because they have not associated falling with the drop-offs. Locomotor experience facilitates the formation of this connection.

Not only gross motor skills may influence cognitive development. Manipulative skills, that is, fine motor skills, may also facilitate cognitive development. Several studies have reported that manipulating an object increases the likelihood that the object will later be recognized or remembered (for example, Ruff, 1982a; Zaporozhets, 1965). This appears to be due to the increased visual attention directed toward the object while it is being manipulated (Weiner & Goodnow, 1970; Ruff, 1982a). Notice that in this example perception and motor development are working together to facilitate cognitive development.

One warning should be added here. The term *cognition* should not be equated with IQ. Motor development may be related to cognitive development, but the rate of motor development does not predict later IQ. It may be related to scores on concurrent measures of infant intelligence (for example, Bayley, 1969). However, such a relationship is inevitable because these scales contain a sizable number of motor development test items.

Locomotion and Personality

Being able to move without assistance also seems to contribute to personality development. Attachment provides an interesting example of this link. In Chapter 4, we discussed Bowlby's four phases of attachment development in which attachment is considered to emerge truly during the third phase—"the phase of active initiative in seeking proximity and contact." The onset of locomotion is important here because it enables the infant to seek and maintain contact at her own initiative (Ainsworth, 1973). She now can play a clearly active role in the attachment relationship. She is no longer simply reacting to her parents' attempts at contact.

Ironically, the behavior that clearly demonstrates the infant's attachment also permits the child to separate gradually from her parents. This "separation-individuation process" is crucial for personality development (see Chapter 10).

Margaret Mahler and her associates (1975) argued that the baby must differentiate himself from his mother. He must develop a sense of himself as an individual. This is a gradual process, taking about 3 years. Locomotor development is an important component of separation-individuation.

First, Mahler suggests that locomotor development provides tangible evidence of the child's gradual individuation. As the child moves toward and away from his mother, we can actually see the conflict between attachment and independence. We can also see the child's increasing interest in doing things himself, in being himself. So, motor development gives us a "window" on the child's intrapsychic development. Parents, too, are aware of locomotor development. It may serve as a "cue" to them to grant the child more independence. This independence granting will facilitate the separation-individuation process.

From the child's perspective, motor development actually permits him to move away from his mother; but, Mahler argues, this is not the most crucial contribution of locomotion. The core issue is that movement is something that the child can do on his own. It is an autonomous behavior. Erik Erikson (1959/1980) has claimed that autonomy is the core personality development issue during the second year. Now, the child starts to realize that he can control his movement. He can "plan" and carry out an activity (Kopp, 1979). He can initiate or end social interactions (for example, Gustafson, 1984; Rheingold & Eckerman, 1970). He can do what *he* wants to do. The child becomes so interested in practicing this independent activity that he often loses interest, at least temporarily, in his mother. This, too, encourages the development of a sense of individuality.

Locomotion and Social Interaction

Locomotion provides the infant with new experiences that may, in turn, alter social interaction. For example, mobile infants touch more, and different, objects than do nonmobile infants (for example, Gustafson, 1984). Parents are more likely to interrupt a locomoting baby's activity than they are a nonmobile baby's (for example, Green, Gustafson & West, 1980). In a somewhat different vein, Meredith West and Harriet Rheingold (1978) found that a majority of mothers' statements to their 1-year-olds were related to exploratory behavior (naming objects, describing the environment, and so on). So, the ability to locomote affects exploration, which in turn affects the social and linguistic interaction between mother and child. These, in turn, would affect the child's social and linguistic development.

The Nature of These Relationships

Looking at these relationships, we are tempted to conclude that motor development "causes" cognitive development (or personality development). Remember, however, that these data are basically correlational, and correlation does not equal causality. The relationship between motor development and cognition, for example, does not mean that cognitive development cannot proceed without motor development. Indeed, a case study of a 3-year-old boy born without any limbs indicated that his cognitive functioning was approximately normal (Kopp & Shaperman, 1973). This boy also was able to achieve relatively normal personality development, including a sense of autonomous functioning (Kopp, 1979).

Although in studying behavior we artificially divide development into discrete categories, the relationships occurring in normal development do allow us to see the interconnectedness of developmental realms. This section has presented a more realistic view of how overall development proceeds.

Having seen the impact of motor development, let's now turn to the sequence of gross motor development.

THE SEQUENCE OF GROSS MOTOR DEVELOPMENT

In the first half of this century, many researchers outlined normative gross motor development (for example, Bayley, 1935; Gesell, 1925; McGraw, 1943; Shirley, 1933). As you might expect, each one came up with a slightly different scheme describing motor development. Each one also generated slightly different age norms. More recently, Nancy Bayley (1969) generated age norms for gross motor milestones while standardizing her infant development scales. These norms are shown in Table 5-1. Note that Table 5-1 contains age ranges for normal development as well as the average age for attaining each milestone. The age ranges serve to emphasize the point (made in Chapter 1) that individual differences exist even within normal development.

Table 5-1 gives us a broad overview of gross motor development. It cannot, however, convey the complexity of each motor skill. We often lose sight of the fact that these are truly skills that take practice and refinement. We tend to think of movements as skilled only when they are of the nature of those performed by Mikhail Baryshnikov. Yet, think of the similarity between Baryshnikov and an infant: Both have a goal in mind (performing a grand jeté; getting over to Mommy).

TABLE 5-1   Milestones in Gross Motor Development: Averages for
American Children*

BEHAVIOR	AVERAGE AGE OF ATTAINMENT (IN MONTHS)	"NORMAL" AGE RANGE (IN MONTHS)
Holds head erect and steady	0.8	.7-4
Turns from side to back	1.8	.7-5
Sits with support	2.3	1-5
Turns from back to side	4.4	2-7
Sits alone (momentarily)	5.3	4-8
Rolls from back to stomach	6.4	4-10
Sits alone (steadily)	6.6	5-9
Early stepping movements (with support)	7.4	5-11
Pulls to standing position	8.1	5-12
Walks with help	9.6	7-12
Stands alone	11.0	9-16
Walks alone	11.7	9-17
Walks backward	14.6	11-20
Walks up stairs (with help)	16.1	12-23
Walks down stairs (with help)	16.4	13-23
Stands on left foot alone	22.7	16-30+
Jumps off floor, both feet	23.4	17-30+
Stands on right foot alone	23.5	16-30+
Walks up stairs alone with both feet on each step	25.1	18-30+
Walks down stairs alone with both feet on each step	25.8	19-30+
Walks up stairs, alternating feet	30+	23-30+
Hops on one foot	30+	30+
Walks down stairs, alternating feet	30+	30+

*These categories, average ages, and age ranges are all from *Bayley Scales of Infant Development* (Bayley, 1969). Bayley used a sample of 1,262 children, ranging in age from 2 to 30 months, in standardizing her scales. Her sample did approximate the general population (as defined by the 1960 Census) in terms of gender, race, education and occupation of parents, geographic location, and birth order. The data were collected between 1958 and 1960.

Achieving the goal requires some planning (for example, starting at a particular spot or moving in a particular direction). A series of intercoordinated movements must be performed. The movements must be coordinated with sensory information (for example, the placement of props or furniture).

To appreciate the infant's accomplishment, let's look closely at the developmental sequence of one of the major gross motor achievements, walking.

Walking

Sequence.   Of the available models, Myrtle McGraw's (1943) outline of the development of walking covers the broadest range of behaviors. She outlined seven steps in the development of "erect locomotion." This sequence focuses on the ability to move forward using only one's legs (that is, not crawling and without external assistance). McGraw treats the other major component of walking—attaining the ability to maintain an erect posture—as a separate phenomenon. Her sequence of walking development is as follows:

1. *Newborn or reflexive stepping.* When held under the arms, neonates will take several steps. McGraw viewed this stepping as distinctly different from the stepping actually involved in independent walking. McGraw noted, for example, that newborn stepping does not involve the same head and upper-body control that independent walking does.

2. *Inhibition.* The newborn stepping reflex is no longer apparent. During this time the infant does, however, develop better head and upper-body control. McGraw suggested that these changes are due to maturation of the cerebral cortex.

3. *Transition.* Bodily activity is increasing. The child may, for example, raise and lower her body while keeping her feet in one position. She may repeatedly stamp one foot. McGraw was uncertain as to whether such behaviors were reflexive or intentional.

4. *Deliberate stepping.* The ability to coordinate posture and stepping is becoming clearer. The child is now more likely to take steps when his hand is being held than when he is being supported under his arms. He also begins to display real pleasure in his own efforts to stand and move relatively independently. However, he is not yet able to walk without support.

5. *Independent walking.* The child can now walk alone, although walking is still far from mature. The child's balance is limited. She may rush to take a few steps before she falls; she may take very slow steps, trying to regain her balance between efforts. She may use her toes to "grip" the floor. Her movements appear exaggerated. Her arms are typically extended, perhaps for balancing. More likely, however, the child is anticipating a fall. Research suggests that children walk just as well with their arms down as with their arms extended. If their arms are not extended, though, they are confused as to what to do when they begin to fall.

6. *Heel-toe progression.* Movements become less exaggerated and more coordinated. The child can now walk using a heel-toe progression. As the heel of the front foot strikes the floor, the back foot is raised onto the toes. The length and timing of steps are more consistent. Leg movements are less exaggerated.

7. *Integration, or maturity of erect locomotion.* The child now synchronously swings her arms in relation to the movement of the opposite foot. The regular, rhythmic swinging of the arms is not always obvious. McGraw viewed its presence as indicative of the integration of all locomotor mechanisms. So, here, as in the preceding step, we are really seeing the refinement of walking.

The refinement of walking continues for some time. For example, 1-year-olds take shorter strides and flex their hip, knee, and ankle joints more when walking than do 4-5-year-olds (Hennessy, Dixon & Simon, 1984). The basic components of walking are the same in the novice as in the mature walker, but the specifics change. This refinement appears to be due to neurological development and to physical growth (Hennessy, Dixon & Simon, 1984).

The length of time it takes the child to attain adultlike walking underscores the complexity of walking. The child has to combine vestibular (balance) information with kinesthetic feedback (information from the muscles) in order to make any forward progress. Information from the other senses—vision, hearing, and touch—must also be integrated if the child is to walk without constantly running into things. Walking represents a clear integration of sensory and motoric phenomena.

The Role of Reflexes.   Notice that the first two levels in McGraw's (1945) sequence are reflexive stepping and inhibition. Although McGraw included reflexive stepping in her sequence, she did not suggest that it was actually the beginning of walking. Instead, she claimed that it had to be inhibited before voluntary walking could appear. Other theorists have made the same argument (for example, Gesell & Armatruda, 1941; Shirley, 1933). This was the dominant view into the 1970s. During this time, practitioners believed that "exercising" this reflex was useless in terms of promoting independent locomotion. In fact, they often actively advised against such exercise on the basis that it might prolong the reflex and thereby interfere with the development of independent locomotion (see Zelazo, 1976).

Research by Philip Zelazo and his colleagues, however, demonstrated that reflexive walking could be maintained through exercise and that such exercise tends to facilitate, not impede, independent walking (Zelazo, Zelazo & Kolb, 1972). This led Zelazo (for example, 1976) to suggest that reflexive walking is a direct precursor of voluntary walking. The problem here is that the link between the two forms was unclear. After all, most American children do not "exercise" the stepping reflex. Yet, they learn to walk. Research by Esther Thelen and Donna Fisher (1982) has provided a clue. They reported that supine kicking, that is, kicking while lying on one's back, is virtually identical to reflexive stepping in terms of motivation, sequential timing, and muscular movements. Kicking, then, provides the baby with a way to "exercise" the movements involved in the stepping reflex. This implies that the stepping reflex does not completely "disappear." Instead, the muscle movement portions simply take a different form—kicking. Stepping itself may disappear because the infant's muscle contractions are not strong enough to move his increasing muscle mass against gravity as must be done in walking but not in kicking. Exercise (such as that provided by Zelazo, Zelazo & Kolb, 1972) may help strengthen the muscles, thus allowing maintenance of stepping.

These data have not completely ended the debate about the role of reflexive stepping in locomotion. For example, the hypothesis that muscle contraction strength is the major hindrance to the continuation of stepping throughout the first year has not been empirically tested. Some recent articles continue to argue that reflexes interfere with intentional walking (for example, Molnar, 1978). However, the data increasingly appear to support the view that reflexive stepping is indeed the first "step" toward walking.

Having examined the sequence of gross motor development, let's now turn our attention to fine motor development.

THE SEQUENCE OF FINE MOTOR DEVELOPMENT

Think for a moment about the skill it takes to feed yourself cereal. First you must hold onto the spoon. You cannot just hold it any old way. The proper position must be maintained even as you move the spoon from the cereal bowl to your mouth. Once you pick up the spoon, you need to guide it to the cereal bowl and dip it into the cereal. Then you have to guide the spoon to your mouth, balancing it carefully so as not to lose all the cereal. You do all this virtually unconsciously. That's because you have had considerable practice at it. Watch an infant learning to feed herself and you will understand that it really *is* a skill, and it is clearly an important one.

Fine motor development is concerned with such manipulatory skill, especially how the hand is used to solve problems. Our hands allow us to make extensive use of tools in solving problems. In fact, it is probably manual dexterity that led to the invention of tools (Bruner, 1973; White, Castle & Held, 1964).

In the cereal-eating example, the importance of coordination between visual information (for example, the location of the spoon relative to the bowl) and hand movements is obvious: This is *eye-hand coordination.* Eye-hand coordination involves two major motor components: reaching and grasping.

Reaching

As with many other areas of gross and fine motor development, considerable debate exists as to when voluntary, that is, self-controlled, reaching first appears. Certainly a newborn moves his arms and may even seem to move them toward a particular object. He may occasionally brush his hand against the object. But is this the same sort of visually directed, goal-oriented reaching of the sort later observed in eye-hand coordination?

Several authors have argued that neonates display no directed reaching. They see neonatal arm movements as simply part of a generalized "mass activity" (for example, White, Castle & Held, 1964). This means that when the baby is aroused, he shows general physical movement that happens to include arm movements that resemble reacing. True visually directed reaching does not appear until much later (around 5 months) (for example, White, 1970).

On the other hand, T.G.R. Bower has suggested that directed reaching is evident during the neonatal period. Bower and his associates, working with infants less than 2 weeks old, found that newborns reached for objects frequently and that 70% of these reaches brought their hands within five degrees of the target object (Bower, 1974; Bower, Broughton & Moore, 1970). In fact, the newborns actually touched the object 40% of the time. Other researchers were not able to replicate Bower's findings, however (for example, Dodwell, Muir & DiFranco, 1976; Ruff & Halton, 1978). Methodological inconsistencies among the studies have only fueled the debate. For example, the researchers employed a variety of definitions of successful reaching and did not always carefully monitor the position of the hand during reaching (a clue to both intentionality and success) (see Lockman & Ashmead, 1983; McDonnell, 1979).

A recent report by Claes von Hofsten (1982) sheds some light on this debate. First, von Hofsten was unable to replicate Bower and his associates' high level of successful reaching by newborns. However, he did find that newborns (less than 9 days old) were showing limited visual guidance of their reaching. The babies reached for objects more frequently when they were staring at the objects. Furthermore, the infants' arm movements came closer to the object when they were intently watching it. These findings suggest that visual attention does contribute to the accuracy of reaching in newborns, even though the reaching is still unsuccessful by adult standards. Von Hofsten calls such movements "prereaching."

Another study by von Hofsten (1984) indicated that prereaching changes during the infant's first 4 months of life (prior to successful reaching). He found that when infants are around 2 months of age, important changes take place in prereaching. Prereaching declines, though it does not disappear. In addition, the prereaching becomes less coordinated. In newborns, the forward extension of the arm is accompanied by an opening of the hand, so the newborn is "ready" to grasp the object, though she rarely actually accomplishes this. In 2-month-olds, the hand is likely to be fisted as the arm extends forward. So, the 2-month-old seems less prepared to grasp the object. Over the next few weeks, the infant begins to open the hand again, especially when she is looking at the object.

Why would the 2-month-old appear less coordinated than the newborn? There is no simple answer to this question. Nor is there an empirically documented answer. Von Hofsten (1984) suggested that the coordinated behavior seen in newborns must be broken down into component parts if it is to be used voluntarily. Each part needs to be mastered and then reintegrated into patterns. Such analysis and reintegration allows the child to "decide" (eventually) which components should be used in solving a particular problem. Since there are no data directly addressing this hypothesis, the role of prereaching in voluntary behavior continues to be debated. Indeed, some theorists (for example, McDonnell, 1979) argue that no causal link exists between prereaching and voluntary reaching. Leaving this question aside, let us now look at the remainder of the sequence of fine motor development. The sequence presented here is based on the work of both Burton White (1970; White, Castle & Held, 1964) and Paul McDonnell (1979).

1. By about 3 months of age, the infant has begun to alternate glances between the object and her hand when reaching. When the baby reaches, she typically strikes the object; but her fist is closed during the reach, and so she does not grasp the object.
2. At about 4 months of age, the infant begins to use the right hand more commonly in reaching. Considerably more reaching activity is also taking place. The child can start to use both hands in reaching. He can even clasp his hands together in front of him. His hand can cross the midline in reaching for objects. In other words, he can use his right hand to reach for an object slightly to his left.

3. By about 5 months of age, the child can reach out to touch and grasp an object. Her reaching is visually directed.

At this point, reaching is more or less mature because it is clearly visually guided. Also, by this time the child is generally successful in actually reaching the object. This does not mean that no further development will take place. The child must still learn, for example, how to reach around barriers in order to get an object. This skill, known as *detour reaching*, frequently does not appear until 10-13 months. Even at 14-17 months it is far from totally mature (Bruner, 1970).

Grasping

Being able to direct your hand toward a toy would be of limited use if you could not then pick up the toy. This is grasping.

Grasping, like stepping, is a reflex during the neonatal period. In fact, grasping is present in premature infants. As with neonatal stepping and voluntary walking, considerable debate revolves around the role the reflex plays in later development.

One view is that voluntary grasping grows out of reflexive behavior (for example, Piaget, 1952; Twitchell, 1970). These theorists argued that the grasping reflex gradually becomes more differentiated or specific. For example, the newborn flexes her entire arm when her palm is stimulated (Twitchell, 1970). By 16-40 weeks, the reaction has become so specific that only one finger may be moved. At the same time, the grasping response is being generalized (for example, Piaget, 1952). This means that grasping is no longer simply elicited. Instead, the baby seems to grope for objects that she is trying to grasp (for example, Twitchell, 1970). This signals intentionality in her grasping. Her grasping, then, is voluntary.

Not all theorists agree that reflexes form the basis for voluntary grasping (prehension). In fact, Jerome Bruner (1970) specifically pointed out that skilled manipulation is not rooted in reflexes. Bruner believed that such reflexes disintegrate and are replaced with an awkward, poorly guided form of motor activity. He argued that manipulatory skills come from this activity.

Regardless of the postulated roots of voluntary grasping, all authors agree that by about 5 months of age, the infant can successfully reach out and grasp an object. However, the grasp is crude. Usually the infant uses both hands in the grasp. If she uses only one hand, she often fumbles the object. When using one hand, the infant may hold the object without using her thumb. At best, the thumb is only partially used. The hand may open in anticipation of grasping when it approaches the object.

The refinement of hand movements is outlined in Table 5-2. Of course, fine motor development continues beyond the skills shown in the table. For example, toddlers often use their entire hand in grasping a crayon while older children use finger-thumb opposition (as adults do).

TABLE 5-2   Milestones in Fine Motor Development: Averages for American Children*

BEHAVIOR	AVERAGE AGE OF ATTAINMENT (IN MONTHS)	"NORMAL" AGE RANGE (IN MONTHS)
Ulnar-palmar prehension (holds cube against the heel of the palm)	3.7	2-7
Partial thumb opposition (radial-palmar) in holding cube	4.9	4-8
Reaches with one hand (unilateral reaching) more often than with both hands at once (bilateral reaching)	5.4	4-8
Rotates wrist	5.7	4-8
Uses scooping motion to obtain small object	6.8	5-9
Holds cube using complete thumb opposition (radial-digital)	6.9	5-9
Obtains small object using inferior pincer (thumb in opposition to several fingers)	7.4	6-10
Bangs two objects at midline	8.6	6-12
Obtains small object using neat pincer (thumb and forefinger in opposition)	8.9	7-12
Claps hands at midline	9.7	7-15

*These categories, average ages, and age ranges are all from *Bayley Scales of Infant Development* (Bayley, 1969). Bayley used a sample of 1,262 children, ranging in age from 2 to 30 months, in standardizing her scales. Her sample did approximate the general population (as defined by the 1960 Census) in terms of gender, race, education and occupation of parents, geographic location, and birth order. The data were collected between 1958 and 1960.

This whole process of reaching and grasping is visually guided. We have, then, eye-hand coordination. We should not underestimate the importance of visual development here, for vision provides the stimulation for the reaching and grasping behavior. It also provides some of the feedback information used to correct arm and hand movements. The importance of vision in this process is clear when we look at the development of blind infants. A blind baby must, of course, reach out and grasp objects on the basis of sound. Typically, blind children cannot do this until they are 9-12 months of age. They may not become proficient at it until they are well past 12 months of age (Adelson & Fraiberg, 1974).

This chapter has so far simply described motor development with only a few brief references to possible causes. Let's now turn our attention to explanations of motor development.

EXPLANATIONS OF MOTOR DEVELOPMENT

As in many developmental realms, a nature-nurture debate exists concerning the roots of motor development. The debate does not so much take the form of "which one" as it questions how nature (biology) and nurture (environment) each contributes to motor development. A quick look at the issue of African precocity will set the stage for this debate.

African Precocity

Beginning in the 1950s, reports indicated that African infants developed motor skills more quickly than did American babies. Marcelle Geber (1958; Geber & Dean, 1957), for example, found that Ugandan babies could sit up and walk a month or two sooner than the average American child. Similarly, Zambian infants tested at 4 months of age obtained an average score of 125.7 on the Bayley Motor Scale (compared to the American average of 100) (Goldberg, 1972).

Early explanations tended to focus on "nature" causes. Genetic differences and prenatal maternal status were offered as explanations (for example, Geber, 1958). Such explanations have not disappeared from the scene. Daniel Freedman (1976) has argued that the Negroid race in general shows quicker motor development than the Caucasian race. He attributed this to genetic differences.

Increasingly, however, the focus has shifted to child-rearing techniques as the cause of the precocity. Susan Goldberg (1972) made this sort of argument. She suggested that the Zambian tradition of carrying babies in slings allowed (required?) more infantile muscular development. This muscular development gave the Zambian babies an edge over their American peers.

What we see then is a clear example of the nature-nurture debate. The issue of African precocity (and other cross-cultural data) is recalled wherever pertinent in the upcoming discussion of explanations of motor development. This issue is also used to draw some conclusions at the end of this section.

The Role of Biology in Motor Development

Back in the 1920s, John Watson and his associates (for example, Watson & Watson, 1921) tried to train motor behavior in young infants. They failed. Since that time, virtually all theorists have agreed that a substantial biological component is involved in motor development. The only debate has been over the nature and extent of the biological contribution. The positions in this debate range from the almost pure maturational view of Arnold Gesell to the skill component theory of Kevin Connolly and Jerome Bruner to the cultural and parenting techniques perspective of Philip Zelazo.

Maturation.   The nature-nurture debate originally took the form of the question, which causes development, nature or nurture? It was during this time that maturationalist Arnold Gesell worked. He believed that motor development basically reflected neurological maturation (for example, Gesell & Armatruda, 1941). This view was shared by both McGraw (1943) and Shirley (1933).

While not all modern theorists agree on its specific role, everyone acknowledges that there is a maturational component in motor development (see, for example, Thelen, 1981; Zelazo, 1976). Most commonly, brain maturation is linked to gross motor development.

As we saw in Chapter 2, the macroarchitecture of the brain develops prenatally. Although the brain is functional prenatally, it is far from fully mature at birth. In fact, considerable postnatal brain development takes place, particularly in the cerebral cortex.

The primary motor area, which is of greatest concern to us here, is the first cortical area to develop (Tanner, 1970). This area controls voluntary muscular movements. It is located in the precentral gyrus, almost in the middle of the cortex (see Figure 5-1). Different portions of the motor area control different muscle groups. In locating these areas, it is helpful to envision an upside-down person superimposed on the precentral gyrus. Thus, those areas closest to the top of the brain control the legs while the areas further down the side of the cortex control the facial muscles (see Figure 5-1).

Development within the motor area is not uniform. The nerve cells that control the upper trunk and the arms develop before those controlling the legs. By the time an infant is 1 month of age (postnatally), the area controlling the arms and upper trunk appears to be functioning. By 3 months, this area, including the area controlling the hands, is quite mature. But as late as 15 months the areas con-

FIGURE 5-1   A Cross-section of the Somatosensory and Motor Cortex Regions of the Human Brain. (Adapted with permission of Macmillan Publishing Company from *The Cerebral Cortex of Man* by Wilder Penfield and Theodore Rasmussen. Copyright 1950 by Macmillan Publishing Company, renewed 1978 by Theodore Rasmussen.)

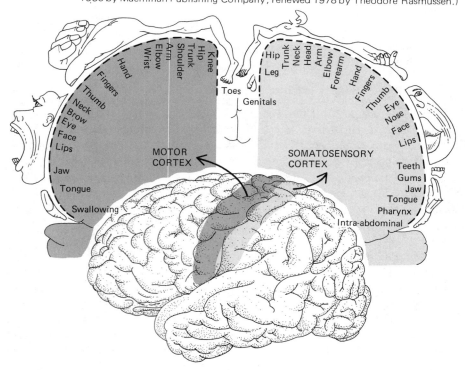

trolling leg movement are clearly less mature than the other portions of the primary motor area. Even at this point, development of the motor area is not complete. In fact, associations among motor neurons probably continue to be made until a child is at least 4 years old (Tanner, 1970).

Clearly, behavioral development tends to follow the pattern of this neurological progression. Infants do typically gain control of upper-body movements prior to walking. It is also evident that walking is far from mature in a child at 15 months of age, when the neurological areas governing leg movement are also relatively immature.

If one adopted a strict maturationalist perspective, any significant individual differences would have to be explained on the basis of differential physiological development. There might be differences in cortical maturation. There might be differences in muscle development or bone structure. These physiological differences might be attributable to a variety of factors, including genetics or malnutrition (for example, Freedman, 1976; Harriman & Lukosius, 1982; Paine & Pasquali, 1982).

Yet, to assume that motor development is simply a question of maturation would be simplistic. Even people making a maturationally oriented argument do not usually completely discount the environment (see, for example, Brazelton, 1972). For example, exercise may improve muscular development and thereby increase the rate of motor development (for example, Super, 1981; Zelazo, Zelazo & Kolb, 1972). Cognitive development, specifically the development of goal-directed behavior, may also be important (Bruner, 1973; Kopp, 1979). Motivation may also play a role. Edna Adelson and Selma Fraiberg (1974) have argued, for example, that motivational issues may account for the differences in motor development in blind vs. sighted infants. They found that blind children with normal brain functioning show a slower rate of motor development than sighted children, but this is true only of movement-related behavior (creeping, walking, and so on). It is not true of postural behavior (for example, sitting). Furthermore, blind children show a slightly different sequence of motor behavior. They can roll over before they raise their heads and chests from a prone position. Sighted children do the reverse. Adelson and Fraiberg (1974) attributed these differences to the fact that blind children do not have the distal visual stimuli to motivate them that seeing children have. In other words, they argued that children usually locomote in order to obtain some object that they see and want to have. Without such stimuli, blind children simply do not even try. Eventually, blind children will be motivated to move toward an object by its sound, but movement based on sound alone develops later than movement based on sight alone.

Modular Theory

These nonphysiological factors in motor development have led modern theorists to reject a strict central nervous system-motor development relationship. Instead, several theorists (for example, Bruner, 1970, 1973; Connolly, 1970) have proposed modular models of skill development. Briefly, these models suggest that there are modules or components of motor skills. Each component is exercised and developed. The practice allows the component to become "automatic." In other words, after enough practice, the baby does not actually have to pay attention to that particular movement. This frees up some of the baby's attention. This is important because babies, like all humans, have limited space to process information. Developing "routines" gives the baby more space to devote to new and challenging problems. Gradually, the components are integrated into complex behaviors. A component does not need to be completely mature before it is integrated with other components. Nor are the components necessarily unmodified by the process of integration with other skills. Rather, the argument is that a complex behavior is formed out of a variety of simpler behaviors.

Von Hofsten's (1984) explanation of the development of reaching and grasping exemplifies this perspective. The reaching with a closed fist displayed by 2-month-olds may be a "subroutine" of reaching and grasping. Once the baby becomes sufficiently adept at reaching, she opens her fist to integrate the subroutine with grasping.

Modular theories are considered "biological" because of the postulated sources of the subroutines. Jerome Bruner (1970) suggested, for example, that one source is innate action patterns. These are behavior patterns that are triggered, or "released," by environmental stimuli. These behavior patterns include such activities as transferring an object from hand to hand. Other modular theorists have suggested that reflexes might be a source of the subroutines (for example, Connolly, 1980; Zelazo, 1976).

The modular theories of skill development (and there are a number of them) are quite popular today. Intuitively, they seem to make sense. However, caution is needed. Few direct tests of the modular perspective have been made. Instead, the theory is almost always invoked as a post hoc explanation for descriptive data (see, for example, von Hofsten, 1984). Part of the reason for this situation is that it is very difficult to identify components of a complex behavior in advance (for example, Bruner, 1973). However, as more post hoc descriptions of components become available, more direct tests of the modular theories can be made.

S.C. Moss and J. Hogg (1983) attempted such a direct test. They examined the modular explanation of fine motor development in 12-to-18-month-olds. Their findings did *not* support the modular theory. The modular theory predicts that more practice should result in more consistent performance of a subroutine. Remember, the subroutine is supposed to become "mindless" or automatic so that the baby can focus on other things. Moss and Hogg did not find such an increase in consistency. Whether these findings point out weaknesses in the modular theory remains to be seen. It could be that Moss and Hogg did not correctly identify appropriate subroutines. By their own admission, they were blazing new trails in trying to define subroutines in advance. Such methodological issues, as well as the adequacy of the modular view, will only be resolved by future research.

Rhythmical Stereotypies

As was noted earlier, many theorists now believe that neonatal reflexes are related to voluntary motor development (for example, Twitchell, 1970; Zelazo, 1976). The question is, how are they linked? Esther Thelen (1981) has proposed that "rhythmical stereotypies" may provide the link.

Rhythmical stereotypies are inborn behavior patterns that involve fairly rapid, repetitious movements of the arms, legs, head, or torso. Thelen (1981) has identified forty-seven different stereotypies in normal human infants including various types of kicking, scratching, bouncing, and rubbing. These rhythmicities predate voluntary behavior in a predictable manner. For example, kicking is most frequent just before the onset of locomotion. Once locomotion appears, kicking declines. In fact, once a voluntary behavior is well established in terms of coordination, the associated rhythmicity disappears. Furthermore, the rhythmicities actually seem to predict motor development. A baby who shows early hand rhythmicities, for example, will also show precocious voluntary manual development (as measured by the Bayley scales).

How do these rhythmic movements lead to voluntary motor development? Thelen sees them as an intermediary stage between spontaneous, random gross movements and voluntary behavior. They allow the baby to formulate and practice muscle coordinations that will be used in intentional movements. In a sense, then, the rhythmicities permit the subroutine development and practice required by the modular theory.

As an example of this phenomenon, Thelen points to her own research on one stereotypy, kicking. She has demonstrated that the movements involved in kicking are virtually identical to those seen in the newborn stepping response (Thelen & Fisher, 1982). As noted earlier, this finding provides a link between newborn stepping and voluntary walking. The innate behavior patterns seen in newborn stepping are exercised in kicking. They are then eventually transferred to intentional locomotion. Although this complete pattern has not been empirically documented, Thelen and Donna Fisher (1983) have demonstrated that spontaneous random kicking does become intentional when it is reinforced. This study also indicated that these kicking movements are very similar to adult walking movements.

Thelen argued that if additional exercise of the kicking or stepping is provided (as in Zelazo et al.'s research), progress will be facilitated. This is interesting in terms of the African precocity issue. African infants tend to be advanced in sitting and walking. According to Charles Super (1981) many traditional African cultures encourage the active training of certain motor skills, especially sitting and walking. Several months before a baby is expected to walk, for example, she will be pulled to an upright position. The parents gradually withdraw support. In other words, the baby gets to exercise these early patterns, much as in the Zelazo study, and they become early sitters and walkers.

The potential value of training reflexes and rhythmicities underscores the argument that motor development is not completely determined by "nature" factors. Let us now turn to a more complete look at the role of the environment in motor development.

THE ROLE OF THE ENVIRONMENT
IN MOTOR DEVELOPMENT

Let's return to the issue of African precocity in motor development. As noted earlier, theorists initially favored genetic explanations of this phenomenon. Charles Super (1981) has pointed out several reasons why an environmental perspective provides a better explanation. Many of his arguments were concerned with methodology. However, he also claimed that the fundamental assumption of the genetic argument is erroneous. Specifically, Super argued that African babies are not truly precocious in motor development. Both the terms *African* and *motor development* are overgeneralizations. Certainly there are some individual differences among African infants. They do not all walk before even "average" American babies (much less all American babies). The point here is that normative data tend to give the impression of greater homogeneity than may actually exist. If all Negroid babies really did walk before all Caucasian babies, then we would be forced to argue some kind of genetic difference. But this is not the case.

The term *motor development* is also too general. When group differences are found, they tend to be in terms of sitting and walking. These behaviors are seen as highly desirable by many traditional African cultures. They are actively taught and practiced (Super, 1981). On the other hand, certain other motor skills may not be actively encouraged. For example, the !Kung San tribe believes that it is bad to lay down a baby. Crawling is delayed among these children. In other words, Super argued that individual behaviors, not general motor development, are accelerated. He also claimed that the behaviors that are most likely to be accelerated are those that are directly trained.

Of course, child-rearing techniques other than direct training may also be influential. In many cultures, babies are carried on their mothers' hips in slings (as were the Zambian infants in the 1972 Goldberg study). This may contribute to more exercising, and therefore quicker strengthening, of back and leg muscles. This, in turn, would contribute to faster motor development, particularly in terms of sitting and walking.

We need to be careful not to overstate the case here. These techniques do not train incredibly young infants (for example, 1 or 2 months old) to sit or walk. A certain amount of maturation is obviously necessary. Furthermore, not all child-rearing techniques have a direct impact on motor development. For example, being carried on cradleboards, which restrict movement, does not seem to delay motor development (for example, Dennis, 1940; Harriman & Lukosius, 1982).

The issue of which child-rearing techniques might influence motor develop-ment is an interesting one. It is possible that we simply have not identified all the techniques and are still underestimating the role of the environment. This possi-bility is underscored by disagreement concerning the impact of the carrying of infants in slings. Freedman (1976) suggests that African infants carried in such a manner develop rapidly *despite* the practice. Goldberg (1972) suggested that rapid development occurred *because* of it. Similarly, the value of walkers, commonly used with American babies, might be debated (see Box 5-1).

BOX 5-1 *THE VALUE OF WALKERS*

Many pediatricians, it was noted in the text, used to warn against "exercis-ing" reflexive walking. Their fears that such exercise might interfere with the development of walking have not been borne out by research.

In many ways, this debate was not particularly relevant to American families. Most parents do not (and never did) encourage their infants to exer-cise the stepping reflex. The more common mode of encouraging the develop-ment of walking has been to put babies in walkers. They enable babies to have the advantages of "erect locomotion" several weeks before they will be able to walk without assistance. No one has demonstrated that using a walker actually "speeds up" motor development. Nonetheless, walkers have enjoyed great popularity among American parents.

The occasional use of walkers, under the watchful eye of an adult, is prob-ably harmless; but this does not mean that walkers are without risk. First, the baby is more likely to have an accident in a walker than while crawling (Gotts, 1972). This is potentially dangerous because the fontanels are not as likely to be closed at this time as they are at "normal" walking age (Gotts, 1972). This makes the baby more susceptible to serious head injury.

Second, the excessive use of walkers (and baby bouncers) with very young infants has been associated with abnormally slow disappearance of reflexes (Simpkiss & Raikes, 1972). Specifically, the grasping reflexes are not replaced with protective responses (such as opening the palms to "catch yourself" when falling). The continuation of the grasp reflex may interfere with fine motor skills, too. These children also seem to have a poor sense of balance. This is probably because of strain on immature leg muscles during walker use, which causes the legs to flex outward in an abnormal position.

Finally, it is possible that early walking actually has *negative* implications for cognitive development (Kopp, 1979). It may decrease the baby's atten-tion to and manipulation of objects. In other words, the baby may become so absorbed in moving that she neglects her exploration of the world.

It is important to reiterate that these negative outcomes are associated primarily with misuse of walkers. They should not be used with very young babies (under about 6 months of age). They should also not be used without close supervision. Finally, they should not be used for lengthy periods of time. Instead, the child should be allowed to explore the world at her own motoric pace.

Furthermore, the child-rearing influences may be at a more general level. Bruner (1973) suggested, for example, that adequate social relationships are necessary for the development of motor skills. For one thing, such relationships provide the models from which complex skills can be learned. Bruner also said that a supportive and challenging environment is necessary for the development of motor skills.

The importance of a warm but challenging environment is supported by Wayne Dennis's studies of orphanage children (for example, Dennis & Najarian, 1957; Sayegh & Dennis, 1965). These children were deprived of both social interaction and general stimulation. The sides of their cribs were covered, so that the babies could see only the ceiling. (This was done to protect the babies from drafts.) Contact with caretakers was restricted to feeding and bathing. In fact, the caretakers did not even stay to feed the infants. Typically, they simply propped the bottle up on a small pillow next to the baby. So, the infants were lying on their backs virtually all the time. In addition, the infants were swaddled until they were about 4 months of age.

When tested between 3 and 12 months of age, these infants showed delayed motor development. They were slow to hold their heads steady, which contributed to delayed sitting. The babies' visuomotor skills, ranging from simply looking at an object to pulling out pegs, were also retarded. Dennis and Najarian (1957) attributed these delays to the children's severely restricted environments. Later research (Sayegh & Dennis, 1965) indicated that additional experience and attention led to dramatic improvements in functioning.

What do these findings tell us about African precocity? Clearly, environmental conditions influence the rate of motor development. In cultures where a particular behavior is trained (or at least encouraged), those specific skills will be advanced. Lack of experiential opportunity may lead to delays in specific behaviors. This does not mean that nonenvironmental explanations (for example, genetic influences) can be ruled out. The research is simply not clear enough to do that. As Super (1981) has noted, the African precocity data are marred by serious methodological problems. Although a definitive statement cannot be made, it appears that the burden of proof currently rests with those who argue for a strong biological component in explaining the precocious development of African children.

A Final Note on Causality.   We have examined a variety of biological and environmental influences on motor development. This is not the full story, however. Development in other areas, particularly perception and cognition, also contribute to motor development. This has been implied throughout this discussion, but it is so important that it needs to be explicitly stated.

A few quick examples will make the point. Perception not only provides the "guidance" for successful prehension but may also provide the motivation (for example, Adelson & Fraiberg, 1974). Cognition contributes intentionality to the behavior (for example, Bruner, 1973). This is, after all, what separates reflex from skilled motor behavior. Even attachment may play a role by providing a child with the security to move out into the world (for example, Rheingold & Eckerman, 1970).

We have come full circle. This chapter began with a discussion of how motor development contributes to development in other areas. Now we see that these relationships are reciprocal. This once again indicates that any divisions among behavioral realms are simply theoretical conveniences. In a real developing child, all behaviors are interrelated.

SUMMARY

Motor development represents the acquisition of complex, skillful movements. It includes both gross motor behaviors such as walking and fine motor skills such as grasping. There is, apparently, a sizable biological component in motor development. This includes maturation of the motor cortex. It may also include reflexes, though the role of reflexes in the development of voluntary movement continues to be debated. Motor development is not, however, strictly a maturational issue. As the African precocity phenomenon demonstrates, training can play a role in the rate of motor development.

Motor development has an impact on many other behavioral realms, including personality, cognitive, and social development. At the same time, motor development is influenced by these other developing abilities. The links between perceptual development and motoric functioning seem to be particularly strong. Let's now turn to an examination of early perceptual functioning.

6

Perceptual Development

Most people have heard of the drug LSD (Lysergic Acid Diethylamide). The drug's main effect is the distortion of perceptual functioning. Objects do not seem to "hold" their shape. They may melt or shrink or expand. A constant sound gets louder, then softer, then louder. Objects, people, or events have no coherency. The world becomes unpredictable and virtually uninterpretable.

People used to believe that an infant's world was just as disorganized and unpredictable. William James (1890) once described the infant's perceptual world as a "blooming, buzzing confusion." Were this true, we would expect the baby's behavior to reflect this disorganization, just as the LSD user's behavior reflects distorted perceptions. This chapter describes infant perceptual functioning and its effects on behavior.

What is perception? It is the process we use to organize and interpret sensory information. One way we organize, for example, is by selective attention. We look at certain stimuli rather than others. Even infants prefer to look at patterns rather than plain stimuli. We are also more likely to look at novel, rather than familiar, patterns.

Within the general area of perception, we examine in this chapter four major areas: the perception of objects, event perception, the perception of places, and social perception. These cannot be discussed without some understanding of the *hardware*, or building blocks, of perception, that is, the visual and auditory systems themselves. Let's first consider, then, the hardware of perception.

THE DEVELOPMENT OF THE SENSORY SYSTEMS

Vision

Structure.   At birth the visual system is functional, though it is far from fully developed. During the first year dramatic changes occur in the eyes' structures. Changes take place in the retina, for example. The retina contains the *receptor cells*, cells that are actually stimulated by light. This, then, is where the experience of vision actually begins.

In the center of the retina is a small depression, the *fovea*, that is distinguishable only in the adult eye. *Visual acuity*, that is, the clarity of the image, is much higher at the fovea than at any other part of your eye. That's why you can see things more clearly when they are right in front of you, and therefore registering on the fovea, than when they are off to one side, and registering on the periphery of the retina.

The periphery of the retina is relatively adultlike at birth, but the fovea is quite immature. In fact, a newborn's fovea is not even clearly identifiable. It has fewer receptor cells, and these cells have not attained adult shape. As a result, foveal functioning at birth is poor by adult standards (Banks & Salapatek, 1983). This is probably one reason for the low visual acuity of neonates (see Chapter 3).

By 4 months after birth, the foveal depression is evident. The receptor cells are more adultlike in number and shape, but they still are not in the adult configuration. Exactly when the fovea becomes adultlike has not been established, though it may be before 11 months after birth (Banks & Salapatek, 1983).

Other components of the visual system, including the visual cortex in the brain, also mature postnatally. Certainly perception requires a functioning visual system. Indeed, some theorists (for example, Fantz, Fagan & Miranda, 1975; Haith, 1980) view such maturation as the basis of visual perception. Others (for example, Banks & Salapatek, 1983; Gibson, 1982) specifically warn against overrating the importance of structural development in perceptual development.

Function.   One thing about structural maturation is clear: The system does not have to be completely mature physiologically in order to function. After all, newborns can see (Chapter 3). However, significant changes in visual system functioning do take place during the first year. For example, visual acuity and visual accommodation improve. *Visual accommodation* is the process of reshaping the lens to see an image more sharply, that is, focusing.

In newborns, neither visual acuity nor accommodation is very good (see Chapter 3), but both improve rapidly during the first 3 months of life. In fact, by the time infants reach 6 months of age, their visual functioning is quite comparable to that of adults (Ruff, 1982b).

Given the newborn's poor visual acuity and her relative inability to focus, researchers used to argue that newborns could see well only at a particular distance. They thought newborns had a "fixed" focal point (for example, Haynes, White & Held, 1965). Newborns do see better at close distances (Ruff, 1982b), but infant visual acuity remains constant across a wide range of distances (for example, in Salapatek, Bechtold & Bushnell, 1976, the range of distances was 30-150 cm). This may be true because the baby fails to notice a significant increase in blurring over this range of distance (Banks, 1980). Banks called this failure poor "depth of focus." As the neural system matures, visual acuity sharpens. The accommodation process responds by increased focusing. The reverse is also true; for example, as the neural system matures, accommodation improves, causing better acuity (Banks, 1980).

Emphasizing development, and thus improvement, in the visual system is risky, for it creates the impression that the newborn or young infant barely sees. Evidence does indicate that the newborn sees well enough to imitate facial gestures (for example, tongue protrusion) modeled by an adult (for example, Meltzoff & Moore, 1983a). They also see well enough to reach with more precision (though it is far from exact) when looking at an object (for example, von Hofsten, 1984). They may not see nearly as well as adults, but they do see well enough to begin immediate exploration of the environment. Furthermore, improvement in functioning is very rapid. Let's now see if the same conclusions can be drawn about the auditory system.

Audition

Structure.   The ear itself (outer, middle, and inner) is fairly mature at birth (Morse & Cowan, 1982). However, some differences between the neonatal ear and the adult ear are evident. The canal in the adult ear, for example, is longer. The shorter neonatal canal may affect the infant's ability to hear differently pitched sounds. However, no research examining this issue has been carried out. In fact, there is virtually no research linking adult-newborn ear differences to any functional differences (see Aslin, Pisoni & Jusczyk, 1983).

Although the ear itself is reasonably mature, the brain structures involved in hearing are not. In fact, maturation of the relevant brain structures continues until the child is about 2 years old (Morse & Cowan, 1982). The brain structures (for example, the inferior colliculus) involved in transmitting the "sound messages" to the cortex are particularly slow to mature (see Aslin, Pisoni & Jusczyk, 1983).

Function.   Does this immaturity mean that hearing does not function well at birth? Newborns can hear almost the same range of sounds as adults can (for example, Aslin, Pisoni & Jusczyk, 1983; Morse & Cowan, 1982). Yet, there are some differences. For example, newborns may need more time between sounds in order to discriminate two sounds (Morse & Cowan, 1982). They may also be less adept at differentiating pitch (Aslin, Pisoni & Jusczyk, 1983).

Newborns are, however, good at localizing sound (Aslin, Pisoni & Jusczyk, 1983). Even 3-day-old babies typically turn their heads toward a sound (Muir & Field, 1979). This ability shows an interesting developmental trend. In a longitudinal study, Jeffrey Field and his associates (1980) found that 1- and 3-month-olds were likely to turn toward a sound, but 2-month-olds were not. At 2 months, infants actually showed a decline in head turning. Field and his colleagues suggested that in the 2-month-old the link between hearing and looking may be "disintegrating" into component parts that need to be reintegrated later. Does this sound familiar? It seems to be similar to the skill building suggested by motor development theorists (though Field and his colleagues do not draw this link). Even the timing is comparable (to, for example, von Hofsten's prereaching study). Once more, we see a potential link between motor and perceptual development.

This evidence concerning head turning toward a sound is interesting for another reason. Namely, it indicates some intercoordination between hearing and vision. The infant *looks for* the source of a sound. Does this mean that even newborns know that things that make sounds have interesting visible properties? If they did, that would indicate a sophisticated innate understanding of objects. The question of inborn hardware coordinating the senses is clearly crucial to our understanding of perceptual development.

Sensory Intercoordination

Theoretical Views. Adults obviously rely on input from more than one sensory channel in trying to evaluate an object or event. Think about Christmas morning, for example. You find one of your presents. You look at it. It's big enough to be that videorecorder you wanted. You pick it up. It's too light to be a VCR. Maybe it's clothes. You shake it. It rattles rather loudly so it can't be clothes. You are using information from a variety of senses to try to identify the contents. Note, also, that you expect that the information you get from looking, touching, and listening will all be related to the nature of the final, whole object. You are using intermodal perception. The question is, when can infants do this?

Major theorists in the field of infant perception have long disagreed on the existence of intersensory coordination in newborns. Jean Piaget (1952), for example, argued that the sensory modalities (for example, vision, hearing, and touch) operate independently of one another at birth. A neonate can look at an object, and she can listen to an object; but she does not look at an object because it made a sound. If she did, it would indicate that she expected any object emitting sound also to have an interesting appearance. Such an expectation is, in Piaget's view, not present at birth. Instead, expectations are actively constructed by the child on the basis of experience. After viewing numerous objects that emit sounds (or are accompanied by sounds), the infant comes to expect that things that make sounds also look like something. The infant is gradually constructing her perceptual functioning.

T.G.R. Bower (Bower & Wishart, 1979) argued virtually the opposite perspective. For Bower, the central task of perceptual development is to differentiate among the modalities. The infant needs to learn to distinguish visual and auditory input. Bower suggested that any event or object elicits a reaction from all the senses. The newborn cannot distinguish a visual sensation from an auditory sensation. So, for example, the infant moves his eyes to look for the source of a sound even when he is in the dark. Eleanor Gibson (for example, Gibson, 1982; Gibson & Spelke, 1983) also believed that intersensory coordination is present at birth. However, she did not agree with Bower concerning its sophistication. Rather, she argued that it was quite immature at birth but developed rapidly.

Research Findings.   Research indicates that newborns will turn their eyes and heads toward a sound (for example, Mendelson & Haith, 1976; Muir & Field, 1979). They do this even in the darkness. Even blind infants will turn their eyes toward a sound (for example, Freedman, 1964). So, there may be some sort of innate tendency to turn toward a sound (Muir & Field, 1979). This does not necessarily mean, however, that sound and vision are intercoordinated in the sense of the infant *expecting* that sounds and sights come from the same source.

In fact, evidence suggests that sound and sight are not truly intercoordinated. Harry McGurk and his colleagues (McGurk, Turnure & Creighton, 1977) found that the addition of sound did not influence a newborn's ability to follow a moving object visually. Working with 1- and 2-month-olds, Katherine Lawson and Holly Ruff (1984) found that sound did result in more visual following of a moving object, but it did not seem to matter whether or not the sound was coordinated with the movement. The sound could come from someplace other than the object and the baby would still pay more attention to the object. Lawson and Ruff concluded that sound simply further aroused the infants rather than aiding in locating the objects.

These two studies both dealt with visual following of moving objects. Studies using stationary objects have indicated that 1-month-olds turn their heads toward the sound source (for example, Butterworth, 1983; Field et al., 1980). Remember, however, that 2-month-olds turned their heads less than 1- or 3-month-olds (Field et al., 1980). The link between audition and vision may change from "listen, look, and see" at birth to "listen, look to see" by 4 months (Field et al., 1980, p. 297).

Thus, evidence indicates that infants both look at and listen to objects. The head turning or eye turning may simply be a reflexive, rather than an integrative, response to sound (for example, Muir & Field, 1979; McGurk, Turnure & Creighton, 1977). For example, 3-month-olds do attend to an object more if it has an accompanying sound, but they remember the object better if it is presented silently (Lawson et al., 1984). Others argue that there is a meaningful intercoordination of sight and sound (for example, Butterworth, 1983). If so, it seems quite immature (for example, in terms of following a moving object). In addition, some change in the nature of the link apparently takes place around 2 months of age (Field et al., 1980).

Such findings seem to challenge Bower's strongly stated view that vision and audition are clearly intercoordinated at birth. They also, however, challenge Piaget's view that the senses are completely independent. The findings are consistent with Gibson's argument that some exploratory mechanisms are present at birth but that the nature and sophistication of the mechanisms improves rapidly during the first few weeks of life.

The extent of the improvement in intermodal coordination is dramatically demonstrated in Elizabeth Spelke's work. In her first study (Spelke, 1976), she showed 4-month-olds two films. A soundtrack was matched to one of the films. She found that the babies preferred to look at the film that matched the sound track. They seemed to expect that sounds and appearances "match" to form a unified whole. In fact, the infants actively looked for the film that "matched" the sound. In a later study, Spelke (1979) found that the babies appeared to be able to match the timing sequence of the sounds and the movements (as opposed to simply matching the locations of the sounds and sights). Although Spelke (1976, 1979) argued that her work supports Gibson's theory, she did work with 4-month-olds. As she notes (Spelke, 1979) Piaget suggested that the initially independent sensory modes are intercoordinated before a child is 4 months of age.

Vision and hearing are not the only senses that show intercoordination in infancy. For example, 1-month-olds can visually recognize objects that they have previously only explored through touching or mouthing (Gibson & Walker, 1984). This suggests intercoordination of the tactile and visual modes.

While information can be transferred from the haptic (touching) mode to vision, simultaneous use of these sensory modes seems actually to interfere with visual learning (for example, Gottfried, Rose & Bridger, 1977). Separate functioning, followed by integration, therefore seems superior to concurrent sensory functioning.

It is possible, though, that haptic exploration might interfere with attending to some visual features, such as color, but facilitate attention to others, such as form (Ruff, 1982a). Research with 1-year-olds supports this argument. Handling an object increases information about texture and form but not color and pattern (Ruff, 1982a). So, haptic and visual exploration do not simply provide redundant information. They provide separate bits of information that are integrated to identify a unified, whole object. The 1-year-old uses intermodal information much as you would in examining that Christmas present.

Gathering information from various sensory channels may be crucial in many developmental tasks. The infant acquiring a vocabulary, for example, has two basic tasks. First, she must pick individual words out of a stream of speech. Second, she must relate that word to an object, a person, and so on (Sullivan & Horowitz, 1983). Using intermodal perception, the child combines language (auditory information) with information about the object (coming through the visual or tactile channel). Interestingly, maternal behavior may help the baby make the connections (Sullivan & Horowitz, 1983). Mothers, for example, typically simultaneously point to and name pictures for their infants (Murphy, 1978). Thus, they bring the object to the baby's visual attention while providing auditory input. Similarly, mothers often name the toys with which their babies are playing (Messer, 1978). In these situations, the infant is receiving information through three perceptual channels—

tactile, visual, and auditory. So, intermodal perception is more than an interesting capability. It may be crucial in the development of complex abilities.

Selective Attention

If we paid attention to everything going on around us, our senses would be overloaded. We would not be able to organize or respond to the massive confusion. So, we "tune in" to some stimuli while "tuning out" others. This is the process of selective attention: Even newborns show selectivity in what they explore. They prefer, for example, to look at complex over simple stimuli (Fantz, 1961). They prefer patterned stimuli to simply brightly colored stimuli. They tend to focus on areas of high contrast, particularly at the outer edges of the patterns (Fantz, Fagan & Miranda, 1975). Very young babies (1 month of age) also prefer to look at larger objects, though this may be a function of their poor visual acuity (Lawson & Ruff, 1984).

As we have seen, information from other sensory modalities may also influence attention. An object that produces sound may draw more attention than a silent one (for example, Lawson et al., 1984). Manual exploration may also increase an infant's interest in an object (for example, Harris, 1971).

Other examples of viewing and listening preferences in infants abound, but these few will suffice to make the point that the infant is selective in what she attends to. In fact, selective attention is such a reliable phenomenon that it forms the basis of the major research model in perception (see Box 6-1). Of course, selective attention does undergo developmental change. This is exemplified in the shift from preference for outer edges to attention to central components of a pattern (Fantz, Fagan & Miranda, 1975). Refinement of selective attention, such as learning to attend to the features of objects that are relevant to a particular task, continues into the school years (see Gibson & Spelke, 1983).

BOX 6-1   *MEASURING PERCEPTUAL FUNCTIONING: SELECTIVE ATTENTION*

Not too many years ago it was commonly believed that neonates and young infants had few, if any, sensory and perceptual skills. This belief was at least partially attributable to our inability to assess infant sensory and perceptual functioning. After all, babies cannot say which ear they hear a sound in or what letters they can read on an eye chart.

In the mid-1950s, Robert Fantz made the first step toward developing appropriate assessment techniques (Fagan, 1982). Fantz (for example, 1961) argued that if a baby looked at one visual stimuli more than another, he must be able to distinguish between the two. The baby's preference was assumed to indicate discrimination. Visual preferences are fairly easy to test: The infant is simply placed before a "stage" which holds the two stimuli. Then an observer watches through a peephole that is between the two patterns. The observer records the length of time each pattern is reflected in the baby's eye. This yields a measure of visual fixation and, thereby, visual preference (Fagan, 1982).

The visual fixation task has been expanded into three methods (Fagan, 1982). In the first, the baby is exposed to one stimulus until she stops attending to it. In other words, the baby habituates to the stimulus. Then a second pattern is introduced. If the baby fixates on the new pattern, it is assumed that she recognizes it as different from the first one. That recognition accounts for her differential response to the two stimuli. It also indicates memory functioning and so is used in memory research.

In the second model, the baby sees a pattern briefly (2 minutes or less). Then that pattern is presented simultaneously with a new stimulus. Infants usually prefer to look at the new pattern. This indicates not only that they distinguish the two patterns but that they remember the first one. Thus, this model is often used in memory research as well as perceptual research.

The third pattern involves using a visual or auditory stimulus to reinforce high-amplitude sucking. After a while, the baby starts to suck less because the stimulus loses its reinforcing property. In other words, the baby habituates to the stimulus and no longer wants to "work" (suck) to see or listen to it. Then, a new stimulus is introduced. If the baby recognizes it as different, then he will again work to see or listen to it.

These models have yielded a huge amount of information concerning visual and auditory functioning. They have been used to examine visual acuity, phonemic distinction, preference for faces over other stimuli, color perception, and recognition of the mother's voice. They have also been used in memory research. Although different models may provide somewhat conflicting information (Rovee-Collier & Fagan, 1981), clearly they have greatly influenced our understanding of perceptual development.

The human newborn is clearly well equipped to explore the environment (although the "environment" can facilitate exploration, as demonstrated in Box 6-2). Further, these exploratory tools develop rapidly during infancy. The basic "system," then, is in place quite early. Does this mean that infants perceive the world the same way that adults do? Do they define objects, events, faces, and voices in an adultlike manner?

BOX 6-2   *FACILITATING EXPLORATION*

As the text indicates, even newborn infants have visual, auditory, and intersensory coordination skills that enable them to explore the environment. This does not mean, however, that their abilities are limitless. If we are to maximize the development that occurs through exploration (for example, cognitive development), we need to "exploit" these perceptual capabilities. A variety of factors should be taken into account.

First, the baby's visual acuity should be considered. Very young babies see objects best at a distance of about 8-10 inches. This means that most of the mobiles we hang over their cribs are out of their visual range, unless the baby is lying directly under the mobile—although from this vantage point the baby's view is often not very interesting. Some mobiles, though, are designed so that the baby sees a pattern when lying under them. These are probably the best choice, particularly for a young infant.

When showing the baby a toy, hold the toy within the baby's visual range. Babies are most attracted to brightly colored toys that move and make noises. Babies also prefer patterns. The pattern might be a face (for example, a doll's or an animal's face or their own reflection in a mirror) or a series of lines and curves (for example, a design in a book). Of course, the toy can be so complex or loud that the baby becomes frightened and withdraws. In this case, remove the toy and then gradually re-present it to the baby (for example, first without sound and movement, then with sound but not movement, and then with sound and movement).

Allowing the baby to manipulate objects is also important. So, objects that the baby can touch make more interesting "crib hangings" than those the baby can simply look at. Books (whose pages can be turned or that can be mouthed) are often of great interest. Of course, very young infants cannot turn paper pages, and so for them the plastic books are preferable (these also withstand mouthing much more effectively). Books are particularly interesting to explore if they contain various textures, smells, or noisemakers. Similarly, things the baby can "make work," like a string of bells hung over the crib that the baby can kick, are interesting.

It is easy to forget that senses other than vision, hearing, and touch also need stimulation. Babies usually like movement. For example, they enjoy sitting in swings or being carried in a pack on their parents' chests or backs. (The backpacks should probably not be used with infants who cannot yet hold up their own heads).

Social stimulation is probably more interesting to most babies than objects. It is important to engage in face-to-face interaction with a baby. It is also important to talk to the infant. The child acquires important social skills through these interactions (see Chapter 10). They probably also help her to gain a sense of trust in the world and to distinguish herself from other people in the environment (see Chapter 11). Again, stimulation during social interaction need not be limited to vision and hearing. You can rock the baby, for example. It is also important to touch the infant. You can stimulate kinesthetic senses by moving the baby's arms (as in the game pat-a-cake or so big). You can also stimulate these senses by offering "resistance" to the baby's movements (for example, letting him push with his feet against your hands). Rough-and-tumble play may be appropriate with older infants; but some caution needs to be exercised here, since the baby can be injured from too much shaking.

Of course, safety needs to be taken into account with all these suggestions. For example, noise-producing toys are of considerable interest to babies, but parents and caregivers need to be sure that whatever produces the noise (the beads in a rattle, for instance) cannot be removed from the toy and swallowed.

OBJECT PERCEPTION

How important is object perception? It is probably not an overstatement to say that it is basic to virtually all development. Without object perception, we would not be able to form categories. Language would be limited because we would have little to name. Much of the motivation for motor development would be gone. All these things, and many others, involve object perception.

At least three major issues are involved in object perception. First is the issue of object discrimination. When do infants distinguish one object from another? Second, what properties of objects does the infant notice? And how well does he recognize the relationships among the object's properties? Finally, once the infant perceives an object, how stable is that perception? Is the object perceived as being the same even when it is viewed from different angles or distances?

Object Discrimination

The first step in perceiving an object is distinguishing it from the rest of the environment. The object must be identified as a unique whole that is separate from everything else. Several factors influence the likelihood that this will occur.

Movement should make an object easier to discriminate (for example, Ruff, 1980, 1982c). Movement should, for example, help an infant identify the object's boundaries (Gibson & Spelke, 1983). It should help the infant separate the object from both the general background and from other objects (Ruff, 1980).

Infants of all ages seem to be aware of movement. Newborns can follow at least some movements (for example, Barten, Birns & Ronch, 1971). Infants 5 months of age attend more to moving objects than to stationary objects (for example, Gibson, Owsley & Johnston, 1978). These abilities and preferences seem to be adaptive because movement does seem to help in object discrimination (for example, Ruff, 1982c). However, only certain types of movement are helpful. Moving the object up and down and from side to side ("translation movements") seems to improve object discrimination, but rotating the object ("rotation movements") doesn't (Ruff, 1982c). Rotation may introduce too much complexity for the infants to absorb (Ruff, 1982c).

Another relevant factor is the distance between two objects. If I put a matchbook on top of a book, you would recognize the matchbook as being separate from the book. Infants under 3 months of age do not (for example, Piaget, 1954; Prather & Spelke, 1982, cited in Gibson & Spelke, 1983). They apparently perceive the two objects as constituting one unit (Piaget, 1954). It is interesting to note that Piaget (1954) found that a baby will reach for an object (for example, the matchbook) if it moves across the supporting object (for example, the book). This again indicates the importance of movement in defining an object's boundaries.

Of course, several factors that we have already discussed also affect discriminatory abilities. Manipulating an object seems to be of some value in its later discrimination (Ruff, 1980). Visual acuity also plays a role. Objects (and patterns) must be large enough to be seen. They must also not be too far away. Adding sound seems to increase attention and, at least in older infants, facilitates recognition (Ruff, 1980).

However, movement and spatial separation seem to be the most crucial elements in object discrimination (Gibson & Spelke, 1983). Gibson (1982; Gibson, Owsley & Johnson, 1978; Gibson & Spelke, 1983) argued that these factors help the infant to discern the object's invariant physical properties. The next question is, what sorts of structural invariants can infants distinguish?

Discriminating Object Properties

Even young infants can distinguish a variety of object properties. In a series of classic studies, Robert Fantz (1961) found, for example, that newborns can discriminate shapes and patterns. This includes the size of the object or pattern and whether the object is three-dimensional or flat. Young infants seem to discriminate shape based solely on the object's external contours. Later, infants pay more attention to the internal contours (for example, Linn et al., 1982). Furthermore, by 9 months of age, infants seem to recognize that the form of an object is constant (Ruff, 1978). They know that a change in the internal configuration of a form signals a novel form.

Infants also seem to be sensitive to an object's substance. Eleanor Gibson and her colleagues (Gibson et al., 1979) have demonstrated that 3.5-month-olds can distinguish a rigid object (made, for example, of wood) from a flexible object (made, for example, of sponge). These discriminations can be based on visual or tactile information (Bahrick, 1980; Gibson & Walker, 1982). Touching an object may also provide information about texture, a property which seems to be discernable by 6-month-olds (Ruff, 1980).

Finally, young infants can distinguish animate from inanimate objects. They approach people and objects differently. They seek information from inanimate things by looking at, touching, or chewing on them. With people, they try to communicate by gesturing and changing facial expressions (Trevarthen, 1979).

So, infants can identify objects and some of their specific properties. However, object perception involves more than simple discrimination. In perceiving an object, adults recognize that it has permanent properties (for example, size and shape). Do young infants have a similar understanding of objects?

The Stability of Objects

Two approaches have been used to investigate the stability of object perception in infancy. First, some researchers have examined part-whole relationships. Does the infant recognize that visible parts of an object signal the presence of the entire object? Let us say, for example, that I'm looking for my daughter's lost shoe. While searching, I see what looks like a shoestring sticking out from under the couch. I would immediately look under the couch on the assumption that where there's a shoelace, there's a shoe. Would an infant make the same assumption?

Research suggests that very young infants (4 months of age or less) would not. They do not search for partially hidden objects (for example, Bower, 1967; Kellman & Spelke, 1981; Piaget, 1954; Uzgiris & Hunt, 1975). So, this approach indicates that young infants do not perceive an object's form as a unified, stable whole.

A second approach used to assess the stability of object perception is to examine the "constancies," especially size and shape constancy. When, for example, you are in an airplane that is taking off, buildings and people on the ground appear to be shrinking, but you know they're not. That's because you have size constancy. You recognize that under normal circumstances, the size of an object does not change. To use Gibson's (1982) terminology, size is a structural invariant of objects.

Gibson also viewed shape as a structural invariant. For example, your best friend's nose looks different when viewed "full-face" than in "profile." Perhaps you can only see the bump on her nose when you look at her profile, but you know that the bump is always there. That's because you have shape constancy.

The question is, do infants perceive size and shape as being constant, or do they live in an "Alice in Wonderland" world where the size and shape of objects seems to change constantly?

T.G.R. Bower (1966) provided the first information on size and shape constancy. He examined the skills of 6-8 week-old infants. Bower found that infants had both size and shape constancy. He suggested that these skills were innate.

Other researchers had difficulty replicating Bower's results (for example, Cook, Field & Griffiths, 1978; Day & McKenzie, 1977). It was suggested, for example, that shape constancy was an illusion caused by the young infant's inability to discriminate forms effectively (Cook, Field & Griffiths, 1978). However, these studies suffered from a variety of methodological problems. More recent studies, which corrected these problems, have demonstrated both size and shape constancy in infants aged 12 and 18 weeks (for example, Caron, Caron & Carlson, 1979; Day & McKenzie, 1981). This does not mean that size and shape constancy are fully mature at this point (Gibson & Spelke, 1983). Think about a much older child trying to do a puzzle and you will be reminded of the infant's limited understanding of shape.

What enables a young infant to perceive constancy? Bower (1966) argued that the child is innately prepared to ignore the changes in retinal image as an object's distance or orientation shifts. Holly Ruff (1982a) disagreed. She suggested that the same movement that caused the changes in orientation or distance provided information about the invariant structural properties of the object (including size and shape) (Ruff, 1980, 1982a). So, rather than being prepared to ignore movement-induced changes, babies are "prepared" to use movement to obtain information about objects (Ruff, 1982a).

Ruff's view exemplifies the functionalist approach to object perception. Let's now examine this, and other, theoretical views.

Theoretical Issues

The major theoretical distinction is between the constructivists and the functionalists.

Constructivism.   Piaget's (1954) theory is the most frequently cited version of constructivism. Piaget saw infants as being naturally curious. This curiosity brings the baby into contact with objects. Each time the infant encounters an object, her understanding of the object changes. The parts and functions of an object are learned individually and are gradually integrated to form a concept of a whole object. A young infant may, for example, see a doll's leg. She doesn't know that it is part of the doll. Nor does she know that the same doll can be used to shake, suck on, and hug. Such structures and uses must be gradually incorporated as the child " constructs" her own definition of a doll. Notice that in the course of this development the child is defining both the physical structure and the functions of the doll. This specific information also leads to the construction of general principles about objects. These principles include the observation that objects have permanent, immutable characteristics and that object parts are related to the whole object. This construction process proceeds through a fixed series of stages, which are summarized in Table 6-1. (See Chapter 7 also.)

Functionalism.   Eleanor Gibson (for example, 1982) presented a functionalistic view of perceptual development. The goal of perception is to identify *affordances*, the function of objects. In order to survive, the child needs to know, for example, whether something can be eaten or walked on. The object's function is discerned on the basis of *structural invariants*, the permanent properties of the objects. With development, the child is able to identify more invariants. The child does not construct the functions or the invariant structures. Instead, both the structures and functions are there to be discovered. A newborn has the exploratory mechanisms needed to begin to perceive affordances. He can hear, see, and feel. He can also integrate the information from these senses, at least to some extent. During the next several weeks, his exploratory abilities improve through maturation and experience. This improvement brings more exact discrimination of invariants and affordances.

Evaluation.   Which theory best fits the available data about object perception? Gibson's theory seems to be favored by the researchers (for example, Butterworth, von Hofsten, Ruff, and Spelke). The data do indicate that Piaget underestimated the rate of perceptual development. Gibson's (Gibson, Owsley & Johnston, 1978) own research, for example, indicates that 5-month-olds can derive information concerning object rigidity on the basis of movement. Piaget (1954) thought this ability would not appear until 9-10 months. These rate errors do not disprove Piaget's theory, however. Indeed, Piaget (1970) emphasized that the sequence of development, not the rate, was the crucial component of his theory.

Some portions of Piaget's sequence can be challenged. Little support exists for the notion that the child's concept of object properties such as texture, size,

TABLE 6-1 **Piaget's Outline of the Development of Object Permanence (all ages are approximations).**

SUBSTAGE	OBJECT PERMANENCE BEHAVIOR
I *(0-1 month)*	No reaction to loss of object, face, and so on. No concept that object continues to exist.
II *(1-4 months)*	Child shows "passive expectation." For example, child continues to stare where object was but does not actively search. Piaget argued that the child is merely continuing an interrupted activity rather than actually expecting the object to return. No object concept.
III *(4-10 months)*	Visually and tactually anticipates the future position of objects. Expects a whole object when only a portion of it is visible. The object exists only in relation to the child's activity with it. It has no independent existence.
IV *(10-12 months)*	In simple search situations (for example, the object is hidden under one pillow), the baby can successfully search. The baby, then, seems to understand that the object continues to exist but can only comprehend this in relatively simple situations.
V *(12-18 months)*	Can successfully search for an object even after a series of hidings, but all hidings must be visible. The child seems to understand that the object continues to exist; yet, since she has no means of symbolizing the object or the hidings, she cannot search successfully if some (or all) of the hidings must be "imagined."
VI *(18-24 months)*	Can now symbolize the object and hidings. He can successfully search for objects even when part of the hiding is not visible. Full object permanence.

(Information from Ginsburg & Opper, 1979.)

shape, or rigidity change significantly during the course of infancy (within the limitations of visual acuity). This suggests that these properties are not constructed by the child. Rather, the ability to discern them appears to be more or less innate.

On the other hand, the infant's perception of the object as a unitary, permanent entity does seem to change significantly. Recall, for example, that part-whole relationships (see Chapter 8 also) are not recognized as early as other structural invariants of objects (for example, shape). At least portions of the constructivist perspective remain very viable.

To summarize, the available data on object perception seem to fit the functionalist view. However, they do not completely refute the constructivist perspective. Only additional research can resolve the debate.

DEPTH PERCEPTION

It would be nice if babies didn't roll off couches, beds, and changing tables. But as any parent knows, young babies cannot be trusted to stay away from the edge of the changing table. Does this mean that they don't see the drop, or does it mean they don't know what the drop means? The research on depth perception provides some clues.

Depth perception is typically assessed using the "visual cliff" (Gibson & Walk, 1960). The "cliff" is made by placing a piece of glass a foot or more above a board, which is on the floor. A piece of patterned cloth is placed flush against half of the glass. A piece of the same material is put on the board below the rest of the glass. This provides the illusion of a drop or cliff, with a shallow and a deep side. The baby is put on a board across the center of the glass. The researchers then try to determine under what circumstances the babies will cross the drop-off.

Gibson and Walk (1960) observed mobile infants (6 or more months old). They found that almost all the babies would crawl onto the "shallow" end, but less than 10% would crawl onto the deep end, even when coaxed by their mothers. Gibson and Walk argued that this indicated that human infants could perceive depth as soon as they could crawl. In fact, they suggested that this depth perception-locomotion link was evident in all species. Thus animals that can walk at birth (for example, chicks) are also born with depth perception. Gibson and Walk's research supported this hypothesis. Gibson and Walk argued that the relationship between depth perception and locomotion was innate, though they did warn that immature motor skills might cause a baby to fall even if depth was perceived.

Joseph Campos and his associates (Campos et al., 1978) agreed that young infants can perceive depth. In fact, their data indicated that infants as young as 2 months of age could perceive depth; but they argued that 2-month-olds were not afraid of the drop. The babies did not seem to understand its danger. Campos and his associates, in fact, found no evidence of fear of the drop until infants were 9 months of age.

Based on these data, they argued that fear of drop-offs was learned through experience. The experience of falling or nearly falling (including parental reaction to such episodes) "teaches" the child not to go over an edge (Campos et al., 1978). This explains why young infants do fall off couches, beds, and changing tables even though they can perceive the drop.

Other researchers have also reported a link between experience and depth perception (for example, Rader, Bausano & Richards, 1980; Richards & Rader, 1981; Walk, 1966), but the relationship is not as simple as Campos proposed. It seems to hold only for babies who first crawl after 6.5 months of age (Rader, Bausano & Richards, 1980; Richards & Rader, 1981). Babies who crawl earlier cross the cliff even though they have had extensive crawling experience.

This led Rader and her associates (Rader, Bausano & Richards, 1980; Richards & Rader, 1981) to suggest that an innate link between the visual system and the motor system emerges at around 6.5 months. Babies who learn to crawl after that time can use vision to guide their crawling. Babies who crawl earlier do not have the benefit of this visuomotor link. They have to rely on information from nonvisual sources, mainly touch, to guide their crawling. Therefore, they attend to the feel of the glass and crawl over the cliff. Whether future research will support this hypothesis remains to be seen.

To complicate the matter further, 8.5-month-olds in walkers will cross the cliff (Rader, Bausano & Richards, 1980). They crossed even though they had extensive experience in the walkers. Even babies who had avoided the drop when crawling crossed over in the walkers. This suggests that the infant does not have a broad understanding that an edge is something you fall off. In other words, the babies did not seem to have a generalized fear of falling. Yet, they did perceive the drop and used that information to guide crawling.

This finding can be interpreted as support for either Gibson's (1982) or Piaget's (1954) theory. Gibson did suggest that a child may be able to perceive an affordance (for example, depth) without an accompanying emotion (for example, fear). On the other hand, concept of depth (including its meaning) does develop gradually. Experience plays some role in this. This is consistent with Piaget's constructivist theory. Once again, the evidence is not sufficient to resolve the debate.

SOCIAL PERCEPTION

Young infants seem to have abilities to process socially oriented information (for example, faces or voices) that exceed their perceptual skills with nonsocial stimuli (T. Field, 1982). When looking at objects, for example, newborns do not scan their interiors. Instead, they focus on the object's outer edges. Yet, even neonates can attend to and discriminate facial movements (for example, tongue protrusion) well enough to imitate them (Meltzoff & Moore, 1983). Such differential perceptual skill has led several reviewers to treat social perception as a distinct realm of perceptual development (for example, Field, 1982; von Hofsten, 1983).

Why would research show that infants have "precocious" social perception? Two explanations are possible (Field, 1982). First, there are methodological issues. Perhaps real social stimuli (for example, faces) are more interesting than the stimuli (for example, bulls-eye patterns) commonly used in perception research.

The second possible explanation is that infants are predisposed to attend to social stimuli. Theorists have suggested that there are inborn "feature detectors" for speech (for example, Eimas, 1975) and faces (for example, Bower & Wishart, 1979). Such predispositions would be adaptive (in an evolutionary sense). They would help infants recognize the sources of their survival, that is, adults. They might also make babies more responsive to adults, thereby increasing the likelihood that adults would want to be around them. This nativist hypothesis can only be evaluated by examining the research on facial, voice, and speech perception.

Facial Perception

A Preference for Faces?   Human infants prefer to look at a face over almost any other kind of visual stimuli (for example, Fantz, 1961). Is this because they are innately tuned to react to the configuration of the human face (Sherrod, 1981)?

Infants under 6 months of age do seem to prefer a "normally" arranged drawing of a face to a "scrambled" facial pattern. However, the preference is not particularly marked (for example, Fantz, 1961). Furthermore, 1-month-olds are less likely than 2-month-olds to scan the interior of faces (Maurer & Salapatek, 1976). So, 1-month-olds are not usually looking at the face's configuration. Instead, they focus mainly on the outer contour of the head. Around 2 months of age, they begin to focus more on the eyes (for example, Maurer & Salapatek, 1976). By about 5 months of age, they begin to concentrate on the nose-mouth area (Sherrod, 1981).

However, under certain circumstances, young infants do attend to the internal configuration of faces. Sound or movement of the head or face increases attention to the interior (Sherrod, 1981), though movement is not as effective as sound (for example, Carpenter, 1974; Nelson & Horowitz, 1983). This explains why infants can attend to and imitate facial movements (for example, Meltzoff & Moore, 1983a).

None of this proves that infants have an innate concept of how a face is arranged. Meltzoff and Moore (1983a) saw the coordination of movement and vision as being the crucial innate component in imitation. Bower and Wishart (1979) argued the innate element is the desire to interact with other people. So, the ability to imitate facial movements may involve an innate component, but that component is not necessarily a special predisposition to perceive faces or their configurations.

Research on facial expressions indicates that young babies have little knowledge of facial configurations. Some studies have reported the ability to discriminate facial expressions in infants 3-4 months of age (for example, Barrera & Maurer, 1981). However, in these studies, only one person modeled the facial expressions. It could be that changes in that person's face, rather than categories of facial expression, were being distinguished (Caron, Caron & Myers, 1982; Sherrod, 1981). When several models are used (for example, Caron, Caron & Myers, 1982) infants cannot distinguish facial expressions (for example, happy vs. surprised) until they are 7 months of age. So, infants do not use configuration information until fairly late. Of course, the changes in facial expression would represent a higher level of complexity than simply knowing where the facial features belong. These data, however, do suggest a lack of attention to features and their configuration during early infancy.

For now, the safest conclusion is probably that infants are very interested in human faces. Although infants may innately prefer faces, one does not need such a nativist explanation to explain the preference. The preference could be based on the simple fact that human faces are interesting—they move, make sounds, have a complex interesting pattern, and so on. In other words, faces have all the characteristics that babies find attractive.

Attention to human faces is only the beginning of social perception. The ability to recognize specific faces represents a crucial advance. After all, this forms the basis of many human interactions. In infancy, for example, facial recognition is an important component of attachment and stranger anxiety.

Facial Recognition. Gary Olson (1981) suggested that there are two types of recognition. The first is "recognition of recurrence." The baby is aware of having encountered this before. For example, placing a breast-fed baby in the position commonly used during nursing frequently elicits rooting behavior. The infant searches for the breast. The baby will show this reaction no matter who is holding him. In other words, the baby does not discriminate among people. He cannot form "classes" of people (such as familiar and unfamiliar). Rather, he is responding to a specific element of the person (for example, how the person holds him). Olson argued that recognition of recurrence but not of class membership is available to infants under 3 months of age. Not everyone agrees. For example, Maurer & Salapatek, (1976) found one-month-olds could discriminate familiar from unfamiliar faces. However, attempts to replicate studies indicating facial discrimination by very young infants have failed (for example, Haith, Bergman & Moore, 1977). This tends to support Olson's argument.

Although disagreement exists concerning the abilities of young infants, everyone agrees that older infants can discriminate familiar from strange faces. Stranger anxiety demonstrates that. The recognitory ability has its limits, though. For example, infants seem to be able to discriminate their mothers from strangers when looking full-face at the adults, but they do not recognize people from a variety of orientations (head positions) until they are 7 months of age (for example, Sherrod, 1979).

Of course, facial recognition is not the only way an infant might recognize her mother (or father). The child might also recognize her parent's voice.

Voice Recognition

For a long time evidence has shown that young infants recognize their mothers' voices (Wolff, 1963). In fact, recent evidence suggests that even newborns prefer their mothers' voices (DeCasper & Fifer, 1980). Voice recognition may precede facial recognition.

When do infants connect the voices and faces? Again, conflict exists over the timing of the intercoordination. Some studies have found that infants as young as 6 weeks of age connect the mother's voice and face (for example, Aronson & Rosenbloom, 1971) while others have not (for example, McGurk & Lewis, 1974). By 4 months of age, infants seem to expect that voices and faces come from the same place (Spelke & Cortelyou, 1981), but connecting a specific voice to a specific face (for example, Dad's face and voice) cannot be clearly demonstrated until slightly later (for example, S. Cohen, 1974; Spelke & Owsley, 1979).

Recognizing people is an important accomplishment. However, it is not the infant's only perceptually based capability that is relevant to social interaction. There is also speech perception.

Speech Perception

As our primary means of communication, language is a crucial factor in social interactions. Therefore, it is important to know how early the infant becomes "tuned in to" language. When do babies first realize that language is different from other auditory input? This recognition may be a first step toward language development.

Skills.   Infants seem to prefer the human voice to other auditory input. Is this simply because of the sound of the voice, or is it because the voice is using language? This question cannot be answered directly, but evidence suggests that infants process language differently than they process other sounds. Young infants process language in the left hemisphere of the cerebral cortex and music in the right hemisphere (for example, Molfese, Freeman & Palermo, 1975). This pattern, which is comparable to the adult pattern, is found even in premature infants (Molfese, Molfese & Carrell, 1982). This indicates that an infant's brain, at least, distinguishes language from other sounds.

Infants can make even more complex distinctions. One-month-olds can differentiate one vowel sound from another. They can also discriminate some consonant sounds. For example, they can distinguish /p/ from /b/ (Eimas et al., 1971). In fact, young infants can differentiate most sounds using cues similar to those used by adults. However, some developmental improvement in these abilities takes place (for example, Morse & Cowan, 1982).

One-month-olds also seem to be attuned to intonation patterns. They prefer intoned speech to flat, nonintoned speech (for example, Mehler et al., 1978). Two-month-olds seem to recognize that speech is divided into syllables (Bertoncini & Mehler, 1981).

How any of these skills is actually related to language acquisition is not clear (see Chapter 10). Young infants do have remarkable language perception skills, though. Where do these skills come from? Are they innate? And are they truly precocious compared to the processing of other auditory input?

Explanations.   Peter Eimas (1975) suggested that innate "feature detectors" in the auditory system pick up the cues needed to distinguish the patterns. These cues include how much air is released prior to the sound and where the tongue is placed when the sound is made (which alters the air flow pattern).

Research indicates that at least some sound discriminations appear early enough to be innate (for example, Trehub, 1976). However, not all discriminations are made by all infants (for example, Eiler et al., 1981). This suggests that not all discriminatory abilities are inborn. The extent of innate abilities, if there are any, is difficult to evaluate because of the lack of studies of newborns (less than 1 month of age). Also, very few studies have been made of vowel-consonant discrimination in other cultures.

Even if we assume that infants have innate speech perception capabilities, the question of whether such abilities are precocious compared to the processing of other sounds remains. The research on this question is sparse, but several studies indicate that music perception is as sophisticated as speech perception (for example, Eimas, 1975; Jusczyk et al., 1977). The research is not unanimous, though (for example, Jusczyk et al., 1980).

Theories of Social Perception

The lack of evidence for precocity in facial and speech perception undermines the position (for example, Bowlby, 1969) that infants are predisposed to perceive social stimuli. We are thus left with the question of how the infant acquires this information. Gibson (for example, Gibson & Spelke, 1983) and Piaget (1952) agree on one thing. Social perception is guided by the same principles as the rest of perception.

In Gibson's view, the infant discovers invariant features of people that lead to the perception of affordances. The infant moves from a global perception to a gradual differentiation of the invariant features. Bower (for example, Bower & Wishart, 1979) also argued that social perception moves from the general to the specific. For example, using structural invariants (for example, movement and configuration) as clues, the baby recognizes the "human-ness" of a face (Bower & Wishart, 1979). The recognition of "human-ness" leads the infant to behave in a certain manner (for example, smiling or differential attention). Eventually, the faces are discriminated to represent particular human beings who have a specific meaning to the child (for example, mother vs. stranger).

Piaget's (1952) view is that the infant constructs his social knowledge. There are bits and pieces of information about a person that are integrated into an understanding of that person. This, in turn, will be generalized to a "concept" of all people. Olson's (1981) suggestion that development moves from recognition of recurrence (based on some element of the stimuli) to discrimination (among integrated wholes) supports this perspective.

There is no simple answer here. This is partially due to the methodological inadequacies that have led to conflicting results. As such problems are alleviated, we should get a clearer picture of social perception.

SUMMARY

In many ways, perceptual development provides the "basics" for other behaviors. It is related to language, cognitive, and social functioning. Once again, then, we see that various developmental realms are linked.

Another theme that has reoccurred in this chapter is the nature-nurture controversy. Newborns do seem to be equipped with perceptual skills. They have not only functioning sensory systems but also preferences (for faces, voices, complexity, and so on). Some of these preferences seem to have functional value.

However, infants are not born with such highly developed systems that experience plays no role. Young infants perceive depth but they need experience to use that information to avoid falling. They like to look at faces, but they cannot translate that into learning to recognize faces quickly. The more advanced skills require experience.

When we talk about experience, part of what we mean is simply exposure. Seeing faces is obviously crucial to recognizing them, but experience is more than simple exposure. It also means forming associations between a stimulus and an event (for example, between an edge and falling). In other words, part of experience is learning. How infants learn is the focus of the next chapter.

7

Learning and Memory

Perceptual skills clearly enable the young infant to explore the environment, but how well can the baby organize and use this information? The value of exploratory skills is mediated by the child's ability to learn from and remember her experiences. In this chapter, we explore infant learning and memory. Because learning principles form the basis of the methodology used in infant memory research, it is necessary to understand learning before examining memory.

LEARNING

Defining Learning

Not so long ago it was commonly believed that babies were born knowing nothing (see Chapter 1). They were seen as blank slates waiting to be written on. This view is obviously an exaggeration. Even newborns have considerable capacities for perceiving, interpreting, and interacting with the world.

However, it is equally evident that newborns have much to learn. They have to learn everyday behaviors like self-feeding, using the toilet, and talking. They also have to learn to differentiate themselves from other people, to interpret objects as constant and immutable, and to organize concepts in relation to one another. Some of these behavioral changes involve a sizable maturational component. Others do not. All involve at least some behavioral changes that are rooted in information obtained from the environment, that is, changes that are learned.

So learning involves behavioral changes. These changes are more or less permanent, although they, too, can be changed. For example, a reaction to a particular object might change. This was exemplified in John Watson's (Watson & Rayner, 1920) classic "Little Albert" experiments. "Albert" was "trained" to be afraid of a white rat, a rabbit, and a dog that he had previously not feared. It is assumed that such fear stays with a child for more than a minute or two (it did in Albert's case).

In addition, the behavioral changes are seen as not being attributable to maturation. So, phenomena like improvement in visual acuity and increased interconnections among cortical neurons are not discussed in terms of learning. Similarly, behavioral changes that seem due to temporary states of the organism are not considered learned. Let's say you have a baby who is good natured and goes to sleep very easily. One day she misses her afternoon nap. That evening she is cranky. Her parents have a difficult time getting her to fall asleep. Would you say that she learned to be cranky and difficult to get to bed? Probably not. You might instead suggest that she was overly tired—a temporary state that caused a change in her behavior.

Learning does refer to behavioral changes attributable to practice or experience. As such, learning has traditionally been viewed as representing the environmental—or nurture—component in development. In fact, in the most extreme traditional views (for example, Skinner, 1974), virtually no role was given to nature. Even the species of the organism was seen as irrelevant. This view was dramatically exemplified by B.F. Skinner, who drew an analogy between a pigeon learning to walk in a figure eight and a child learning to talk (Skinner, 1957). More recent writers (for example, Lipsitt, 1982; Sameroff & Cavanaugh, 1979; Seligman, 1970) have argued that biological predispositions are involved in learning.

Many models of how learning occurs have been constructed. In terms of infant learning, these fall into four major catetories: classical conditioning, instrumental conditioning, habituation, and imitation. Each one of these models will be briefly described and evaluated in terms of infant learning.

Classical Conditioning

Definitions.   Everyone has heard of Pavlov's dogs (for example, Pavlov, 1927). Pavlov used meat powder to elicit salivation in the dogs. He then paired the meat powder with a tone. He did this several times. Eventually, the tone alone elicited salivation.

This was the first demonstration of *classical* or *respondent* conditioning. *Classical conditioning* involves finding a stimulus (the unconditioned stimulus) which elicits a response (the unconditioned response). This unconditioned stimulus is then paired with a neutral stimulus. The neutral stimulus initially has no effect on the unconditioned response. However, after multiple pairings of the unconditioned stimulus and the neutral stimulus, the previously neutral stimulus, now termed the conditioned stimulus, comes to elicit the reponse, now called the conditioned response, too (see Figure 7-1). In Pavlov's original experiments, meat powder was the unconditioned stimulus, salivation was the unconditioned response. The tone was the neutral stimulus that eventually became the conditioned stimulus.

In the traditional classical conditioning paradigm, it was assumed that neutral stimuli were all equal. In other words, any neutral stimulus could become a conditioned stimulus in any situation. Martin Seligman (1970, p. 407) has called this the "assumption of equivalence of associability." Pavlov viewed the choice of the tone as arbitrary. The neutral stimulus could have just as well been a light, a hand movement, or even a cat. Keep this assumption in mind, for it has been the focus of several evaluations of infant classical conditioning (for example, Fitzgerald & Brackbill, 1976; Lipsitt, 1982; Sameroff & Cavanaugh, 1979).

Classical Conditioning in Infancy.   Can newborns and infants be classically conditioned? Evidence exists to suggest they can be. Lewis Lipsitt and his associates demonstrated that neonatal sucking could be classically conditioned to the presentation of a tube or a tone (Lipsitt & Kaye, 1964; Lipsitt, Kaye & Bosack, 1966).

However, Lipsitt (1982) and other reviewers of the infant classical conditioning literature (for example, Fitzgerald & Brackbill, 1976; Olson & Sherman, 1983; Sameroff & Cavanaugh, 1979) argued that infant classical conditioning has

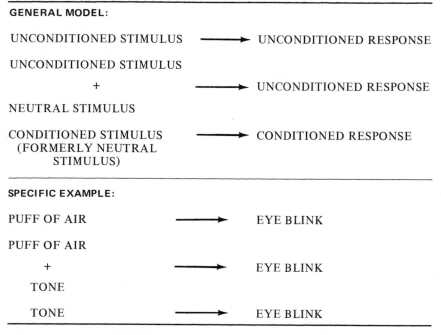

GENERAL MODEL:

UNCONDITIONED STIMULUS ⟶ UNCONDITIONED RESPONSE

UNCONDITIONED STIMULUS

\+ ⟶ UNCONDITIONED RESPONSE

NEUTRAL STIMULUS

CONDITIONED STIMULUS ⟶ CONDITIONED RESPONSE
(FORMERLY NEUTRAL
STIMULUS)

SPECIFIC EXAMPLE:

PUFF OF AIR ⟶ EYE BLINK

PUFF OF AIR

\+ ⟶ EYE BLINK

TONE

TONE ⟶ EYE BLINK

FIGURE 7-1   Classical Conditioning.

limitations. First, infant state (see Chapter 3) affects conditionability. Certain behaviors that might serve as the unconditioned reponse may, for example, be obtainable only during a particular state or states. The Babkin reflex, which has served as the unconditioned response in several studies (for example, Kaye, 1965; Sostek, Sameroff & Sostek, 1972) can be elicited only during the wakefulness and irregular sleep states (Sameroff & Cavanaugh, 1979). State or state changes may also affect the type, speed, and strength of the association being made (see Fitzgerald & Brackbill, 1976, or Sameroff & Cavanaugh, 1979). Thus, classical conditioning is constrained by the infant's state during the testing.

The findings concerning the effects of state may not particularly surprise you, but the second limitation on infant conditioning might. This is that infants seem to be prepared to make some conditioned associations but not others. The "little Albert" research provides an example. Recall that Albert was conditioned to fear a white rat, a dog, and a rabbit (Watson & Rayner, 1920). In a later study using the same technique, infants could not be trained to fear blocks or curtains (Bregman, 1934). So, animals can become conditioned objects of fear, but blocks and curtains cannot.

Martin Seligman (1970) has argued that such findings undermine the "equivalence of associability" assumption made by traditional classical conditioning theorists. He argued that people do not make arbitrary associations. Rather, people are *prepared*, biologically, to make certain associations. He suggested that there is a continuum of preparedness. Associations we are prepared to make will be formed very quickly. At the other end of the continuum are contraprepared associations. These are associations that either cannot be made at all or can be made only with many pairings. In the middle of the continuum are the unprepared responses. These associations are made with a moderate amount of training. The amount and type of preparedness of a particular association is assumed to have evolutionary significance.

An example might be helpful. Recall that even young infants emit a variety of cries (see Chapter 3). With development the cries become even more differentiated (Wolff, 1973), and mothers interpret the cries more and more (for example, Ainsworth & Bell, 1977). Now, a mother might associate a particular type of cry with fatigue or general fussiness, and so she may not respond immediately. However, when she hears a pain cry, she runs to her infant (Wolff, 1973). Mothers do not interpret pain cries as "nothing to worry about." We might say that mothers are contraprepared to associate pain cries with minor events or upsets. The evolutionary advantage of such contrapreparedness is clear: It would protect the baby and maximize his chances for survival.

This notion of preparedness has received widespread acceptance in the infant classical conditioning literature (for example, Fitzgerald & Brackbill, 1976). Lipsitt (1982) took the argument a step further. He suggested that learning is fundamentally a biological process. It is basically an indicator of the infant's ability to adapt to the environment and its demands. This view is obviously quite different from the traditional stance.

However, Lipsitt's position is not the most radical one available. Arnold Sameroff and Patrick Cavanaugh (1979) go even further. Citing a variety of methodological issues, they argued that true classical conditioning has not been demonstrated in infants. They point out that many studies did not have adequate control groups, that instrumental and classical conditioning were combined so that the results are unclear, or that state was not monitored. Take, for example, conditioned sucking. Evidence indicates that sucking can be conditioned to an auditory stimulus. However, an auditory stimulus can also elicit unconditioned sucking. In other words, when a tone sounds, an infant may suck even if the tone has never been paired with food. So, it is difficult to prove that classical conditioning occurred in such studies.

Sameroff and Cavanaugh do acknowledge that the infant forms some associations. However, these associations are constrained by preparedness. Furthermore, they are not associations between conditioned stimuli (for example, tone) and conditioned responses (for example, eye blink). Instead, they are associations between unconditioned (for example, puff of air) and conditioned stimuli (for example, tone) (see Figure 7-2). To Sameroff and Cavanaugh, this is an important

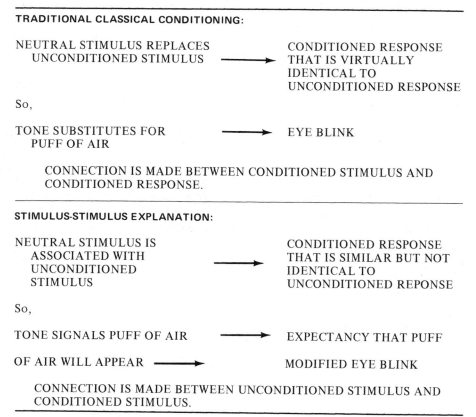

TRADITIONAL CLASSICAL CONDITIONING:

NEUTRAL STIMULUS REPLACES
   UNCONDITIONED STIMULUS   ⟶   CONDITIONED RESPONSE
                                     THAT IS VIRTUALLY
                                     IDENTICAL TO
                                     UNCONDITIONED RESPONSE

So,

TONE SUBSTITUTES FOR   ⟶   EYE BLINK
   PUFF OF AIR

   CONNECTION IS MADE BETWEEN CONDITIONED STIMULUS AND
   CONDITIONED RESPONSE.

STIMULUS-STIMULUS EXPLANATION:

NEUTRAL STIMULUS IS
   ASSOCIATED WITH
   UNCONDITIONED   ⟶   CONDITIONED RESPONSE
   STIMULUS   THAT IS SIMILAR BUT NOT
                                     IDENTICAL TO
                                     UNCONDITIONED REPONSE

So,

TONE SIGNALS PUFF OF AIR   ⟶   EXPECTANCY THAT PUFF

OF AIR WILL APPEAR   ⟶   MODIFIED EYE BLINK

   CONNECTION IS MADE BETWEEN UNCONDITIONED STIMULUS AND
   CONDITIONED STIMULUS.

FIGURE 7-2   Two Interpretations of Classical Conditioning.

distinction. If the infant formed associations between stimuli and responses, we could argue that a totally new association was formed. If the association is between the stimuli, however, we could argue that the new (conditioned) stimuli is simply being integrated into an existing behavioral pattern. The latter case, which is what Sameroff and Cavanaugh argued actually happens, is much closer to Piaget's concept of assimilation (see Chapter 8) than to traditional classical conditioning.

To conclude, there is some debate about whether infants can be classically conditioned, at least in the traditional sense. However, there is widespread agreement that the associations that can be made are significantly constrained by biological predispositions. As we shall see, similar conclusions seem to apply to instrumental conditioning.

Instrumental Conditioning

Definition.   Classical conditioning can explain how existing responses come to be controlled by new stimuli. So, it can explain why a baby eventually comes to cry in the presence of a variety of objects or people. But, classical conditioning cannot tell us how totally "new" behaviors, such as toilet training, are acquired. *Instrumental conditioning* offers an explanation for such behaviors.

The basic premise of instrumental conditioning is that behavior is controlled by its consequences (for example, Skinner, 1974). If a behavior is rewarded (for example, has positive consequences), it will be performed more frequently. If it is punished (for example, has negative consequences), it occurs less often. Since the environment determines the consequences, environment controls behavior. Little or no role is ascribed to biology. No inherent link between the behavior and its consequences exists. Rather, the behavior appears almost randomly, is positively reinforced, and, therefore, recurs.

Instrumental Conditioning in Infancy.   Again, evidence suggests that infants can be instrumentally conditioned (see, for example, Lipsitt, 1982). Indeed, instrumental conditioning has become a common methodological technique. For example, in Bower's studies of size constancy (see Chapter 6), infants were conditioned to turn their heads when they saw a particular cube. The reward for head turning was a game of peek-a-boo. Bower then tested to see whether the babies would turn their heads to objects that were the same size as the original object but placed at different distances. Also, conditioned kicking has been an important methodological tool in the memory research we will be examining later (for example, Rovee-Collier's work).

Of course, this does not mean that infants can be instrumentally conditioned to do anything. Preparedness also seems to be an issue here (for example, Lipsitt, 1982; Olson & Sherman, 1983; Sameroff & Cavanaugh, 1979). For example, social behaviors are much more likely to be conditioned by using socially oriented rewards, such as vocalizations, than by using nonsocial rewards, such as looking at a pattern (for example, Weisberg, 1963). Again, preparedness seems to have adaptive significance. Pairing a social behavior (for example, infant vocalizations) with a social consequence (for example, paternal vocalizations) increases social interaction. This affords the child increased protection and stimulation. This preparedness component may explain why some things are rewarding and others aren't (Seligman, 1970). This is an issue that traditional instrumental conditioning models have considerable difficulty explaining.

Once again, Sameroff and Cavanaugh (1979) go beyond simply modifying the conditioning model to include preparedness. They argue that instrumental conditioning has not been well-demonstrated. They cite two major reasons for this. First, the effects of instrumental conditioning often disappear quite quickly. An infant might be trained to suck on a tube to get sugar water, but once the sugar water stops coming, the infant soon stops sucking. This is not the more or less permanent change in behavior required by the definition of learning.

Second, it is possible that the rewards elicit rather than train the behavior. So, the behaviors do not appear randomly. They are preprogrammed (at least in newborns). Part of this program is that certain events will elicit certain behaviors. So, social behavior from an adult elicits social behavior from an infant. With experience, the baby connects his behavior with adults' behavior and comes to expect the social interaction. This, in turn, does modify his behavior. However, according to Sameroff and Cavanaugh, the modification is controlled, not by the environment, but by the child's existing behavioral structures. Once again, this is a modified Piagetian approach.

Sameroff and Cavanaugh's use of a Piagetian model to explain both classical and instrumental conditioning underscores another major issue concerning infant learning. In both research and real-life settings, separating the effects of classical and instrumental conditioning is often difficult. Let's say, for example, that a baby is being breast-fed. His mother often wears a shirt that zips up the front. After a few days, the baby begins to turn his head when he hears the zipper. Is this because he associates the sound with the tactile stimulation (the touch of the breast against his face) that elicits head turning? This would be classical conditioning. Or is it because his head turning at the sound of the zipper is rewarded with milk? This would be instrumental conditioning. Which model explains this behavior?

Obviously, infants can form associations between their own behaviors and environmental responses to them. Whether these behaviors are truly determined by the environment, as proponents of instrumental conditioning would argue, remains a matter of debate. Clearly, however, there are biological predispositions that influence the likelihood of instrumental conditioning. There are also developmental changes in conditionability. All this suggests that the traditional models of instrumental conditioning and classical conditioning are too simplistic to explain infant learning.

Before moving onto habituation and imitation, let's consider the possible implications of conditioning for a particular behavior—crying.

Crying and Conditioning

I often speak to parents' groups. I always go to such meetings knowing I will be asked about crying. Can you spoil a baby by going to her every time she cries? If you don't go, will the baby feel neglected and unloved? Is it ever appropriate to simply let the baby cry? Should you rock a baby just because he's crying? Feed him? Hold him?

There are two real questions here. First, how can I stop my baby from crying? This is an understandable question, given that most parents find the crying at least annoying and often distressing. The response to this question is complicated by the second question. How can I stop my baby from crying without spoiling him? Again, this is an understandable question. No parent wants to *encourage* crying.

These issues clearly relate to conditioning. You want to train the baby to act in a certain way, that is, to stop crying. You don't want the baby to train you, that is, you don't want the baby's crying to dominate your behavior so that you are always running to him. What should you do?

Early research concerning conditioning and crying seemed to support the popular belief that going to a crying baby quickly served as a positive reinforcer of crying (for example, Etzel & Gewirtz, 1967; Moss & Robson, 1968). For example, the faster mothers responded to the fussing of their 1-month-olds, the more the babies fussed at 3 months of age (Moss & Robson, 1968). These findings seemed to be consistent with research concerning older children. Such research indicated that crying in preschoolers could be controlled by reward and punishment (for example, Hart et al., 1964).

However, these studies were criticized by Silvia Bell and Mary Ainsworth (1972). They suggested that few of the studies were done in truly naturalistic settings (except for the Moss & Robson study). Furthermore, Bell and Ainsworth pointed out that these were all relatively short-term studies. They argued that infant behavior needed to be monitored for a longer time if we were to understand the dynamics of mother-infant interaction.

So, Bell and Ainsworth (1972) observed infants throughout the first year of life. The observational pattern was somewhat different for individual infants, but it began with infants either 1 or 3 weeks of age and lasted until they were 52 weeks of age. All observations were done in the infants' homes.

Bell and Ainsworth found that ignoring a baby's crying contributed to more crying at later ages. "Ignoring" included both failure to respond and delayed responding. Whether mothers ignored the cries of their tiny babies seemed to be a function of their own style, but by the end of the year a cycle had developed. Ignoring the crying contributed to more crying, which led to more ignoring, resulting in more crying, and so on. Leila Beckwith (1972) reported similar results.

Bell and Ainsworth interpret their findings as supporting Bowlby's view on attachment (see Chapter 4). In this theory, crying is seen as a signaling behavior designed to bring the mother near. When it works, the baby is comforted and can develop a secure attachment. When it fails, the baby is left uncertain and insecure.

This, according to Bell and Ainsworth (1972; Ainsworth & Bell, 1977) explains why ignoring contributes to increased crying. This position has been supported in more recent research (for example, Ainsworth et al., 1978; Belsky, Rovine & Taylor, 1984).

It is interesting to note that the crucial issue, according to Bell and Ainsworth, is simply whether the mother responds. How she responds seemed less important. They did find that picking the baby up was more effective than any other intervention. However, feeding the baby, touching the baby, and simply entering the room were almost as effective in stopping the crying. Simply vocalizing to the baby was the least effective way to stop the crying, particularly during the first 4 months. These differences were not great, and so although the type of maternal response may differentially affect the immediate episode to some extent, it is *responding* that has the long-term effects (Bell & Ainsworth, 1972).

The Bell and Ainsworth study has been roundly criticized by Jacob Gewirtz and Elizabeth Boyd (1977), who pointed out a variety of methodological short-comings in the study. Most important for our purposes is Gewirtz and Boyd's claim that Bell and Ainsworth failed to define *crying* carefully. Gewirtz and Boyd argued that some cries, particularly those of very young infants, probably do not respond to conditioning techniques. Such cries may well signal distress that requires maternal attention. Failing to respond to such cries may result in the pattern demonstrated by Bell and Ainsworth.

Later, though, crying becomes more voluntary and can be used intentionally to control the behavior of others. In other words, the baby begins to recognize the "contingent effects" (for example, Watson, 1979) of her crying. If she cries, Mom comes running. At this point, Gewirtz and Boyd argue, the crying can be increased by maternal responding. Of course, even at this point, some crying is meant to signal a "need" (for example, injury) and will require immediate response.

In their counterresponse, Ainsworth and Bell (1977) note that Gewirtz and Boyd provided no data to support their view. The Gewirtz and Boyd paper was a critique, not a research report. In addition, Ainsworth and Bell point out that it would be virtually impossible for a researcher to distinguish an infant's "need" cries from her "conditionable" cries. They do agree that such a distinction exists, but they believe it probably does not emerge until after the infant reaches 4 months of age. Hence, during at least the first 4 months, Ainsworth and Bell argue, parents ought to respond promptly to infant cries if they want to foster secure attachments.

So what advice can we give parents concerning crying? During early infancy (the first 4 months or so) cries ought to receive prompt attention. We do not want to overstate the case here. Failing to respond promptly every now and then will not cause irreparable damage. Indeed, none of the mothers in the Bell and Ainsworth (1972) study responded every time. Rather, the general pattern should be one of quick response. As the baby gets older and starts to recognize the "power" of crying, mothers (and fathers) may need to be more discriminating in their responses. The key word here is *discriminating*. There is never an age at which all cries should be ignored, even temporarily. How discriminating parents should be varies from baby to baby. Parents who have been responding sensitively during the early months should be able to make such discriminations.

Having examined a behavior that is related to the two forms of learning already outlined, let's now look at another form of infant learning—imitation.

Imitation

Imitation is not discussed in every review of infant learning. However, imitation does seem to fit the broad definition of learning given at the beginning of the chapter. Imitation involves acquiring a new behavior by attending to the actions of another person (model) and then producing a behavior similar to the modeled one.

Imitation is of considerable interest to psychologists. Many of our social behaviors are learned through imitation. The range of such behaviors runs from dress styles to phobias. Piaget (1962) has outlined a major role for imitation in cognitive development. Also, researchers have long acknowledged the role of imitation in language development (for example, Slobin & Welch, 1973).

It may be surprising, then, to learn that imitation during the neonatal and early infancy period has only recently become the focus of considerable research attention. There is a good reason for this: The major theories of imitation suggested that newborns were not capable of imitating behaviors.

Instrumental Learning.   One explanation of imitation is that it is a special case of instrumental conditioning (Gewirtz & Stingle, 1968). In this view, imitation is reinforced much like any other behavior. Let's say a parent wants to teach his baby to wave bye-bye. He begins by waving his hand at the baby. He may even wave the baby's hand for her. When the baby produces a similar movement, he rewards her with smiles, cheers, and so forth. Eventually, the bye-bye behavior is shaped into an adultlike form. The baby is imitating (Meltzoff & Moore, 1983a).

Gradually the child learns that imitation is a source of potential reinforcement. Only occasional reinforcement is needed to keep the child imitating. However, it takes a while to reach this point, making it clear that the newborn would be considered incapable of imitation. How long it takes for imitation to be possible is unclear, though it is probably not an incredibly lengthy process. So, researchers working from this model would not be likely to investigate neonatal imitation.

Piaget.   Jean Piaget (1962) also argued that neonates could not imitate. However, that is the only similarity between his model and the instrumental learning model. Indeed, the two models do not even examine identical behaviors (Meltzoff & Moore, 1983a). The instrumental learning model focuses on behaviors that are "trained" by adults. Piaget considered such behaviors "pseudo-imitation." He was only concerned with behaviors that were spontaneous imitations.

Piaget proposed that the ability to imitate developed in six invariant stages (summarized in Table 7-1). Note several things about the stages. First, newborns are incapable of imitation. A behavior such as crying may appear to be imitated, since a baby may start crying when he hears another baby cry; but, Piaget argued, such instances are simply reflexive. The crying of the other baby triggers the reflex. So, there is no true imitation in the neonatal period.

TABLE 7-1 Piaget's Stages of the Development of Imitation (ages are approximatons).

STAGE	DESCRIPTION	EXAMPLE
I *(0-1.5 months)*	No imitation. Preparation through reflexes.	One infant cries. A second infant then begins crying. The second infant is not imitating. Rather, the crying of the first infant has triggered a reflex reaction.
II *(2-4.5 months)*	Imitation begins. Only familiar sounds and movements are imitated. Imitation of a familiar sound not currently being produced is possible but sporadic. Only movement visible to the infant or causing visual changes (for example, head shaking) can be imitated.	A child produces a *raa* sound. When the child is silent, the parent produces a similar sound. The baby imitates the sound.
III *(5-8 months)*	Imitation becomes more systematic. It is still confined to familiar behaviors. Imitation of gestures is confined to gestures the child has seen.	A child holds up his thumb and looks at it. He moves it. The parent does the same thing. The child imitates.
IV *(8-12 months)*	The child can begin to imitate invisible movements if she has already performed the movement herself. She can also imitate new sounds and movements, but the movements must be visible during her imitation of them.	The child bites her lower lip. The parents bites his lip. The child imitates.
V *(12-18 months)*	Imitation of new models is now systematic. The child can imitate even behaviors that are invisible to her while she is imitating them.	The adult pulls a piece of his hair across his forehead. The child has never done this before, but she imitates.
VI *(18-24 months)*	Deferred or representative imitation. In all previous stages, the child could not	A visiting playmate throws a tantrum. It involves all sorts of

FIGURE 7-1   (continued)

STAGE	DESCRIPTION	EXAMPLE
	"delay" imitation. She had to imitate immediately or the behavior would be "lost" to her. Now, she has the representational capacity to rehearse the behavior mentally. This allows her to reproduce the behavior at a later time.	new behaviors. The observer child does nothing at the time. The next day, though, she throws a comparable tantrum.

(Information, including examples, is taken from Piaget, 1962.)

Second, the earliest imitations are of behaviors that are familiar to the baby. The model's behavior is incorporated into an existing behavioral pattern. If an infant has already produced a particular sound, she will imitate that sound when an adult produces it. The child does not need to be making the sound immediately before the adult models it. The important thing is that the sound is already in the baby's repertoire.

The same process occurs with gestures, but an additional factor is involved here. While the young baby will imitate hand movements he has seen himself make, movements that are not directly visible to the infant (such as facial movements) cannot yet be imitated. Indeed, Piaget (1962) argued that the baby cannot imitate even familiar facial movements until the fourth stage, when the infant is 8-9 months of age. It is also not this stage that infants become capable of imitating some novel behaviors, that is, behaviors not already included in their own repertoires.

Finally, Piaget distinguishes between immediate imitation of a model and "deferred imitation." Deferred imitation is the ability to model a behavior some time after it is first demonstrated. For example, Piaget's daughter, Jacqueline, once threw a temper tantrum that was similar to one she had watched a friend throw the day before. Since she had never done this before, Piaget (1962) concluded that she must have been imitating her friend even though there was a full day between her observation and her performance of the behavior. In order to imitate following this sort of delay, the infant must have a mental means of rehearsing and remembering the behavior. In other words, the baby must have mental symbols. In Piaget's view, this symbolic functioning is not available until late in the second year.

To summarize, the Piagetian view makes three important points. First, neonates do not imitate. Second, imitation of facial movements, particularly unfamiliar ones, is very difficult and does not occur until an infant is at least 8-9 months of age. Third, deferred imitation is not possible until mental symbols develop toward the end of the second year.

Neonatal Imitation. We have seen two theories—instrumental learning and Piagetian—that predict that neonates do not imitate. Their rationales are quite different, though their conclusion is the same. Research by Andre Meltzoff and M. Keith Moore (1977, 1983b) has seriously challenged this conclusion.

Working with 12-21-day-old infants, Meltzoff and Moore (1977) demonstrated imitation of facial movements (for example, tongue protrusion and mouth opening). The design of their study eliminated the possibility that the infant's increased tongue protrusion and mouth opening was attributable simply to increased arousal levels, which had been a problem in earlier studies (for example, Gardner & Gardner, 1970). Interestingly, they also demonstrated that the infants could imitate tongue protrusion or mouth opening even after a momentary delay between the model's presentation and the infant's imitative attempt.

These results raise serious doubts about Piaget's position. Not only were young infants capable of imitation, but they were also able to delay, or defer, imitation. However, this study did not eliminate an instrumental conditioning explanation as a possibility. After all, the babies were 2-3 weeks of age. It was possible that they had already "learned" the value of imitation.

A more recent study by Meltzoff and Moore (1983b) seems to eliminate the instrumental conditioning explanation. In this study, the infants ranged in age from 42 minutes to 72 hours. Again, the infants seemed to imitate tongue protrusion and mouth opening.

Meltzoff and Moore (1983a) argued that their results cannot be explained by either the instrumental learning or Piagetian model. They suggested that infants have an innate ability to match their own behavior to a model's. Since this matching can occur even when the infant cannot visually monitor her own reproduction, they argued that the infant makes the match using intermodal information. The infant recognizes the relationship between the visual display and her own facial muscle movements. It is not that she has learned to "integrate" the information from various modalities. Rather, she starts out with a "supermodal" representation of events in which sensory modalities are not differentiated. Only later does she learn to separate the modalities. This view is consistent with Bower's theory (Bower & Wishart, 1979; see Chapter 6). It is dramatically opposed to Piaget's view that the sensory modalities are initially separate and are only gradually integrated (Piaget, 1952; see Chapter 6).

Meltzoff and Moore's findings have not gone unchallenged. Sandra Jacobson (1979), for example, found that 6-14-week-olds could imitate tongue protrusions. They also "imitated" protrusions "modeled" by a moving ballpoint pen. Jacobson concluded that young infants are not capable of selective imitation. Instead, movement in a model's face "releases" movements in a baby's face. Other forms of movements (such as that by the pen) also release the baby's movements. Other researchers have made similar arguments (for example, McCall, Parke & Kavanaugh, 1977).

Louise Hayes and John Watson (1981) also disagreed with Meltzoff and Moore's conclusions. Hayes and Watson could not replicate the Meltzoff and Moore (1977) study. They found no evidence of imitation in 17-22-day-old infants. Although Meltzoff and Moore (1983a) have criticized Hayes and Watson's methodology, these findings remain a challenge to Meltzoff and Moore's model.

Even if Meltzoff and Moore are correct, we are left with many unanswered questions. Where does imitation go after the neonatal period? It certainly is not fully developed at birth (for example, Meltzoff & Moore, 1983a). In fact, the ability to imitate seems to decline in infants of about 2 months of age (Jacobson, 1979). One might suggest, therefore, that neonatal imitation is comparable to reflexive walking. In support of this agrument, Jacobson (1979) reported that exercise did help to maintain levels of imitative behavior. This seems comparable to the report by Zelazo, Zelazo, and Kolb (1972) that exercise helped to maintain neonatal walking (see Chapter 5).

How neonatal imitation, assuming it exists, is related to later imitative skills remains unclear. We can say a few things about later imitation, however. For one thing, some research indicates substantial improvement in imitative abilities. McCall, Parke, and Kavanaugh (1977), for example, found that 1-year-olds could not imitate single-element actions, such as sliding a block from one edge of a table to another, as reliably as could 18-month-olds. Two-year-olds were even better. The differences were even more dramatic when two-element actions, such as picking up a string to suspend a cup and then striking the cup, were modeled. These were virtually impossible for the 12- and 15-month-olds to imitate. Yet 2-year-olds could imitate them most of the time. Some of the research indicating progression in imitative abilities also supports Piaget's stages (for example, Uzgiris & Hunt, 1975). These findings support both the content and sequence of behaviors outlined by Piaget.

On the other hand, Piaget argued that deferred imitation was not possible until 18-24 months of age (see Table 7-1). Although some research (for example, McCall, Parke & Kavanaugh, 1977) supports this view, other research does not. Andrew Meltzoff (1985), for example, reported that 45% of the 14-month-olds he tested could imitate a novel behavior even after a 24-hour delay. How seriously Meltzoff's findings question Piaget's theory is unclear. After all, Piaget himself claimed that his age ranges were only approximate. It may be that Meltzoff's infants were simply reaching the final stage of imitation sooner than Piaget originally predicted. The real contribution of Meltzoff's study is to provide a simple, usable means of testing deferred imitation so that deferred imitation can be more thoroughly investigated.

So, by 2 years of age, children have become quite adept at imitation. Imitative skills are particularly useful in acquiring social behaviors. There are, of course, some individual differences in their use. For example, some children use imitation as a means of acquiring language much more frequently than do others (Nelson, 1981). Also, more socially oriented 2-year-olds seem more inclined to imitate (McCall, Parke & Kavanaugh, 1977).

One social behavior where imitation may be combined with conditioning to shape behavior is toilet training. Given the interest of this topic to parents, let's take a few moments to see how learning plays a role in toilet training.

Toilet Training

In my experience, toilet training is second only to crying as a topic of paramount interest to parents. I am constantly amazed at how early parents start asking about toilet training. It is not unusual for parents of 6-month-olds to ask when and how they should train their babies.

My experiences are not inconsistent with existing data. A number of studies have reported that a substantial number, often a majority, of mothers place their infants on the pot prior to 1 year of age (for example, Douglas & Blomfield, 1958; Sears, Maccoby & Levin, 1957). Of course, these studies are old and trends may have changed, but they nonetheless do underscore the interest of even young babies' parents in toilet training.

Most modern authors agree that toilet training should be delayed until the child is "ready" (see, for example, Shaffer, 1980). This may not be until a child is past 2 years of age. However, Nathan Azrin and Richard Foxx (1981), authors of a manual based on a learning theory technique, suggest most children are ready by 20 months of age. They suggest assessing readiness on the basis of bladder control, physical (motor) readiness, and language development. Once the child is ready, they suggest using imitation and conditioning techniques to train him rapidly.

In order to use Azrin and Foxx's method, the parents need to set aside an afternoon (or even a day) for intensive toilet training. During that time the training process should not be interrupted for errands, telephone calls, and the like. The child is given a great deal to drink during this time and is frequently reminded about the use of the toilet, for example, "Do you need to go potty?" Briefly summarized, the method begins with demonstrating toilet use with a doll that wets. The child is then encouraged to imitate the doll. He is also reminded that Daddy, Mommy, and other significant people (such as siblings and babysitters) use the toilet. If he does use the toilet, he receives a treat. He is also given enthusiastic approval by parents, siblings, friends, and others. This process is repeated continuously throughout the day. Thus, both imitation (of the doll and parents) and instrumental learning (rewarding successful toileting) are used in this method.

How well does this method work? Azrin and Foxx report excellent results. In a study of thirty-three children over 20 months of age, only two were not trained. In both cases the father was opposed to the training. The average time it took to train a child was less than four hours. (This is four hours of concentrated effort on toilet training.)

These results seem to give startling support to the method, but a few warnings are in order. First, many of the children in the study were older. The oldest ones were more than 4 years of age. A method that works with an older child—who clearly has the physical and cognitive maturity to accomplish the task—may be less

Both imitation and reinforcement play a role in successful
toilet training. Courtesy of Jacqueline Spencer.

effective with a younger child. This is underscored by Azrin and Foxx's finding that
the older children trained more quickly. In fairness, it should be emphasized that
these older children had been quite resistant to toilet training. So, this method
seems to work where others have failed.

How important is the imitation-conditioning component itself? The answer
to this is not clear, since Azrin and Foxx had no control group. However, other
researchers (for example, Brazelton, 1962) have reported that children frequently
can be trained in under a week without such intensive techniques as long as they are
ready to be trained.

What can we conclude about learning theory and toilet training? Well, the real
central component to toilet training seems to be physiological and cognitive readiness. Children cannot be trained effectively without this. Once ready, many
children will train with little or no parental effort. In fact, some will virtually train
themselves. Even in these cases, learning obviously plays a role. The children are
imitating parents, peers, siblings, and other role models. It is likely that at the very
least they will be praised (a form of positive reinforcement) for their efforts.

Some children, on the other hand, will be more difficult. They may express
no interest in using the toilet. They may even resist parental attempts to train them.
In such cases, a more intense, direct application of learning theory techniques (as
in Azrin and Foxx) may be helpful.

Habituation

The last form of infant learning to be considered is habituation. *Habituation*
is the tendency of a response to gradually diminish with repeated presentations of

the eliciting stimulus. So, the first time you ring a bell near the baby's head, he will "startle." With successive rings, however, the startle response becomes weaker and weaker. Eventually, the baby seems to be "ignoring" the bell.

Habituation can be considered a form of learning because it involves behavioral changes (which last for a measurable amount of time) in response to the environment (Lipsitt, 1982). However, it is quite different from the other forms of learning. Most notably, it does not involve either the formation or strengthening of associations as in conditioning and imitation (Lipsitt, 1982). So, "preparedness" of association does not apply to habituation as it does to classical conditioning (Olson & Sherman, 1983).

Although habituation seems a very simple process, it is a very important one. Habituation is often used as an indicator of central nervous system integrity (see Chapter 3). Children with Down's syndrome, for example, seem to show less habituation than do normal children (Barnet, Olrich & Shanks, 1974).

Of greater interest to us here is habituation's usefulness in assessing other behaviors. Habituation has been used to test perceptual development. Take, for example, studies of sound discrimination (for example, Eimas et al., 1971). An infant is trained to suck vigorously to a sound. With repeated presentations of the sound, the sucking diminishes; that is, it *habituates*. Then a new sound is presented. If the sucking increases, that is, if the baby *dishabituates*, it is assumed that the baby perceived the second sound as different from the first. Similar techniques have been used to assess visual memory (see, for example, Fagan, 1982).

Individual differences in habituation make the use of this habituation-dishabituation paradigm somewhat problematic (Olson & Sherman, 1983). Getting babies under 10 weeks of age to complete the entire cycle is often difficult (Lipsitt, 1982). For example, in one study (Friedman, 1972) only 32% of the babies tested showed the entire habituation-dishabituation pattern. Some of the failures seemed attributable to state changes (Olson & Sherman, 1983). This is important because individual differences in habituation-dishabituation are often interpreted as indicating individual differences in memory. Joseph Fagan (Fagan & Singer, 1983) has argued that such individual differences in memory may predict later intelligence. Olson and Sherman have suggested that such conclusions are premature.

With this warning in mind, let's now turn our attention to the question of memory development in infancy.

MEMORY

People often think that infants do not have good memory functioning. There seem to be two reasons for this. First, most adults cannot remember much from early childhood, much less infancy. Second, infants seem able to "forget" negative events more quickly than adults. For example, one minute a pair of 2-year-olds may be fighting over a toy. The next, they are the best of friends. They act as though the fight never occurred. Does this mean that infants have little or no memory?

No, it does not. We have already reviewed a substantial amount of evidence suggesting that young infants have functioning memories. Any recognition of voices, faces, visual patterns, and so on, implies memory is working (see Chapter 6). Infants' ability to learn, which we just examined, also requires memory functioning (Rovee-Collier & Fagan, 1981). We will not reexamine all these data here but instead provide a systematic summary of memory functioning.

Memory functioning falls into two broad types: recognition and recall. *Recognition* memory is simply the ability to differentiate between a familiar and an unfamiliar face, voice, event, and so on. The familiar stimulus is actually present during a recognition task. In *recall* tasks, on the other hand, few, if any, cues concerning the to-be-remembered stimulus are available. Instead, the memory has to be spontaneously reconstructed by the individual. This makes recall a more difficult task than recognition (for example, Olson & Sherman, 1983). Indeed, recall may require more complex cognitive skills such as symbolic functioning (for example, Kagan, 1979) (see Chapter 8). We would therefore expect that recognition precedes recall in development. This makes recognition memory a logical starting point for our discussion.

Recognition Memory

Two major approaches have been used to study infant recognition memory. The first focuses on recognition of visual stimuli such as faces and patterns. The methodology used in these studies is the same as that used in visual preference research (Fagan, 1982) (see Chapter 6). Thus, for example, a baby is exposed to an object or pattern—a *familiarization trial*. Later, that object is presented along with a new object—*retention trial*. If the baby stares at the new object, it is assumed that he recognized, and therefore remembered, the old object. This approach has a longer, richer history than the second one.

The second approach examines recognition of learned associations (for example, Sullivan, Rovee-Collier & Tynes, 1979). For example, the baby's foot may be tied to a mobile so that when she kicks, the mobile moves (a sight that is very interesting to a young baby). Later, she will be placed in the same situation. If she kicks immediately, it is assumed that she remembers that kicking causes the mobile to move.

Both approaches need to be considered here because the visual preference approach may be more influenced by perceptual than memory development (Rovee-Collier & Fagan, 1981). On the other hand, the debates about the existence of conditioning in young infants necessitate consideration of an alternative model.

The first question to address is, when does memory functioning begin?

Onset of Memory.   The presence of visual recognition memory has been demonstrated in newborns (Fagan, 1982). It is even apparent in premature infants (Werner & Siqueland, 1978). However, infants under 3-4 months of age can only distinguish familiar from unfamiliar patterns if gross differences between the stimuli are evident. The patterns have to differ on more than one dimension (such as size and number of pattern elements) for recognition to occur (Fagan, 1982). By 5 months of age, babies are able to make more subtle pattern distinctions (Fagan, 1982). This is probably due to improved perceptual functioning (Fagan, 1977a) (see Chapter 6). By 6 months of age, babies are able to recognize familiar stimuli even if they are presented in new positions (Fagan, 1982).

The learning approach to memory study has not yet been applied to newborns (Olson & Sherman, 1983). There is, however, evidence of retention across daily learning sessions in 1- and 2-month-olds (Weizmann, Cohen & Pratt, 1971).

Clearly, then, memory for a variety of objects and events begins functioning early in infancy. In fact, the skill is so well developed that the baby needs very little exposure to a stimulus in order to remember it. For example, two training sessions, with 9 minutes of reinforcement per session, are sufficient to establish an association in 3-month-olds that will be remembered for at least 8 days (Sullivan, Rovee-Collier & Tynes, 1979). More amazingly, 5-month-olds can remember a simple visual stimulus after seeing it for less than 5 seconds (Fagan, 1974; Rose, 1981).

How strong are these recognition skills? Are the learned associations and familiar visual patterns easily forgotten?

Forgetting. By 3 months of age, infants can remember learned associations between foot kicking and movement of a mobile for at least 8 days (Sullivan et al., 1979). Indeed, some 3-month-olds can remember the association for 2 weeks (Sullivan et al., 1979). Similarly, research with 5-month-olds has demonstrated that they retain visual patterns for at least 2 weeks (Fagan, 1982).

These studies were performed under optimal conditions for memory retention. Specifically, no factors within the situation itself interfered with memory functioning. No stimuli were presented between the familiarization training and the retention testing within the research setting. Of course, the baby may well have had new experiences outside the setting, but these would not be expected to interfere with memory as much as directly competing stimuli would.

An example might be helpful. Imagine you are learning material for a test. Imagine how easy it would be if you only had to learn one fact. Unfortunately, when you study for an examination you must retain many facts and theories. These compete for your memory space. One fact may well interfere with your memorizing another, so that one (or both) is forgotten.

How much interference can infant memory tolerate? The research suggests a substantial amount of interference can be ignored. Even at 3 months of age, babies are able to remember visual patterns when other patterns are presented between the familiarization and retention testing. The more similar these patterns are to the originals, the greater the interference (Fagan, 1977b). However, similarity alone does not always produce interference (for example, McCall, Kennedy & Dodds, 1977; Cohen, DeLoache & Pearl, 1977). It seems to depend on the type of stimulus and the testing method used in the research. In general, it seems that once an infant has learned to recognize a particular pattern, he does not forget it easily (Fagan, 1977b; Cohen, Deloache & Pearl, 1977).

The likelihood of remembering can be improved. The duration of memory in 3-month-olds can, for example, be increased from 8 days to 4 weeks by a short re-exposure to the reinforcer (for example, a moving mobile) used in training the infant (Rovee-Collier et al., 1980).

However, under some conditions infants are more likely to "forget." Specifically, short familiarization trials contribute to increased forgetting even when no interfering stimuli are present (Rose, 1981). This is true only when there is a delay between the familiarization and the retention testing (Rose, 1981). It also applies only to young infants. Nine-month-olds are much less affected by shorter familiarization times than are 6-month-olds (Rose, 1981). Keep in mind that these are very short familiarization sessions—5-20 seconds in the Rose study compared to 120 seconds in the Fagan (1977b) study.

Although infant recognition memory has been convincingly demonstrated, the processes that guide it remain poorly understood. Let's now examine several theories that attempt to explain recognition development.

Explanations of Recognition.   It appears that maturation plays a substantial role in recognition memory functioning, at least in visual recognition memory. Improvements in perceptual functioning (see Chapter 6), particularly in terms of discriminating among stimuli, are part of this. In addition, cerebral cortex matura-tion may play a role. Premature infants perform more poorly on visual recognition tasks than do full-term infants (Rose, 1980). However, preterms who received extra sensory stimulation during their hospital stay performed virtually the same as full-term infants. Such sensory stimulation is associated with an increased rate of cortical maturation. So, cortical maturation is at least implicated as a factor in visual recognition development (Rose, 1980).

Theoretical explanations of recognition memory functioning revolve around two popular models. First, Joseph Fagan (1977a) has presented a discrimination learning model. He suggested that the baby takes one "look" at the novel and familiar stimuli in the retention testing. Two processes occur during this look. First, the infant attends to a particular dimension. The baby then makes a fixating response to a cue. If the dimension the baby selects contains a cue that differen-tiates the familiar from the novel, then she will fixate on the novel stimulus (indicating recognition). The probability of attending to a dimension or fixating on a cue is influenced by both the saliency of the feature and by perceptual develop-ment (for example, the preference for contours over interiors in young babies).

Probabilities of focusing on certain dimensions and cues can be determined empirically. When these probabilities are established, the model does seem to predict visual recognition performance (Fagan, 1977a). Furthermore, the link between perceptual development and visual recognition performance helps to explain why developmental changes in memory functioning take place.

The second model is rooted in information processing theories of adult memory (Cohen & Gelber, 1975). This model suggests that there are several levels of memory processing and storage (see Table 7-2). Once the infant attends to and fixates on a stimulus, the memory process begins. The child, by repeatedly or con-

TABLE 7-2 Levels of Memory in Information-Processing Model

LEVEL	DESCRIPTION	DURATION	ROLE OF REHEARSAL
Sensory Registers	Briefly "registers" stimuli exactly as they are occurring.	Less than 2 seconds	None possible
Short-term Memory	Processing of stimuli begins, for example, new information may be related to existing concepts or it may be grouped into "chunks" for easier recall. Short-term storage.	Up to 30 seconds	Necessary if information is to be retained
Long-term Memory	Long-term storage.	Indefinite	Probably needed if information is to remain readily accessible

(Based on Craik, F., & Lockhart, R. (1972). Levels of processing: A framework for memory research. *Journal of Verbal Learning and Verbal Behavior, 11,* 671-84.)

tinuously looking at the object, builds a representation of the object. This representation is in a short-term memory store. In other words, it is held only in immediate memory and will not be available several hours later. In order to be useful in delayed-recognition tasks, this representation must be transferred to long-term memory. If the transfer is made, the child will be able to use the representation to recognize the object later on (by comparing the representation and the actual object) (Cohen & Gelber, 1975). These models propose that forgetting occurs when the representation "decays" so that the memory is "lost" to the child (Rovee-Collier & Fagan, 1981).

Carolyn Rovee-Collier and Joseph Fagan (1981) argued that the memory is never "lost." They suggested that, instead, the memory simply cannot be easily retrieved. The memory is in the system but is not readily available to the child. This argument is supported by *reactivation* studies (for example, Rovee-Collier et al., 1980). In these studies, the infant is reexposed to a portion of the learned association. For example, a 3-month-old acquires an association between foot kicking and mobile movement because her foot is connected by a ribbon to the mobile. Two weeks later, the baby will not remember this association, and she will not kick in the presence of the mobile (Sullivan, Rovee-Collier & Tynes, 1979). If, however, on the thirteenth day the baby is exposed to the mobile moving independently of her kicking, she will remember the association on the fourteenth day. Indeed, she will remember the association for several more days (Rovee-Collier et al., 1980). Notice that the reexposure to the moving mobile was not sufficient for the baby to "re-learn" the association. After all, her foot was not moving the mobile. Rather, exposure to the moving mobile reactivated the memory, thereby making it easier to retrieve when the baby was tested later (Rovee-Collier & Fagan, 1981).

This model, then, can explain how babies build up memories in their day-to-day lives. As long as the baby is occasionally reexposed to some portion of the original situation, her memory will remain accessible (Rovee-Collier & Fagan, 1981). When such exposure stops, we lose access to these early memories.

Rovee-Collier and Fagan (1981) argued that these findings clearly indicate that very young infants use mental representations to remember events. Other theorists (for example, Kagan, 1979; Piaget & Inhelder, 1973) disagreed. These young babies can remember the associations only when the retention testing situation is very similar to the acquisition context. Even the reactivation has to be similar to the acquisition context. Reactivation does not work if, for example, the baby is simply reexposed to the mobile when it is not moving (Rovee-Collier & Fagan, 1981). This reliance on context indicates a lack of representation as defined by Piaget (1962) (see Chapter 8). Within his definition, representation is evidenced only when the baby no longer needs extensive contextual cues to "remember" an event. His view, then, argues for a sharp distinction between recognition and recall memory.

Recall

In adults, recall memory is easy to assess. You can simply ask an adult to recite a recently learned list of words, or you can ask him to recount an experience or event. These adult measures rely heavily on verbal skills. Infants simply do not have comparable skills. As a consequence, infant recall memory ability must be inferred from other behaviors.

Symbolic Functioning. One behavior which allows us to infer recall memory functioning is deferred imitation, discussed earlier in this chapter (Olson & Sherman, 1983). Recall that in deferred imitation, the baby spontaneously reproduces a behavior that she observed some time before. Cues are not necessary, though they may be present. Piaget (1962) argued that deferred imitation requires the ability to use mental symbols. Therefore, this behavior is not possible, according to Piaget, until infants are 18-24 months of age (see also McCall, Parke & Kavanaugh, 1977).

It can be argued that any behavior requiring use of symbols involves memory (Olson & Sherman, 1983). (See Chapter 8 for a description of these behaviors.) So, for example, pretending in play implies that the child remembers the event he is reproducing in his play. Searching for a hidden object suggests that the baby has some memory of the object itself.

The ability to search for hidden objects first appears, in an immature form, toward the end of the first year of life (Kagan, 1979). Other indicators at this point demonstrate that recall memory is functioning. For example, attachment and its related behaviors (for example, separation distress) first appear. This has led Jerome Kagan (1979) to suggest that a major shift in memory functioning occurs at the end of the first year. This view has been supported by research reporting dramatic improvements in delayed recognition in infants around 9 months of age (Rose, 1981).

Relying on these behaviors to mark the onset of recall memory imposes a serious problem. All these behaviors involve other skills (for example, motor development). Thus, recall memory may become available considerably earlier than these behaviors appear. This problem is much less severe in the second approach—cued recall.

Cued Recall. The premise of this method is relatively simple. The baby learns a task that has two clearly separate components. The two components may be separated by time or space (Brody, 1981). In order to respond to the second component, the baby must recall the first one. In Leslie Brody's (1981) study, for example, infants were rewarded for touching a picture of a face that had been illuminated 250 milliseconds (9 second earlier.)

This research also indicates dramatic improvement in, and perhaps onset of, recall memory toward the end of the first year (Brody, 1981). Eight-month-olds could choose the correct face if the delay between illumination and response was only 250 milliseconds (one quarter of a second), but they could not hold the illuminated face in memory long enough to respond correctly if the delay was 3-9 seconds. One-year-olds could tolerate the longer delays, with 16-month-olds performing even better (Brody, 1981).

Brody (1981) used an information-processing approach to explain her data. She suggested that the 8-month-olds could not transfer information from their sensory registers to short-term storage (see Table 7-2). Once the sensory "image" was lost, the "memory" was gone. The older infants, however, were able to make the transfer and hold the information in short-term memory. She suggested that this improvement might be due to neurological maturation.

Thus, the assumption that recognition memory predates recall memory appears justified. Although this sequence is probably universal, some individual differences in memory development exist. These individual differences are of special interest because they appear to have applied value.

Memory and Intelligence

Infants do show individual differences in memory. For example, although most 3-month-olds do not recognize a learned association after 2 weeks, a few do (Sullivan, Rovee-Collier & Tynes, 1979). Infants also display individual differences in visual recognition memory. Joseph Fagan has suggested that these individual differences may be related to intelligence (Fagan, 1982; Fagan & Singer, 1983).

Research with Down's syndrome babies and premature babies has indicated that these infants show deficits in visual recognition memory (for example, Caron & Caron, 1981; Cohen, 1981; Miranda & Fantz, 1974; Rose, 1980). Other groups of at-risk infants (for example, infants born to diabetic mothers) also show memory deficits (Fagan & Singer, 1983). Furthermore, babies of "average" intelligence mothers are less adept at memory tasks than those born to "high intelligence" mothers (Fantz & Nevis, 1967). Thus, visual recognition memory tests may be useful in differentiating among infants who are ultimately expected to show varying levels of intelligence.

These results are intriguing, particularly since current tests of infant intelligence do not adequately predict later intellectual functioning (see Chapter 8). They are only suggestive, of course. After all, they do not demonstrate that infants with poor visual recognition memory actually will show intellectual deficits later in life.

However, research provides some evidence linking early recognition memory performance to later IQ (for example, Fagan, 1981; Fagan & McGrath, 1981; Lewis & Brooks-Gunn, 1981). In fact, relationships between visual memory assessed in individuals at 4-7 months of age and IQ performance as late as 7 years of age have been reported (Fagan & McGrath, 1981). Meaningful relationships have been found for infants of both genders, different races, and different socioeconomic classes (Fagan & Singer, 1983). Moreover, visual performance at 7 months was a stronger predictor of 3-year-olds' IQ than was race, parental education, or maternal vocabulary (Fagan, 1981).

None of these studies can be viewed as absolutely conclusive. The number of infants tested is small by test validation standards. Yet this research does suggest an exciting path for future research. If visual recognition does indeed prove to be related to later intelligence, we would finally have a reliable means of indentifying infants at risk for poor intellectual development. Right now, no such measure is available (see Chapters 3 and 8).

SUMMARY

Once again, we have seen that infants have capabilities that exceed most people's expectations. Even young babies are capable of learning. This in and of itself suggests that they have functioning memory systems.

The precise nature of infant learning remains the subject of some debate. Some theorists suggest that the infant can indeed form new associations. Others argue that the infant can only integrate new stimuli into his existing cognitive structures. Although the theories predict different mechanisms (and, perhaps, levels) of learning, they all agree that young infants are acquiring new information.

Similarly, the precise mechanisms involved in infant memory are poorly understood. One current debate concerns the role of representational thought in early memory. This issue is clearly related to debates concerning infant cognitive development. It is considered in more detail in the next chapter.

8

Cognitive Development

Americans seem to have developed almost an obsession with what babies know. We are even more concerned with how much they *can* know. This is obvious even in the popular press. The largest-selling issue of *Time* magazine in 1983 carried a cover story entitled "What do babies know? When do they know it?" The August, 1984, issue of *Glamour* magazine carried an article titled "Can you make your baby a genius? Should you try?" (Span, 1984).

This issue of knowing is the core of cognitive development theory and research. *Cognition* is a broad term. It includes all behavioral realms related to knowing including perception, memory, and thought. The focus of this chapter is thought (see Chapters 6 and 7 for discussions of the other issues). Let's begin with a description of Piaget's theory of cognitive development.

PIAGET'S THEORY

No theorist has had a greater impact on American developmental psychology in the past 20 years than Jean Piaget. We have already seen his theory used to explain perceptual, learning, and memory development. His theory also appears in discussions of social and language development. Some of these explanations are extrapolations from Piaget's work, but many reflect the breadth and diversity of Piaget's own writings. There is no way to cover all aspects of his theory. What follows is a selective discussion of those portions of his theory most relevant to the development of thought during infancy.

Basic Concepts

Piaget (for example, 1952, 1954) has outlined specific accomplishments that occur during infancy. Before we can understand these stages, we need to examine the basic principles of Piaget's theory. This discussion will also help us understand why Piaget has had such an impact on American psychology.

Constructivism and Interactionism.   Piaget was a constructivist. He did not believe that thought patterns are inborn. Nor did he believe they are "given" to the child by the environment. Rather, the child actively constructs her thought. She builds her understanding of the world, including herself. This is evident in at least two ways. First, the child actively builds her understanding of specific aspects of the world. This is exemplified in our earlier discussion of object perception (see Chapter 6).

A second indicator of construction is found in the cognitive structures that Piaget believed underlie thought. These structures are a framework for thought, for they contain general information about how to approach, analyze, and solve problems. These structures change dramatically during development. The most major changes are used to differentiate the four broad stages of development: sensorimotor, preoperations, concrete operations, and formal operations. These are summarized in Table 8-1, though we will be examining only sensorimotor development in this chapter.

TABLE 8-1   Piaget's Stages of Cognitive Development

STAGE	DESCRIPTION
Sensorimotor *(0-2 years)*	Child moves from reflex-dominated behavior to a "practical" intelligence based on her own actions with objects, people, and so on.
Preoperations *(2-7 years)*	Child can now use mental symbols, but the symbols are "static" and "inflexible." The child defines concepts in "black and white" terms. Ability to take other people's perspective is limited but improving.
Concrete Operations *(7-12 years)*	Thought is now flexible. Child is able to use "reversibility" (for example, she knows that addition can be reversed through subtraction). Is still tied to perceptible reality.
Formal Operations *(12 + years)*	The logic that appeared in the previous stage is now extended to the abstract realm. The child is no longer tied to reality. He can now form a variety of hypotheses about a situation and devise ways to test them. Becomes aware of the *possible*, not just the real.

(Information from Ginsburg & Opper, 1979.)

Piaget (for example, Piaget & Inhelder, 1969) claimed that at each stage the child builds the new structures. Actually, he argued that the structures are "reconstructed." This means that thought does not just get "better" from stage to stage. It actually becomes "different." Each successive stage leads to a greater balance, or *equilibrium*, between the child and her environment. She encounters fewer and fewer problems that she cannot appropriately analyze with her cognitive structures. Again, these shifts are exemplified in Table 8-1. This restructuring is not limited to between-stage shifts. It also occurs within stages. Nowhere is this more evident than during the sensorimotor stage.

Where does the child get the information to perform these constructions? Piaget did not believe thought is either innate or learned. Rather, he was an interactionist (see Chapter 1). He believed that both the environment and biology contribute to cognitive development.

Specifically, Piaget (for example, Piaget & Inhelder, 1969) outlined three "sources" of cognitive development: maturation, environment (including social interaction), and objects. Maturation of the nervous system and sensory organs provides the child with new opportunities for exploring the environment. For an example of this, recall the discussion on the improvement in visual acuity during infancy and how this affects exploration. The environment provides information. Mothers may, for example, point to objects while naming them, and they may thereby facilitate the child's connection of a specific object with a name (for example, Murphy, 1978). Such information is actively interpreted within the child's existing structures. Active exploration of objects, such as sucking them and grasping them, provides the "raw" material for concepts. Again, the child's structures influence the construction of a concept of objects. But the relationships among the environment, objects, and the child's structures are reciprocal. Hence, the structures that are guiding the interpretation of the environment and objects are also being altered by them.

No one of these three sources can, in and of itself, account for cognitive development. They interact to produce development. The environment and biology both play crucial roles. The child, of course, is the agent of the development. She is actively using and integrating the opportunities and information from all three sources as she adapts to the environment.

Adaptation.   Adaptation helps us to understand the purpose of cognitive development. In fact, for Piaget (for example, 1952), adaptation and intelligence are virtually synonymous. Understanding the world and being able to cope with new situations increases the likelihood of survival. In this sense, Piaget uses adaptation in the same way that many other theorists (for example, Bowlby and Gibson) do.

Piaget provided a specific description of how adaptation works. Adaptation, according to Piaget (for example, 1970), consists of two processes: assimilation and accommodation. *Assimilation* involves altering the environment to fit existing structures. So, a baby may suck on a pencil rather than write with it. Sucking is an existing structure to which the pencil is being adapted. *Accommodation* involves altering structures to fit the environment. So, the mouth has to be held in a slightly different shape to suck a pencil than to suck a bottle. In any situation, some elements of both assimilation and accommodation are present.

Summary. Piaget provided a picture of children as active beings who gradually construct an understanding of the world. Universals in cognitive development (for example, the stages) can be explained by the maturational constraints on the child's development. The necessity of adaptation also contributes to the universals. However, such biological factors are not the sole determinants of cognitive development. Rather, cognitive development is based on the child's active interaction with the world. The information obtained from the environment is just as important as the biological component.

Having introduced these fundamental concepts, let's now examine the stages of sensorimotor development.

Stages of Sensorimotor Development

Piaget's belief that the underlying structures of thought change with development is clearly exemplified in the six substages of sensorimotor development. He presented descriptions of both the general form of thought (for example, Piaget, 1952) and specific content areas such as imitation, play, spatial relations, and object permanence (for example, Piaget, 1954, 1962).

The changes in thought during the sensorimotor period are dramatic. At the beginning of sensorimotor development, the infant is basically a reflexive being. Her activity is poorly differentiated. She does not know the difference between a goal and the behavior that achieves that goal. Thus, for example, the baby does not "plan" to suck to get food. Sucking and getting milk are indistinguishable from the baby's perspective: They are one and the same thing. Since the behavior cannot be "planned," the baby cannot really generate her own behavior. Instead, behavior is triggered by environmental events or stimuli (such as the presence of the nipple) (Piaget, 1952).

By 2 years of age, when the sensorimotor period ends, the child has developed a "practical intelligence." She can differentiate a goal from the behavior to obtain that goal. She can coordinate behaviors to use in obtaining a goal. She can even "plan" a course of action mentally. Of course, her ability to plan is quite limited (see Table 8-1 for some later developments). Most notably, her behavior is tied to the immediate here-and-now. It is rooted in active manipulation of objects rather than in conceptual thought. Yet she is, in Piaget's view, capable of intelligent activity. This means that she can adapt to new circumstances by devising more or less appropriate actions to solve a problem.

Sensorimotor Substages. More specifically, the child's behavior is dominated by reflexes during substage I. This period covers approximately the first month of life (note that the ages are approximations). Some of the reflexes, such as sucking and grasping, will be "exercised." In other words, the infant will suck just to suck, that is, with no "goal." Breast-fed babies, for example, often will nurse at each breast for 20-30 minutes; yet they get virtually all the available milk in the breast during the first 7 minutes or so. They just seem to enjoy sucking. Piaget (1952) called this kind of behavior "functional assimilation." This functional assimilation strengthens the behavior involved in the reflex. Eventually, the behavior is extended to new objects (such as sucking the hand or the corner of the blanket). Piaget called this "generalized assimilation." Also, the behavior will begin to "anticipate" the stimuli. The baby will, for instance, start to suck as soon as he is placed in the position for breast-feeding, before the nipple is actually presented. Piaget (1952) calls this "recognitory assimilation." Thus, the reflex extends beyond the level of unconditioned stimulus-unconditioned response. The behavior itself remains basically unchanged, however. It is simply repeated over and over again in its original form.

In substage II (1-4 months of age), considerable repetition of behaviors still occurs, but now the behaviors are not limited to reflexes. These repetitions are *primary circular reactions.* In primary circular reactions, the infant repeats an interesting behavior that involves his own body. The baby might, for example, repeatedly try to get his hand into his mouth (Piaget, 1952). He discovers such behaviors by chance. But then through the processes of assimilation and accommodation, he practices them until they become habits. The assimilation is evident because the baby moves his head to search for his hand much as he has been doing to search for the nipple during feeding. Accommodation is evidenced by changes in his arm movements to get his hand closer to his mouth (Ginsburg & Opper, 1979). In this manner the baby is "learning" a behavior, but the learning occurs through adaptation rather than through classical or instrumental conditioning.

Primary circular reactions are limited to the child's own body because he cannot separate the means from the goal. The motions themselves and the final outcome (for example, his hand in his mouth) are synonymous. During substage III (4.5-8 months of age), goal and means begin to be differentiated. The child is able to begin to use previously developed behavior patterns to obtain external objects or interesting events. So, the baby may kick at bells strung across her crib in order to hear them ring. Such behaviors are *secondary circular reactions.* Secondary circular reactions differ from primary circular reactions in that the repetitive behavior patterns are no longer limited to the child's body. According to Piaget (1952), these indicate that the baby's behavior is becoming intentional. Although intention is not fully developed at this stage, the behavior is almost intentional because it involves searching for the appropriate behavior to get the desired effect. On the other hand, this searching is simply rediscovering a behavior pattern. It does not involve inventing new behaviors or applying known behaviors to new circumstances. As such, it is not truly intentional (Piaget, 1952) because the baby only distinguishes the cause (kicking) from the effect (bells ringing) *after* completing his "searching."

This after-the-fact distinction eventually leads to the development of intention. The infant becomes able to apply old behavior patterns to new situations.

This occurs during substage IV (8-12 months of age). If you put your hand in front of an object that a substage III baby wants, for example, she makes no organized attempt to move your hand; but at substage IV she might slap at your hand until she moves it (Piaget, 1952). Thus, the child for the first time is actually adapting to a new situation. This, according to Piaget (1952), marks the beginning of true intelligence. The child is also better able to see relations between things (for example, that an *object* is behind a *screen*). So, the child's behavior is no longer restricted to reproducing interesting events. Now he can combine behaviors such as slapping your hand and then reaching for the desired object in order to initiate interesting results such as getting the object.

However, the substage IV child cannot devise new behaviors to achieve a goal. This ability first appears during substage V (12-18 months of age) in the form of *tertiary circular reactions*. Tertiary circular reactions represent "the first real experimentations" (Piaget, 1952, p. 151). In these experimentations, the child is searching for novelty by introducing variations in familiar events. You can see this if you give a baby a rattle. He might start by shaking it with one hand as he always has. Then he might try shaking it harder. Then he might shake it hard enough to hit it on the table. Then he might drop it. All these variations are instituted intentionally by the child. This does not mean that the variations are preplanned. Even at this point the behaviors are basically trial-and-error, but they clearly are not simply repetitive. The baby is "experimenting," trying to find *new* means to produce interesting events, including solving problems.

Although the substage V infant can discover new "means" through experimentation, he cannot "plan" this experimentation in advance. The substage VI (18-24 months of age) baby can. She can make her new combinations of behaviors and objects or situations on a mental level. This is made possible by the development of representational skills. The baby can now use some kind of symbol to stand in for the actual activity. Piaget (1952, pp. 333-338) provided the classic example, which is summarized here.

Piaget presented his daughter Lucienne with a problem. He placed a gold chain in a matchbox. She had seen this problem before. She had developed two behaviors to solve it. She either dumped the chain out of the box or placed her finger in the opening of the matchbox to get the chain. She did not know how to "open" the box. This time Piaget made the matchbox opening too small to use either of the established behaviors. Lucienne's subsequent behavior demonstrated the use of representation to plan a behavioral solution to the problem.

Lucienne paused and stared at the opening in the box. Then she began to open her mouth. She gradually opened her mouth wider and wider. She was imitating the slit in the box! Such imitation is a form of representation because a simple motor act, such as opening the mouth, is used to substitute for a more complex action. This was, according to Piaget, Lucienne's way of thinking about a solution before trying it out. Shortly after her "imitation," she put her finger in the matchbox opening, pulled open the slit wider, and got the chain out. Remember, she had never opened the box before. In fact, she didn't even "know" the box could be

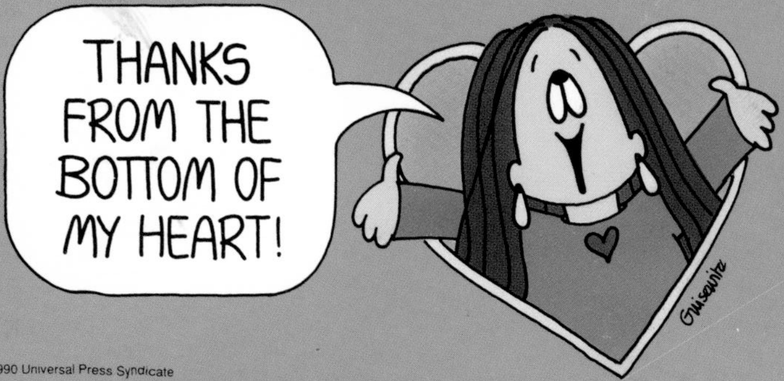

© 1990 Universal Press Syndicate

Gord memo, Kid

Thanks for being
here!

Joey

opened. She had, then, invented a new means to solve a problem by first thinking about it.

Summary. This outline provides a general impression of the dramatic changes Piaget believed occurred during infancy. Two more points need to be made. First, each substage is a relatively discrete entity. All the child's specific behaviors will be at the same level. You would not, for example, find only primary circular reactions involving reaching when grasping had already been integrated into secondary circular reactions. This does not mean there can be absolutely no differences in the rate of development of individual behaviors. One may lag slightly behind another—Piaget called this lag "horizontal decalage"—but the lag is not so great as to endanger the integrity of the stage. Also, such lags are the exception rather than the rule.

Second, the stages are linked by more than the fact that one builds upon the other. In each stage, behavior is always marked by organization and adaptation. The child is always seeking a better equilibrium between his cognitive structures and the problems he encounters in the environment. Clearly, the substage VI baby is better equipped than a younger infant to deal with new problems.

Although Piaget's theory has dominated the field of infant cognitive development, it is not without its critics. Let's now turn to some of the criticisms of Piaget's theory, as well as to some of the alternative models such criticisms have fostered.

CRITIQUE OF PIAGET'S THEORY

Two of the most fundamental aspects of Piaget's theory are the stages and constructivism. Both have been challenged by other researchers and theorists.

Stages

Piaget's argument that each substage represents a unique entity has become the focus of considerable controversy. Ina Uzgiris and J. McVicker Hunt (1975), for example, tried to replicate Piaget's sequence of sensorimotor development. They did replicate the sequence, but they did not find that all behaviors were at the same level. In other words, Piaget seemed to be correct in the sequence of development of specific behavior patterns, such as imitation or object permanence, but not in his assumption that these sequences formed unified stages. Other researchers have reported similar findings, particularly in the area of symbol development (for example, Bates et al., 1979; Chapman, 1981; Fischer & Corrigan, 1981). These results have led several theorists, including Kurt Fischer (1980), to argue that decalage is the rule, not the exception.

Fischer (1980) conceptualized development as proceeding through ten levels which fit into three tiers (sensorimotor, representational, and abstract). In some ways, this sounds similar to Piaget's view, only with different numbers and titles Fischer argued that his levels are not comparable to Piaget's stages because the levels are not unitary entities. Instead, Fischer uses them to describe the level of a particular skill. A child may be at different levels for different skills. Which skill is most advanced will depend upon which one the child has had the greatest opportunity to practice. So, a child whose hands have been covered with mittens to stop him from scratching himself might be more advanced at reaching than at grasping objects. Such unevenness in development is to be expected. Therefore, one could not characterize a child as being at a particular level (as Piaget did with his stages). Instead, the assessment of the child's functioning must involve rating the various levels of many skills. This is quite different from Piaget's conceptualization of stages. Within Piaget's stages, one could, supposedly, assess one skill (such as object permanence) and then assume that the baby would function at a similar level on other skills (such as imitation or means-ends).

Constructivism

Piaget's claim that the child constructs his intellectual structures has also been challenged. Several theorists have suggested that infants do not start with simple behaviors and integrate them into wholes. Rather, they argue that infants begin with global behaviors and gradually differentiate them into mature behaviors. These models are usually offshoots of the Gibsons' theory of perceptual functioning and development (for example, E. Gibson, 1982; J. J. Gibson, 1979).

T.G.R. Bower's theory exemplifies this perspective (Bower & Wishart, 1979). Bower believed that the child begins her exploration of the world in an undifferentiated state (see Chapter 6). She does not distinguish the sound of an object from the appearance of an object. This is different from saying that the infant integrates information from various senses. Integration implies that the two can be, and at some point have been, separated. Bower argued that the infant cannot do that. So, perception is not intermodal; it is supramodal (Bower, 1982). Everything starts out unified and poorly differentiated. The child's understanding of events becomes more specific as development proceeds. Each individual skill is then practiced and eventually integrated into complex wholes. This process makes it look as if skills are reacquired. It is also means that practice may increase a skill.

An example, taken from Bower and Wishart (1979), might be helpful. Babies were shown an object moving through a tunnel. The babies had to figure out that it was the same object at the beginning of the tunnel as at the end of the tunnel. They also had to develop some idea about where the object was while it was in the tunnel. If babies have limited experience with this situation, they seem able to transfer their knowledge to new situations. So, they will look in a cup for a cube that is placed in it. This, according to Bower and Wishart, indicates that they understand that even an out-of-sight object still exists. With more practice with the tunnel, the babies are less able to transfer the information about continued existence. Instead, they seem to learn to track an object so well in the tunnel situation that they can no longer transfer the information. In other words, with practice, the originally global information becomes highly specific. In fact, the information is now too specific to transfer. When given the cube-in-the-cup situation, it seems as if the babies have to re-learn that the cube still exists within that specific situation. Eventually, such specific information will be reintegrated into concepts.

George Butterworth (1983) has also questioned Piaget's view of constructivism, albeit in a different behavioral realm. Piaget (1952) suggested that infants and young children are fundamentally egocentric. They are unable to adopt the visual, emotional, or attitudinal perspectives of other people. Infants are still in the process of constructing their own view of the world. They haven't had the time or experience to construct alternative perspectives. Experience, in the form of acting upon a variety of situations from diverse perspectives, is particularly crucial. Piaget (for example, Piaget, 1926) believed that such egocentrism declined very slowly.

Buterworth (1983) diagreed. He presented data suggesting that 6-month-olds will follow their mothers' line of vision. In other words, they look where their mothers look. This is true even if there is nothing to look at. It is as if the child thinks the mother must be looking at something. This suggests that the baby is aware of the mother as a separate individual with her own perspective. These and other findings led Butterworth to conclude that infants are not remarkably egocentric. They also do not need particular experience to construct other people's spatial perspectives. Rather, such information is built into the objects and spaces they encounter (as per E. Gibson's view discussed in Chapter 6). Infants simply discover these regularities. They do not construct them.

This does not mean that Butterworth (or Bower) has "disproven" Piaget's theory. Many unanswered questions remain. In the Butterworth (1983) study, for example, infants followed their mothers' gaze only when the mothers looked in a direction in front of the infant. Babies would not follow a gaze directed behind them or to their side. Thus, infants do not follow a gaze so well that we could argue that they completely adopt their mothers' perspectives. In fact, one could argue, in line with Piaget, that the infant is simply following the mother's head in order to maintain an interesting sight (her face) (Butterworth, 1983).

What can we conclude? First, Piaget's theory has been, and continues to be, a major force in understanding infant cognition. The theory has been challenged, however. Challenges concerning the unitary nature of the stages seem particularly well founded. It is unusual to find a research paper nowadays that discusses the "sensorimotor" child. Instead, a specific skill is investigated, often in relationship to another specific skill (for example, Gopnik, 1984; Smolak & Levine, 1984). We will see this exemplified when we talk about representation later in this chapter. What is interesting, though, is that it is still Piaget's outline of the development of each skill that dominates the literature. Although researchers are no longer convinced that the stages are unitary, they still see Piaget's model of development of the individual behaviors (imitation, object permanence, and so forth) as quite viable.

The question of whether development moves from the specific to the abstract (Piaget) or the abstract to the specific (for example, Bower) is more difficult to answer. In support of Bower, Butterworth, and others working from the Gibsons' theories, the young infant's perceptual world does seem to be much better organized than Piaget suggested. The evidence suggests that infants do not have to construct size constancy, shape constancy, and the like gradually. On the other hand, we are lacking certain crucial information about how the very young infant interprets the world. For example, Bower, Butterworth, and Fischer (but not Piaget) predict that babies can use information from two or more senses simultaneously to interpret an object or event. This ability indicates a global understanding of objects by young infants. Yet the research that most clearly addresses this question (such as Spelke's work; see Chapter 6) is with children who are old enough, by Piaget's standards, to have made the intermodal integrations. This issue obviously requires further research.

Bower's reports of behaviors that seem to appear, disappear, and then re-appear do seem to pose a challenge to the constructivist view. However, keep in mind that in Piaget's view, the structures underlying thought are constantly being changed and reorganized. Thus, a child may appear to give a correct response at one age, an incorrect one at another, and a correct one later on. Piaget's explanation for this phenomenon would be that the "rationale" for the child's answer changed as the child's understanding of the problem changed. He never argued that development was simply a building-up process. Instead, shifts in the nature of thought might explain such shifts in behavior. In fact, there is some research supporting the existence of shifts that seem fairly consistent with Piaget's model (McCall, Eichorn & Hogarty, 1977).

We have seen considerable debate about Piaget's broad model of development. Let's now look at how some of these issues are exemplified in specific areas of cognitive development.

OBJECT PERMANENCE

Probably no other area of Piaget's theory of infant development has attracted as much attention as object permanence. This may be because, of the behaviors he outlined, object permanence best lent itself to assessment (Brainerd, 1978). Scales of object permanence are more easily developed than scales of, say, primary circular reactions.

No doubt object permanence attracted attention because Piaget's (1954) presentation of it was fascinating. Basically, Piaget suggested that the infant had to construct a concept of objects. Neonates, he argued, know nothing about objects. They do not know that objects retain a particular size or shape. They do not know that objects always exist. For the infant, objects exist only when he is using them. In other words, objects are defined only in relation to the baby's own activity (indicating the infant's egocentrism). Gradually, the infant constructs a concept of objects that does include immutability (of shape, size, and so on) and permanence.

Piaget (1954) based this model on his observations of infants' search behavior. He would hide an object and see what the infant did. Young infants would not search even if the object was still partially visible. Older infants only searched when they had seen where the object had been hidden. Toddlers searched successfully even when part of the hiding process was out of their view. Piaget identified six stages (the sensorimotor substages) in search development. These stages of object permanence development, which take about 2 years to complete, are summarized in Table 8-2.

TABLE 8-2 **Piaget's Stages of Object Permanence**

STAGE	AGE	DESCRIPTION*
I	Birth- 1 month	No reaction to the loss of an object. Does not search.
II	1-4 months	Does not search for objects that "disappear." But, will continue activity that was in progress at the time of disappearance.
III	4-9 months	May react to object disappearance by crying. Can anticipate future position of object. Can find partially hidden object. Does not search successfully for completely hidden object.
IV	9-12 months	Can successfully search for hidden objects in relatively simple situations (for example, only one probable hiding place). This indicates that child believes that objects have a permanent existence and certain immutable characteristics.
V	12-18 months	Can follow successive hidings of an object as long as the object remains visible between hidings. No longer defines object primarily in terms of her own actions with it.
VI	18-24 months	Can follow hidings even when object is not visible between hidings. This requires the presence of representational thought.

(Information from Ginsburg & Opper, 1979. All ages are approximate.)

Piaget was making a shocking suggestion (Schuberth, 1983). Imagine what the world would be like if you didn't know objects were immutable and permanent. What would your social relationships be like? Could you form categories and concepts? What would your language be like? Would you even have language? What would guide your behavior from situation to situation? It is not surprising, then, that Piaget's position has been questioned.

While Piaget's work has been attacked on many levels, two issues seem particularly crucial. First, several authors, most notably T.G.R. Bower (for example, 1974, 1982), have argued that even very young infants do understand that objects exist all of the time. Second, it appears that factors other than the child's understanding of objects heavily influence search behavior (for example, Butterworth, 1983). Let's look at each of these issues.

Onset of Object Permanence

As you may recall from Chapter 6, T.G.R. Bower demonstrated that very young infants understood a good deal about objects. His work suggested, for example, that infants understood both size and shape constancy. He argued, contrary to Piaget, that information about the structure (and function) of objects was inherent in the objects themselves. Infants used supramodal perceptual functioning to discern such information (Bower & Wishart, 1979).

Bower extended these ideas to include permanence. If an object maintained its shape, size, and so forth, why wouldn't it also maintain its existence? Bower demonstrated that young infants follow objects well even when the object "disappears" temporarily behind a screen. The infants "anticipate" the object's "future" position (that is, where it will emerge from behind the screen) (for example, Bower & Paterson, 1973). He also found that 5-week-olds could recognize an object after seeing only part of it (Bower, 1967). Other studies indicated that infants would search successfully if the object was hidden in certain ways (for example, behind a screen rather than under a cover, by turning out the lights rather than under a cover) (for example, Bower & Wishart, 1972). Finally, studies indicated that infants made the same errors retrieving visible objects (hidden under a transparent cover, for example) as retrieving hidden objects (for example, Bower & Paterson, 1973).

According to Bower, all these behaviors indicate that infants understand object permanence by 2 or 3 months of age. Their problems in searching come from not understanding that two objects such as a screen and the hidden object can be in the same place. Very young infants do not always understand that objects are not changed by their relationship to other objects. In other words, they know an object is permanent as long as that object does not come into direct contact with another object. If it does, the original object loses its identity for the baby. So, an infant will have a difficult time reaching for a matchbook placed on top of a book because the matchbox and book become a new, single object for the infant (see Chapter 6). Similarly, when an object is covered during a hiding task, the cover and object are no longer well differentiated. That is why a baby is no more successful searching under a transparent than under an opaque cover. Gradually, infants come to understand the relationship between screen and hidden object and can search.

Thus, Bower and Piaget reached radically different conclusions concerning object permanence. Neither one appears to be completely right. It is clear that Piaget underestimated the young infant's knowledge of objects. He also underestimated their ability to use intermodal perceptual information. (See Chapter 6.) On the other hand, Bower may have overestimated the young infant's understanding of object permanence. Virtually every one of his studies has been attacked on methodological grounds ranging from a failure to employ appropriate control groups to not monitoring visual following properly (see, for example, Gratch, 1977; Harris, 1983; Schuberth, 1983). Several attempts to replicate his findings have failed (for example, Muller & Aslin, 1978, failed to replicate Bower's findings concerning visual following). Overall, reviewers seem to agree with Richard Schuberth's conclusion that "the evidence that Bower marshals in support of the claim that the young infant is aware of object permanence is equivocal" (1983, p. 155).

In addition, Bower's theory cannot explain a form of search failure known as the AB error (Gratch, 1977; Schuberth, 1983). In this error, the substage IV (see Table 8-2) infant searches successfully when an object is hidden under the first of two screens (A). When the object is removed from under the first screen and placed under a second screen (B), the infant often continues to search under the first one. Piaget (1954) explained this perseverance in searching at A as indicating that the infant defined the object in terms of his own actions. He had found the object at A so it must still be there. This also indicates her egocentrism. Bower's theory cannot explain it. However, other researchers, most notably George Butterworth, have built upon Bower's theory to try to explain the AB error. Butterworth's explanation focuses on the issue of whether search failure in older infants is due to conceptual or perceptual difficulties.

The AB Error

If Piaget was right, stage IV infants should make the AB error quite consistently. Babies should also make the error the first time the object is hidden at B. Characteristics of the screen or background upon which the objects and screens are placed should not affect performance.

Infants do seem to make more errors when an object is hidden under the second screen than when it is hidden under the first. Gerald Gratch and William Landers (1971) reported, for example, that ten of thirteen babies who had passed the A hiding trial continued to search at A when the object was first hidden at B. Similarly, in a cross-sectional study, George Butterworth (1977) found that 56 of 144 infants failed the first B trial, and only one of these infants failed the first A trial. This may seem to support Piaget, but take a closer look. Most of the infants in the Butterworth study did not persevere in searching at A. Similar findings were reported in a later study (Butterworth, Jarrett & Hicks, 1982).

Even more damaging to Piaget's model are findings suggesting that the likelihood of the AB error is heavily influenced by the context of the task. Infants are least likely to commit the error if two different-colored covers are used and the background behind the two covers is identical (Butterworth, Jarrett & Hicks, 1982). In other words, cues about location (as opposed to the object per se) seem to help in the solution of the AB task.

Such findings have led Butterworth (1983; Butterworth, Jarrett & Hicks, 1982) to conclude that perceptual rather than conceptual issues determine the AB error. Contrary to Piaget's model, Butterworth suggested that infants can follow the movement of an object from one screen to the other. But, the baby needs certain perceptual information to do this. Babies will use the information provided by the context if it is sufficiently clear, as when the location is marked by color or pattern. The baby will rely on such information. This reflects the Gibsonian view that information (affordances) inherent in an object or situation can be perceived and used by the baby. Without such information, the baby will rely on her own position in relation to the object as her major clue. According to Butterworth, this creates a conflict. The situation looks the same from where the baby is seated. She cannot use color or pattern, for instance, to distinguish one situation from the other. Yet the object has moved. Because babies are not adept at reconciling the apparent stability with an actual change in location, they tend to respond almost equally to A and B until they get enough experience to search at B. This theory, then, can explain why some infants in a situation without landmarks search at A and some at B when an object is first hidden at B. It also explains why infants commit the AB error only under certain conditions.

However, Butterworth's work does have its limitations. First, the babies in Butterworth's research may have been old enough to be beyond the true AB error (Gratch, 1977). The percentage of AB errors in the Gratch and Landers study (1971) was substantially higher than that in the Butterworth (1977) study, you will recall. Gratch and Landers, in their longitudinal study, found that the average age for the appearance of the AB error was 8 months, 2 days. By 9 months, 8 days (median age), infants in their study were likely to search successfully at B. The average age of the infants in the Butterworth (1977) study was about 9.5 months. Perhaps younger children would have made the AB error independently of landmarks.

Second, Butterworth's theory cannot explain why infants are more likely to make the AB error if they are not allowed to search immediately (for example, Gratch et al., 1974). As Schuberth (1983) noted, the perceptual information remains constant whether search is immediate or not.

Finally, Butterworth's theory is confined to a very narrow component of search behavior. It does not explain why very young infants fail to search altogether. It also does not explain later difficulties in search.

Yet Butterworth's work, like Bower's, does highlight some shortcomings in Piaget's theory. Can the data be reconciled?

Summary

We can start with Paul Harris's (1983) contention that no theory currently available has replaced or can replace Piaget's because no other theorist has presented such a complete model of object permanence development. Furthermore, Piaget's model has received considerable support. Several longitudinal studies (for example, Uzgiris & Hunt, 1975) have replicated his sequence of object permanence development. Indeed, reviews of the object permanence research have generally concluded that Piaget's theory holds up well (Schuberth, 1983).

It is also clear, however, that Piaget's model needs to be modified if it is to explain all the available data. Once again, Piaget apparently underestimated infant abilities. Paul Harris (1983) has proposed a model which represents a beginning toward such a modification.

Harris suggests that Piaget was correct in arguing that the infant is constructing hypotheses to guide her search, but Piaget erred in defining the question that the infant tries to answer. Piaget thought babies were forming hypotheses about the nature of objects. Harris thinks that babies try to figure out where and how to search for objects. This involves first learning that a single object can have successive, though not simultaneous, locations. Very young infants do not understand this and so do not search for, or even follow, objects that have moved. Once the infant recognizes that a given object can move, she must construct schemes that allow successful search. These search plans will be greatly influenced by, and perhaps defined by, environmental cues.

Harris's model borrows from Gibson, Butterworth, Bower, and Piaget. Of course, it is not as complete as Piaget's and leaves many questions unanswered. However, as Schuberth (1983) notes, it does offer a "promising alternative" to Piaget (and the others). Only additional research can fill in the gaps.

As we leave our consideration of object permanence development, take one more look at Table 8-2. Look at stage 6. In this stage, the child is able to search successfully for an object even when part of the hiding process is invisible. Piaget argued that this implied that the baby's search must be guided by some kind of mental representation of the object and the hiding pattern. This, according to Piaget, is but one indicator of the baby's newly developed mental ability—to represent.

MENTAL REPRESENTATION

When I say the word *Christmas*, you are likely to have some kind of "mental" reaction. You might picture a Christmas tree with presents under it. You might try to recall the words to the song "The Twelve Days of Christmas." You might start to sketch a wreath or a tree. In all these activities, you are using representational skills. No tree is in front of you; yet you can picture, draw, or talk about one. You are able to provide an image or drawing or word to "stand in" for the tree. In other words, you can use a *symbol*. This is the essence of mental representation.

Mental representation is an important accomplishment. Try to imagine what thought would be like if you could not use words or images. You probably cannot do it; but if you could, you would realize the advantages of representational thought over nonrepresentational or sensorimotor thought. Without representational thought, you have to follow events as they actually happen. You cannot mentally "speed them up." You also are tied to immediate events. You cannot think about the future or the past. Finally, without representation you cannot link events together and think about them simultaneously. You are restricted to the step-by-step unfolding of individual events (Piaget & Inhelder, 1969). So, representation allows you to separate thought from the action or event it stands in for (Piaget & Inhelder, 1969). The emergence of representational thought is such a milestone that Piaget used it to mark the transition into a new stage of cognitive development (see Table 8-1).

It should be pointed out that mental representations are not synonymous with concepts. Concepts go beyond the actual symbolized event (Piaget, 1962). They may, for example, include emotional reactions (such as the excitement you associate with Christmas). Or, they may include relationships among specific events (for example, caroling, putting up the tree, and opening presents on Christmas morning). The representations are narrower, referring only to the concrete event they signify. This is, of course, a theoretical distinction. In real life, the two are almost indistinguishable. They also develop almost simultaneously (Piaget, 1962). For the purpose of this discussion, though, they will be kept separate.

Piaget View

Piaget (1962) believed that representational thought emerges during the last stage of sensorimotor development. He believed it is gradually constructed, evolving from the action patterns of earlier sensorimotor development. It is probably this idea of action roots that led Piaget to suggest that imitation is the most basic form of representation (Piaget & Inhelder, 1969).

Imitation involves the replication of a modeled action (see Chapter 7). The early forms of imitation are not considered representational. Imitation becomes representational only when it becomes deferred (see the temper tantrum example in Chapter 7). Piaget argued that deferred imitation forms the roots of all other forms of representation. He saw it as both the sensorimotor precursor of representation (because it involves direct action) and the transition to true representation (because it involves mentally condensing and rehearsing the action) (Piaget & Inhelder, 1969).

Forms of Representation.   There is not a huge gap between the appearance of deferred imitation and the other forms of representation. Indeed, Piaget (for example, Piaget & Inhelder, 1969) believed they appeared almost simultaneously. This reflects his notion of unified stages of development. Deferred imitation does come first, however, followed by symbolic (pretend) play, drawing (or graphic image), the mental image (visual imagery), and representational language.

Symbolic play first takes the form of pretending at your own activities (Piaget, 1962). Lorraine McCune-Nicolich (1981) has called this "autosymbolic play." So, the child may pretend to be asleep or to feed himself. Later the child pretends at his parents' activities (for example, cooking dinner or fixing a "broken" toy). At this level, the child seems to be aware that he is pretending. It is a game for him. Notice, too, that the child is pretending at activities. According to Piaget (for example, Piaget & Inhelder, 1969), this shows how symbolic play is related to imitation. Only later will the child be able to use objects as symbols in play (such as using a stick as a laser gun) (McCune-Nicolich, 1981; Piaget, 1962; Piaget & Inhelder, 1969).

Piaget had little to say about the graphic or mental images. He did claim that the graphic images (drawing) were an intermediary step between play (an activity) and mental images (truly mental representation) (Piaget & Inhelder, 1969). He also noted that mental images were required for stage 6 object permanence functioning (Piaget & Inhelder, 1969).

Finally, we come to language as a form of representation. It is a more difficult form of representation than the others because it is socially rather than personally defined. Therefore, it is expected to appear after the other representational forms (Piaget, 1962; Piaget & Inhelder, 1969). This prediction has been the focus of a great deal of controversy. Before we turn to that controversy, we need to emphasize that Piaget suggested that *representational language* followed other forms of representation. Representational language is language used to refer to absent objects, people, and so on, or past events (Piaget, 1962; Piaget & Inhelder, 1969). The earliest words, according to Piaget (1962), are tied to actions and are sensorimotor phenomena. So, if a child can say *ball* while playing with the ball but cannot use the word to refer to a ball that is out of sight, then the child is not using the word in a representational manner (see Smolak & Levine, 1984). According to Piaget, such a child may or may not show stage 6 functioning in other forms of representation.

Interrelationships in Representation

In examining the relationships among the various forms of representation, researchers have not considered all forms equally. First, almost all of the research involves language. Much of it involves object permanence, which could be interpreted as a measure of visual (mental) imagery. A few researchers have looked at symbolic play. Almost no one has considered imitation, which is ironic given Piaget's emphasis. Graphic imagery has also been excluded from this type of research.

Piaget suggested that the various forms of representation are intercorrelated. The data do indicate a relationship among the nonlanguage forms of mental representation, though it is not a very strong one. Researchers have found, at best, moderate correlations among object permanence, symbolic play, and imitation (for example, Bates et al., 1979; Chapman, 1981; Smolak & Levine, 1984; Uzgiris & Hunt, 1975). Such findings have led many researchers to conclude that decalage is indeed the rule in the nonlinguistic forms of representational development (for example, Bates et al., 1979; Chapman, 1981; Fischer & Corrigan, 1981).

What about language? More research exists on the relationship of language to other forms of representation than on interrelationships among the nonlinguistic forms. There are two questions here. How strongly is language related to nonlinguistic representation? And, does nonlinguistic representation predate language?

The largest body of research addressing these questions looks at the relationship between stage 6 object permanence and language. The results are mixed, but they do not point to a strong relationship. For example, several researchers have reported moderate correlations between object permanence and language (for example, Corrigan, 1978; Smolak, 1982; Zachry, 1978). Bates (Bates et al., 1979) found no correlation. All these findings apply to language production skills. The relationships are even weaker when language comprehension is investigated (for example, Chapman, 1981; Smolak, 1982).

Although the relationship between object permanence and language is not a strong one, it does not preclude the possibility that stage 6 object permanence predates representational language. If the gap between the attainment of stage 6 object permanence and language was fairly large (as decalage theorists like Fischer might suggest), correlations between the two would be low. Nonetheless, the precursor relationship would still be there (see Smolak & Levine, 1984).

In reviewing the object permanence research, Roberta Corrigan (1979) concluded that the data did not generally support the predicted precursor relationship. She also noted that the literature was full of methodological problems. Different investigators, for example, used different definitions of object permanence and language. Some used nonrepresentational language as defined by Piaget. Some used more difficult search tasks to define stage 6 object permanence than Piaget himself suggested were necessary. Such definitional problems could affect the findings. In a study controlling for these problems, we found that definitions did indeed have an effect (Smolak & Levine, 1984). When Piaget's own definitions were used, his theory was confirmed in that stage 6 object permanence did predate representational language. This study looked only at language production, however. Other studies looking at language comprehension have failed to find that stage 6 object permanence is a "prerequisite" for representational comprehension (for example, Chapman, 1981).

The relationship between symbolic play and language has also received some attention. Researchers have been somewhat more able to find correlations between symbolic play and language than between object permanence and language (for example, Bates et al., 1979; Rosenblatt, 1977). Also, considerable evidence indicates that the first pretending behaviors and the first words appear at about the same time (McCune-Nocolich, 1981). However, the first words may or may not be representational. So, these findings do not really address Piaget's contention concerning the sequence of representational development. In directly examining the relationship between autosymbolic play (the earliest form) and representational language, researchers found no clear-cut precursor relationship (Smolak & Levine, 1984). This issue obviously needs more research attention.

Overall, then, Piaget's views concerning the relationships among various forms of representation have not received strong support. At the same time, given the methodological problems (for example, definitions), they have not been discounted. The difficulties in supporting Piaget's view have led to the development of other models. For example, Elizabeth Bates (for example, Bates et al., 1979) suggested that language and cognition have shared roots, but language does not grow directly out of cognition as Piaget argued. Rather, other factors such as biological preparedness for language or environmental input may contribute to a distinction between language and cognitive development. We will take up this view more completely in the next chapter. For now, we can make the same statement we made concerning object permanence development: No theory has yet taken the place of Piaget's, though the data have clearly indicated that Piaget's views need to be modified if they are to explain representational functioning.

As mentioned earlier, Piaget treats concept development and representational development as two separate issues. As our final example of cognitive development in infancy, let's look at concept acquisition.

CONCEPT DEVELOPMENT

We use the term *concept*, or category, to represent the common characteristics of a group of similar events or objects (Reznick & Kagan, 1983). This representation is generalized rather than specific (Anisfeld, 1984). Thus, for example, the concept *table* refers to a group of objects with legs and a flat top that can have things (dishes, books, papers, and so on) placed upon it. It does not refer to one specific table, although it can be exemplified by a specific table. The definition of *table* is specific enough to allow us to distinguish it from *desk, bench,* or *counter,* though many of us may be hard pressed to explain how we make such distinctions (Anisfeld, 1984). In short, a concept permits us to simultaneously group things together and distinguish among things.

Why are categories important? If we could not use concepts, every object we encountered would have to be treated as a completely unique entity. Every time we came across a table, we would have to explore its surfaces and uses. We wouldn't just "know" what it was and how to use it. We would even have to name each table separately. This would remove much of the shared social nature of language and would severely limit our ability to communicate. Categories are clearly important in determining how we approach and interact with the environment.

Piaget (for example, Inhelder & Piaget, 1964) and other early writers (for example, Bruner, Oliver & Greenfield, 1966) believed that infants could not form true categories. They thought that infant concepts were defined subjectively in terms of the infant's own activity with the objects. Infants could group objects into "objects to be sucked" or "objects to be grasped," but they could not categorize objects on the basis of more objective perceptual or functional characteristics such as size, shape, or use. Piaget (1962) argued that objectively defined concepts did not appear until after mental representation emerged. Therefore, within Piaget's model, conceptual thought was not possible until the preoperational period (see Table 8-1). Early research supported this view (for example, Bruner, Oliver & Greenfield, 1966; Inhelder & Piaget, 1964). However, later studies, using new measurement techniques, uncovered evidence of categorization in infants as young as 12 months of age (for example, Nelson, 1973b; Ricciuti, 1965).

How do young children categorize objects? Nelson (1973b) suggested that both perceptual characteristics (for example, shape or color) and functional characteristics (what the object does or is used for) were important. She believed that object function formed the core of the concept (Nelson, 1974). This is consistent with Piaget's model. The child's direct, active experience with an object (for example, what the object does or can have done with it) is the central defining characteristic. The concept is then extended on the basis of perceptual characteristics. So, for example, *ball* might first be defined as "something that bounces when you throw it." Other objects that bounce will be considered balls. Later, the child will recognize that balls are round. He will assume that round things are balls and will try to bounce them. This is *overgeneralization* of the concept. Nelson (1973b, 1974) argued that such concept development begins before the child has the words to name the concept. Again, this is consistent with Piaget's view that language is based on cognition.

These findings apply to children between 12 and 24 months of age. What about younger children? Can they categorize objects? Do they use functional characteristics as the core definitions of their concepts?

Researchers have demonstrated that even newborns are capable of forming certain simple categories. Two-day-old infants can discriminate a category of patterns containing two elements from a category of patterns containing three elements (Antell & Keating, 1983). They cannot discriminate categories involving five or six elements (Antell & Keating, 1983). Development of object categories apparently takes place later, somewhere around 7 months (for example, Cohen & Caputo, 1978, cited in Caron & Caron, 1982; Ross, 1980). Infants under 1 year of age can also form categories relevant to facial recognition. For example, 30-week-old infants can categorize faces as happy or surprised (Caron, Caron & Myers, 1982). They can also recognize facial orientations (for example, profile vs. full faced) and gender of the face as categories (Cohen & Strauss, 1979). Such concepts, particularly those involving pattern recognition in newborns, seem to be rooted in perceptual rather than functional characteristics. This has led some authors (for example, Reznick & Kagan, 1983) to suggest that babies under 1 year of age define concepts on the basis of perceptual characteristics. Older babies would, though, rely more heavily on functional characteristics.

Thus, even newborns seem to be capable of some concept formation. Certainly these capabilities are limited, and we have no idea what the concepts actually mean to the baby or how she uses them. The ability to form concepts does underscore two themes for us. First, once again, it appears that Piaget has underestimated the capabilities of the young infant. The data seem to support Gibson's (for example, 1982) arguments that infants are simply perceiving what is there rather than constructing a world view. Second, infants right from the beginning seem to live in an organized world. Again, this is more consistent with Gibson's position than Piaget's.

The discussion so far has provided information about how thought processes might develop. The questions most asked by parents and clinicians have not yet been addressed. These questions are, "How smart is this baby?" and "How can I make this baby smarter?" Let's conclude this chapter with an examination of these issues.

HOW INTELLIGENT?

Measuring Intelligence

When parents ask, "How smart is my baby?" they basically want to know how their baby compares to other infants. Is he ahead of most infants his age? Is he behind? Is he on target?

Any experienced developmentalist or clinician can, of course, give the parents a global impression of the infant's intelligence. We can say, "Well, he has a larger vocabulary than most children his age" or "He walked a little late, but he's within the normal range." Much of the time, only global impressions are needed. Sometimes, though, we need a more specific, scientific answer. This may be needed for research purposes, such as evaluating early education programs, or for clinical purposes, as when retardation is suspected.

In other words, we sometimes need a test of infant intelligence. Two types of tests might be used. One type is the tests based upon Piaget's theory (for example, Uzgiris & Hunt, 1975). These tests are designed to assess the substages of sensorimotor development within chosen conceptual realms (for example, object permanence, causality). Examples from the Uzgiris-Hunt (1975) scales can be found in Box 8-1.

BOX 8-1 *THE UZGIRIS-HUNT SCALE*

Piaget's theory of cognitive development caused a revolution in our conceptualization of children's intellectual functioning. The existing DQ scales (for example, Bayley or Gesell) were inappropriate for the task of identifying developmental stages. The DQ scales took a quantitative approach to intelligence, emphasizing a building up of specific skills without assuming any change in the structures underlying those abilities. Piaget, of course, argued that such qualitative structural changes were at the root of cognitive development. Therefore new scales had to be devised to test children's intellectual development from a Piagetian perspective.

Several attempts have been made to construct Piagetian scales of sensorimotor development (for example, Mehrabian & Williams, 1971). Perhaps the best known and most widely used of these scales was developed by Ina Uzgiris and J. McVicker Hunt (1975).

The Uzgiris-Hunt scales actually consist of six separate scales. These scales measure various facets of sensorimotor development including object permanence, means-ends, causality, spatial relations, imitation, and the coordination of schemes. Each scale consists of items derived from Piaget's descriptions of infant behavior. Piaget's sequence for the development of each behavioral realm is reproduced more or less intact. The accuracy of each sequence has been confirmed by empirical data (Uzgiris & Hunt, 1975).

In line with Piaget's theory, there are changes not only in the complexity of items (quantitative shifts) but also in the nature of the task. So, for example, the vocal imitation scale begins by assessing the presence of noncry vocalizations. Later items try to elicit familiar sounds (for example, cooing) and sound patterns (for example, words) from the baby. The highest-level items are designed to measure the ability to imitate unfamiliar sound patterns. Similarly, the object permanence scale starts with measures of visual following skills. It then proceeds to tasks involving simple hidings. The baby is asked to search for a partially hidden object and then an object hidden under one screen. Later, the child is asked to follow multiple displacements. For example, on a table are three scarves. The object is hidden under the first scarf, then the second, and then the third, where it is left. As the object is moved from under one screen to the next, it is shown to the child. Finally, there are invisible displacement tasks. In these tasks, the object is first hidden in a box or in the tester's hand. Then the box or hand is moved from under one scarf to another, and the object is left under a particular scarf. Thus, the child does not see the object move from one hiding place to another. She must be able to represent the object mentally in order to follow the invisible displacements.

Each scale is scored individually. In other words, no overall level of sensorimotor functioning is assigned. This is because the scales are not highly intercorrelated. The scales do not indicate, or at least do not tap, any unified stage functioning (see text).

Uzgiris and Hunt (1975) provide a variety of test validation data, including test-retest stability and interrater reliability. They also provide age norms for each item of each scale. The availability of these data has probably contributed to the popularity of the scales. Nonetheless, the scales are of limited usefulness. Their ability to predict later intellectual functioning is limited (see discussion in main text). Also, the standardization samples used in developing the scales was relatively small by test validation standards. This seriously limits the diagnostic value of the scales.

In addition, it should be emphasized that the Uzgiris-Hunt scale assesses a much narrower range of behaviors than the infant DQ scales (for example, the Bayley or Gesell). Again, this limits its value, particularly in diagnostic situations.

The other type of test is the developmental quotient (DQ) scales (for example, Bayley, 1969; Gesell & Armatruda, 1941). The DQ is comparable to IQ (intelligence quotient). Like IQ tests, the DQ scales consist of items meant to tap a wide range of abilities (see Box 8-2 for examples). These items have been "standardized." In standardization, the items are given to a large number of infants. This allows the test designer to establish *norms*, that is, the average age at which a child passes particular items. An individual baby's performance can be compared to these norms and be assigned a developmental quotient. A perfectly average baby would have a DQ of 100.

BOX 8-2   *THE BAYLEY SCALES OF INFANT DEVELOPMENT*

One of the best known infant DQ scales is the Bayley Scales of Infant Development (BSID). The first form of the scales was published in 1933 and was entitled the California First-Year Mental Scale. The BSID now applies to children up to about 30 months of age.

The BSID consists of three subscales (Bayley, 1969). First, there is the mental scale. This subscale assesses social behaviors (for example, response to a voice at about 1 month of age), responses to objects (for example, visual following), fine motor skills (for example, removing a pellet from a bottle, the ability to reproduce a drawn line), and language skills (for example, pointing to pictures on request, producing noncry sounds and, later, words). Norms, based on a study of 1,262 children, are provided so that a mental DQ can be assigned (Bayley, 1969).

The second subscale focuses on motor development. Fine and gross motor skills are both included, though the emphasis is on gross motor skills. Rolling over, sitting, walking, standing, jumping, and using stairs are among the gross motor skills assessed. The major fine motor skill tested is grasping. Again, norms are provided so that a motor DQ can be assigned.

The final subscale is the Infant Behavior Record. This scale includes the tester's subjective rating of infant characteristics such as responsivity, fearfulness, tension, activity level, attention span, and goal directedness. Although average scores at each age are presented for this scale, they are not sufficiently detailed to yield a behavior DQ.

The Piagetian and DQ scales have both been criticized. Gerald Gratch (1977), for example, argued that the relationship between Piagetian scales and Piaget's theory is not well defined. The scales use Piaget's sequence to measure specific behavioral realms. A series of hiding tasks may be used to assess object permanence, but the broad concepts that form the core of Piaget's theory—such as primary or secondary circular reactions—are never assessed.

The most common criticism leveled against the DQ scales is that they do not predict later intelligence (for example, Brooks & Weinraub, 1976; McCall, 1979). Knowing an infant's DQ at 6 months tells you virtually nothing about what her IQ will be at 5 years. This is particularly true if the infant test is given at a very young age (less than 6 months old). It is also true if a large gap exists between the infant test and the childhood IQ measure. The exception to the trend of low predictability is with low-functioning children. In these cases, DQ and IQ are much more stable.

Why don't DQ tests predict future IQ? It does *not* seem to be attributable to sloppy test construction. On a variety of indices of test validity, DQ tests have met the criteria for valid tests (see, for example, Bayley, 1969; Harris, 1983; McCall, 1979). In fact, the only statistical criterion that the DQ scales have consistently failed to meet is predictive ability; that is, the tests do not predict future performance on IQ.

That this is the only statistical criterion that is consistently problematic may give us a clue. Perhaps DQ scores do not predict IQ scores because the two tests measure different abilities. We have already seen that infant intelligence seems quite different from childhood or adult intelligence. Particularly during the first few months, where predictive validity is poorest, the infant has no language, no symbol use, and few problem-solving strategies. DQ items for this age range focus on motor skills (for example, sitting), manual skills (picking up a cube), and visual following (see Box 8-2). How these skills are related to IQ test skills (vocabulary, verbal analogies, picture completion, and so on) is unclear. In other words, the shift in measured abilities from early infancy to childhood may preclude prediction (for example, Harris, 1983; McCall, 1979).

This argument is bolstered by two other findings. First, DQ scores do not seem to have a strong genetic component (Harris, 1983; McCall, 1979). In other words, DQ tests do not seem to be measuring *native intelligence*. Instead, they are measuring current abilities in a variety of areas. These abilities do seem to be strongly influenced by the stimulation available in the baby's current environment and by the parent-infant relationship (McCall, 1979). Second, some abilities do predict from infancy to later childhood. Memory functioning is an example of this (Fagan, 1983). Measuring the same thing repeatedly (for example, memory) provides more predictive validity than measuring different skills (as in DQ vs. IQ skills) and trying to correlate them. Again, this suggests that DQ tests and IQ tests are probably *not* measuring *native intelligence*, if there is such a thing. Rather, they are measuring *skills*.

Since DQ tests do not predict future intelligence test performance, many developmentalists feel the tests are not particularly useful. Robert McCall (1979) pointed out that this conclusion is probably extreme. Since we expect change in development, why should we expect that all tests will be able to predict that change? Is a test useless if it cannot? McCall argued that a test could validly measure present functioning without having the ability to predict. Knowing where a baby scores relative to other infants right now is a useful piece of information! Indeed, DQ tests may be useful in assessing current functioning. The researcher or clinician simply needs to keep in mind that the present functioning cannot be used to predict future development. A similar statement can be made about the Piagetian scales: They have limited predictive power, but they can provide valuable information about a child's current abilities.

Whatever DQ tests measure, it certainly is not a fixed capacity. Furthermore, environment seems to affect performance on these tests. This suggests that it may be possible to take an "ordinary" baby, place him in an "optimal" environment, and produce a high DQ. A good deal has been written in the popular press about doing just that. Let's look at this issue now.

Improving Intelligence

Several years ago a family in rural Ohio created a national sensation. They had "made" their children into geniuses. The mother began talking to the babies while they were still in the womb. She worked with the infants, from birth, with books and flashcards. The parents claimed that before 6 months of age their children had talked in complete sentences. All the children could, they said, read by 1 year of age. Testing of the children, who ranged in age from preschool to adolescence, indicated that the children were all "talented." Whether the children talked and read at such extraordinarily early ages, of course, could not be documented.

This family was not alone in claiming that young infants could be taught to do "incredible" things. Glenn Doman (for example, 1975, 1982) has presented programs for teaching babies to read and do arithmetic. His programs involve showing the baby flashcards for a few seconds at a time several times a day. He claimed that you can start to teach your baby to read as early as 10 months of age, and you ought to start by the time the baby is 2 years of age. If you do, and you follow his program, Doman (1975) suggested you can teach even brain-injured preschoolers to read.

Doman and others (for example, Engelmann & Engelmann, 1981) claim that parents typically waste the learning potential of the first few years. Parents bore their children with meaningless toys. They even actively deny the child the opportunity to learn—by using playpens, denying access to certain objects, and so forth. The children come to associate curiosity and learning with punishment and boredom. No wonder, says Doman, so many of our children have learning problems!

Is it true? Can babies learn to read, add, and subtract? Are learning problems the creation of the way most of us raise our children? Could we all have genius children?

There is little doubt that young children can learn to recognize words. As Doman (1975) pointed out, many preschoolers do this automatically. They may recognize words like *Coke* or *McDonald's* or *Sesame Street*. There is no reason to believe that this "recognition vocabulary" cannot be expanded to include other words.

Two serious questions remain, however. First, what is the relationship of such recognition to more complex reading? Kurt Fischer (quoted in Span, 1984) argued that little continuity between such early skills and true reading is evident. One could draw an analogy between such phenomena and the skill-building theories of motor and cognitive development (for example, Bower & Wishart, 1979; Connolly, 1980; Fischer, 1980). It is not at all clear that the earliest forms of any skill, be it stepping, imitation, or reading, are simply building blocks for more complex skills. The early skills may have to be reorganized, and even relearned, before the more complex ones can appear. If this is the case, early instruction may be lost.

The second question is perhaps even more important. What is the price we pay for instructing our infants? Doman (for example, 1975) is probably correct in arguing that infants are curious and enjoy learning opportunities. His programs are designed to be "low pressure" and "fun." Yet can parents institute his programs without pressure? Think for a moment about the kind of parent likely to try such a program. Who would pay almost $500 to Doman's Better Baby Institute (the price is quoted in Span, 1984) to get a "smarter" baby? Although we cannot be sure because there is no research on this issue, it is likely that many of these parents are achievement oriented. They want "smart babies." There is a real possibility that they will pressure their babies. What if the baby doesn't "learn" to read? One must conclude that either the program, the parent, or the baby is a failure. Concluding that the parent or child has failed has obvious dangers. Even if the child does learn to read, the pressure to "hurry up" and be more adultlike may create serious adjustment problems (see Elkind, 1981).

Unfortunately, neither of these questions can be answered right now. Virtually no empirical research has been undertaken to answer them. In fact, Doman (for example, 1975) and other program creators (for example, Nippert, quoted in Bridgman, 1984) actively discourage testing their "pupils." Indeed, most developmental psychologists seem to be skeptical about these programs. However, there is no "proof" that these programs do not work; there is also no "proof" that they do. Further, they *may* have deleterious effects.

More importantly, no evidence exists to indicate that special programs are needed to encourage intellectual development. This doesn't mean that parents cannot encourage intellectual development. The research suggests that parents can do several things (see, for example, McCall, 1979).

Parents can first of all provide emotional and physical support for the baby's curiosity. As Piaget suggested, babies seem to learn best when they are allowed to actively explore objects, places, and so on (see Ginsburg & Opper, 1977). So, the environment should be designed to maximize exploratory opportunities. Babies should not spend too much time confined to playpens or cribs. This doesn't mean that free rein is necessary, but that restrictions should be limited.

The baby should also be given the opportunity to explore *various* objects, not just toys. Babies can play with many safe, "real" objects—pots and pans, spoons, magazines, furniture, and clothes, for instance. Of course, in the process of the baby's explorations some objects may be damaged or even destroyed (especially magazines). From such opportunities, however, the baby does learn. He learns not only about restrictions on what is acceptable behavior but about cause and effect and the properties of various materials.

It is also important for the parents to interact with their babies. The child needs the parents' approval for her learning attempts. The child also gains from the parents' verbal input. Babies whose parents talk to them and read to them seem to do better. Again, this does not mean constantly entertaining the baby. As with restricting activity, balance is needed.

SUMMARY

We have seen that cognitive development makes significant advances during infancy. Jean Piaget's theory is the dominant mode of explaining these changes. However, the theory has faced serious challenges during the past decade. These challenges cover broad concepts such as the idea of stages in development. They also address progress within specific realms such as object permanence development. The best conclusion to draw at this point is that Piaget's theory is in need of revision. He apparently seriously underestimated infant abilities. However, currently, there does not seem to be any theory on the verge of replacing Piaget's.

Practical issues of measuring and improving infant intelligence were also addressed in this chapter. Again, no simple conclusions can be drawn. We can say that infant DQ tests do not predict later IQ. However, they do seem to be useful for defining an infant's current level of functioning. Improving IQ is a trickier issue. Certainly the environment can be designed to facilitate cognitive development, but the value of programs specifically intended to teach infants reading, math, and so on, remains questionable. In fact, Elkind (and others) have argued that such programs may even be harmful.

Frequent references to language development have been made in this chapter. Language and thought are closely related topics. Indeed, Piaget (for example, 1962) viewed language as simply a form of thought. However, language is, in many ways, a unique entity. It is therefore treated as a separate topic in the next chapter.

9

Language

You might wonder what a chapter on language development is doing in a book about infancy. After all, the word *infant* comes from the Latin *infans*, which means "without language." This bit of information reinforces our idea that infants don't talk. They cry. They babble. They may even say a few words. Yet we tend to think of toddlers rather than infants when we think of children really learning to talk.

This popular conceptualization of language development is true to some extent. Children under 2 years of age (infants) certainly do not usually talk well, but the foundations of language are laid during these first 2 years. Considerable progress is made toward using "real" language. A brief look at some of the language-related accomplishments during the first two years demonstrates this.

AN OVERVIEW OF LANGUAGE

Sequence

During the first 6 months of life, babies do not "intentionally" communicate. That is, they do not think about what idea they wish to convey and then try to express it. This does not mean that there is no communication. Parents do, for example, react differently to "pain" cries as opposed to "hunger" cries (for example, Wolff, 1973). The baby's "need" is therefore communicated to the parents.

However, the communication lies in parental willingness to interpret the cry rather than in the infant's intention.

Initially, cries are about the only form of vocal communication available. By about 3 weeks of age, the child has developed a "fake cry." *Cooing*, the vowellike sounds such as *aaah* or *ooo*, also appears now (Wolff, 1973), though it does not become strong and regular until the child is about 2 months old. So, the baby's vocal communication repertoire grows markedly during the first month. Parents do interpret these sounds as if they were communicative. There is no evidence, however, that the babies are aware of the communicative value of the sounds.

Since language is a tool for social interaction, it is also important to consider advances in interactional capabilities during these first 6 months of life. At birth, infants can produce a variety of facial expressions that become quite clear by 2-3 months (Trevarthen, 1979). The expressions include facial and tongue movements that give mothers the impression that the baby is "about to speak." The child often combines these facial expressions with more or less appropriate gestures. Similarly, by 2 months of age the infant can control eye contact. These behaviors encourage social interaction, which is imperative for language acquisition. In addition, these behaviors may be important as a foundation for communicative development (Trevarthen, 1979).

When the baby is between 6 and 12 months of age, three major developments occur. First, sounds become more differentiated. The baby begins to babble, that is, to combine consonant and vowel sounds as in *ba, goo,* or *da.* These sounds become increasingly speechlike. In fact, by the end of this period, the child may produce his first word.

Second, the baby starts to communicate intentionally. This happens by 8-10 months. It is related to the development of understanding means-ends relationships (for example, Harding & Golinkoff, 1979; Harding, 1982).

These two accomplishments are nicely exemplified in Michael Halliday's work (for example, 1975, 1979) on "protolanguage." Protolanguage is like regular language in that it expresses meaning. Unlike language, though, it has no socially agreed upon vocabulary or grammatical rules. The child uses sounds, typically combined with gestures, to convey a particular meaning, so that a particular sound is associated with a particular meaning. Halliday's son Nigel, for example, used the sound *na* to mean "I want that" (Halliday, 1975). Because interpreting such utterances obviously requires considerable familiarity with the child, protolanguage is not considered language; but protolanguage does indicate that the child has learned that she can communicate feelings and desires to other people by means of vocalizations.

The final accomplishment of the 6-12 month period is the onset of language comprehension. Children apparently start to understand single words around 10 months of age (for example, Benedict, 1979; Huttenlocher, 1974). This means that they can respond to a word without any gestural cues (including the mother staring at the object while she asks for it). They can also retrieve a requested object that is not currently visible.

During the next 6 months, when the child is 12-18 months of age, language comprehension skills develop rapidly. For example, Benedict (1979) reported that, on the average, the eight children in her study understood 50 words by about 13.5 months of age. By 16 months of age, six of the children understood 100 words or more. Two of these children understood 200 words.

Progress in language production is much slower. Benedict (1979) reported that, on the average, children understood over 60 words when they were able to produce just 10. The average age for producing 50 words was just over 18 months— almost 5 months after the children had reached this milestone for comprehension. Clearly, then, comprehension vocabulary development predates production skills.

Between 18 and 24 months, production skills make their major advances, although these advances may come considerably later than this and still be considered "normal." Generally, in children between 18 and 24 months of age two things happen. First, the production vocabulary grows considerably. Some children even experience a "vocabulary spurt." It seems as though they now understand that everything has a name and they start naming everything. Entering this period, the baby may have a vocabulary of about 30 words. By the end of it, she may be producing 400 or more words (Brandstadter-Palmer, 1982).

Second, the child begins to express grammar. The first words are produced one at a time. They are not combined into sentences or even two-word utterances. Now, utterances of two or more words make their appearance. In fact, by 24 months of age, the child may be producing four- or five-word sentences (Brandstadter-Palmer, 1982). The child's grammatical knowledge is still immature, however; he does not, for example, usually use plural or past-tense forms. Nonetheless, his ability to communicate a desire or feeling has clearly improved remarkably.

In sum, during the first 2 years of life the baby moves from communicating only by crying to using small sentences. Her first communications lack intentionality. By the end of the first year, she can intentionally communicate. She can also understand language and has started to say a few words. By the middle of the second year, she can understand a good deal of what is being said around her. And, by the end of that year, she can say enough to carry on a conversation.

All the things a baby needs to learn to acquire language—grammar, vocabulary, and intentionality—are implied in this sequence. If we are to discuss how language is acquired, we need to define explicitly what it is the child is learning. In other words, we need to define language.

Definition

Language may be defined as a system of socially defined symbols (or, in Piaget's terminology, signs) that is organized phonologically, semantically, and syntactically. Language is used for communication and for representation. Let's examine this definition in terms of its two broad components—form and function.

Form.   Language contains three elements that determine the form of an utterance. First is *phonology*, the sound system of the language. It defines which sounds are included in a language. For example, the Japanese language does not have an *l* sound as ours does (this is why the Japanese often have trouble pronouncing *l*). The phonological system also defines how the sounds may be combined. These rules vary somewhat from language to language. Just think of how difficult it is to pronounce (and spell) non-English names. This has been well exemplified with the multiple spellings and pronunciations of Libyan leader Mummar Khadafy's name (also spelled Gaddafi and Khaddafi).

The second formal system is *semantics*, the meaning system of the language. Semantics includes the definitions of words as well as the interrelationship among words. How do we know, for example, that the words *cat, mammal,* and *animal* are related? How do we learn synonyms and antonyms?

Syntax, or grammar, is the last formal component. The syntax of a language contains the rules and categories for combining words into sentences. You remember being taught these in school: For example, every sentence needs a subject and verb. The subject and verb must agree; that is, if the subject is plural, the verb must be plural. You can add to any sentence by using coordination conjunctions such as *but, and,* and *or*. Learning all these rules for a test may have been torture for you, especially if you also had to diagram the sentences. The fascinating thing is that you had already been using most of the rules for years, for even the first one-and two-word utterances seem to be guided by some rules.

Thus, language is organized into phonological, semantic, and syntactic systems, though these systems can be quite immature when language first appears. But, infants apparently have some understanding of phonology, semantics, and syntax. Without it, infants could not produce utterances that can be comprehended by other people.

Function.   Being understood by others—communication—is one of the goals of language. We might want to communicate information about objects or events. We might communicate our feelings or desires. We might ask someone to clarify his attempts at communication. The study of these various forms of communicative intent is *pragmatics*. Researchers studying pragmatics in infancy address a number of questions: When and how does the baby develop intentional communication? When does she distinguish among the various types of communicative intentions? What does a baby need to know about communication before language will appear?

The other function of language is representation (see Chapter 8). Language is a symbol, or sign, system. Words "stand in for" real objects, people, and events. Language thus allows us to talk and think about objects or people who are not present. The earliest words may not serve this function, leading Piaget to argue that they are not truly language.

If not every word is representational, it is also true that not every representation is a word, for representation and language are not synonymous (see Chapter 8). The same can be said of communication, for not every word is communicative. We sometimes talk to guide our own activity. Conversely, we can communicate without talking. The old adage "one picture is worth a thousand words" demonstrates that.

The definition of language as given so far could well apply to a variety of animal communication systems. Birds, for example, often have songs defined as set patterns of notes that communicate particular meanings (mating, danger, and so on) (for example, Frings & Frings, 1964). However, two characteristics seem to distinguish human language from other animal communication systems. First, human language can be used to discuss abstract ideas. In other words, our words can be used to express ideas that do not have specific referents. We can debate the merits of communism as opposed to capitalism, for example. Second, our language has infinite generativity (for example, Chomsky, 1975). We have a finite vocabulary (contained in an unabridged dictionary), but by using that limited vocabulary we can produce an infinite number of meaningful utterances. Their meanings may overlap. I could say, for example, "Give me the ball" or "Give the ball to me" or "You give me that ball" and so on. The many variations of this simple sentence demonstrate that it would be impossible to count every possible sentence in any language.

Language seems to be a uniquely human capability, at least as far as we know. It is also an incredibly complex skill. Yet, it is one that is acquired by almost every child. More incredibly, children seem to acquire language with little or no *direct* training and with relative ease. All this might lead you to think that the newborn brings with him some special capacity for language. Let's now look at what predispositions for language that newborn and young infants might possess.

LANGUAGE PREPAREDNESS

In this section we discuss several factors that may be viewed as "preparations" or "predispositions" for language, but be aware that any clear link between these behaviors and language remains undefined. The research that would link early facial expressons to language communication patterns, for example, is simply not yet available. Thus, the links proposed here must be treated as hypothetical.

Brain Lateralization

In most adults, language is processed in the left hemisphere of the cerebral cortex (for example, Geschwind, 1979). Other sounds, such as music, tend to be processed in the right hemisphere. This hemispheric specialization appears to be present even at birth. For example, the language processing area of the left hemisphere is measurably larger than the comparable area in the right hemisphere in newborns and even fetuses (Wada, Clarke & Hamm, 1975; Witelson & Pallie, 1973). This suggests a possible anatomical basis for language responsivity and acquisition.

EEG data show the same pattern. EEG activity is greater in the left hemisphere than the right when the infant is listening to language (for example, Davis & Wada, 1977; Molfese, Freeman & Palermo, 1975). In fact, the newborn brain seems to be quite specialized for language. For example, /b/ and /g/ sounds elicit different patterns of brain responses (Molfese & Molfese, 1979). The neonatal brain, then, appears to be prepared to process language in a way comparable to, though of course not identical to, adult processing. The ability to distinguish language from other sounds is imperative for language acquisition. The ability to distinguish sounds and sound patterns within the language is equally important.

Phoneme Distinction

The smallest units of sound in a language are *phonemes*. The ability to distinguish among phonemes is a prerequisite to recognizing various words. Research indicates that even infants less than 4 months of age can distinguish among a wide variety of phonemes. (See Chapters 3 and 6.) This has been demonstrated using a variety of techniques (which strengthens the reliability of the findings) (for example, Eimas et al., 1971; Leavitt et al., 1976; Moffitt, 1971; Molfese & Molfese, 1979). The ability to make some distinctions seems to be present at birth. Other distinctions seem possible only as development proceeds (Molfese, Molfese & Carrell, 1982). Note that these infants are simply distinguishing sounds. There is no evidence that very young infants ascribe any meaning to the sounds.

Social Interaction

Three social interaction patterns present at or shortly after birth may affect language acquisition. First, newborns seem to synchronize their movements with adult speech (Condon, 1979; Condon & Sander, 1974). This could be interpreted as showing that the baby is sensitive to the rhythms of language. It also might show how attuned infants are to human interaction. Not all researchers agree with these interpretations. Some believe, for example, that the movements may simply reflect the baby's natural "rhythms" (Trevarthen, 1979). (Recall Thelen's work on rhythmicity discussed in Chapter 5.) The infant's movements would as a result be guided by an "inner pacemaker" rather than by the adult's speech. Nonetheless, synchrony appears to affect the parent's interactional behavior and thereby the child's language acquisition.

The second social behavior is turn taking. The ability to take conversational turns is crucial for effective communication. Learning about interactional turns starts at a very young age (for example, Kaye, 1979). This is evident in the feeding situation. Initially, the mother jiggles the nipple when the baby pauses in his nursing. This seems to speed up the renewal of sucking. In fact, the baby often starts sucking before the jiggling stops. After 2 weeks, though, the pattern changes. The pause in sucking is still followed by jiggling, but now the jiggling stops before the sucking is reinstituted. Although the mother is probably doing most of the adapting here (Kaye, 1979), turn-taking patterns are being developed.

Finally, newborns can recognize their mothers' voices (see Chapter 3). This is important because it may increase attention to maternal vocalizations.

Summary

About 30 years ago, B.F. Skinner (1957) argued that infants bring nothing special to the language-learning process. Data collected since then suggest that he was wrong. Newborns' brains seem to be ready to discriminate and process language. Babies can differentiate sounds within the language. They have social skills that may encourage exposure to language, so that they are likely to make use of these available skills. Whether these capacities actually form the roots of language or set the stage for language acquisition is unknown. They do, however, fuel the nature-nurture debate concerning the roots of language. Let's now consider how language acquisition might be explained.

EXPLAINING LANGUAGE

What causes language to develop? Is it the maturation of the biological structures? Is there an innate mental structure specially designed for language? Is it rooted in general cognitive development? Or, is language learned primarily through imitation? These are some of the explanations of language development considered here.

Chomsky: A Nativist View

Nature theorists, or *nativists*, argue that language abilities are innate. This position implies that the child comes to the task of language acquisition with some sort of bias (Maratsos, 1983). In ancient times, this bias was thought to be toward the "natural language" of humanity. The ancients believed that humans were pre-programmed to speak the language of the first race of people. This ability was so extensive that no training or even exposure to language was needed for language to develop. Even the language's vocabulary was innately available to children (Dale, 1976).

The modern nativist view is much less extreme. All nativists agree that children must be exposed to language to learn it and that vocabulary is an acquired skill. For example, Noam Chomsky (1957, 1965) argued that the semantic and syntactic systems are entirely separate. It is syntax that he viewed as innate.

To be more specific, Chomsky distinguished between the "deep structure" of utterances and the "surface structure." The deep structure is the syntax that underlies a sentence. It includes information such as whether the past tense is needed or the relationship between the subject and predicate of the sentence. The surface structure is what we actually hear (or read). It includes the -*ed* that marks past tense and the actual placement of the subject in front of the predicate. The deep and surface structures, which are dramatically different, are connected by rules of transformation: how to form the past tense, how to mark a particular word as being the subject, and so on. It is the deep structure and the rules of transformation that Chomsky thought to be innate.

Chomsky thought this information was innate rather than learned for two reasons. First, there are linguistic universals. These are regularities that occur in every studied human language. For example, all languages are divided into parts of speech comparable to nouns, verbs, adjectives, and so on. All languages require a subject and a predicate to form a complete sentence. Such regularities are evidence that some universal, underlying structure guides language development.

Second, Chomsky (for example, 1957) argued that children acquire language with incredible speed and ease. He suggested that they acquire language so quickly that it cannot possibly be guided by the principles of normal learning (as was argued, for example, by Skinner, 1957). (See Chapter 7.) The environment does not really support language acquisition in the way learning explanations require, for children are exposed to degenerate models of language, full of incomplete sentences and false starts. Furthermore, Chomsky argued, parents do not directly reinforce their children for proper syntax use.

These factors led Chomsky to postulate an innate structure that guided language acquisition. This hypothetical structure is the LAD (Language Acquisition Device) (McNeill, 1970). Describing the LAD as a hypothetical structure emphasizes it is not physiologically defined. It is not the equivalent of any of the areas of the brain that have been associated with language (for example, Broca's area or Wernicke's area). Rather, the LAD is part of the "mind."

Thus, the LAD is a mental structure (Chomsky, 1975) just like Piaget's cognitive structures. However, it differs from Piaget's mental structures in at least two important ways. First, because the LAD is mature at or shortly after birth, it is not constructed in stages (as in Piaget's model). Rather, the structures are givens that remain constant throughout life. Second, the syntactic structures postulated by Chomsky are not rooted in cognitive development.

If the LAD is innate, then children must be aware of syntax before the first word is spoken. This contention puts the nativists in a tricky situation. When most children first begin to speak, they say only one word at a time. In other words, children's first utterances do not express syntactic relations. The nativists claim that this inability reflects a surface structure problem. The child simply has not yet learned how to express grammar in his language. In fact, McNeill (1970) claimed that the words that children use during this period indicate an understanding of syntax. For example, children's vocabularly during this one-word period is dominated by nouns. Nouns, unlike any other part of speech, occur in every grammatical relation. They are, therefore, the most flexible part of speech, allowing the child to maximize the likelihood of adult comprehension of the entire thought that the child is trying to express (McNeill, 1970).

In short, the nativists argued that syntax development is guided by an innate, linguistically oriented mental structure. Although this view was extremely influential during the 1960s and early 1970s, it has gradually fallen into disfavor for a variety of reasons.

Criticisms of Chomsky's View

The nativist view can be criticized on both empirical and theoretical grounds. First, semantic and syntactic development do seem to be heavily intertwined

(Maratsos, 1983). In fact, several theorists have suggested that syntax is rooted in semantic categories (for example, Fillmore, 1968). These theorists suggested, for example, that the child conceptualizes categories such as actor (or agent) and action rather than categories like subject and verb. The former categories are clearly related to the prelinguistic sensorimotor categories (discussed later in this chapter). Also, there is little reason to believe that deep and surface structures are radically different (Maratsos, 1983).

Questions have also been raised concerning the nativist position concerning development per se. Research on maternal speech (discussed later in this chapter) clearly indicates that children hear well-formed language. Chomsky was therefore erroneous in arguing that children are exposed to degenerate linguistic models. His claim that children are not directly reinforced for using correct syntax has received some support (for example, Brown & Hanlon, 1970; Hirsh-Patek, Treiman & Schneiderman, 1984). However, it does appear that mothers may provide clues about correct syntax in a more subtle manner (Hirsh-Patek, Treiman & Schneiderman, 1984). Mothers are more likely to repeat their children's utterances when they contain syntax errors. Within these repetitions, the mothers correct the children's errors. These repetitions may provide the child with cues about the proper use of syntax. This possibility is supported by the finding that children whose mothers frequently repeat child statements tend to develop language more quickly (for example, Cross, 1978; Smolak & Weinraub, 1983; Wells, 1980).

Another issue that has been debated is whether or not single-word utterances encode syntax (for example, Bloom, 1973; Dore, 1975). Lois Bloom (1973), for example, eliminated a variety of explanations for why children 12-18 months of age might "know" syntax, as McNeill claimed, and yet not encode it. She noted that children of this age have the memory, articulatory, and vocabulary abilities needed to produce multiword utterances, but they don't. Bloom claimed that this was because the children do not understand syntactic relations. Such views are bolstered by findings suggesting that nouns do not dominate all early vocabularies as McNeill had suggested (for example, Nelson, 1973a, 1981). Language comprehension research also suggest that young children know nothing about syntax. There seems to be a substantial lag between understanding single words and understanding even two-word utterances (for example, Chapman, 1981).

On a more theoretical level, Hermina Sinclair de Zwart (for example, 1973) argued that a nativist explanation raises more questions than it answers. Why doesn't the child express syntax sooner? Exactly what is innate? How can we distinguish an innate structure from an acquired structure? Why would certain transformations be innate? Do they serve some evolutionary purpose (Maratsos, 1983)? What is the relationship between cognition and language?

Sinclair de Zwart's Alternative: A Cognitive Developmental View

Sinclair de Zwart's basic premise was that language development is rooted in general sensorimotor development (for example, Sinclair de Zwart, 1973). The linguistic universals noted by Chomsky are simply reflections of cognitive universals. Thus, for example, in developing an understanding of causality, the child comes to distinguish actor from action. This relationship is later reflected in the subject-verb relationship found in sentences. Sinclair de Zwart's model, then, is an expansion of Piaget's views (see Chapter 8). Indeed, all of Piaget's basic tenets (for example, constructionism and stages) are also found in Sinclair de Zwart's model.

Sinclair de Zwart's model has certain advantages over the nativists'. For one thing, Sinclair de Zwart's model is better equipped to explain the continued development of language into the school years. It also helps us understand why very young children use only one word at a time. However, as noted in Chapter 8, general relationships between cognition and language development have not been well supported. Such findings undermine Sinclair de Zwart's position. On the other hand, recent data do suggest a relationship between very specific cognitive and linguistic skills. The ability to use the word *gone* for example, is related to the development of object permanence (Gopnik, 1984).

Another problem undermines Sinclair de Zwart's position. Let's assume, for the moment. that cognition *is*, as she suggested, the basis for language. How does the child get from cognitive understanding to language? Certainly there is nothing inherent in cognition that would lead to language. The rules of language seem to exist separately from cognition (Bates et al., 1979; Bruner, 1983). Nothing about understanding time, for example, automatically leads to being able to indicate that a verb stands for past, present, or future tense (Bruner, 1983). Such tense marking is part of the language, not part of the time concept per se, though the time concept may be part of the tense marking. Furthermore, early concepts are formed on the basis of personal interaction with the environment. As such, they may be idiosyncratic. How do these individualized concepts become the socially agreed-upon signs of language (Bruner, 1983)?

Jerome Bruner (1983) suggested that the only solution to these problems is to view language and cognition as distinct developmental entities. This does not mean they are totally unrelated. Instead, Bruner meant that language is not simply a reflection of cognition, as Piaget and his followers argued. Language has its own rules, separate from those guiding cognitive development. Bruner argued that social interaction, especially maternal speech patterns, provided the basic information about these rules.

A Social Interactionist View

The Linguistic Environment.   Adults do not speak to young, language-learning children the same way they talk to adults. Some of the differences are obvious to almost any observer. For example, we tend to use "cute euphemisms" in talking to young children. Just think of the words mothers use for toileting functions and body parts. We also talk to babies with a high-pitched, sing-song intonation.

Other differences may be somewhat less obvious. The statements directed toward children are shorter, containing fewer verbs and modifiers. They also have fewer embedded and subordinate clauses. Mothers use more interrogative and imperative forms when talking to children. Their speech is more fluent and intelligible. They are also more likely to repeat themselves when talking to children (Elliot, 1981).

This "special" pattern of talking to babies is not unique to American mothers. Similar patterns have been found among Latvian, Polish, Lithuanian, Russian, Arabic, Comanche, Greek, Japanese, Maltese, and Spanish mothers (Ferguson, 1977). Furthermore, even preschoolers seem to realize that one speaks differently to babies than to peers or adults (Sachs & Devin, 1976; Shatz & Gelman, 1973).

Fathers, too, speak baby talk, though their speech patterns may not be identical to maternal speech (Golinkoff & Ames, 1979; Masur & Gleason, 1980; Rondal, 1980). Fathers may use a wider vocabulary range when talking to children. They also seem to be more demanding than mothers. They request more labeling and more function explanations, for example, "What does that do?" Further, they are more likely than mothers to ask children to repeat or clarify a statement. Nonetheless, more similarities than differences exist between maternal and paternal speech, indicating that fathers are capable of sensitive parenting (see Chapter 3). However, the differences are important, too. They indicate that the father is not simply a secondary mother. Rather, he may be making a unique contribution to child development. Perhaps the mother provides the "basics" of language to the child while the father prepares the child to interact with the outside world by demanding greater clarity and complexity (for example, Clark-Stewart, 1978).

The differences between mothers and fathers are not the only ones observed in the use of baby talk. First, baby talk seems related to the age of the child. Surprisingly, we do not talk baby talk to very young infants (for example, Kaye, 1980; Snow, 1972). Baby talk probably does not appear until the baby is at least 7 months of age. Significant changes in baby talk take place with infants between 18 and 30 months of age (for example, Bellinger, 1980). Similarly, some evidence suggests that maternal speech patterns change as the child's linguistic skills improve (for example, Cross, 1977, 1978).

On the other hand, other data suggest that mothers' speech to children is based more on the child's age than on language level (Smolak & Weinraub, 1983). These data seem to indicate that mothers adopt a way of speaking to children of a certain age and stick with it. This is consistent with evidence that different mothers adopt different styles of baby talk (McDonald & Pien, 1982). Some mothers use language primarily to elicit conversation from their babies while others try to control or direct the baby's physical behavior. Nonetheless, these mothers still demonstrate considerable similarity. They all maintain the basic baby talk pattern (for example, Smolak & Weinraub, 1983).

The regularity and widespread use of baby talk suggests that the linguistic environment is designed to facilitate language acquisition. Yet the sheer presence of baby talk does not prove that it facilitates language development in general or in specific realms, such as syntax. Let's look at the research that has examined the relationship between baby talk and child language development. We will do this as we examine each major system of language development.

LINGUISTIC SYSTEMS

The four linguistic systems are phonology (sound system), semantics (meaning system), syntax (grammar), and pragmatics (language functions). Semantics, syntax, and phonology work together to form language. Through these systems, a person is able to go from simply making sounds to making sounds that are organized into meaningful words and sentences (Bruner, 1983). In a way, then, these systems serve language. At the same time, language serves pragmatics (Bruner, 1983). Pragmatics is the study of how we use language. We use it to get what we want, to promise people things, to humiliate people, to provide warnings, and so on. These goals can be accomplished without language. Gestures, facial expressions, and even silence itself can serve to convey these "messages." We do use such nonlinguistic methods, but many messages are best conveyed linguistically.

If we agree that language serves pragmatics, then it makes sense to argue that pragmatics influences the organization of the other systems (Bruner, 1983). Going a step further, Bruner (1983) argued that language development is actually rooted in pragmatics.

Pragmatics

Jerome Bruner (1983) has pointed out that when we talk about pragmatics, we are really talking about social interaction. The child needs to develop some ideas about social interaction before she can use language effectively. Therefore, the development of pragmatics must begin prior to the onset of language.

Intentional Vocalizations. Somehow around 8 months of age, infants begin to use vocalizations intentionally to communicate with others (for example, Harding, 1982). Intentional communications are sounds or gestures that seem to serve a specific goal or purpose *for the baby.* Behaviorally, they are distinguished from nonintentional vocalizations because they are accompanied by gazing at the communicative target, such as the mother or father. In other words, these vocalizations are more clearly directed to a specific person.

By 8 months of age, then, the child has come to realize at least two things: she can influence the behavior of other people, and sound patterns are an effective means of influence.

Knowing that you can influence others' behavior implies that you have some understanding of cause and effect. This is a cognitive skill. Before infants can use vocalizations intentionally, they must understand that

1. They can "cause" things to happen.
2. Other people could behave independently of them.
3. They could develop goals that included affecting the behavior of others and devise means to achieve such goals.

This means that substage 5 sensorimotor functioning would be a prerequisite for intentional communication (Harding, 1982, 1983). The data support this argument (for example, Harding & Golinkoff, 1979; Harding, 1983). Thus, there does appear to be a cognitive prerequisite to pragmatic development.

Social Interaction and Intentionality.   Of course, we are left with the problem of how the infant would get from a cognitive understanding of causality to intentional vocalizations. Mother-infant interaction may be the key (Bruner, 1983; Harding, 1983). Mothers treat early vocalizations such as cries and babbles *as if* they were meaningful (Harding, 1983; Trevarthen, 1979). The baby makes a sound and the mother responds. Baby and mother even take turns, as if engaged in conversation. Yet mothers seem to know that such sounds are not really intentional communications (Harding, 1983). By their responsivity they may teach the baby that sounds have an effect on behavior. At the very least, the baby should learn that her sounds will elicit a response from her mother.

This experience might lead the baby to try sounds as one means of influencing maternal behavior. Since she is trying to affect her mother, she will look at her and then make a sound. Mothers seem to attribute special significance to this. The eye contact accompanying the sound gives *them* the impression that the baby is really trying to communicate. Thus, the mothers respond more vigorously to these sounds than they do to "nonintentional" vocalizations (Harding, 1983). This should further encourage the use of sounds to influence others.

This model sounds sensible and neat, but there is a problem. This model assumes that the mother responds to infant vocalizations. Middle-class American mothers do. Even during the neonatal period, mothers talk to their infants and engage them in conversationlike behavior (for example, turn taking). Not all mothers in all cultures do this.

Bambi Schieffelin and Elinor Ochs (1983) have reported that Kaluli mothers talk to their infants very little. (The Kaluli are a New Guinean tribe.) The Kaluli believe that young infants cannot understand anything. They see talking to an infant as a waste of time. In fact, direct mother-infant interaction does not occur frequently. The mothers do not even regularly look into their babies' eyes. Instead, the babies are carried so that they face away from the mother. This way, babies can see other people and observe the interactions among others. The baby is also indirectly involved in interaction. In talking to an older child, for example, the mother will speak for the baby, although her statements on the baby's behalf are not rooted in the infant's own behavior.

This is a very different pattern of mother-infant interaction than is commonly observed among middle-class American mothers. No true dyadic interaction among Kaluli mothers and their babies has been observed; yet Kaluli children do develop language normally (Schieffelin & Ochs, 1983). Thus, the dyadic interaction so emphasized in many current models is more a cultural phenomenon than a true "requirement" for language acquisition.

Both Kaluli and American babies are exposed to social interaction, albeit in different ways. This exposure probably contributes to the development of pragmatics. Specifics of how this contribution is made are not available (for example, Bruner, 1983; Harding, 1983). Much more research is needed on this issue.

Even if we knew how infants first come to use vocalizations intentionally, we would be left with another major question. In claiming that these intentional vocalizations form the basis of pragmatics, researchers are implying that these vocalizations can be used to convey a variety of messages. None of the research presented here thus far "proves" that assumption. For this we need to return to the research on protolanguage.

Protolanguage.   Michael Halliday (for example, 1975, 1979) has identified several functions that may be conveyed in protolanguage. (These functions are summarized in Table 9-1.) Sounds—which are not yet words—in conjunction with intonation patterns convey these messages. The messages range from functional (for example, getting things done) to more reflective (for example, interactional and personal) communications.

Pragmatic functions seem to appear, in association with sounds, prior to language; but are these really the roots of linguistic pragmatics? There is no simple way to draw relationships between prelinguistic and linguistic phenomena (for example, Bruner, 1983; Harding, 1983). However, we can ask whether the functions seen in protolanguage are the first to appear during early language use.

Early Language.   Although most children speak only single-word utterances initially, by combining these words (few though they may be) with various intona-

TABLE 9-1   Pragmatic Functions in Protolanguage

PRAGMATIC FUNCTION	DESCRIPTION
Instrumental	A demand for a specific object or "service." The requests involve objects but are "person-mediated." The "statement" is addressed to a particular person with the goal of obtaining that person's assistance.
Regulatory	A demand designed to regulate a person's behavior. No object is involved. The child might, for example, want a person to repeat an act (such as picking up the baby).
Interactional	An utterance intended to "encourage" social interaction. For example, the child may respond to his name being called. Or, he may "ask" a parent to look at or play with something together. This category includes "greetings."
Personal	The child is trying to convey something about his own attitude or interests. "Statements" of pleasure (the equivalent of "I like") and interest are included here.
Heuristic	This develops later than the previous four functions. It serves to organize experience by "asking for" labels for objects, people, and so on.

(Information, including examples, from Halliday, 1971).

tion patterns, children are able to convey a variety of meanings (for example, Dore, 1975). These meanings include labeling, repeating, answering, requesting action, requesting answers, calling, greeting, protesting, and practicing. Clearly, the functions Halliday (1975) identified in protolanguage are also in evidence here. However, not all functions are available at the onset of language. Indeed, the number of pragmatic functions expressed by children increases dramatically when the children are between 1 and 2 years of age (Dale, 1980).

Although improvement in pragmatic functioning seems to be a developmental trend, other facets of pragmatics seem more individualized. For example, there does not appear to be a universal sequence in the acquisition of pragmatic functions (Dale, 1980). In fact, a particular child might focus on one subset of pragmatic functions. So, one child might use language mainly to discuss objects (labeling, commenting on attributes of objects, requesting objects, and so on). Another might use language mainly for social interaction (requesting answers, greetings, attention-seeking, and so on) (Dore, 1975; Nelson, 1973a, 1981). These pragmatic preferences may be related to the type of maternal speech the child hears (Della Corte, Benedict & Klein, 1983).

The role of protolanguage in pragmatic development remains unclear. Halliday (1979) himself suggests that all children may not go through a protolanguage period. Also, we do not know whether individual differences in early language use are first evident during protolanguage. As in virtually all aspects of the transition from prelinguistic functioning to language, not enough research exists to answer these questions.

Halliday (1979) did, however, emphasize that during the protolanguage period, specific sound patterns conveyed meaning. Though these sound patterns were not actual words, he saw them as the precursor of semantic development (see also Harding, 1983).

Semantic Development

There can be no doubt that the environment plays a major role in the acquisition of first words. Otherwise why would some children speak French and others English? However, many theorists have argued that this is not the whole story. They (for example, Clark, 1978; Nelson, 1974; Nelson et al., 1978) have suggested that cognitive development is also crucial. These theorists have argued that early words are matched to existing concepts.

Concepts and Words.   Eve Clark (for example, 1973, 1978) suggested that each word is defined in terms of a "set" of features. This set is the concept underlying the word. According to Clark, infants' sets consist of only one or two features that are typically perceptually based. So, the features associated with *dog* might be four-leggedness and furriness. Because of this narrow definition, the child may have "extension" problems. Extension problems involve including too many (overextension) or too few (underextension) objects within the word's definition. That's why a child might call all four-legged, furry animals dogs (overextension). On the other hand, he may be willing to call only his dog or only familiar dogs dogs (under-extension). Eventually, as the child tries to communicate more effectively, his definition improves and becomes adultlike.

Katherine Nelson (for example, 1974; Nelson et al., 1978) has criticized this model. She wondered how the infant would pick out specific features of an object and then generalize them into a concept. She argued that being able to recognize the specific features seemed to presuppose an existing link (a concept?) among the objects. How could a child recognize, for example, that all dogs have four legs unless she already knew that they were all dogs?

Therefore, Nelson developed an alternative model to Clark's. She too argued that words were matched to existing or developing concepts in the early phases of language development. She believed, however, that the infant first identified an object as a whole rather than on the basis of its parts or features. By interacting with the object, the child comes to identify its functions. The function may be what the object does (for example, a dog barks). It may be what is done to an object (for example, a ball can be thrown). These functions serve as the "core" of the concept. Words may be matched to the concept at any point during its develop-ment (see Box 9-1). The relative maturity of the concept accounts for at least some of the extension problems. Eventually (at about 16-20 months of age), the child will be able to form concepts to fit a newly acquired word. We do this every time we look up or figure out the definition of a word we hear for the first time.

BOX 9-1 *EARLY VOCABULARY*

In the text, much is made of early vocabulary. The first words provide clues to the development of the pragmatic, syntactic (for example, McNeill, 1970), and semantic (for example, Clark, 1983) systems. They also provide information about how language is acquired (for example, through imitation or by "attaching" words to concepts). What are these first words? Is there really a set of early words that most (or at least many) acquire?

Apparently there is. First, most children's early words are primarily nouns. Helen Benedict (1978) found that 61% of the first fifty words produced by her subjects were names of either people or objects. The comparable figure in Katherine Nelson's (1973a) study was 65%.

What things do children name? Of course, most of them will have a word to refer to Mommy, Daddy, and themselves (this word is often *baby*). There are usually several words related to food (for example, *juice, milk, cookie, water*). Animal words, especially *dog* and *cat*, are popular. Toys are also named: usually *ball, block, book,* and *doll.* Body parts, particularly the parts of the face, are also frequently named (Clark, 1983).

Two points need to be made about these early object names. First, chil-dren often use some variant of the common word. So, a dog may be a *doggie* or a *bow-wow.* This effect is intensified by the children's limited pronuncia-tion skills (so, a dog may actually be a *wow*). Second, as noted in the text, it is not unusual for children's word meanings to differ from adults'. For example, the word *daddy* may be applied to all adult men (overextension), while the word *dog* might be applied only to the child's own pet (underextension).

Of course, not all early words are nouns. Most children have a word for *no* (though *yes* does not commonly appear in the first fifty words). They also regularly use greeting words such as *hi* or *bye* (Clark, 1983). Many of them can use language to play interactive games. For example, they commonly produce animal responses within the context of the game "What does the ____ say?" (Benedict, 1978).

We can, then, identify a relatively common set of first words. Both the Benedict and Nelson studies were done in the 1970s using primarily white, middle-class American children. If early vocabulary is to provide clues toward a universally applicable theory of language, we must be able to assume that early vocabulary items are universal. Historically, such an assumption seems justified. The vocabulary items listed in Benedict's and Nelson's studies are similar to those found in studies 50 years ago (Clark, 1983). The cross-cultural validity of the assumption cannot be evaluated, for virtually no cross-cultural research has been done on the specific vocabulary content of young children (Blount, 1981).

Both Clark's and Nelson's original models were based on available information concerning spoken words (language production). It was at least tacitly assumed that they would also apply to language comprehension: Concepts should begin to develop before the object name is comprehended. Recent evidence concerning language comprehension has led to questions concerning this view.

Comprehension vs. Production.   The assumption that comprehension and production development are similar leads to several corollary assumptions. First, as already noted, at least rudimentary concept development should predate comprehension. Second, comprehension development should be slower than production development because the link between word and object is first formed during comprehension. The comprehended word would then simply be produced. This leads to the third assumption. Early comprehension and production vocabularies ought to be similar.

None of these assumptions has been supported by the research. First, the composition of the production and comprehension vocabularies is quite different. Helen Benedict (1979) compared the first fifty words comprehended by eight children to the first fifty words they produced. The two vocabularies had comparable percentages of naming words, but the comprehension vocabulary included twice as many action words (for example, *give, kiss*). Modifiers (for example, *pretty, hot*) and personal-social words (for example, *hi, yes*) were considerably more common in the production vocabulary.

Second, comprehension develops at a faster rate than production. This means not simply that comprehension develops before production, but that new vocabulary words are added more quickly in comprehension than in production. Benedict

(1979) reported, for example, it took the children in her study an average of 2.69 months to enlarge their comprehension vocabularies from ten to fifty words. Yet it took 4.8 months for their production vocabularies to grow from ten to fifty words.

Finally, there is at best weak support for the contention that comprehension development has cognitive prerequisites. As noted in Chapter 7, several researchers have failed to find links between comprehension and object permanence (for example, Bates et al., 1979; Chapman, 1981; Smolak, 1982). Smolak (1982) also reported only a marginal relationship between categorization abilities and comprehension. Robin Chapman (1981) found that understanding of causality was related to early comprehension development. Others (Bates et al., 1979) have not found a causality-comprehension relationship.

These data have led some researchers (for example, Bates et al., 1979; Smolak, 1982) to conclude that cognition and language development, especially comprehension, may be less tied together than the Clark and Nelson models suggest. Bates, for example, suggested that language and cognition might share common roots in social interaction. However, she argued, they follow somewhat separate paths (Bates et al., 1979).

Katherine Nelson and her colleagues (Nelson et al., 1978) believed that the cognition-language link needs to be modified rather than dismissed. They thought that comprehension simply needs to rely on less-developed concepts than production does because the child can rely more on the context in comprehension than production. Anisfeld (1984) made a similar suggestion. The child, then, understands a word only in the presence of the object to which it refers. Research has supported this element of the argument. Young infants do seem to comprehend words only in association with the situation or object for which the word was first learned (for example, Chapman, 1981; Oviatt, 1980, 1982; Snyder, Bates & Bretherton, 1981). The child just acquiring comprehension may simply be attaching the label to an incipient concept. This means that the concept-matching model of vocabulary development is questionable but not dead.

When a child wishes to convey a message, he needs more than just individual words. The words must be organized in a certain manner to maximize effectiveness. This organization of words into sentences is known as syntax.

Syntax

When does the child first become aware of the grammar of the language—the syntax? We have already seen the considerable debate concerning syntax during the one-word-at-a-time period. Let's look more deeply into that debate.

One-word Utterances. Some time around the end of the first year, children usually begin to talk. Most of the time they produce only single-word utterances. David McNeill (for example, 1970) and others (for example, deLaguna, 1927; Greenfield & Smith, 1976) have argued that the children are encoding syntactic relations in these utterances. They suggested that such speech is "holophrastic"; that is, the relationships of an entire simple sentence or phrase are represented in one word. Other researchers (for example, Bloom, 1973; Sinclair de Zwart, 1973) have contended that the child does not have syntactic knowledge at this point.

To add to the foregoing arguments against the holophrastic position, developmental sequences during the one-word period also seem to argue against the existence of syntax. It appears that at the beginning of this period only one word is produced in a specific situation. A child drinking milk from a Mickey Mouse cup might say "milk." Later, though, the child produces several single-word utterances concerning one situation. The child might now say "milk," "cup," "Mickey," and "more." Each one of these utterances is distinct and has a separate intonation pattern (for example, Bloom, 1973). The utterances do not form a sentence because pauses between the words are too long for that (Branigan, 1979). Nonetheless, the utterances do appear to be closer to sentences than to the earlier single-word utterances in terms of intonation patterns (Branigan, 1979). These "successive single-word utterances," then, appear to be an intermediary phase between no encoding of syntax and a fluent, clear-cut use of syntax (for example, Bloom, 1973; Branigan, 1979).

Does this mean that early single-word utterances are simply single-word comments about a situation or event (Bloom, 1973)? Such a position seems too extreme. Think of a young child pointing to a bowl of apples and saying "apple." Her mother looks at her and answers, "Yes, that's a bowl of apples." The child repeats, more forcefully, "apple." The mother replies, "Yes, those are apples." Again, the child, now on the verge of tears, says "apple." Finally, the mother answers, "Oh, you want an apple?" The child, calming down, says "apple."

Right from the beginning of this exchange, the child seems to be trying to do more than just say "apple." Furthermore, the meaning of the word seems to change a bit during the exchange. Initially, "apple" seems to mean "I want an apple." In the last child utterance, though, the word *apple* seems to substitute for a *yes* response to the mother's question. The different messages are conveyed by combining the word with specific intonation patterns, and often with gestures (for example, Dore, 1975). By doing this, the child is able to convey a relatively complex thought without using or even understanding syntax. John Dore (1975) has labeled such utterances *speech acts*. He suggested that speech acts consisted of two components: the "rudimentary referring expression," that is, the word itself, and the "primitive force," which is usually intonation. The force is used to convey the specific meaning of the word. It is, in a sense, the pragmatic element of the utterance.

Dore's position is less extreme than either Bloom's or McNeill's. It enables us to see how a child might convey a sentencelike thought. Yet it does not require any understanding of complex syntactic relations. It has gained considerable popularity in recent years because of this (for example, Bruner, 1983). It does, however, leave us with the question of how syntax develops. In recent years, two major theoretical models have been proposed. One relies on cognitive roots. The other views syntax as growing out of semantics.

Cognitive and Syntax.   This model, based on Piaget's (for example, 1962) work, suggests that syntax reflects cognition (for example, Sinclair de Zwart, 1973). The infant first cognitively separates the components of an event. He comes to understand, for example, that the person rolling the ball is separate from the ball itself. He can distinguish the agent, or actor, from the action and the action from the recipient, or target, of the action. These component parts are reflected in language. The actor becomes the subject of the sentence. The action is represented as the verb. The target is represented as the verb's object.

The question, as always, is how the child makes the cognitive-linguistic links. How does he get from actor to subject? Cognitive theorists, like Sinclair de Zwart, did not provide the answer to this question. This has led many theorists to suggest that cognition alone is not the basis for syntax. Rather, syntax, they arued, grows out of semantics.

Syntax and Semantics.   A rudimentary semantic system exists by the time the first words appear. These first words do not, however, appear to be organized syntactically. Sometime between 18 and 24 months of age most children will begin to produce two-word sentences. It is clear that these sentences are guided by rules (for example, Braine, 1976). The children do not produce random combinations; they do not say things like "the more" or "more fall." Do the rules guiding these productions reflect knowledge of syntax or of semantics?

How important and real is the distinction between syntactic and semantic categories? Syntactic categories are considerably more abstract and complex than semantic categories. Semantic categories include agents, patients (recipients of an action), locations (for example, the word *table* in the statement *book table*), and modified objects (for example, the word *book* in the statement *red book*). It is entirely possible that words included in all these categories are nouns. The syntax-category noun, then, is diverse. Its definition is broader and less concrete than any of the aforementioned semantic categories. It is also less clearly tied to sensori-motor cognitive development (see earlier discussion of Sinclair de Zwart's work) than are the semantic categories.

There is widespread agreement that the early multiword utterances are organized on the basis of semantic relations (Bloom, 1970; Brown, 1973; Maratsos, 1983). This means that children organize and order words depending on what the words mean in that particular situation. Table 9-2 exemplifies several semantic relations commonly found in early multiword utterances.

It is probably not until 3-4 years of age that children have truly syntactic categories (Maratsos, 1983). Although development of these categories falls outside the realm of this book, it should be noted that many theorists believe that the semantic categories form the core of the syntactic categories. Other theorists believe that the semantic categories are somewhat less central in developing syntax (Maratsos, 1983). Nonetheless, most theorists think a relationship exists between semantics and syntax.

TABLE 9-2 Some Semantic Relations Encoded in Early Two-word Utterances

SEMANTIC RELATION	DEFINITION	EXAMPLE
Agent-Action	Encodes the "cause" of the action and the action itself	Car go; Mommy push
Action-Object	Encodes the action and the person who "receives" that action	Hit mommy; Push Billy
Entity-Locative	Encodes an object (or person) and its location	Lady home; Baby talk
Possessor-Possession	Encodes "owner" and owner's possession	Daddy chair; Mommy shoe
Entity-Attribute	Describes a characteristic of a thing	Little dog; hot soup
Demonstrative-Entity	Specifies which particular object is being discussed	That chair; this dog

(Derived from Brown, 1973).

Maternal Speech and Syntax.   Although a link may exist between syntax and semantics, they are clearly distinguishable systems. One indicator of this is the role of maternal speech in syntax and in semantics. Maternal speech obviously plays a major role in semantic development, at least in terms of vocabulary acquisition. The role of maternal speech in syntax acquisition is less clear.

Overall, studies have found few relationships between syntactic construction in maternal speech and child syntax development (for example, Barnes et al., 1983; Brown, 1973; Gleitman, Newport & Gleitman, 1984; Newport, Gleitman & Gleitman, 1977; Smolak & Weinraub, 1983). Of course, there are exceptions to this trend (for example, Furrow, Nelson & Benedict, 1979; Moerk, 1980). However, these studies have been roundly criticized and have not been replicated (for example, Gleitman, Newport & Gleitman, 1984; Pinker, 1981).

It is possible that the failure to find links between maternal speech and children's grammar is attributable to methodological problems. Most notably, the majority of these studies observed white, middle-class American mothers, who are all quite similar in their syntax use. Perhaps with more linguistically diverse mothers relationships would emerge (Smolak & Weinraub, 1983; Wells, 1980). It is premature to dismiss maternal speech completely as a major factor in syntax development. However, current evidence suggests that maternal speech plays only a small role in syntax development.

Pragmatics, Semantics, and Syntax.   We have seen that pragmatics, semantics, and syntax seem to be related linguistic systems. Pragmatics seems to contribute to the development of semantics. Semantics seems to contribute to the development of syntax. To say that one system "grew" exclusively from the other would be an oversimplification. We have seen, for example, that each system has its own links to cognitive development. Furthermore, maternal speech may play a different role in the development of each system.

The three systems also appear at different times. Of the three, pragmatics seems most clearly rooted in prelinguistic development. True syntax, on the other hand, may not appear until a child is 3 or 4 years of age. Of course, children show considerable individual differences in the timing of language development. They may also show individual differences in language acquisition strategies. These differences have received some attention in the preceding discussions. Let's now take a closer look at them.

INDIVIDUAL DIFFERENCES IN LANGUAGE ACQUISITION

You would not have to observe very many children before noticing that the rate of language development can vary dramatically. About 5% of all 16-month-olds, for example, produce two-word utterances. At just under 21 months of age, half of the children produce two-word utterances. It is not until they reach 30 months of age that 95% of the children will be using two-word utterances (Bayley, 1969).

Rate is not the only area of language acquisition where individual differences can be observed. Children also display different styles or strategies in developing language (Nelson, 1981). Some children seem to focus on nouns. Others emphasize social expressions. Both rate and style differences have received some research attention.

Rate

A variety of reasons explain why one child might develop language more quickly than another. Physiological maturity might play a role. Some children may be genetically predisposed to quicker language development. Certain maternal speech styles might also encourage language acquisition. Indeed, all three factors have been implicated as causes of differential rates.

Maturity. Two types of evidence suggest that maturation rate may also play a role. First, girls as a group develop language more quickly than do boys (for example, Maccoby & Jacklin, 1974; Schachter et al., 1978). At birth, girls are physiologically more mature than boys (see Chapter 3), and girls continue to mature more quickly through puberty. Some authors have suggested that this differential maturation rate may affect brain functioning. More specifically, children who mature quickly may develop the brain specialization needed for language more quickly. In other words, the localization of language in the left hemisphere may take place sooner in these children (for example, Waber, 1977).

Although girls generally mature more quickly than boys, gender is not the sole determinant of maturation rate. Individual boys may mature more quickly than certain girls. Given what we know about growth at puberty, it is possible that maturation rate is influenced by genetics. Although the three-way link between genetics, maturation, and language has not been investigated, current evidence suggests that genetics may play a role in language.

Genetics.   The role of genetics in language development has not received much attention. However, research with adopted children indicates that the cognitive abilities of the birth mother, but not of the adoptive mother, are significantly related to infant language development (Hardy-Brown, Plomin & DeFries, 1981). For example, the memory skills of the birth mothers are positively related to the 12-month-olds' use of vocal imitation, vocal signals, and production vocabulary. The researchers hypothesized that the memory-language link is based on the ability to use mental representation. The birth mothers' general cognitive functioning is also significantly related to infant language. However, birth mothers' vocabulary is not related to infant language (Hardy-Brown, Plomin & DeFries, 1981).

These data suggest a genetic component in language. The component seems to be in terms of general cognitive, rather than specifically linguistic, skills. This does not mean that the environment does not affect the rate of language acquisition. Indeed, the same study (Hardy-Brown, Plomin & DeFries, 1981) found that adoptive mothers who imitated their babies' vocalizations had babies with better language skills. As we are about to see, this is not an unusual finding.

Environment.   Recall that specific elements of maternal syntax appear to be only minimally related to the rate of language acquisition. However, syntax is only one component of maternal speech. It is possible that other components do have an impact on the rate of child language development.

Discourse features of maternal speech do seem to be related to rate of child language acquisition. Discourse features refer to the nature of the mother's conversational turn. Does she repeat some or all of what she said in her previous turn? Does she repeat some or all of what the baby just said? Is her statement related in any way to the baby's?

Several investigators have reported that the relatedness of maternal speech to infant speech is an important influence. The more contingent the mother's statements are on the baby's, the faster the rate of language acquisition (for example, Barnes et al., 1983; Cross, 1978; Hardy-Brown, Plomin & DeFries, 1981; Smolak & Weinraub, 1983; Wells, 1980). In most of these studies, the "contingent responses" took the form of partial or complete imitations of the child's statements. Not all studies have found such relationships, however. Some studies, for example, have actually reported negative relationships between maternal imitations and child language development (for example, Newport, Gleitman & Gleitman, 1977; Gleitman, Newport & Gleitman, 1984).

Other discourse features that might be related to language acquisition rate are amount and complexity of maternal speech. Mothers with "quick learning" children do seem to address more speech to their children (for example, Smolak & Weinraub, 1983; Wells, 1980). The relationship between complexity and child language is less straightforward. It does seem to be important to talk "on the child's level." Too much complexity overwhelms the child's processing capabilities, resulting in slower acquisition (for example, Gleitman, Newport & Gleitman, 1984). On the other hand, the mother or adult speaker needs to provide some challenge to the child. Otherwise, the child would never move beyond her present level of functioning. Thus, introducing new words and constructions at a moderate pace may be important also. The child, then, needs exposure to moderately complex language for optimal acquisition (Gleitman, Newport & Gleitman, 1984).

Although we can claim that maternal speech affects the rate of language development, we have no evidence that certain forms of maternal speech are necessary for language development (think of the Kaluli children). We also have no evidence that a certain form of maternal speech guarantees rapid acquisition. Many other factors (for example, maturation) may also influence the rate of language acquisition. One such factor is the language-learning strategy adopted by the child.

Strategies of Language Acquisition

In "normal" language development children's first utterances are single words. Later, children produce two-word utterances. This is actually the sequence for the majority of children. A sizable minority of children, however, approach language learning with a different strategy (for example, Nelson, 1981). They begin by producing short, socially oriented phrases. This makes their speech less intelligible. It also means that their vocabularies will be smaller, since there are fewer social phrases than object names. This makes their rate of language development appear to be slower.

The acquisition style marked by a predominance of nouns is the *referential* style. The alternative style, focusing on social interaction, is the *expressive* strategy (Nelson 1973a). Both end in essentially normal levels of language functioning well before the children start school (Nelson, 1981).

One possible source of this style difference is maternal speech (Della Corte, Benedict & Klein, 1983; Lieven, 1978). The strategies may also be rooted in a more general symbol use style (Bates et al., 1979). Play styles provide an example of this (Wolf & Gardner, 1979). Some children do not like to use imaginary objects in their play; they want real objects. These object-oriented, reality-tied children show the referential, or object-oriented, strategy. Other children seem to thrive on imaginary play. In fact, they spontaneously introduce imaginary objects and people into their play. These children, who seem to care less about the realistic nature of objects, typically show the expressive language strategy (Wolf & Gardner, 1979).

To summarize, then, rate and pattern of language acquisition are related. Both may be affected by maternal speech patterns. Genetics and maturation may also play a role in rate of development. In addition, cognitive style may affect language acquisition style. The range of influences gives us an idea of the complexity of the language acquisition task. Although this complexity makes it difficult to provide parents with a simple formula for facilitating language development, in the final section of this chapter we explore some suggestions for facilitating language development in normal and special children.

FACILITATING LANGUAGE DEVELOPMENT

Language acquisition is of paramount concern to most parents (see Box 9-2). For several reasons few events are as eagerly awaited as the first word. We often use language, both formally and informally, to gauge intelligence. The onset of language can also make child care an easier task. When a child can talk, the parents no longer have to guess what the child wants. So, parents often want to know what they can do to encourage language development.

BOX 9-2   *DOES MY CHILD HAVE A LANGUAGE DISORDER?*

As has been noted, parents anxiously await their child's first words. They are concerned if the words do not come soon enough or are too difficult to understand or if the vocabulary does not grow quickly enough.

In one way, parents are justified in their concerns. Language is an important skill in and of itself. It is also central to cognitive, social, and personality development. In addition, language problems during infancy do predict later language problems. A child whose language is noticeably lagging at 2.5 years, for example, is more likely than other children to develop language problems later on (Zelazo, Kearsley & Ungerer, 1984).

On the other hand, parents of children under 2 years of age often over-react to what they perceive as language problems because they do not really know what early language development is like. Several normal developmental phenomena occur during the first 2 years of life that parents misinterpret as indicative of problems. These include the following:

1. *Vocabulary size.* A normal vocabulary in a child of 18 months consists of 10-20 words. By 24 months, this increases to 50-250 words (Zelazo, Kearsley & Ungerer, 1984). Note the wide range. This is why parents often believe that a 50- or 60-word vocabulary in a 2-year-old is "slow." Every parent seems to know a child with a 200-250 word vocabulary. This makes their own child seem "slow."

2. *Sentence use.* Most children begin to combine two words by the time they are 2 years of age. Three-word sentences appear when children are around 2.5 years of age (Zelazo, Kearsley & Ungerer, 1984). Keep in mind that the appearance of sentences relies to some extent on the child's language acquisition style (see text). By the way, grammar is very limited at this time. The 2-year-old uses few, if any, word endings (marking plural, past tense, and so on). Again, many parents seem to expect more. They think that 2-year-olds should truly "carry on conversations." Although 2-year-olds can communicate quite well, their sentences are still clearly at the "novice level."

3. *Pronunciation.* Children have pronunciation problems well into the school years (Zelazo, Kearsley & Ungerer, 1984). It is common for very young children (under 2 years of age) to drop the beginning or end of words. "Cookie Monster," for example, was simply "kee" to my daughter. Many children call a ball just "ba." Normally, all vowel sounds are not intelligible until the child is 2.5 years of age. Indeed, even

7-year-olds have trouble with certain consonant sounds (for example, *tw, dw, bl, thr*) (Zelazo, Kearsley & Ungerer, 1984). It is therefore normal for a 2-year-old to be difficult to understand, especially in terms of consonants and combinations of consonants.

4. *Stuttering.* Many toddlers stutter, especially when upset or excited. This differs from "problem stuttering" in that it is not usually restricted to one or two particular sounds. Again, such stuttering is not unusual, and there is little need for concern unless the problem worsens as time goes on. Note, though, that this "developmental stuttering" does not usually start until language development is well under way, when the child is 2-4 years of age. So, if a child does not stutter initially but does stutter at 2 years of age, the condition may well be this *nonproblem*, or developmental, stuttering. If the stuttering continues unabated past age 5, a specialist should be consulted.

If a child does appear to be language delayed by these standards, certain things should be done. First, the child's hearing should be tested. If the baby's hearing is normal, then the parent should determine whether the cause is simply a language delay or generally delayed development. Motor, social, and cognitive development can be evaluated. If all or much of development is delayed, then a special preschool program becomes a viable option.

If the problem is restricted to language, a special preschool program may also be helpful. Sometimes the problem can be corrected at home, though. Many "slow talkers" simply don't talk because they don't want to or don't have to. Perhaps older siblings talk for them, or they can get what they want by just pointing and whinning. In such cases, modifying the family interactions and the child's behavior may alleviate the problems (see Zelazo, Kearsley & Ungerer, 1984 for some specific ideas about how to do this).

Normal Children

Assuming that the child is exposed to language, the normal child will eventually talk. As we have seen, no specific environment is required for language development. The noninteractive mode of the Kaluli tribe seems as adequate as the heavily interactive middle-class American style (Schieffelin & Ochs, 1983).

However, certain forms of parental speech may speed up the process. Since many of these have been mentioned earlier, they are just summarized here. First, the more langue the child hears, the better (for example, Smolak & Weinraub, 1983; Wells, 1980). Whether the language has to be directed to the child to be effective is unclear (think, again, of the Kalulis), but some evidence suggests that the more related the mother's speech is to the child's speech, the better (for example, Cross, 1978; Smolak & Weinraub, 1983).

In addition, giving the child the opportunity to talk seems important. Using questions directed toward the child seems to help (for example, Barnes, Gottfried & Wells, 1983; Smolak & Weinraub, 1983). The mother's use of yes-no questions seems to encourage language development in young children (for example, Gleitman, Newport & Gleitman, 1984), perhaps because the yes-no questions encourage linguistic processing. On the other hand, more open-ended questions are more likely to get a response (Olsen-Fulero & Conforti, 1983). These types of questions may involve a child more in the conversation and thus allow him to practice and refine his language skills.

Aspects of maternal speech that encourage a referential style, such as the infrequent use of directives, are also helpful (for example, Della Corte, Benedict & Klein, 1983). Remember, the referential style is associated with a faster rate of development. Also remember, however, that referential and expressive children both ultimately end up with adequate language.

Factors other than maternal speech affect language development. Katherine Nelson (1973a), for example, reported that children who watched more television during their first 18 months of life had slower language development than those who watched less television during the same time. The show most frequently watched by these children was "Sesame Street." This may seem counterintuitive. After all, the show is designed to encourage language as well as other skills. Possibly, the early viewing interfered with language because it reduced direct mother-infant interaction. The television may not provide the cues linking objects and words that mothers provide. An alternative explanation is that mothers who put their infants in front of the television to watch "Sesame Street" may not be as sensitive to their children as other mothers are to theirs. The show *is* designed for children considerably older than 18 months of age. Perhaps these mothers cannot judge the needs of their children well (Nelson, 1973a). If this is true, these mothers might not, for example, be able to achieve that "moderate complexity" of speech that seems to facilitate language acquisition (for example, Gleitman, Newport & Gleitman, 1984).

Experiences outside of the home also seem to encourage language development (Nelson, 1973a). It may be that outings provide additional social interactions that allow the baby to practice his growing language skills (or the prerequisite skills). It may be that the outings give the mother and baby more to talk about.

On the other hand, the presence of siblings seems to slow language development. This may be because the mother simply does not have time to interact with later-borns as much as with a first-born. It may be that the older children talk for the younger ones. Obviously, parents cannot get rid of older siblings. However, the effects may be mediated by ensuring that the parents get some opportunity for one-on-one interactions with the younger child. The parents can also monitor older siblings to make sure that the younger one has the opportunity to talk.

Overall, then, several factors *may* facilitate language acquisition in normal children, but they do not form any clear-cut training program. Indeed, no clear need for direct language training is evident. In addition, there is no strong evidence suggesting that language training programs are helpful. Let's see if this is also the case with deaf children.

Deaf Children

Evaluating hearing in infants is very difficult. It can be done, but it is not routinely done until children are close to school age. Because of this, many deaf and hard-of-hearing children are not diagnosed until the toddler years or later. Obviously, this means their language development is usually delayed. Indeed, it is often the delayed language that first leads to the hearing evaluation.

Once their hearing problem has been identified, deaf children can learn language. In fact, the developmental progression in sign language is not remarkably different from that in spoken language. Signs will, for example, be spontaneously combined into short sentences (for example, Goldin-Meadow & Feldman, 1977). However, this type of relatively normal (in terms of rate and pattern) language acquisition is found only in children who learn some form of sign language.

Traditionally, many educators argued that deaf children should not learn sign language. They contended that the children would "fit in" better if they learned to speak. The appeal of this arrangment to a frustrated, disappointed parent is evident. However, not all parents are frustrated or disappointed by their child's deafness. Deaf parents, of course, are often more able to accept their child's deafness (Kopp & Krakow, 1982). They are thus more willing to teach their children to use sign language. Such children may have better language skills, higher educational attainment, and better personal adjustment than other deaf children (for example, Maxwell, 1983).

A deaf child can learn numerous sign systems (for example, Maxwell, 1983). Which sign system a child learns first does not seem to be important. Learning one sign system does not appear to preclude learning another. In fact, contrary to the fear of earlier educators, learning signs does not interfere with acquiring spoken language. In fact, signing children are somewhat *more* likely than other deaf children to learn to speak (Maxwell, 1983).

The key to language training in deaf children, then, appears to be the introduction of a manually based language. Indeed, if such a system is used, real language training is no more necessary than with hearing children. Certainly a child must be "taught" the signs, but this is no different from a hearing child learning vocabulary words. The biggest barrier to language learning among deaf children does not seem to be an inherent language disability. Rather, the parents' inability to accept the child's deafness or to use sign language is the most likely obstacle to language development.

SUMMARY

Language is a system in which symbols stand in for objects, people, events, and ideas. It is organized on a variety of levels, including pragmatics, syntax, semantics, and phonology. It is used for communication and mental representation.

Many factors contribute to language development. There do appear to be cognitive prerequisites. However, language is much more than simply a reflection of cognition. Social interaction also plays a role in acquiring general skills such as turn taking, as well as specific skills such as vocabulary acquisition.

Although remarkable advances in language functioning take place during a child's first two years of life, these accomplishments are attained at very different rates in different children. Again, a variety of factors affect the rate of acquisition. Style of acquisition also varies from child to child. Typically, however, neither the rate nor style of acquisition has implications for the long-term outcome.

Despite the incredible complexity of the language-learning task, language does not seem to require much if any direct training in normal children. Even deaf children can acquire language with little more training than hearing children need provided that the deaf child is learning a manual language.

The ability to understand and produce language provides the child with a powerful learning tool. Among other things, it helps the child to learn about herself and about social roles (Olsen-Fulero & Conforti, 1983). The acquisition of knowledge concerning self and social roles is the focus of the next chapter.

10

Personality and Social Development

Some time ago a friend of mine became a father for the first time. He was totally enthralled with his daughter. I hadn't seen him for several months (his daughter was now 9 months old). So, when I ran into him, I asked about her. He replied, "Oh, she's great. She's really starting to become a person now."

What my friend meant was that his little girl was more clearly an individual. She had her own moods, reactions, and preferences. He also meant that she was becoming more "human": She was starting to show some truly social behaviors, such as carrying on "conversations."

These issues of individuality and social skills are the focus of this chapter. At first glance, these may seem like opposing topics. Yet, they are clearly related. Our individual personalities influence our social interactions, and our social interactions influence our personalities. Self-esteem, for example, is an important component of a personality. People with poor self-esteem behave differently in social interactions than those with strong self-esteem: They may be aggressive or disruptive in order to gain attention, or they may withdraw. On the other hand, social interactions may influence self-esteem. Being labeled a failure or a disappointment may lower self-esteem. A seeming lack of parental interest or low responsivity by the parents might contribute to the development of low self-esteem. Thus, personality and social interactions are reciprocal forces in development.

It is not absolutely clear developmentally that personality predates social interactions, or vice-versa. Some evidence does indicate that certain elements of personality, particularly temperament, may appear very early in infancy. In fact, they may be present at birth (see Chapter 3). Because of these findings we will begin with a discussion of infant temperament.

TEMPERAMENT

Defining Temperament

The concept of temperament was introduced in Chapter 3. At that point, temperament was defined as one's characteristic way of reacting to the environment (Thomas et al., 1970). The emphasis, then, is on individual behavioral styles (Thomas & Chess, 1980), which are assumed to be somewhat consistent across time and situations.

This is a rather broad definition of temperament. As noted in Chapter 3, researchers have not agreed on a single, widely accepted definition of temperament. Some definitions include causal factors. Arnold Buss and Robert Plomin's (1975) definition, for example, included that temperament must be genetically rooted and have some evolutionary, or adaptive, purpose. Alexander Thomas and Stella Chess (1977), in contrast, tried to avoid including a specific etiology in their definition. Such definitional differences imply that researchers do not always agree as to what behaviors constitute temperament. They also, of course, disagree on how to measure temperament (see Hubert et al., 1982, for a review.) Because of such conflicts, interpretations of the temperament research must be made cautiously.

Describing Temperament

The classic descriptions of infant temperament come from the work of Thomas and Chess (for example, Thomas, Chess & Birch, 1970; Thomas & Chess, 1977; Thomas & Chess, 1980), who identified nine categories of temperament. These categories are defined in Table 10-1.

These categories were used to identify three general types of babies: "easy," "slow-to-warm," and "difficult" temperaments. These types are also defined in Table 10-1 in relation to the nine categories.

Several points need to be made about these types. First, babies can be grouped into one type or the other as early as 2 or 3 months of age (for example, Thomas, Chess & Birch, 1970). (Note that Thomas, Chess, and Birch did not study newborns.) This suggests that the patterns are apparent very early and may even be innate. Second, not all babies fit neatly into the typology. In the original study, 40% of the babies were classified as easy, 15% as slow-to-warm, and 10% as difficult. This means that 35% of the babies they studied could not be categorized. Instead, these babies showed a mixture of traits.

TABLE 10-1 Typology of Infant Temperament

	TYPES OF TEMPERAMENT		
CHARACTERISTIC	EASY	SLOW-TO-WARM	DIFFICULT
Activity Level (ratio of active to inactive periods)	Can vary	Low to moderate	Can vary
Rhythmicity (regularity of body functions)	Regular body functions	Variable body functions	Irregular body functions
Distractibility (effectiveness of extraneous events in affecting child's behavior)	Variable	Variable	Variable
Approach or Withdrawal (initial reaction to novel object or person)	Approach	Partial withdrawal	Withdrawal
Adaptability (response to environmental changes)	Adapts easily	Adapts slowly	Adapts slowly
Attention Span and Persistence (time spent on an activity and ability to maintain attention in the face of distractions)	High or low	High or low	High or low
Intensity of Reaction (response's energy level)	Low or mild	Mild	Intense
Threshold of Responsiveness (level of stimulation needed to elicit a response)	High or low	High or low	High or low
Quality of Mood (ratio of pleasant to unpleasant behavior)	General positive	Slightly negative	Negative

(Adapted from Thomas, A., Chess, S., & Birch, H. (1970). The origin of personality. *Scientific American, 223,* 102-9. Also from Thomas, A., & Chess, S. (1977). *Temperament and development.* New York: Brunner/Mazel).

Since theorists do not agree on a definition of temperament, it is not surprising that they also disagree on descriptions of temperament. For example, Buss and Plomin (1975) listed four temperament dimensions (as opposed to Thomas, Chess, and Birch's nine). These dimensions are emotionality (fear, anger, distress, and so on), activity, sociability (interest in people), and impulsivity (how long it takes to react to a person or event). Mary Rothbart and Douglas Derryberry (1981) presented yet another description. They broadly divided temperament into reactivity and self-regulation factors. The reactivity factor included chracteristics that mark the individual's reaction to events. This might include motoric reactions such as activity or affective reactions such as positive or negative mood. The self-regulation factor refers to the baby's ability to control or moderate the reactivity. This includes things like selective attention.

Of course, these descriptions overlap somewhat. All the theorists include activity level and emotional reactions as components of temperament. They also all have characteristics that reflect the infant's style of social interaction. Yet, there are also important differences among the descriptions. These descriptive differences reflect the theorists' disagreements concerning the determinants of temperament.

Determinants of Temperament

Most of the major theorists assume that temperament is present at birth (for example, Buss & Plomin, 1975; Rothbart & Derryberry, 1981; Thomas & Chess, 1977). Many people will automatically equate "present at birth" with "genetically determined." As we saw in Chapter 2, this assumption is often erroneous. Characteristics evident in a neonate may be attributable to genetic influences, and evidence suggests that identical twins are more similar in temperament than fraternal twins (Torgersen, 1981). Although the temperament dimensions of sociability, emotionality, and activity appear to be particularly heavily influenced by genetics (Goldsmith, 1983), newborn characteristics may also be due to prenatal (for example, exposure to alcohol) or perinatal (for example, exposure to anesthesia or anoxia) influences. Thus, for example, children born to alcoholic mothers seem to be more irritable and have more disrupted sleep patterns than children born to nonalcoholic mothers (for example, Abel, 1984; Rosett & Sander, 1979). The characteristics may even reflect "constitutional" differences among children. All these potential factors are represented in current conceptualizations of the origins of temperament.

At one extreme, we have Buss and Plomin's (1975) theory. In defining temperament, they required that temperament characteristics be inheritable. In other words, for Buss and Plomin, temperament is by definition genetically determined. They also assumed that temperament characteristics are stable. Finally, they argued that temperament has evolutionary origins. The evolutionary component is included in two ways. First, the temperament characteristic must be adaptive; it must serve some survival purpose. Second, temperament characteristics may well be evident in nonhuman animals.

Buss and Plomin emphasized genetic and evolutionary causes, but they did not completely ignore environmental influences. They suggested that the child's temperament influences parental behavior. The effect of such parental behavior is a function of the child's temperament. Similarly, the likelihood of a child imitating parental behavior is a function of the child's temperament. More specifically, children are more likely to imitate parents who share the child's temperament characteristics. In this manner, the child's temperament interacts with the environment, but the environment does not alter the child's temperament.

Rothbart and Derryberry (1981) shared Buss and Plomin's view that temperament is basically biologically determined. However, they defined temperament as being constitutionally determined. Constitution refers to the "relatively enduring biological makeup of the organism" (Rothbart & Derryberry, 1981, p. 37). This biological makeup is "influenced over time by heredity, maturation, and experience" (Rothbart & Derryberry, 1981, p. 37).

How might this biological makeup determine temperament? Recall that Rothbart and Derryberry's definition of temperament focused on reactivity and self-regulation. It could be hypothesized that individual nervous systems have different reactions to stimulation. Some people seem more readily able to perceive sound, light, or touch. How many times have you heard someone say, "I have a high pain threshold" or "I just don't tolerate drugs well?" Such differences may well be attributable to biological makeup. These differences would, of course, affect behavior, especially reactivity and self-regulation. By the way, this model is consistent with several adult models of temperament, particularly that of Hans Eysenck (for example, 1967). Rothbart and Derryberry's model is overwhelmingly biological in nature. They assigned virtually no role to environmental (or parental) influences on the child's temperament.

Thomas and Chess (for example, 1977) also saw biology as an important determinant of temperament. They recognized a "sizable" genetic component. They also discussed prenatal and perinatal influences. They noted, for example, the possible adverse effects of maternal anxiety during pregnancy on the infant's temperament. Finally, in the biological realm, Thomas and Chess suggested that differences in biochemical, endocrine, perceptual, and other physiological systems might influence temperament. This is, of course, consistent with Rothbart and Derryberry's view.

However, Thomas and Chess (1977, 1980) do not view temperament characteristics or their expression as being solely or even primarily biologically determined. They argued that temperament will only be stable as long as environmental influences are stable. In other words, the environment can alter a child's temperament, or at least its expression.

The importance of biological and environmental influences on temperament is nicely demonstrated in a study by Denise Daniels and Robert Plomin (1985). They examined shyness—one aspect of sociability—in adopted infants. They found that the shyer and less sociable the adoptive mother (who provided environmental but no genetic influences), the shyer the child at both 12 and 24 months of age. They also found that the less sociable the birth mother (who provided genetic but no environmental influence), the shyer the child at 24 months. These data suggest that both environment and heredity contribute to the development of shyness in infants and toddlers.

The interplay of environment and biology in determining temperament raises another interesting question. How stable is temperament?

Stability

Theories.   Temperament is of interest to us because we assume that it represents a more or less stable component of personality functioning. Ideally, infant temperament should provide us with clues concerning future development. It is also frequently assumed that as a "behavioral style," temperament will be displayed consistently across situations. These attitudes are often reflected in parents' statements about their children. They might say, "Oh, he was always a fussy eater" or "It always takes her a while to get used to new people." They are startled by instability. A friend of mine once told me that she was surprised how quickly her son took to me. "He never likes new people right away. I just don't understand it. You must really have a way with kids," she told me.

Despite such parental assumptions, theorists actually have quite disparate views on the stability of infant temperament. Buss and Plomin (1975), for example, argued that temperament is by definition stable. A child who is excitable in one situation (for example, a fear-provoking situation) will also be excitable in another, very different situation (for example, a joy-provoking event). Because they view temperament as genetically determined, Buss and Plomin also argued that temperament would by definition be stable across an individual's life.

This position has been criticized as too narrow. Joseph Campos and his colleagues (Campos et al., 1983) believed that different emotional reactions ought to be expected in different situations. A child might, for example, be very passive in the face of a frightening situation but very excitable in a pleasurable setting. There has also been disagreement concerning temporal stability. Rothbart and Derryberry (1981), for example, have suggested that we ought to expect maturational and experiential changes in temperament. Both reactivity and self-regulation are subject to such developmental changes. The precise nature of these changes remains undefined.

Thomas and Chess (for example, 1977, 1980; Thomas et al., 1970) also believed that temperament characteristics would be reflected differently at various ages though the characteristics themselves would remain stable (see Table 10-2). However, Thomas and Chess did not suggest that such stability is automatic. They believed that the environment strongly influences the nature and expression of temperament. To them, the basic question was how well the environment and the child's temperament "fit" together. If there was a "good fit," any child would be

TABLE 10-2   Expression of Temperament Characteristics at Different Ages

	EXPRESSION AT AGE			
CHARACTERISTIC	2 MONTHS	1 YEAR	2 YEARS	5 YEARS
Activity Level: High	Wiggles during diaper changes	Get into things; eats quickly	Climbs on furniture	Always runs; gets up during meals

Rhythmicity: Irregular	Wakes at different times each day; eats different amounts each day	Slow to go to sleep	Naps at different times each day; no pattern to bowel movements	Food intake and timing of bowel movements varies
Distractibility: Not Distractible	Will not stop crying during diaper changing	Will not be comforted by substitute toy	Screams if not given a desired object	Ignores mother when engaged in favorite game
Approach/Withdrawal: Positive	Has always liked bottle	Approaches strangers easily	Slept well first time overnight at grandparents	Went into school building without hesitation
Adaptability: Not Adaptive	Resists diaper changing	Keeps refusing foods that have been offered before	Cries and screams each time hair is cut	Bounces on bed despite spankings
Attention Span and Persistence: Long	Repeatedly rejects water if wants milk	Plays alone in playpen for over an hour	Works on puzzle until it is done	Spends over an hour reading a book
Intensity of Reaction: Mild	Whimpers rather than cries when hungry	Doesn't fuss much when shirt is pulled over head	When a child hits her, does not hit back	Drops eyes and is silent when parent says no
Threshold of Responsiveness: High	Not startled easily by noises	Eats food he likes even if mixed with disliked food	Can be left with almost anyone	Does not hear loud, sudden noises when reading
Quality of Mood: Negative	Fusses after nursing	Cries when left alone	Cries when given haircut	Cries when frustrated

*Examples are given for one dimension of each characteristic. Generally, the other dimension is more or less the opposite of the one given.
(Adapted from Thomas, A., Chess, S., & Birch, H. (1970). The origin of personality. *Scientific American, 223,* 102-9).

relatively easy to handle. With a "poor fit," even a temperamentally easy child could become difficult. If the fit between temperament and environment changes, then the child's temperament may also change.

A few examples might help clarify this concept of goodness of fit. Difficult children typically adapt slowly to new situations. One way this is evident is in their reaction to new foods. They may turn their heads, close their mouths tightly, or spit out food. Now imagine a parent who just "gives up" and doesn't even try to introduce new foods. The child will grow up knowing that he doesn't even have to try to adapt. He may, as did one subject in the Thomas, Chess, and Birch (1970) study, eventually live on a very restricted diet. A negative outcome might also result if the parents were excessively punitive or impatient.

On the other hand, imagine a parent who is patient. She repeatedly introduces the new food, expecting the baby to take only a little bit at a time. She gives him the opportunity to accept new foods at his own pace. Her child may, ultimately, be much more adaptable than the other "difficult" child.

Easy children can tolerate a much broader range of parental styles than can difficult children. This does not mean that their adaptive capabilities are endless, however. Thomas, Chess, and Birch (1970) provide the example of a little girl named Isobel. Isobel was an easy baby. Her home environment was quite open, encouraging freedom of expression and creativity. When she went to school, however, she had to follow relatively strict rules and routines. She reacted with resistance and withdrawal. The difference between the home and school environments was too much for her to reconcile. She became, temporarily, a difficult child. When the problem of conflicting demands was resolved, Isobel returned to her old self.

Obviously, the environment can affect the expression of temperament. It seems to be able to change, or at least mask, a child's behavioral style. Of course, many children live in relatively unchanging environments. This may give the impression of temperamental stability. What does the research suggest about temperamental stability?

Data.   If biology is a major determinant of temperament, then we might expect a child's temperament to be relatively stable across situations. We might also expect at least some stability across time. Notice that we do not expect complete stability over time. As has already been noted several times, even biological influences are not immutable.

Several studies have looked at how similarly babies' temperament is rated across situations (for example, home vs. day-care center). When the same observer rates the baby's temperament in roughly comparable situations (for example, one-to-one interaction with mother vs. one-to-one interaction with caregiver), considerable consistency is evidenced within most measures of temperament (for example, Greenberg & Field, 1982). This is more true of specially trained observers than of people simply familiar with the baby (for example, mother vs. father or two nursery teachers) (Field & Greenberg, 1982; Greenberg & Field, 1982). Furthermore, when two different raters (for example, teacher and parent) evaluate temperament in different settings (for example, school and home), the ratings are also not very similar (Field & Greenberg, 1982; Greenberg & Field, 1982).

These findings raise an important issue about trying to assess temperament stability. When different people rate the baby's temperament, they are more likely to differ in their ratings than when one person rates the infant in two different settings. This implies that the rating of temperament may reflect the raters' biases more than the infant's actual behavior. Different raters may have different expectations of infant behavior, or they may have different comparison groups they use in rating temperament. Think, for example, of a first-time mother. She may believe that most babies are like hers. That her baby does not sleep on a regular schedule or resists new food, for example, does not indicate a difficult temperament to her. On the other hand, a person with wide-ranging experience might recognize that most babies adapt more easily and sleep on a more predictable schedule.

The subjectivity of the rater is also an issue in measuring the stability of temperament across time. In addition, it is possible that the expression of temperament may be masked by environmental consistency (Thomas & Chess, 1980). When the environment does not demand adaptability, a difficult child may appear to be adaptable, regular in body functions, and pleasant (Thomas & Chess, 1980).

These problems may partially account for the mixed results concerning temperament stability. When studies examine stability over a period of one year or less, several traits show some continuity. Most notably, activity, sociability, and affect seem fairly stable (for example, Clarke-Stewart et al., 1980; Matheny et al., 1981; Rothbart, 1981; Thompson & Lamb, 1983). Typically, however, the correlations between the temperament measures are low to moderate. Furthermore, not all studies find such stability. The results depend to some extent on how temperament is measured and which temperament dimensions are being assessed (Hubert et al., 1982) (see Box 10-1).

BOX 10-1   *MEASURING TEMPERAMENT*

In most research, temperament is measured by having the parents or care-givers fill out a questionnaire. Given the divergence in definitions of temperament, it is not surprising to find that many different questionnaires are available. In fact, there are at least twenty-six different infant-toddler temperament surveys! (Hubert et al., 1982). We cannot possibly review all these instruments, but we can get a better idea of what these surveys tap by looking at one of the more popular ones—the Infant Temperament Questionnaire (ITQ) (Carey, 1970).

The ITQ was designed for use with infants under 1 year of age. It consists of seventy items designed to elicit information about nine different categories of temperament. These categories include activity, rhythmicity, adaptability, approach, threshold, intensity, mood, distractibility, and persistence. Items examine the baby's behavior in specific situations: They ask for information about sleep and elimination habits (part of rhythmicity), reactions to bathing and dressing, and responses to new situations or visits to the doctor. Parents are also asked to provide their global impressions of the baby's "difficultness."

Despite the popularity of the ITQ, statistical analyses have not generally shown the test or its revision, the Revised ITQ (Carey & McDevitt, 1978b), to be a very reliable assessment tool. For example, a child's rating in several categories, especially persistence and intensity, are typically not very stable

(Hubert et al., 1982). Similarly, the correlation between ITQ ratings and behavioral observations of temperament is not usually very high (Hubert et al., 1982).

Of course, similar charges could be leveled against virtually all the available surveys. We do not currently have a clearly valid, reliable temperament assessment survey. This may be because of the lack of information on some of the questionnaires (that is, we may have a reliable tool for assessment but not know it yet); or it may reflect a more fundamental problem in our understanding of temperament.

Several authors have measured temperament without the benefit of these surveys. Some have made observations of activity level, mood, and so on, in naturally occurring situations (for example, Clarke-Stewart, 1973). Others have designed laboratory situations to assess characteristics such as sociability (for example, Lamb, 1982). However, we do not know if such measures are any more reliable or valid than the parent questionnaires. Furthermore, certain temperament dimensions (for example, rhythmicity) would be almost impossible to measure using observational techniques.

As the length of time between measurements increases, the stability ratings tend to decrease. For example, measures of infant temperament taken at 4-8 months were more related to measures taken at 3-5 years than to those at 5-7 years (Carey & McDevitt, 1978a). In this study, the researchers assessed the stability of ratings of easy vs. slow-to-warm vs. difficult. They found that the difficult children were most likely to stay in the same category (40% of them had the same rating at 4-8 months and 3-7 years of age). Thomas and Chess (1977) also found that stability decreased with increasing time between measurements. By the time they compared 1-year ratings to 5-year ratings, they found significant stability on only one temperament dimension—threshold of response.

In contrast, some researchers have reported significant stability even over lengthy intertest intervals. Anneliese Korner and her associates (Korner et al., 1985), for example, reported significant correlations between neonatal activity and daytime activity level in children 4-7 years of age. Again, some conflicts in the data are probably attributable to the methodological problems mentioned earlier.

One of those methodological problems was, of course, the possibility that the environment altered the expression of temperament. It is also possible that infant temperament affects the environment.

Effects of Temperament on Parent Behavior

We have already seen that temperament characteristics can affect newborn-mother interaction (for example, Greene et al., 1983; see Chapter 3). These neonatal characteristics can continue to affect maternal behavior, even after the baby's behavior has changed. The research reported in Chapter 3 applied only to infants 3 months of age. What happens beyond that time?

Researchers have reported that the effects of temperament tend to become more pronounced as development proceeds. John Bates (1980), for example, investigated the relationship between infant temperament (easy vs. difficult) and maternal responsivity, teaching, and affection giving. When the infants were 6 to 13 months of age, few relationships were evident between maternal behavior and infant temperament. By the time their infants were 24 months of age, however, the mothers of the difficult children were showing more controlling behavior in interacting with their children. There was also more conflict between these mothers and children. These mothers were more likely to take a toy from their children. They were also more likely to repeat warnings to them. Eleanor Maccoby and her colleagues (Maccoby, Snow & Jacklin, reported in Maccoby & Martin, 1983) found a similar trend. Mothers of difficult sons between the ages of 12 and 18 months declined in their attempts to teach their children. The mothers basically "backed off" from trying to socialize their children. Similar findings have been reported for older children (for example, Olweus, 1980).

In the Bates and the Maccoby studies, the children's behavior seemed to influence maternal behavior. The difficult children in Bates's study, for example, tended to persist in negative behaviors longer than other children. They tended to ignore orders from the mother. This might well explain why such mothers repeated commands more frequently. Maccoby (Maccoby & Martin, 1983) also suggested that the "backing off" by the mothers she observed was attributable to their children's temperament.

The effects of child temperament and parental behavior seem to be reciprocal. Maccoby's study provides an example of this reciprocity. The child's difficult temperament leads the mother to withdraw her socialization pressures. This, in turn, seems to intensify the difficulty of the child's temperament (Maccoby & Martin, 1983). Although Maccoby and her colleagues did not follow the children beyond 18 months of age, we might expect that we are seeing the beginning of a cycle of mother-child interaction. This cycle may result in an uncontrollable child by the time school starts. This is an exemplification of the transactional model (see Chapter 1). One behavior affects another, which in turn affects the original behavior. Interpretations by the parents and child probably play some role in this process.

In fact, some researchers have suggested that parental interpretation actually "causes" infant temperament (see, for example, Thomas, 1982, for a discussion). In other words, temperament is viewed as a parental perception rather than a child characteristic. This position appears to be overstated. John Bates and his colleagues (Bates, Freeland & Lounsbury, 1979) reported that maternal perceptions of infant difficultness were significantly related to "objective" observers' ratings of the same babies. This suggests that mothers' (and fathers') perceptions are rooted in actual infant behaviors. However, maternal characteristics also affected the way mothers rated their babies. Mothers who had more than one child and who were extraverts were less likely to rate their babies as difficult. Thus, parental reports of infant temperament are based both upon infant characteristics and parent characteristics, which include parental perceptions. Such findings, again, support a transactional model.

Infant temperament affects parent-child interaction, even if the temperament characteristics are not terribly stable. Indeed, the environment seems to influence that stability. Given the temperament-parent behavior relationships, it is not unreasonable to expect that temperament might have at least an indirect effect on self-development. This hypothesis is supported by findings that temperament is related to the development of psychological disorders in children (for example, Thomas & Chess, 1980; see Chapter 11). With this in mind, let's now turn to an examination of the development of self.

SELF-DEVELOPMENT

Every human being is unique. As we have already seen, some of this uniqueness is attributable to temperament differences. The differences go well beyond temperament, however. We each have a unique appearance (except, perhaps, for identical twins), talents, shortcomings, and aspirations. These differences are not simply visible to others. They are also part of our own system of knowledge. In other words, we all have concepts of self.

We have all heard and used terms like *self-esteem, self-concept,* and *self-image,* and we all have somewhat different definitions of these words. Researchers, though, need to be specific about the meaning of *self.* This need for clarity has lead to distinctions being drawn among certain elements of self (Brooks-Gunn & Lewis, 1982). Three elements of self—self-recognition, categorical self, and self-concept— are discussed here.

First, an individual must be able to distinguish herself from other people. Michael Lewis and Jeanne Brooks-Gunn (1979) referred to this ability as the "existential self." The development of the existential self is first signaled by self-recognition. We might note that recognizing yourself as distinct implies that you also recognize the individuality of other people. Thus, this process is, according to Margaret Mahler and her colleagues (Mahler et al., 1975), "self-other differentiation." Knowledge about others does not necessarily develop at the same time as self-knowledge. Indeed, knowledge of "other" seems to develop later (Harter, 1983). More sophisticated knowledge about others, including their unique thoughts, feelings, and perspectives, develops even later (Kaye, 1982). Such knowledge is part of the realm of social cognition, which is discussed later in this chapter.

Once you recognize yourself, you begin to associate yourself conceptually with others who are similar to you. You form categories that are used to classify you and others. These categories are also used to ascribe value to behaviors and other people. In forming a *categorical self*, then, you define yourself in terms of these categories (Brooks-Gunn & Lewis, 1982). In American society, age and gender are important elements of the categorical self. The assignment of such categories is, as we shall see, related to self-concept.

Self-concept, the final element of self-knowledge to be defined here, is not an easily defined term. In fact, there is virtually no consensus concerning its definition (Brooks-Gunn & Lewis, 1982). For our purposes, the term simply means all other knowledge about self not covered by self-recognition and categorical self. As such, self-concept includes what has often been called self-image, self-esteem, and self-consciousness.

Before you can know "who" you are, you must know "that" you are. In other words, you must recognize yourself as distinct from other people. As noted earlier, this is the first step in self-development (for example, Kaye, 1982; Lewis & Brooks-Gunn, 1979). Self-recognition, therefore, is discussed next as the first step in self-development.

Self-recognition

Sequence.   Researchers can measure self-recognition in young infants in several possible ways. They can test whether infants behave differently when looking at pictures of themselves and pictures of others. The pictures can be either still photographs or videotapes. They can also see how the infants behave in front of a mirror. Do they recognize the relationship between the movements of the baby in the mirror and their own movements? Do they react to another person's entry into the mirror image (for example, an adult coming up behind them). Indeed, these are the sorts of techniques that have been used by researchers (for example, Berenthal & Fischer, 1978; Lewis & Brooks-Gunn, 1979) to investigate self-recognition development. Lewis and Brooks-Gunn (1979) found that the different techniques yield somewhat different results, with the earlier signs of self-recognition evident when the mirror is used.

The mirror task deserves a bit more description. The baby is seated in front of a mirror. Measures of smiling, body touching, pointing, and so on, are obtained. Then the baby's nose is wiped with a tissue. This leaves a spot of rouge on the baby's nose. The baby is placed in front of the mirror again. The measures are then taken again. Presumably, the baby will touch his nose more when the rouge is on it if he recognizes the baby in the mirror as himself.

Before about 9 months of age, babies seem totally unaware of any relationship between themselves and their mirror image (Harter, 1983). They may smile at their image and even move rhythmically in front of it, but they do not, for example, try to touch rouge placed on their nose when they see it in the mirror.

By 9 months of age, infants begin to show self-recognition (Lewis & Brooks-Gunn, 1979). For example, they touch their own bodies while looking at the image. However, they still do not react any differently to a rouged vs. clean nose. Such a reaction is not evident until infants are about 15 months of age. The majority of babies do not show differential behavior to the rouge until they are 18-20 months of age (Brooks-Gunn & Lewis, 1982).

A variety of other behaviors first appear around this time to bolster the impression that the infant is becoming aware of herself as an individual (for example, Kagan, 1982). For example, after 19 months of age, children start to smile when they complete tasks. These "mastery smiles" seem to indicate pride in accomplishing a goal. Also, between 19 and 24 months of age, children increasingly use self-descriptive phrases (for example, "I do it myself") (Bloom, Lightbrown & Hood, 1975; Kagan, 1982). Both mastery smiles and self-descriptive statements indicate a growing self-awareness (Kagan, 1982).

By 2 years of age, then, the child has clearly started to define himself as an individual. Of course, considerably more self-defining is still to be done; but self-recognition, at least, seems to be established. In fact, by 2 years of age, children can even recognize themselves in pictures (Brooks-Gunn & Lewis, 1982). The question now is, what factors enable them to develop this capability?

Dynamics.   There is virtually universal agreement that social interaction is required for the development of self-recognition; how heavily, and even exclusively, social interaction is viewed as the cause of self-development varies from theorist to theorist.

Two general approaches have been taken in the study of self-development. Some theorists focus on the development of the concept of other. These writers focus particularly on the development of the concept of the mother. John Bowlby's ethological theory, outlined in Chapter 4, is an example of this approach. Margaret Mahler's (Mahler et al., 1968) theory of separation-individuation also fits into this category.

Mahler suggested that initially the child is in an "autistic" phase. During the first few weeks, the child simply attempts to maintain physical equilibrium. He does not distinguish between himself and the environment. Within a few weeks, he has established a symbiotic relationship with his mother. Again, he is not yet distinguishing himself from his mother.

Around 5 months of age, the infant begins the separation-individual process. (The four phrases of this process are summarized in Table 10-3.) Several points should be emphasized here. First, Mahler's focus is on the emerging conceptualization of the mother. The conceptualization of self is only implied. The theory says little about how the infant develops a sense of herself as a separate and unique person (Harter, 1983). Second, Mahler did not emphasize mother-infant interaction as a determinant of this process. She provided a description of the sequence without clearly outlining the dynamics that moved the sequence along (for example, Campos et al., 1983; Harter, 1983). This does not mean that Mahler never considered the role of mother-infant interaction. She suggested, for example, that predictable behavior by the mother would facilitate self-other differentiation (Mahler et al., 1975). Thus, social interaction as a factor in self-development is not ignored, but it is not emphasized.

TABLE 10-3 Mahler's Phases of Separation-Individuation

STAGE	AGE	DESCRIPTION
FORERUNNERS OF SEPARATION-INDIVIDUATION:		
Autistic Phase	0-2 months	The infant does not respond to external stimuli. Instead, behavior is determined by internal, physiological stimuli. The newborn is simply trying to establish homeostatis within his new environment. There seems to be a "stimulus barrier" between the newborn and the environment.
Symbiotic Phase	2-5 months	The child is aware of the mother and her fulfillment of his physical needs, but he does not distinguish himself from her. He does not understand that he and his mother are distinct people. Instead, he acts as if he and his other form one "ominipotent system."
SUBPHASES OF SEPARATION-INDIVIDUATION PROCESS:		
Differentiation Subphase	5-10 months	The child begins to "hatch" out of the symbiotic relationship. She begins to discriminate her mother from other people and develops a special attachment to her.
Practicing Subphase	10-18 months	The infant becomes aware that his body is separate from his mother's. Locomotor development contributes to this realization. The child's concept of his mother is further differentiated and consolidated so that she becomes even more important to the baby.
Rapprochement Subphase	15-22 months	Toddlers seem more attached to their mothers. There is often intense separation and stranger anxiety. Thus, after moving away from the mother in the practicing subphase, the child now seems more attached than ever to her mother. She still recognizes that she and her mother are separate, however.
Consolidation of Individuality and the Beginnings of Emotional Object Constancy	24-36 months	The child has a well-formed concept of her mother. This includes understanding that her mother is a permanent entity with both positive and negative characteristics. The child can tolerate increasingly lengthy separations from the mother.

(Information from Mahler, Pine & Bergman, 1975, and Campos et al., 1983).

On the other hand, George Herbert Mead (for example, 1934) argued that self arose exclusively through social interaction. Mead falls into the second broad category of theorists. The authors in this group focused more on the development of the concept of self than the concept of other. According to Mead, the infant processes social experiences to form a sense of self. Parental statements about the child and their reactions to the child's behavior form the basis of self-development. The infant's organization and anticipation of these reactions become the self that guides behavior. Language is needed in order to organize and anticipate these reactions. The roles and concepts that are so organized are actually practiced through play (as opposed, for example, to simply being imitated). This underscores, again, Mead's belief that the infant is actively involved in self-development. Overall, then, Mead suggested that the infant was constructing a sense of self rooted in environmental reactions to him.

Michael Lewis and Jeanne Brooks-Gunn (1979) also argued that social interaction was central to self-development. More specifically, parental reactions contingent upon infant behaviors were viewed as crucial. Regular, consistent, and contingent responses allow the baby to develop expectations about the world. Thus, for example, an infant might come to expect to be picked up when she cries because this is what her mother usually does. This response helps her learn that she can influence her mother's behavior. This understanding implies the beginning of self-other differentiation. In other words, these expectations facilitate the differentiation of self from other.

In many ways Lewis and Brooks-Gunn's analysis borrowed from Mead's view. However, Lewis and Brooks-Gunn added a component of cognitive development to their theory. They noted, for example, that object permanence development (see Chapter 8) is related to the ability to define a continuously existing self. This "self permanence" is a prerequisite for the organization of characteristics or categories of self (Lewis & Brooks-Gunn, 1979).

While Lewis and Brooks-Gunn emphasized a cognitive component in addition to social interaction, Jerome Kagan (1982) focused on central nervous system development as important. In fact, Kagan viewed central nervous system development as more important than some specific form of social interaction. This is not to say that he dismissed social interaction as a contributing factor in self-development. He acknowledged that self would not develop in a child reared in social isolation. What he doubted was that specific forms of social interaction, such as imitation or contingent responding, were important. Rather, any form of interaction with people and objects is sufficient. Central nervous system maturation allows the infant to remember, organize, and interpret these experiences. There is an interaction here: The experience influences central nervous system development just as central nervous system development influences the organization of the experience. It is this maturation that enables the child to develop the skills that ultimately lead to self-awareness, however.

Social interaction is thus a crucial component of self-development. Whether a specific form of social interaction is important is unclear, but it seems unlikely that a specific form is required. Child-rearing techniques vary too dramatically from family to family and culture to culture (remember the Kalulis in Chapter 9) to support such an argument. There may be a form of social interaction that facilitates, or speeds up, self-development. But, that does not mean this form of interaction is necessary for self-development. We need more cross-cultural research to resolve these issues.

What is important beyond social interaction in determining self-awareness? Is self-awareness rooted in cognitive development, central nervous system maturation, both, or neither? Again, such questions are unresolved. It is probable that both factors, and perhaps other factors, play a role. These, too, are issues to be resolved in future research.

We have thus far been discussing only self-recognition and self-awareness here. It may well be the case that certain forms of social interaction are related to how categories defining the self develop. Let's explore this issue next.

Categorical Self

Self-recognition (in mirrors, pictures, and so on) implies that you recognize yourself as a unique individual. You realize that you have a face, a body, and so on, that is different from that of other people. Developing this recognition requires that you know certain things about yourself. Included in this knowledge is information about yourself in relation to the rest of the world. Some of this information is in terms of cultural categories, such as age and gender, used to define individuals. The question here is, when do children become aware of and start to use these categories to define themselves?

Age.   Using age to define broad categorizations of people (for example, baby vs. child vs. adult) is a relatively easy task, for you can use height, body features (for example, breasts, facial hair), facial characteristics, voice, clothing, and so on, as clues. In addition to using these physical characteristics, you can make age distinctions on the basis of behavior (for example, who is "in charge" in a situation or who has money). With all these clues available, it is not surprising that infants can make age distinctions fairly early (Brooks-Gunn & Lewis, 1982).

Between 6 and 12 months of age, infants give several indications of the ability to differentiate age groups. They can, for example, distinguish adults from babies in slides, papier-mâché heads, and pictures (for example, Lewis & Brooks-Gunn, 1979). By 12 months of age, they prefer to interact with infant rather than adult strangers (Lewis & Brooks, 1974). Even infants still in the earliest phases of language acquisition rarely confuse names on the basis of age. They might call all men Daddy, but they almost never call a baby Daddy (Brooks-Gunn & Lewis, 1979). They seem able to use height and facial features as cues in making such distinctions (Brooks & Lewis, 1976). Although these data demonstrate that young infants are aware of age categories, they do not tell us whether infants apply such categories to themselves. As already noted, babies begin to recognize themselves at about 15 months of age. Brooks-Gunn and Lewis (1982) argued that at that time babies were using age to categorize self and others. In fact, even at 9-12 months of age, infants seemed to respond differently to strange babies than to adults (Lewis &

Brooks-Gunn, 1979). In addition, limited evidence indicated that babies this young could differentiate themselves from other babies—an ability clearly evident by 21 months of age (Lewis & Brooks-Gunn, 1979). However, the Lewis and Brooks-Gunn (1979) study overlooked an important comparison: It did not compare infant reactions to pictures of self vs. adult stranger with pictures of self vs. infant stranger. In other words, we do not know whether babies can more easily distinguish themselves from adults than from children.

In sum, the evidence suggests that infants use age as a category early in life. They become aware of age distinctions before 12 months of age. They seem to apply the age category to themselves well before 24 months of age. However, additional research is needed to identify the complete sequence of application of age categories to self.

Age as a component of categorical self is of interest for two reasons. First, the salience of age characteristics increases the likelihood that the category will appear early in development. Second, age is used virtually universally to distinguish among individuals. Only one other social category clearly shares these characteristics. That category is gender.

Gender.   Children do not use labels such as *girl* and *boy* appropriately until they are 2.5 or 3 years of age (for example, Lewis & Brooks-Gunn, 1979). In addition, children under 2.5 years of age are not particularly adept at identifying sex-appropriate clothing, work, tools, and games (see Huston, 1983, for a review). Such evidence might lead us to conclude that infants have no categories to define gender.

Yet other research indicates that infants do have at least rudimentary gender categories. During the first year, for example, they respond more negatively to male than to female strangers (for example, Morgan & Ricciuti, 1969). More interestingly for our purposes, they seem to be including themselves in these categories. Lewis and Brooks-Gunn (1979) found that infants looked and smiled more at pictures of same-sex than at opposite-sex peers. Note that this distinction was based on the relationship between the gender of the observer infant and that of the pictured baby. There was no simple preference for pictures of girls over boys (or vice versa).

How much do these gender categories affect infant behavior? That is not an easy question to answer. Remember, the categories are far from completely developed. Despite their inability to label gender and gender-appropriate activities, children under 2.5 years of age do show some "sex-typed" behaviors. Greta Fein and her colleagues (Fein et al., 1975) found, for example, that even 20-month-olds played more with toys that were "appropriate" for their own gender. More recently, Margaret Snow and her colleagues (Snow, Jacklin & Maccoby, 1983) reported that 1-year-old girls were more likely than 1-year-old boys to play with a doll when it was given to them. The boys in this study also showed more "mischievious" behavior (for example, getting into a full ashtray). Evidence also suggested that boys engage in physically active play more often than girls do (for example, Goldberg & Lewis, 1969), though not all researchers find this difference before the age of 2 (see Rubin, Fein & Vandenberg, 1983).

From where do these gender differences in play come? Is there, for example, a biological component? Perhaps the greater physical play by boys is related to temperament. After all, some research suggests that boy newborns are more physically active than girls (see Chapter 3). Similarly, one might argue that the girls' preference for dolls reflects an innate maternal instinct. These arguments are weak, however. Lack of maternal instinct cannot, for example, explain why boys prefer trucks; and its presence cannot explain why preschool girls have an affinity for art or other quiet play. In fact, in some cultures, girls engage in more rough, physical play than do boys. In other cultures, the proportion of rough-and-tumble play is about equal for boys and girls (see Rubin et al., 1983, for a review). Furthermore, little evidence supports the notion that adult women are better or more interested parents by nature (see, for example, Maccoby & Jacklin, 1974; see also Chapter 3). So, there does not seem to be strong evidence for an innate basis for the gender differences in play.

Socialization seems to be a more likely causal factor. *Socialization* refers to the direct and indirect training of children into appropriate social roles, including roles defined on the basis of age, gender, social class, and race. In the United States, sex-role socialization begins early in life. In fact, parents have different impressions of boy and girl newborns. Girls are rated as smaller, softer, and less alert than boys despite the absence of real physical differences. Fathers of newborns rate boys as stronger and hardier (for example, Rubin, Provenzano & Luria, 1974). Such differences in perceptions may result in differential treatment of boy and girl infants. This is certainly what the transactional model predicts. Also, this argument is supported by the data. Parents, particularly fathers, play more rough-and-tumble games with boy infants (for example, Parke & Suomi, 1980; Power & Parke, 1980). Indeed, this is one of the most consistently documented findings in the sex-differences literature (Huston, 1983).

Parents not only play differently with boy than with girl infants, they create different environments for the children. The decor and objects in the rooms of boys are different from those typically found in girls' rooms (Rheingold & Cook, 1975). Boys are more likely to be given trucks, construction sets, and sports equipment. Girls' toys are more likely to include dolls and their accompanying paraphernalia (Rheingold & Cook, 1975). It is more unusual for boys to receive "girl" toys than vice-versa (for example, Fein et al., 1975). These parental patterns of toy choice are even evident in a laboratory setting where a variety of toys are available (for example, Snow et al., 1983). The parents' choices are not simply a question of what they buy for their children, for parental preferences extend into other nonhome play situations. The children's toy preferences mirror the parents' preferences.

These parental techniques, in conjunction with role modeling by the parents and in the mass media, probably strongly influence the child's early definition of gender. Gender categories appear to develop early and are applied to the self early, so that they influence behavior during infancy.

Other Categories. Of course, categories other than age and sex are socially defined. In the United States, race is certainly such a category. Others might include social class, family lineage, ethnicity, and even physical appearance attributes such as attractiveness and height. Although many of these categories probably contribute to our self-definition, their development in infancy has not been studied. While some of these categories are probably not self-defined until later in life, others may well influence eary self-definition. These issues can only be resolved by future research.

The categories discussed here contain a substantial social element. In other words, different social values are attached to being a boy as opposed to being a girl, a baby as opposed to an adult, black as opposed to white, and so on. Such differential social values might influence the development of self-esteem in a child. Let's now examine the limited information available concerning self-esteem in infancy.

Self-esteem

A friend of mine was visiting with her 17-month-old son. The little boy was behaving like most 17-months-olds, exploring and getting into almost everything. He apparently behaved the same way at home. During the course of the visit, his mother said to him, in a playful voice, "Are you a brat?" The little boy would answer "yes" or "brat." He even used the word *brat* to refer to himself spontaneously.

Some people might think that this mother was cruel or, at best, thoughtless. They might believe that she was instilling in her son a negative self-image. They might also think that the boy would eventually become a brat in order to fulfill his mother's expectations. On the other hand, some people (including the mother, I'm sure) would argue that this labeling was harmless. They would suggest that the child had no more understanding of the word *brat* than young children have of the profanity that they so often parrot. They would argue that as long as the child was generally treated with love, he would not develop low self-esteem.

This example raises several interesting questions. Do young children have any sense of self-esteem? If so, is it based mainly on the behavior of other people? What behavior of others is particularly salient? Do the child's own accomplishments influence her level of self-esteem? Does she compare herself to other young children?

These questions may all be subsumed under the general question of when and how children begin to develop self-esteem. What is self-esteem? As you might expect, many definitions are available. William James's (1890/1963) definition seems particularly popular. He suggested that self-esteem is the ratio of success to pretensions or expectations. In other words, self-esteem is a question of interpretation (for example, Maccoby, 1980). If you expect to get an A on an exam and you only get a B+, your self-esteem may suffer. On the other hand, if you expected a C and you get a B+, your self-esteem may be bolstered. Your self-esteem is thus a function of your ability to live up to your own expectations (which are probably related to the expectations of others).

When do these expectations emerge? Where do they come from? Let's begin by looking at Erik Erikson's (1959/1980) theory of personality development.

Erikson's Theory.   Erik Erikson (for example, 1963) suggested that personality development proceeded through eight stages. At each stage, a psychosocial crisis is to be resolved. (These eight crises are summarized in Table 10-4.) The resolution of each crisis is dependent on the resolution of the previous crises, as well as on cultural and social supports. The first two crises, occurring in infancy, therefore form the foundation of all personality development. As the foundation, the resolution of these two crises may well influence self-esteem throughout a person's life. In addition, the resolution of each crisis will influence current functioning, and Erikson (1959/1980) does include self-esteem as an element of that current functioning.

TABLE 10-4   A Brief Summary of Erikson's Eight Stages

CRISIS	AGE RANGE	DESCRIPTION OF POSITIVE OUTCOME
Trust vs. Mistrust	First year	Child develops confidence that his needs will be met and that there is a constancy of the environment that can be counted on.
Autonomy vs. Shame and Self-doubt	Second year	Child gains sense of "having a choice" that will result in pride rather than embarrassment.
Initiative vs. Guilt	3-5 years	Child learns to trust her ability to select, plan, and carry out activities that will gain approval from self and others.
Industry vs. Inferiority	5-12 years	Child acquires basic societal skills (for example, reading, manners) on the way to preparing for adult life. He has the sense that such skills and tasks are performed at least adequately.
Identity vs. Role Confusion	Adolescence	Teen develops sense of continuity of self. She sees self as unique and yet as "fitting in."
Intimacy vs. Isolation	Young adulthood	Young adult establishes a relationship within which he can share feelings, confidences, work, child-rearing, and leisure.
Generativity vs. Stagnation	Middle age	Adult passes on wisdom, skills, and so on, to the next generation (including his own children).
Ego Integrity vs. Despair	Old age	Senior citizen is dominated by a sense that she has done the best she could with her life. She has a "trust" in her own life cycle and in humankind generally.

(Based on Erikson, 1963).

The first crisis in Erikson's model centers on trust vs. mistrust. Trust is an unconscious faith in your own body to be able to regulate itself. This element of trust is exemplified by regular, uneventful patterns of sleep, eating, and elimination. Trust also involves an unconscious faith in other people to help meet your needs. This "social trust" is exemplified by the infant's increasing tolerance of short separations from her mother (Erikson, 1963).

What happens if this sense of trust does not develop? Over the long term, pathology may develop. Erikson (1959/1980) related extreme mistrust to disorders such as depression, sadism, and schizoid personality. These disorders obviously have an element of low self-esteem. Depressed people, for example, believe that they cannot do anything well and that no one can do anything to help them (for example, Beck, 1967). They can never live up to their expectations. They feel worthless. They do not trust themselves or others.

The effects of mistrust are also evident during infancy. The mistrustful infant may engage in haphazard activity to try to get what he wants or needs (Erikson, 1959/1980). He may cry excessively, for example; or he may fail to go to sleep even when exhausted. The mistrustful infant may, on the other hand, withdraw. To use Erikson's phrase, "he will find his thumb and damn the world" (Erikson, 1959/ 1980, p. 60). One could, then, argue that the child is already building negative expectations concerning his ability to influence his own happiness and others' behavior. Of course, this cannot be proven. Erikson himself suggested that all this was unconscious. Theoretically, however, this may well be the beginning of self-esteem (for example, Harter, 1983).

Self-esteem is more clearly involved in the second crisis—the crisis of autonomy vs. shame and self-doubt. The major issue here is the child's sense that she can make choices (Erikson, 1963). Through saying no, moving toward or away from something, and so on, she has the sense of making her own decisions. Again, this sense of autonomy is unconscious, and the child must have a sense of trust in order to make such moves effectively. She must know, on an unconscious level, that such moves will not result in the loss of parental love.

What if she develops a sense of shame and self-doubt instead? Erikson (1963, 1959/1980) suggested that shame may be indicated by trying to hide things. In other words, the child may try to "get away with" things. An extreme example is the child who defecates in hidden, out-of-the-way areas of the house. The child may, on the other hand, develop a sense of shamelessness. She may become excessively defiant. No punishment will be effective because the child just doesn't care. This is a *pseudoautonomy*. It is based on "knowing" that no one cares anyway, and so it doesn't matter what you do.

These outcomes imply that the 1-to-2-year-old child has begun to build expectations about others' reactions to his behavior. Empirical research supports this assumption. Jerome Kagan (1982), for example, reported the onset of mastery smiles in infants between 19 and 25 months of age. These children smile when they have completed a task. This suggests that they know they have done well, that they have lived up to expectations. Similarly, they show distress over potential failure.

When a model demonstrates a task that is too difficult to remember or perform, young children show signs of anxiety. They may cling to their mothers or whine. Again, this indicates that the children have expectations of themselves. They think they have to imitate the model (although they were not told to) and fear that they cannot (Kagan, 1982). Their self-esteem is threatened.

By the end of the second year, then, children appear to have developed beliefs about what others expect of them. They also have some sense of whether or not they are living up to those expectations. In other words, self-esteem has started to emerge. If we believe Erikson's model, this self-esteem is not new. Rather, it is becoming more obvious, more tangible. It actually began to develop during the infant's first year of life.

Going back to my friend and her son, we are still left with the question of how parental behavior influences the development of self-esteem. Let's turn our attention to that issue.

Parental Behavior and Self-esteem.   The theroretical constructs just examined are somewhat vague. How would you measure a sense of trust in an infant? Given this, there is little research directly addressing self-esteem development in infancy. Erikson does make some suggestions as to how parents may influence this development. By combining his advice with empirical work with older children, some suggestions to parents can be formulated.

According to Erikson (1959/1980), the development of trust is rooted in the quality of the mother-infant relationship. The amount of feeding, diaper changing, and so on, is less crucial than the overall quality of the relationship. The mother must respond sensitively to the baby's needs. She must treat the baby as an individual. She must also convey a sense that there is some reason for what she does or doesn't do for the baby. In other words, her reactions to the baby should not seem arbitrary. In order to convey this sense of purpose, she, too, must have an overall sense of why she is doing what she is doing. She should not be guided by temporary influences such as fatigue, anger at other people, or suggestions by others. Instead, she should have some principles (perhaps culturally determined) guiding her behavior. Such principles lend consistency to the mother's behaviors, a consistency that is crucial if the baby is to develop a sense of social trust.

Erikson's emphasis on consistent, sensitive parenting is supported by research with older boys (for example, Coopersmith, 1967). Fifth- and sixth-graders with high self-esteem had parents who were consistent in their discipline. They set reasonable, reliable rules for the child to follow. At the same time, these parents were affectionate. They also were involved in their children's lives. They were aware of their children's problems and tried to help with them. In other words, they were strict but sensitive parents.

Coopersmith also found that parents of high-self-esteem boys were democratic. In other words, they let the child express his wishes. They took these wishes into account, though they made the final decisions. This characteristic seems to be related to Erikson's advice to parents of autonomy-crisis children. He suggested parents must be firm with these children, but they should also support the children in their efforts to make decisions and do things alone. They should neither smother nor shame the child for trying. According to Erikson, parents' ability to provide this kind of support is determined by their own sense of personal independence. Parents who feel powerless are less able to let their children gain power. This may be one explanation for the frequent finding that lower-class parents are more likely to use coercive discipline than middle-class parents. They are also less likely to be democratic in their discipline (Maccoby, 1980). This may come from their own sense of powerlessness outside the home. So, they exercise extreme power within the home. Such nondemocratic parenting has been linked to low self-esteem in children (see Maccoby & Martin, 1983, for a review).

In sum, parents ought to be aware that self-esteem begins to develop during infancy. They should be responsive to their infant, aware of his needs as an individual. When independence starts to emerge, they should allow him to express that independence. This does not mean they should have no rules. They should, but the rules should be explainable. They should serve a purpose (other than "because I said so"). The rules should be combined with love and, preferably, visible affection. In this way, the child will come to understand that the parents make rules because they care about the child. When possible, the child's wishes should be seriously considered. This does not mean that the child should always gets her way, but that the parents let the child sometimes make the decisions. When the child can't have her way, the parents explain why.

By following these guidelines, parents may facilitate the development of positive self-esteem. What about my friend? Well, given that she was affectionate and loving to her son, calling him a brat probably wasn't incredibly serious. On the other hand, it wasn't particularly helpful, either. Such labeling should be avoided because the child could interpret it as disrespect or even dislike. This interpretation could damage the emerging self-esteem.

In discussing self-esteem, we have seen the influence of other people. This implies that the child has some understanding of other people and their expectations. Indeed, throughout the discussion of self, the understanding of other has been implied. Let's now turn to a more detailed examination of how the concept of other develops and how it influences social behavior.

THE CONCEPT OF OTHER

It is clear from the preceding discussion that infants differentiate themselves from other people. Infants can also distinguish among people. They can, for example, distinguish themselves from adults, their mothers and fathers from other adults, and adults from peers. These abilities are supported by the data presented in Chapter 4 concerning attachment and peer interaction.

Being able to distinguish people from one another does not necessarily signify a fully developed concept of other. You can recognize a person without being able to anticipate his thoughts, feelings, or behaviors. Indeed, Jean Piaget (for example, 1926) argued that infants, and even preschoolers, are incapable of assuming another person's perspective (see Chapter 8). This implies that infants' behavior cannot be guided by any comprehension of other people's needs, emotions, and so on. Piaget's view has been challenged by research on the infant's ability to comprehend, and react to, emotion in other people.

Judging Emotions of Others.   As we saw in Chapter 6, even very young infants are capable of discerning facial expressions indicative of very basic emotions (for example, surprised vs. happy). The ability to discriminate among facial expressions may emerge by the time the infant reaches 6 weeks of age. The evidence suggests that these young infants do not yet appreciate the emotional state associated with the facial expression (Campos et al., 1983); this ability does not emerge until infants are about 4-5 months of age. Infants younger than 4-5 months of age will become distressed if their mothers looked depressed or still-faced (for example, Cohn & Tronick, 1982), but the babies' distress seems more attributable to the interruption of social interaction than to any understanding of the maternal facial expression (Campos et al., 1983).

Harriet Oster (1981) has suggested several explanations for the young infant's failure to recognize emotions. It could be that they lack the perceptual skills necessary to make fine discriminations in facial expressions. There is some empirical support for this argument. Oster and Ewy (1980, cited in Oster, 1981), for example, reported that 4-month-olds could only discriminate smiles from sad expressions if teeth were visible in the smile.

Oster also suggested that infants may be predisposed to make positive responses to any facial expression. The baby would respond with a smile to either a happy face or a sad face. Such responses could be adaptive, in the evolutionary sense; they would, perhaps, facilitate the development of attachments. Negative responses by babies to facial expressions, on the other hand, might interfere with attachment formation. If this tendency does exist, it would mask the ability (if there is any) of the young infant to discriminate among facial expressions.

In keeping with the theme of this chapter, another explanation might be offered. Perhaps young children fail to respond to the emotional state of others because they do not yet have a functioning concept of other. Without a concept of other, the infant could not possibly understand the feelings or behaviors of another person. In other words, the child may not be cognitively ready to discriminate emotions.

Around 5 months of age, children do begin to react to different facial expressions. They are more likely to smile at happy faces. They tend to react negatively to angry or sad faces (Campos et al., 1983; Oster, 1981). This emerging ability coincides with the onset of self-awareness. According to Mahler (Mahler et al., 1975; see Table 10-3), the differentiation phase is beginning. Studies of self-recognition suggest that it is around this time that the infant becomes aware of her own body as a source of movement (Harter, 1983). The precise relationship between self-other differentiation and recognition of emotions has not been explored. Perhaps recognition of emotion is simply another indicator of self-other differentiation. Perhaps recognition is directly dependent on self-other differentiation. Or perhaps recognition of emotions contributes to the ability to distinguish other people. Only future research can answer these questions.

The ability to recognize emotions continues to be refined. Around 10 months of age, the child starts to actively seek clues about the emotional states of others (Campos et al., 1983). By 18 months of age, children are showing clear signs of empathetic reactions. They no longer simply cry or look sad when another person is distressed. Instead, they appear concerned. They may even try to comfort the distressed person (Radke-Yarrow, Zahn-Waxler & Chapman, 1983). Later still, children can appreciate that a person can feel two emotions simultaneously. It is not until 9 or 10 years of age that children understand that a person can feel two conflicting emotions at once (Campos et al., 1983). Again, the increased ability to understand what another person is feeling *may* be related to the improving concept of other.

These findings all undermine Piaget's view that infants are completely egocentric. Even relatively young infants seem aware of other people's emotions and react to them appropriately. These studies indicate a fairly sophisticated concept of other people. They also imply that children have already started to learn socially acceptable responses (for example, helping a distressed peer) to others' emotional states.

SUMMARY

Each one of us is a unique individual. We react differently to new situations. We require different levels of quiet in order to concentrate. Some of us are more easily irritated than others. Many people need to eat and sleep on a fairly set schedule; others do not.

What accounts for these individual differences? Some of them appear at or shortly after birth. These temperament differences may be due to genetic factors. Prenatal (for example, alcohol) or perinatal (for example, anesthesia, anoxia) factors may also play a role. Does this mean that personality is set by biological factors? Perhaps. But, many theorists and researchers (for example, Crockenberg & Smith, 1982; Thomas & Chess, 1980) argue that parental perception of infant temperament is a major determinant of how consistently and strongly particular characteristics are displayed.

Another potential source of individual differences is self-concept. The child begins to differentiate himself from others during the first year. By 2 years of age, the child has a concept of himself in relation to societal categories (for example, a "boy baby"). At the same time, the child is beginning to form an impression of his worth as an individual. These developments seem to be heavily rooted in early social interactions.

These findings all suggest that personality development begins early. Does this mean that abnormal personality functioning is always rooted in infancy? Can children who begin with difficult temperaments or poor self-concepts overcome these negative beginnings? How important are biological factors in such problems? Do social interaction patterns "cause" abnormality? These are some of the issues discussed in the next chapter.

11

At-Risk Infants

Some people just seem to start out life with a disadvantage. Perhaps they are born prematurely. They might be ill at or shortly after birth, or they might be born mentally retarded or physically handicapped. Maybe their parents have a psychological disorder, or maybe their parents are divorced or were never married. Maybe they are abused or neglected by their parents.

Some of these disadvantages seem primarily biological (for example, being born mentally retarded). Others appear to be environmental (for example, being abused). Still others appear to combine biological and environmental risk (for example, being born to and raised by disturbed parents). Regardless of the nature of the factor, it is commonly assumed that any of these situations endangers a child's development. We assume that babies in these situations are at risk. We anticipate problems in their development.

The question is, what factors are most likely to influence a child's development negatively? Is one factor (for example, premature birth) sufficient to "cause" abnormal development? Or do you need some combination of factors before problems appear? Are the problems permanent? For example, if an infant is abused and begins to show abnormal development, is she forever set on a path of developmental problems? These are some of the issues addressed in this chapter.

THE CONCEPT OF RISK

Definition. *Developmental risk factors* are conditions or situations that increase the likelihood of abnormal development (Kopp, 1983). A child may be at risk due to biological or environmental conditions or some combination of the two. Some risk factors are virtually guaranteed to affect development negatively. Downs syndrome, a chromosomal defect causing mental retardation (see Chapter 2), is such a factor. Other risk factors, such as prematurity or being raised in a single-parent home, carry less certain risks. The effects of risk factors may be evident in any realm of development. Motor, perceptual, personality, cognitive, social, or academic functioning may be negatively affected.

Models of Risk. The same four models outlined in Chapter 1 to explain development are evident in explanations of risk. Thus, for example, some authors emphasize biological factors. (Some examples of biological risk factors are given in Table 11-1.) These factors include genetic disorders and predispositions, prenatal and perinatal complications, postnatal trauma or accidents, and postnatal illness (see Chapter 2 also). Other researchers emphasize environmental factors. (These factors are exemplified in Table 11-2.) Most of these are concerned with the structure and functioning of the family (for example, divorce, single-parent homes, abuse). Some are broader, cultural factors (for example, poverty).

TABLE 11-1 **Perinatal and Postnatal Biological Risk Factors and Their Associated Outcomes**

RISK FACTOR*	ASSOCIATED OUTCOMES
Anoxia or asphyxia (oxygen deprivation during birth)	Most show no long-term effects but can result in brain injury, cerebral palsy, or, possibly, minimal brain dysfunction (for example, hyperactivity).
Malnutrition	Depends on length, duration, and severity of malnutrition. Can result in apathy, overall developmental retardation, and brain dysfunction.
Accidents	As many as 50,000 children per year may have accidents severe enough to result in neurological damage or dysfunction (for example, hyperactivity, learning problems).
Meningitis	Effects vary but can include brain damage, mental retardation, and hearing loss.
Reyes syndrome	Effects vary but can result in mental retardation and neurological dysfunction.
Lead poisoning	Depending on level of lead in blood stream, can result in seizures, mental retardation, cerebral palsy, and behavioral disorders.

*For genetic and prenatal risk factors, see Tables 2-1 and 2-4.
(After Kopp, C. (1983). Risk factors in development. In P. Mussen (ed.), *Handbook of child psychology* (4th ed) (Vol. 2). New York: John Wiley).

TABLE 11-2 Environmental Risk Factors and Their Associated Outcomes

RISK FACTOR	ASSOCIATED OUTCOMES
War	If parents remain available and supportive, long-term effects are usually minimal. However, if child is separated from family, a variety of behavioral disorders may result.
Divorce	The outcomes for very young children do not appear to be as severe as for children over 5 years of age. Most children of all ages will show short-term (1-2 years) behavioral problems. The severity and duration of problems vary greatly depending on adjustment of parents, custody arrangements, and disruption of other aspects of family life (for example, moving or mother going to work).
Working mother	No clearly negative long-term effects of day care have been documented. There is, however, an increased rate of illness in day-care children. More research is needed.
Single-parent home	Effects depend on the adjustment of the parent and available support systems outside the home. An intact family does not appear to be an important variable in predicting normal development.
Poverty	Effects vary depending on family adjustment and support. Availability of extrafamilial support also appears to be important. There is a somewhat higher rate of child abuse in poverty-level families.

(Information from Garmezy, 1983; Wallerstein, 1983; Weinraub &Wolf, 1983).

Increasingly, however, theorists are adopting interactional or transactional models to explain the development of at-risk infants. Norman Garmezy (1983) and Michael Rutter (1983) have suggested that a triad of factors influences developmental outcome. The first factor is the infant's own characteristics. These characteristics might include temperament, birth defects, illness, and cognitive level. So, a child with a difficult temperament may be more likely to develop a problem than a child with an easy-going disposition.

The second factor is the family. The family may be disorganized due to poverty, divorce, death, or psychological disturbance in one or both parents. The family may thus be unable to provide the kind of support a child needs to develop normally (as outlined, for example, by Erikson; see Chapter 9). However, this lack of support can be ameliorated by the third factor.

The third factor is cultural or societal systems. These are people outside the family who may support or hinder the child's development. Teachers, babysitters, grandparents—all may serve as attachment figures and role models. Of course, very broad cultural factors, such as racism or war, may also influence a child's development.

These three factors interact to produce a positive or negative outcome for the child. A child born with Downs syndrome whose parents are accepting and supportive is likely to develop a higher level of intellectual functioning than one who is raised in an institution (for example, Kopp, 1983). Children who experience birth complications may show few, if any, developmental problems unless they are raised in stressful family environments (for example, marital instability or maternal psychiatric problems) (Werner, Bierman & French, 1971; Werner & Smith, 1982).

Increasing numbers of theorists are arguing that the effects of combining a poor environment and some form of biological risk are not simply additive: You do not simply have a "problem" child who happens to be born into a "problem" environment. Rather, the child and the environment mutually influence each other (for example, Rutter, 1983; Sameroff & Seifer, 1983). Neither the baby nor the environment is passive or stagnant. The way the mother interprets the baby's condition influences how she interacts with the child (see Chapters 3 and 10). This, of course, is the transactional model of development (see Chapter 1). It is probably the case that some mothers are more likely to make negative appraisals of infant behavior. Mothers who have little education or who are stressed by poverty, for example, may be more likely to make negative appraisals. Those appraisals can be changed through an intervention program, however. Such intervention can dramatically improve the likelihood of a positive outcome (Sameroff & Seifer, 1983).

As noted in Chapter 10, parental appraisals are probably more influential than child appraisals in determining the course of early interactions. This does not mean that the child makes no appraisals. Even young infants react to changes in stimulation levels and, perhaps, facial expressions (Campos et al., 1983). By 2 years of age children are clearly reacting to approval, disapproval, and even adult expectations (Kagan, 1982).

Children's reactions to adult behavior can be dramatically exemplified by looking at the effects of war. Adults conceptualize few things as more stressful or traumatic than living in a war zone; yet children tend to show immediate behavior problems only if the adults around them are incapable of supporting them emotionally (see Garmezy, 1983). We see similar effects in children's reactions to divorce (for example, Wallerstein, 1983). This raises an interesting point. Adults have a variety of behaviors available for coping with stress. They might drink or use drugs. They can talk to other adults, including a therapist. They can involve themselves in their work. They can read or watch television. The list is almost endless. Very young children, in contrast, have limited coping strategies (Maccoby, 1983). They can cry or withdraw, but they have not yet developed problem-solving skills for specific situations; and so when they are stressed, their behavior completely disintegrates. Think of how many times you have seen an infant reduced to uncontrollable crying by a problem that to you seems easily solvable. Infants and young children rely heavily on others to structure their environments and provide coping mechanisms. They particularly rely on their attachment figures (usually their parents) (Maccoby, 1983). In this manner, parental coping influences how a child reacts to a situation, even if the child is not cognitively able to completely appraise the situation. The child's reaction will, in turn, affect adult behavior, which will again influence the child, and so on.

Given this general framework for understanding risk in infancy, let's now turn to three specific risk factors and examine how they influence development. The factors—prematurity, child abuse, and parental psychiatric disturbance—were selected because they represent a range of biological and social influences. They were also chosen because of their interest to parents and professionals. In addition, all three are commonly seen as major developmental risk factors.

PREMATURITY

Definition.   The best-known feature of premature infants is that they are small. By most definitions, they weigh less than 2,500 grams (5.5 pounds). However, this feature alone cannot adequately identify prematurity. Some babies are carried to term (38-40 weeks) but weigh less than 5.5 pounds. These small-for-gestational-age (SGA) babies are at risk, but they are not premature.

A premature baby is one born before the 38th week of pregnancy. Since many women do not remember the date of their last menstrual period prior to pregnancy, it is often difficult to distinguish SGA babies from true premature infants. Some differences between SGA and premature infants can help in differential diagnosis. For example, the reflexes of the SGA baby are likely to be stronger than those of the premature infant. Indeed, some reflexes may be completely absent in a preterm. The newborn stepping reflex, for example, does not appear until 32 weeks' gestational age. It is not in a mature form until 34 weeks' gestational age (Holmes, Reich & Pasternak, 1984). Also, physical appearance differs between premature and SGA babies. For example, premature infants have more lanugo and less well defined ears (Holmes, Reich & Pasternak, 1984). While these and other features may help distinguish preterm from SGA babies, none is perfectly reliable. Our inability to absolutely discriminate SGA from prematurity (except in cases where the mother does remember her last menstrual period) probably contributes to the conflicting research findings concerning the premature infant's developmental outcome.

Developmental Outcome.   Within the past 20 years, the outlook for preterms has improved dramatically. They are much more likely to survive the neonatal period, and they are *less* likely to develop serious impairments. Interestingly, this is partially attributable to less aggressive treatment of preterms. During the 1950s and 1960s, preterms were often given dramatic medical treatment, but the treatments were often untested. Those treatments, such as administering pure oxygen to preterms, apparently caused some of the problems that doctors of the time attributed to prematurity. These problems included blindness, cerebral palsy, and mental retardation (for example, Kopp, 1983). This implies that research conducted during this time should be cautiously interpreted.

Of course, our improved technology, such as better temperature and light control, waterbeds, and better diet, has also improved the preterm's chances (for example, Kopp & Parmelee, 1979; Liederman, 1983). This does not mean that premature infants are no longer at risk. There continue to be somewhat higher rates of infant mortality and disorders such as cerebral palsy, particularly in very small preterms (those weighing less than 1,500 grams) (for example, Holmes, Reich & Pasternak, 1984; Kopp, 1983). Although the difference between preterms and full-terms in mortality and serious disorders is smaller, it is still there. For example, about 2% of full-terms suffer from serious neurological problems. Probably around 20% of all preterms do (for example, Holmes, Reich & Pasternak, 1984).

Even in the absence of severe disorders, preterms appear to develop more slowly than full-terms. During infancy, they appear to lag behind full-terms in gross motor, cognitive (for example, object permanence), personal-social, perceptual, and language development skills (for example, Crnic et al., 1983; Holmes, Nagy & Pasternak, 1984; Ungerer & Sigman, 1983). Many of the differences between preterms and full-terms seem to disappear by about 3 years of age (for example, Ungerer & Sigman, 1983). This suggests that some portion of the difference is attributable to the biological immaturity of the preterms. However, simply correcting for biological immaturity does not eliminate all the differences, particularly after the babies are more than a few months old (for example, Siegel, 1983a). This suggests that other factors, such as social interaction patterns and illness, are also influencing early development (for example, Greene, Fox & Lewis, 1983; Rocissano & Yatchmink, 1983).

Although many "deficits" are limited to the first 3 years, some problems seem to continue throughout the school years. Visual processing problems are frequently noted. This is reflected in both nonverbal IQ performance (for example, Caputo, Goldstein & Taub, 1979) and an increased risk for learning disabilities (for example, Siegel, 1983b). Preterms also display deficits in visual attention (for example, Fantz, Fagan & Miranda, 1975; Rose, 1980, 1981). The children showing the clearest visual attention deficits are also like to have lower IQs at 5 years of age (for example, Cohen & Parmelee, 1983).

Preterm birth thus appears to have both short- and long-term consequences. However, to simply say that prematurity causes developmental lags or learning disabilities is neither accurate nor informative. The real question is, what components of prematurity increase the likelihood of problematic development? Are the problems biologically based, or are they due to differences in parent-infant interactions?

Biological Factors in Prematurity.   At least three biological factors may put the premature infant at increased risk. First, premature infants are less physiologically mature. Their central nervous systems are underdeveloped (for example, Holmes, Reich & Pasternak, 1984). Their immature reflexes may contribute to feeding problems. They also show more sleep disturbances. Furthermore, their immaturity means they are more likely to develop infections, to be vulnerable to drug effects, to be less able to regulate their bodies' homeostatic balance, and so on.

This contributes to the second factor: They are more likely to be ill (for example, Holmes, Reich & Pasternak, 1984). And third, they are more likely to suffer from other complications (for example, delivery problems). Recall, for example, that alcoholic mothers are more likely to deliver preterms, and alcohol can affect the newborn and her future development (see Chapter 2).

The physiological immaturity factor most clearly affects behavior during the first few months. When statistical procedures are used to "correct" the age of the young preterm (under 12 months old), the behavioral differences between preterms and full-terms are reduced. This is not true of older preterms (for example, Siegel, 1983a). This is not necessarily because the preterms "catch up" biologically for in fact research suggests that preterms continue to be smaller than full-terms, at least into the preschool years (for example, Holmes, Reich & Pasternak, 1984). Rather, it is because the effects of the environment become more noticeable (for example, Siegel, 1983a). Simply correcting for gestational age will not erase or diminish the differences between older preterms and full-terms.

Preterms are also more likely to be ill than are full-terms. This is particularly true of smaller, less-developed premature infants. Some of the illnesses are directly attributable to prematurity. The immaturity of the preterm's lungs, for example, may lead to respiratory distress syndrome. This is considered a life-threatening disorder, although the actual mortality rates have declined dramatically in recent years (for example, Field, Dempsey & Shuman, 1983). The immaturity of the preterm's immune system means increased susceptibility to disease, including serious diseases such as meningitis (for example, Holmes, Reich & Pasternak, 1984). This increased susceptibility is one reason why premature infants have traditionally been kept in isolettes, removed from substantial amount of human contact (for example, Holmes, Reich & Pasternak, 1984).

Finally, certain groups of women are somewhat more likely to give birth to preterms. These groups include women who have had serious prenatal infections such as rubella; women who smoke, drink, or abuse drugs; and women who are poor (Holmes, Reich & Pasternak, 1984; see also Chapter 2). The children of women in all these groups are at risk even if they are not premature. This makes it difficult to sort out the effects of prematurity per se from the effects of other prenatal or perinatal complications.

To further complicate the issue, all these biological factors may influence the way parents interact with newborns. The physical immaturity of the preterm may render him less "appealing" to adults (for example, Goldberg, 1981). Illness may contribute to a more difficult temperament during the neonatal period, thereby affecting mother-infant interaction patterns (for example, Green, Fox & Lewis, 1983). Other complications may only intensify these effects. Let's now look more systematically at parent-premature interaction.

Parents and Preterms. There are really two issues here. First, how does parent-premature interaction differ from parent-fullterm interaction? What accounts for these differences? Are there characteristics of preterms that in and of themselves affect the parents, or are most of the differences attributable to hospital treatment of preterms and their parents? The second series of questions grows out of the first. How do these differential parent-infant interactions affect later development? Do parents of preterms continue to treat their babies differently than parents of full-terms treat theirs? Is any such continued differential treatment potentially detrimental to the preterm?

In answer to the first issue, there is little doubt that preterms are treated differently than full-terms. Studies of the neonatal period indicate, for example, that mothers of preterms are less actively involved with their babies. These mothers are less likely to cuddle, talk to, and touch their babies while feeding them (for example, DiVitto & Goldberg, 1979). Research with slightly older infants suggests that these mothers are less likely to smile at and look into the face of their babies (for example, Crnic et al., 1983). This does not mean that preemies receive little or no stimulation from their mothers. Mothers of 4-8-month-old preterms may actually talk to and touch their babies more frequently than mothers of full-terms. In fact, evidence suggests that during the first year, mothers of preterms inappropriately overstimulate their babies (for example, Crnic et al., 1983). These mothers and babies are less able to maintain an appropriate "rhythm" in their interactions. Their cycles of social interaction and inattention are not well matched (Lester, Hoffman & Brazelton, 1985). The differences are particularly dramatic if you compare sick preterms to healthy full-terms (for example, DiVitto & Goldberg, 1979; Green, Fox & Lewis, 1983).

Effects of Preterms' Characteristics on Parental Behavior.   What causes mothers of prematures to interact differently with their babies? One possibility is the characteristics of premature babies. Prematures sleep more than full-terms (for example, Holmes, Reich & Pasternak, 1984). When they are awake, prematures appear to be less responsive than full-term babies. They also initiate fewer interactions (for example, Lester, Hoffman & Brazelton, 1985). As newborns, they are less likely to orient to visual or auditory stimuli (for example, DiVitto & Goldberg, 1979). Premature infants look away from other people more frequently (for example, Field, 1979). During their first year, they smile and vocalize less than full-terms do (for example, Crnic et al., 1983).

Researchers disagree over whether preterms are more irritable than full-terms. Some researchers argue that they are (for example, Field, 1979a), while others argue they are not (for example, Holmes, Reich & Pasternak, 1984). However, it does appear that whatever crying and fussing preterms do may be more irritating to their parents. The cries of preterms are higher pitched and are perceived as more aversive (for example, Frodi et al., 1978) than the cries of full-terms. Again, these behaviors are particularly pronounced in sick premature infants.

Aside from these behavioral characteristics, the physical appearance of the newborn may also be important to the parents. Preemies have less body fat and so appear thin and drawn. Their eyes are often partially closed and may be surrounded by dark circles. Skin tones may be grey and mottled instead of pink (Holmes, Reich

& Pasternak, 1984). All these characteristics may contribute to adults' perception of preemies as relatively unattractive (for example, Frodi et al., 1978), although this perception may be ameliorated by continued interaction with one preterm (which would, of course, be what happens to specific parents) (for example, Corter et al., 1978).

Try to imagine the response of the parents to a premature infant. You have a baby who doesn't fit the "perfect baby" image physically or behaviorally. She is not "cute." She is not particularly alert. She doesn't respond well to social overtures. Recall how much of the mother's evaluation of the baby and of her own competence as a mother is based on the baby's behavior (see Chapter 3). Mothers of these babies are getting less feedback from their babies than other mothers get, and much of the feedback is negative. The mother is therefore more likely to evaluate herself and the baby more negatively. This may lead her to withdraw from the baby. It may, on the other hand, cause her to try harder to get the baby to interact. Indeed, the patterns of parent-infant interactions reviewed here suggest some mixture of these reactions. Such parent-infant interaction fits a transactional model quite nicely. The behaviors of the preterm affect the parents' impressions of themselves and their babies. These expectations, in turn, affect the way the parents treat the child.

Withdrawal and overstimulation are two possible parental reactions to prematurity. There is a third possibility. Research suggests that premature children are more likely to be abused than full-terms (for example, Lynch, 1975). This has been linked to their characteristics. The aversive cry of the premature, for example, may increase the likelihood of abuse (for example, Frodi et al., 1978), although this link has not been empirically documented. On the other hand, another element of the parent-premature relationship may contribute to abuse—the early separation of parents from their prematures due to hospitalization (for example, Kennell, Voos & Klaus, 1979).

The Effects of the Hospital Setting.   It is important to keep in mind that a premature birth is a medical emergency (Holmes, Reich & Pasternak, 1984). Explanations given to the parents may be brief. There may be little time to provide them with emotional support. This is particularly true in cases of very premature or ill children. The overall emotional tone probably intensifies the effects of the hospital setting that will now be considered.

As soon as the premature is born, he is removed from the delivery room. He may be placed in a neonatal intensive-care unit in the hospital where he was born. However, it is also possible that he will be transferred to another hospital where more specialized care is available (Holmes, Reich & Pasternak, 1984). The point here is that the parents and newborn are going to be separated. In very serious cases, the physical distance separating them may be sizable.

Since the infant is removed to facilitate medical care, he will already be "under treatment" when his parents first see him. Even relatively healthy preterms will be attached to an array of tubes and wires. More medical personnel hover

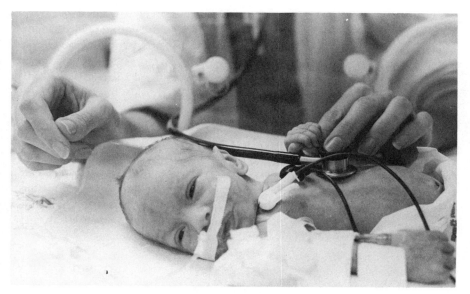

A premature infant in neonatal ICU. Courtesy of Children's Hospital, Columbus, Ohio.

around than in most other areas of the hospital. No wonder that parents find this first visit a shocking, often frightening experience. The parents were not prepared for this birth to begin with. Now they are faced with dealing with the birth of an endangered child (Holmes, Reich & Pasternak, 1984).

Given the psychological status of the parents and the hospital setting, it is not surprising that parents of preterms may not form normal early attachment bonds to their babies. These mothers may actually feel that the babies belong more to the medical staff than to them (for example, Leiderman, 1983). They are unsure of their ability to care for the child. In fact, they occasionally refuse to take the baby home (for example, Klaus & Kennell, 1976).

Researchers have found that such negative attitudes continue even after the baby is well enough to go home (for example, Leifer et al., 1972; Seashore et al., 1973). For several months after the baby is released from the hospital, these mothers seem less confident in their mothering abilities than do mothers of full-terms. This may be particularly true in first-time mothers (for example, Leiderman & Seashore, 1975). They also have lower self-esteem. These attitudes may well influence the way they interact with their babies. Indeed, they do not hold their babies as close as the mothers of full-terms hold theirs. They are also more rigid when holding their babies. These attitudes may also be related to the higher rates of child abuse directed toward preterms. Several researchers (Holmes et al., 1984; Kennell, Voos & Klaus, 1979; Leiderman, 1983) have postulated a connection between this early separation, negative attitudes about self and the baby, and abuse of preterms.

The early separation of mothers and babies due to medical needs may increase preterm risk. It may contribute to a poor mother-to-infant attachment bond, which may negatively influence interaction patterns. Among middle-class mothers, such effects appear temporary. They may disappear by the time the preterm is 2 years of age. Lower-class mothers may be more dramatically affected by the separation (for example, Leiderman, 1983). In short, while bonding may not be crucial in normal births, the severe disruption often seen in preterm births may negatively affect early parental functioning (for example, Leiderman, 1983).

Summary. Prematurity as a risk factor is often conceptualized as a primarily biological problem. The research clearly indicates that this is an oversimplification. In fact, characteristics of the premature infant as well as of her treatment influence the social environment. This, in turn, has implications for the child's outcome. Let's now turn to a risk factor that is commonly thought of as fundamentally social to see if it actually contains a biological component.

CHILD ABUSE

Definition. It seems as though it should be easy to define child abuse. We think of the dramatic cases we see chronicled in the newspaper or on television and can all agree that those children have been abused. Most Americans also agree that parents have a right to hit their children (see, for example, Belsky, 1980; Korbin, 1981a). The question, then, is where does discipline stop and abuse begin?

To further cloud the issue, at least four types of child abuse can be identified (Kempe & Kempe, 1978). There is physical violence, where a parent intentionally harms the child through slapping, kicking, burning, and the like. There is emotional and physical neglect. In such cases, the parent fails to provide the proper emotional and physical care to the child. As a result, the child may be malnourished, dressed inappropriately, or left without proper supervision. Neglect can be difficult to detect and can go on for a long time before it is discovered.

The third form of child abuse is emotional abuse. The parents may constantly denigrate the child and his actions. They may try to frighten him. They may ridicule him. Again, this type of abuse is difficult to identify. Finally, there is sexual abuse. This may involve rape, incest, or molestation. Such cases often go unidentified for long periods of time, particularly in cases of incest.

While all forms of abuse have potentially serious effects on the child, the focus here will be on physical violence. This does not mean that the other forms of abuse do not happen to children under 2 years of age. They do. However, the available research offers the most information about physical violence abuse.

Effects. Child abuse has both physical and psychological effects. The physical risks include central nervous system damage. Physically abused children are at risk for mental retardation, cerebral palsy, motor dysfunction (such as clumsiness or lack of coordination), and learning disorders (for example, Jones, 1981). It is not clear in every single case that the abuse actually caused the damage (Jones, 1981). Indeed, it is quite likely that in many cases the child was retarded or palsied or had learning disorders before the abuse. However, such damage may be the result of abuse. This damage may be attributable to repeated severe blows to the head. Such injury can occur without any visible damage to the skull or face. This is because in young children, violent shaking can also cause brain injury (for example, Caffey, 1972, 1974).

Abused children also often show retarded growth (Jones, 1981). This pattern is often referred to as *failure-to-thrive* syndrome. Quite simply, these children fail to grow. There is no known medical cause for the problem. In some cases the children are malnourished, although the malnutrition cannot account for the extent of the growth failure. An 18-month-old, for example, might weigh only 10 pounds. While some of these children will "catch up" when their home situation is remedied, others continue to fail to grow (Jones, 1981).

Even in the absence of these physical effects, there may be psychological damage. The psychological effects of child abuse can emerge early. Abuse disrupts infant-to-mother attachment, for example (Schneider-Rosen & Cicchetti, 1984). Abused and neglected infants do attach to their mothers, but these attachments are more likely to be insecure. This may hold implications for both social and cognitive development (see Chapter 4).

Although the direct link between attachment and social and cognitive development in abused children has not been investigated, it is apparent that abuse affects development in these realms. By 2-3 years of age abused children are more aggressive than their peers (for example, George & Main, 1979; Hoffman-Plotkin & Twentyman, 1984). They also harass and threaten their caregivers more frequently (George & Main, 1979). They are less likely to make friendly overtures to caregivers, and they tend to avoid attempts by peers and caregivers to make friendly contact with them (George & Main, 1979). This is an interesting pattern because it indicates that at a very early age abused children begin to do things that may result in social isolation, which is one characteristic of abusive parents. The development of this pattern may be one reason that abused children are at risk for becoming abusive parents themselves (Belsky, 1980).

Cognitive development also appears impaired in abused children. Both abused and neglected preschoolers score lower than their peers on IQ tests (Hoffman-Plotkin & Twentyman, 1984). They also show language deficits (Jones, 1981), including small vocabularies (for example, Hoffman-Plotkin & Twentyman, 1984).

Finally, these children may have impaired personality development (for example, Green, 1978). They may fail to develop the basic trust described by Erikson as the foundation of development (see Chapter 10). They may have poor self-concepts. Self-abusive behaviors (such as self-biting or headbanging) are also more common among abused children.

Clearly, then, abuse puts a child at risk in a variety of ways. Virtually every major area of development can be negatively affected by abuse. Furthermore, these abused children are more likely to become abusive parents. This creates a self-perpetuating cycle of risk.

What we seem to have is an environmental factor (abuse) serving to increase the likelihood of poor development. In fact, one might be left with the impression that abuse causes these negative effects independently of the child involved. This is an oversimplification, for the type of home environment available after the period of abuse influences the ultimate outcome (Jones, 1981; Main, 1981). Furthermore, it seems that only some children are likely to be the victims of abuse. In other words, even within an abusive family not all children are equally likely to be abused (for example, Parke & Collmer, 1975). Thus, in addition to the risk factors attributable to the abuse itself, another element of risk must be considered: That is the question of what characteristics put a child at risk for child abuse.

Children at Risk for Abuse.   We have already seen that premature infants are more likely to be abused than full-terms. Children with handicaps are also at risk for abuse (for example, Burgess, 1978). These handicaps may be physical, such as Downs' syndrome or a deformity or chronic illness; or they may be psychological, such as hyperactivity or a difficult temperament (though, in such cases, it is difficult to know which came first, the abuse or the behavioral problem).

Obviously, these childen all present a special challenge to their parents. They are all more difficult to raise than the average child. They may require extensive, and expensive, medical treatment. This may result in separations that may impair parent-to-infant attachment (for example, Leiderman, 1983; see above discussion). They may need special schooling or psychological treatment. Further, on a day-to-day basis, they may require more or special attention. They may also be less responsive to parental stimulation or interaction. Overall, their parents are more likely to perceive them as disappointments.

It is important to emphasize that none of these characteristics "causes" abuse. Instead, each increases the likelihood that a child will be abused by certain types of parents. Hence, for example, parents who were abused themselves are more likely to be abusers. So are parents who have little experience with child care (Belsky, 1980).

Even this combination of a particular type of child and a particular type of parent is not sufficient to explain child abuse. Broader familial issues are involved, too. Typically, there are marital problems in abusive families. These may cause a parent to look to the child for emotional support and sustenance (Belsky, 1980). While this would be a difficult role for any child, it is particularly unlikely that the "special" children described above could fill this role. The resulting disappointment and frustration may increase the risk of abuse.

The situation gets even more complex. The supports available in the family's immediate social situation also play a role. Unemployment or job dissatisfaction increases the likelihood of abuse (Belsky, 1980). So does social isolation. The social isolation may be due to cultural attitudes of not "getting involved" in other families' business. In China, for example, where a person can be held morally and legally responsible for a neighborhood child's abuse, child maltreatment is rare (Korbin, 1981b). The pattern of social isolation may also be attributable to parental behaviors such as withdrawal and avoidance that first developed in childhood (Belsky, 1980; see the preceding discussion of childhood social behaviors among abuse victims).

Finally, cultural values may contribute to the likelihood of abuse. In the United States, children are viewed as the property of parents (Belsky, 1980). Contrast this to China, where children are viewed as belonging to (and being the future of) the state. China's government, therefore, takes a much greater role in monitoring the health and well-being of children (Korbin, 1981b). In addition, violence is an integral part of American society (Belsky, 1980). This is evident in our media preferences, high murder and assault rates, and our high rates of child abuse (Belsky, 1980). Such cultural norms may further increase the likelihood of abuse.

What we see, then, is that a variety of social and biological factors interact to produce child abuse. No one factor can explain the presence (or absence) of abuse in a particular family. Similarly, no one factor can determine the child's developmental outcome. As with prematurity, risk is a multifaceted phenomenon. Nonetheless, the balance of risk factors is not identical in prematurity and in child abuse. Prematurity contains a large component of biological risk, while child abuse is a more socially oriented risk factor. In the final example of at-risk development, there is a greater balance of biological and social factors.

CHILDREN OF DISTURBED PARENTS

Parental psychiatric disorders are frequently cited as a major risk factor in child development (for example, Sameroff & Chandler, 1975; Werner & Smith, 1982). Children whose parents have psychiatric disorders are more likely than their peers to develop abnormal behavior in either childhood or adulthood.

Traditionally, researchers have focused on the most seriously ill parents. These include schizophrenic, seriously depressed, and personality-disordered parents. Schizophrenia, which has received the most attention, is the focus of this section.

Defining Schizophrenia.   *Schizophrenia* is a severe thought disorder in which the victim may have unrealistic ideas *(delusions)* about people persecuting him or about his own importance. Hallucinations, especially "hearing vioices," are common. Thought is illogical and is marked by poor associational patterns, that is, one thought is not connected to either the preceding or subsequent ones. Often, schizophrenics exhibit bizarre behavior that may include inappropriate laughing, failure to find pleasure in anything *(anhedonia)*, lack of sexual inhibitions, or maintaining the body in some contorted position for hours (American Psychiatric Association, 1980). There are several different types of schizophrenia, which are summarized in Table 11-3.

TABLE 11-3   Types of Schizophrenia and Their Associated Risk to Offspring

TYPE	DESCRIPTION	RISK TO OFFSPRING
Hebephrenic (disorganized)	Delusions and hallucinations are bizarre and do not focus around a single theme. Shallow, inappropriate affect. Loss of modesty and concern for appearance. Severely disordered thought.	The children of hebephrenics are at very high risk. If both parents are schizophrenic (one hebephrenic), nearly 21% of the children will develop schizophrenia. If one parent is normal, the risk is about 17%.
Catatonic	Delusions are fantastic and changeable. Alternates between periods of catatonia and mania. In the catatonic state, the person assumes and holds a fixed position. He appears oblivious to his surroundings and bodily needs. The position may hold some symbolic meaning for the person. In the manic state, the person is highly agitated, moving and speaking rapidly. May be dangerous to self or others during the manic state.	The risk to offspring of catatonics is also quite high. If a catatonic mates with another schizophrenic (non-catatonic), the risk of the child developing schizophrenia is nearly 22%. If the other parent is normal, the risk is about 16%.
Paranoid	Delusions center around themes of persecution and grandeur. As disorder progresses, the delusions become increasingly complex and bizarre. May be dangerous.	Risk to offspring is about 10% if the paranoid mates with another schizophrenic. If the other parent is normal, the risk is about 8.5%.
Simple	Delusions and hallucinations are present, but the person does not fit any of the above categories.	The risk to offspring is almost 12% if the second parent is a schizophrenic. If the other parent is normal, the risk is less than 2%.

(Gottesman, I., & Shields, J. (1982). *Schizophrenia: The epigenetic puzzle.* Cambridge, MA: Cambridge University Press.)

A recent survey by the National Institute of Mental Health suggested that about 1% of all Americans suffer from schizophrenia (*Time*, 1984). This translates to about 1.5 million Americans. A little more than half of these people are receiving treatment, which typically involves drug therapy. Such therapy can be quite effective, although not all schizophrenics recover. The availability of such effective therapy has probably increased the number of schizophrenics who bear and raise children (Sameroff, Seifer & Zax, 1982). In addition, schizophrenia often does not require treatment until the victim is in her 30s. This implies that many schizophrenics, particularly women, will have children prior to the onset of the illness (for example, Gottesman & Shields, 1982). So, a significant number of schizophrenics do become parents.

Although the risk rate of developing schizophrenia is only about 1% in the general population, about 10-15% of the children born to one schizophrenic parent will develop the disorder (for example, Walker & Emory, 1983), while about 45% of the children with two schizophrenic parents will develop the disorder (for example, Gottesman & Shields, 1982). Certain forms of schizophrenia seem to carry higher risk than others. Thus, for example, the children of hebephrenic or catatonic schizophrenics are at greater risk than those born to paranoid or simple schizophrenics (see Table 11-3) (Gottesman & Shields, 1982). Furthermore, some evidence suggests that children of schizophrenics are more likely to develop some form of mental illness, even if it is not schizophrenia, than their peers (for example, Higgins, 1976; but see also Gottesman & Shields, 1982, for an opposing view).

The children of schizophrenics differ from their peers in a number of ways. For example, motor deficits are more common among these children. These deficits are apparent at birth, when the motor reflexes of schizophrenic offspring are weaker (for example, Mednick et al., 1971). These children continue to show deficits, at least throughout the first year (see Walker & Emory, 1983, for a summary). The children of schizophrenics also display attentional problems. They seem to be particularly poor at distinguishing a signal from background noise (see Rutter & Garmezy, 1983, for a summary). Also, some evidence suggests that these children are excessively sensitive to stimuli (for example, Walker & Emory, 1983). However, not all researchers have reported this finding (Rutter & Garmezy, 1983).

It should be emphasized that it is not known which, if any, of these behavioral differences predicts the later development of schizophrenia (Rutter & Garmezy, 1983). Not all the children born to schizophrenics show these deficits; and, or course, not all of them will develop schizophrenia. Researchers simply do not know if the ones showing the early deficits are also the ones most likely to develop schizophrenia themselves.

Nonetheless, it is clear that the children of schizophrenics are considered a high-risk population. What is the source of the risk? Are these children genetically "predisposed" toward developing schizophrenia? Or is the stress of being raised by a schizophrenic parent or parents the culprit?

Genetic Factors.　No doubt genetics plays a role in the increased risk of the offspring of schizophrenics (for example, Gottesman & Shields, 1982; Walker & Emory, 1983). However, the precise nature of the transmission of the genetic predisposition is not known (Walker & Emory, 1983). We do not know, for example, if just one gene is involved in schizophrenia or if a number of genes are responsible. In fact, the nature of the predisposition itself is not known (for example, Walker & Emory, 1983).

What is clear is that genetic factors alone are not enough to explain the development of schizophrenia. First of all, almost 90% of the schizophrenics who have been studied do not have schizophrenic parents (Rutter & Garmezy, 1983). Second, studies of twins clearly point out the importance of nongenetic influences.

Indeed, studies of twins, particularly monozygotic (MZ) twins, are an important source of information about genetic effects. Monozygotic, or identical, twins develop from the same zygote (fertilized egg). They therefore have exactly the same genetic makeup. If a trait is completely determined by genetics, both will have that characteristic. This is 100% *concordance*. Any lower concordance rate would indicate that nongenetic factors are involved.

Concordance rates for schizophrenia among MZ twins vary from study to study. Typically, they average about 45-65% concordance (Gottesman & Shields, 1982). This means that even with the higher estimates, about one-third of all identical twins with schizophrenia have a nonschizophrenic twin. (However, the reverse of this statement, that is, that one-third of all nonschizophrenic MZ twins have a schizophrenic twin, is not true.) Since MZ twins have identical genetic material, some other factors must be operative. The question is, are those other factors biological or social or both?

Other Biological Factors.   Prenatal and perinatal complications appear to increase the risk that a child born to schizophrenic will later develop the disorder (Walker & Emory, 1983). These complications do not seem to be more common among babies born to schizophrenics (Walker & Emory, 1983). But when they occur, they tend to have more dramatic effects (Walker & Emory, 1983).

The research provides several examples of these effects. Maternal water retention, vaginal bleeding during pregnancy, and the use of anesthesia were associated with lower IQ among the school-age children of schizophrenics (for example, Reider, Broman & Rosenthal, 1977). A similar relationship was *not* found for a peer group. Similarly, low birth weight was associated with neurological and motor deficits among schizophrenics' children (for example, Marcus et al., 1981). Again, no such relationship was found for peers, even for peers whose mothers were suffering from disturbances other than schizophrenia (for example, depression and personality disorders).

Such findings indicate that schizophrenics' children may by nature be more vulnerable to trauma. Elaine Walker and Eugene Emory (1983) suggested that this vulnerability may be rooted in the central nervous system's balance-maintaining mechanisms. Walker and Emory argued that these children's central nervous systems may be thrown more off balance, and show less recovery, when exposed to trauma. This is only a hypothesis. Yet the presence of perinatal complications is the only factor that predicts the development of schizophrenia in both the male and female children born to schizophrenics.

Interestingly, not all authors believe that this vulnerability is always genetically determined (for example, Brodsky & Brodsky, 1981). It apparently can be acquired. This helps us to understand how 90% of schizophrenics are born to nonschizophrenic parents.

Thus, the major biological factor involved in the development of schizophrenia seems to be the presence of vulnerability, particularly in conjunction with prenatal or perinatal complications. This does not mean that social factors play no role in the development of the disorder. In fact, schizophrenic parents may well contribute to the development of the disorder through the type of environment they provide.

Schizophrenic Parenting. Many theorists (for example, Bateson et al., 1956) have argued that schizophrenia can be caused by early parent-child interactions. Although this view is no longer dominant, it does point out that the family lives of schizophrenics can differ dramatically from that of other people. Furthermore, most theorists agree that family environment, perhaps in conjunction with constitutional vulnerability, is a contributing factor in the development of schizophrenia.

This belief has lead researchers to examine the parenting style of schizophrenics. The assumption here is that these parents are particularly likely to display the patterns that encourage schizophrenic development. In addition, the children of these parents are, of course, more likely to have the constitutional vulnerability that many believe enhances the negative impact of poor parenting.

Do schizophrenic parents treat their infants differently? Some research suggests that they do. Schizophrenic mothers have been described, for example, as insensitive and even rejecting (see Brodsky & Brodsky, 1981, and Walker & Emory, 1983, for reviews). Their parenting does not seem to be based on the infant's needs or signals. This implies that their parenting is inconsistent, at least from the baby's perspective. It also means that the mother is of limited value in helping the baby adapt to environmental demands.

According to Patricia and Marvin Brodsky (1981), this inability to assist in infant adaptation is critical. They argued that the "constitutional vulnerability" in the offspring of schizophrenics takes the form of an inability to regulate incoming stimuli. In other words, these babies are particularly poor at tuning out stimuli. They are easily overaroused and have a difficult time calming themselves. If their mothers cannot help in regulating the environment, the mothers themselves may become sources of overstimulation. Thus, the mother herself becomes aversive. Brodsky and Brodsky (1981) suggested that this is why so many of these children show anxious-avoidant attachments to their mothers. This poor attachment holds negative implications for later development (see Chapter 4).

Children of rejecting mothers often show anxious-avoidant attachment patterns, even when schizophrenia is not a factor (for example, Main, 1981). However, the combination of this type of parent-child relationship and a constitutional vulnerability may place the children of schizophrenics at particular risk (Brodsky & Brodsky, 1981). In such cases, there is a poor fit between child and environment. As noted in Chapter 10, a poor child-environment fit puts a child at risk for psychopathology (Thomas & Chess, 1977).

So, the emotional responsiveness of the mother may be a factor in the development of schizophrenia. However, such unresponsiveness is not limited to schizophrenic mothers. Indeed, some researchers report that it is less common in schizophrenics than in depressed mothers (for example, Fisher et al., 1980; Sameroff, Seifer & Zax, 1982). A study by Arnold Sameroff and his colleagues (Sameroff, Seifer & Zax, 1982), for example, found few differences between the way that schizophrenic and normal mothers treated their infants (from birth to 30 months of age). Neurotically depressed mothers, however, were more anxious and showed less competence socially than the other mothers. They were less involved with their young infants. When the babies were 30 months of age, depressed mothers were more likely to report their children as being difficult, though direct observations did not always support this. This means that depressed mothers made negative appraisals of their children, even if their children's behavior didn't warrant it. Under the transactional model (see Chapter 1), such appraisals are expected to have negative effects on parent-child interaction and on child development.

Why would depressed mothers show more aberrant parenting patterns than schizophrenics? On a day-to-day basis, the depressed mothers may be more "disturbed" than the schizophrenic mothers (for example, Fisher et al., 1980); that is, the effects of their disorder on their behavior are more consistent. Schizophrenic symptoms tend to be episodic and can be controlled with drugs. Moderate neurotic depression looks less severe and is therefore less likely to be treated immediately. It is also somewhat less easily treated. So, these mothers show the symptoms more regularly and for longer time periods than do schizophrenics.

In general, then, the presence of schizophrenia does not guarantee poor parenting. In fact, disorders other than schizophrenia may be more closely associated with aberrant parenting. However, the children of schizophrenics are still more likely to develop severe behavioral problems than their peers (for example, Werner & Smith, 1982). This is probably because of their constitutional vulnerability. These vulnerable children cannot adapt to poor parenting as well as others can (for example, Brodsky & Brodsky, 1981). Those most likely to develop serious problems also tend to be exposed to nonparenting environmental stressors (for example, poverty, divorce) (Werner & Smith, 1982). It seems to be a combination of vulnerability and stress that leads to the development of psychiatric disorders. This combination is more likely to occur in the offspring of schizophrenics. Of course, the combination does not occur in all children born to schizophrenics. Remember, 90% of these children will not develop schizophrenia themselves.

CONCLUSION

The development of at-risk infants is of interest for at least two reasons. First, there is concern for the infants themselves. We are interested in maximizing every child's chances for normal, healthy development. Second, the development of at-risk infants provides clues as to how normal development proceeds. It is often easier to identify a deviant pattern than a run-of-the-mill one.

The research on at-risk infants tends to support the transactional model of development. There is little doubt that these children possess characteristics that make them more difficult to raise. However, the reaction of their parents to these characteristics is crucial. Parental interpretation of child behavior heavily influences their own behavior toward the child. The development of a negative parent-child relationship increases the likelihood that these children will develop abnormally. On the other hand, positive parenting can mediate the effects of even severe biological risk; so, for example, a child born with Downs' syndrome can attain a close-to-normal IQ when raised in a stimulating, supportive, warm environment (for example, Kopp, 1983).

It is clear, then, that no child is biologically predestined to develop problems. Rather, it is the interaction of biological and environmental factors that determines the child's developmental outcome.

12

Challenges and Caveats

When you were born, your parents may well have wondered if you could see or hear. They may have wondered when you would be able to understand them or recognize their voices. They may have thought that you had no thoughts, that you understood absolutely nothing about the world around you.

Now, many new parents are concerned about when to start teaching their babies how to read. They may even grapple with the question of when to purchase a home computer for the infant. These shifts are at least partially attributable to our increased knowledge of neonatal and infant abilities. You have already seen that infants are well equipped to organize their worlds and to gain knowledge. They have individual personalities. They are ready to interact with other human beings.

All these data suggest that infants, and even newborns, have much greater capabilities than we formerly believed. In one sense, this is a positive step. It enables us as parents and professionals to better tap into the baby's needs and abilities. We may be getting closer to being able to construct environments that may truly optimize development. However, this knowledge also carries risks.

Risky Assumptions

Overestimating Abilities. One risk is that we will overestimate and over-emphasize the capabilities of infants. As a society obsessed with achievement, we may be particularly likely to focus on the perceptual and cognitive skills. We may at the same time ignore (or at least underestimate) the emotional needs of the child. This may lead us to expect too much of the child.

We often see this sort of situation arise with talented children. A friend of mine has a very gifted preschooler. When he was 4 years of age, he read on a fourth-grade level. He could spell a variety of words, including words as difficult as *pharmacy.* He assigned numbers to each letter of the alphabet and then wrote words in the number "code." The child's abilities were so striking that people often forgot that he was only 4. They were amazed (and a bit disappointed) when he threw temper tantrums or refused to share or displayed separation fears. Indeed, even his mother reported that she often "forgot" that he was still a preschooler.

David Elkind (1981) has noted that this may be happening to increasing numbers of children. He suggested that we are "hurrying" our children into adulthood. He pointed out several causes of this "trend," one of which is our emphasis on intellectual achievement. We have clearly seen this trend extended into infancy with programs like Glenn Doman's (1982) and articles in popular magazines on how to make your infant brighter.

The Stability Assumption.   There is another danger in our increased knowledge of infancy. We have come so far in our knowledge during the past 20 years that we may lose sight of how much we have to learn: We still cannot reliably predict future intellectual functioning (see Chapter 8). We still cannot define the effects of maternal speech on child language development (see Chapter 9). We still cannot identify which children will develop schizophrenia or other serious disorders (see Chapter 11).

However, we continue to assume that one day we will be able to make such predictions. This is attributable not only to our faith in our abilities and technology but also to our belief that infancy is an important, if not the most important, period of development. We assume that early experience shapes later experience. This is at least partially rooted in Freud's argument that personality is formed by age 5 (for example, Hall & Lindzey, 1970). It is bolstered (and reflected) by other major theorists such as Piaget and Erikson.

Yet, little evidence indicates that infancy by definition lays an immutable foundation for later development. Indeed, we have seen that attachment patterns can change (see Chapter 4). Temperament may be so affected by environmental circumstances that a difficult temperament is all but forgotten (see Chapter 10). Indeed, negative effects of early separation appear to be reversible (Rutter, 1979). Substantial evidence suggests that the resiliency of human beings far outweights most individual experiences (see, for example, Garmezy & Rutter, 1983).

None of this means that infancy experiences cannot affect later behavior. If the child continues in the same environment, her behavior may show considerable stability (for example, Chapters 4 & 10). This, of course, is likely to be the case for two reasons. First, most children are reared by the same parent or parents most, if not all, of their lives. Even in cases of divorce, one of the biological parents will retain custody, and the noncustodial parent is quite likely to continue to play a role in the child's life.

Second, genetic predispositions shape the environment (Scarr & McCartney, 1983). A highly active child will choose certain friends and activities that a lower-activity child would not. In addition, the child's behavior affects the behaviors and attitudes of the people around her. As the transactional model suggests, these people start to treat the child as if they expect he will behave in a certain manner. This treatment may maintain or even intensify certain child behaviors. For example, I have a nephew who as an infant was very active. He was into almost everyting. His mother labeled him hyperactive. She put him on a sugar-free diet (though she permitted him to have honey). Occasionally, though, the boy would get something with sugar in it. When he did, she expected him to "act out." He always did— as long as she or another family member was around. When he went to nursery school, on the other hand, there was no evidence of high activity level much less hyperactivity. It appeared his behavior was maintained more by his mother's expectations than by his own predispositions.

Of course, some behaviors such as certain aspects of temperament or visual memory functioning appear to remain quite stable independent of environmental forces. These behaviors may be affected by extreme environments (for example, being isolated from human contact); yet, they seem to account for at least some of the individual differences observed in both rate and style of development. Some of these characteristics may be genetically mediated. Others may be attributable to prenatal or perinatal influences. The source of other stable individual differences remains unclear.

Future Research

Individual Differences.   The study of individual differences is a growing area of child development. Developmentalists now recognize that normal language development takes more than one path (see Chapter 9). And some children seem to be more vulnerable to stress than others, placing them at risk for pathological development (see Chapter 11). Some infants seem to develop visual recognition memory more quickly than others; this may indicate differences in intellectual capabilities (see Chapter 7).

These and other individual differences serve to remind us of the warnings about normative data (see Chapter 1). Although normative data provide useful information, they may serve to impede our understanding of child development. In the late 1960s and early 1970s, for example, it was generally accepted that the first vocabulary words were predominantly nouns. This belief, which reflects normative data, influenced the popular theories of language acquisition (for example, McNeill, 1970). When research indicated that not all children showed this pattern (for example, Nelson, 1981), theories of language development had to be revised.

In addition, emphasis on normative data may interfere with successful teaching and intervention. Education and intervention programs are often designed as if age-mates will all be functioning at the same developmental levels (in terms of attention span, conceptual development, social development, and so on) and will be able to tolerate comparable levels of stimulation and social interaction. Programs which minimize individual differences may well miss the opportunity to develop a particular child's talents. Conversely, such programs may frustrate a child who cannot keep up. In both cases, the child's self-esteem may well be threatened. Other areas of development may also be negatively influenced. Thus, a fuller understanding of individual differences will have both theoretical and applied value.

Ethnocentrism.   Much of the available research has involved observation of American children. Such research forms the core data base for theorizing about universal principles in child development. We build theories based on the assumption that virtually all parents treat their children as Americans do, at least on certain fundamental issues. So, for example, we assume that all parents talk to their infants. We then build theories of language development emphasizing mother-infant interactions. Yet, not all parents do talk to their babies (for example, Schieffelin & Ochs, 1983) (see Chapter 9). Thus, mother-infant interaction cannot be as crucial as some theorists suppose. Similar arguments can be made about sex-role development (for example, Bronstein, 1984) or a child's ability to responsibly care for herself without parental supervision (for example, Korbin, 1981).

Clearly, then, we need to expand our data base. More cross-cultural research is needed before "determinants" of child development can be identified. Without such data, we run the risk of assuming that culturally determined behaviors reflect predispositions of the human species.

Context of Development.   It is, of course, important to understand how cultural values themselves influence development. Similarly, differences among families need to be examined in order to account for child development. Indeed, we have seen numerous studies of how parenting differences might affect the development of attachment, self-concept, gender roles, language, and psychopathology.

Unfortunately, these studies typically set up cultural or familial factors as *independent variables*; that is, these factors are treated as causing the child's behavior or development. Much less attention has been given to the way the child affects parental behavior. We have often lost sight of the transaction between child and parent. The use of the transactional model to guide research on child development represents another important advance (Maccoby & Martin, 1983).

Emphasis on the transaction between parent and child is only one way in which child development is being placed in context. We also need to understand how parents are affected by one another and by societal institutions, norms, and so on (Maccoby & Martin, 1983). Much of our research looks at the interaction of mother and child together. Again, we build theories of development based on such observations. Yet, when fathers or siblings are introduced to the situation, the behavior of both the mother and the infant changes (for example, Clarke-Stewart, 1978; Dunn, 1983). Understanding how the interactions among all family members influence development represents another challenge for future researchers.

Similarly, we need to understand how situational factors affect parenting, which in turn may affect the child. We have little information about how mothers of day-care children differ from those who choose to stay home (for example, Belsky & Steinberg, 1978; Hock, 1980). Yet, we assume that any differences between day-care and home-reared children are attributable either to the daily separation of the day-care children from their mothers or the day-care program per se. It is equally likely that differences may be due to differences in attitudes or behaviors of the mothers and fathers when they are with their children. Indeed, even the differential effects of various programs may be at least partially attributable to differences among the parents. After all, the parents selected the program. It may well be that the selection reflects some differences in parenting attitudes or behaviors.

The argument here is that development will only be fully understood when it is placed in context. The context includes the culture and the family. It involves how members of the family influence one another. We also need to understand how the society and the family interact. How does a family make a decision about child-care or educational programs? What does that tell us about their parenting styles? How does that influence child development?

Conclusion

Since the early work on child development (for example, Watson, 1928), we have come a long way in our conceptualization of human infants. We now view them as complex, well-functioning human beings. We see them as being distinctively individual right from birth. These attitudinal shifts have dramatically affected our patterns of child care.

There are, of course, risks attendant to our increased knowledge. We may overestimate the child's ability. We may even overestimate the importance of the infancy period. Both risks are exemplified in our increasing concern that we are permanently losing the best opportunity to teach our children reading, arithmetic, and so on, if we don't start during infancy.

Despite our increased understanding of individual differences, we frequently cling to the idea of the average child. This, too, carries risks for theorizing about child development and designing effective intervention programs.

Future research in infant development is being shaped by an increasingly complex view of developmental context. We are moving toward a transactional model that recognizes the reciprocal interaction of child and parent. We are also increasingly aware that the child has more than one parent (the mother) influencing development and that the parents have influences on their own functioning—influences that in turn affect their interactions with their children.

While such models will make infant research a more challenging and difficult endeavor, they also carry with them the possibility of great rewards. Despite the massive increase in knowledge concerning infants, we have only begun to approach an understanding of infant development. The challenge of the future is to expand not only our knowledge but also our conceptualization of how human infants function and develop. In that challenge lies our best hope for maximizing individual developmental potential.

References

ABEL, E. (1981). Behavioral teratology of alcohol. *Psychological Bulletin, 90,* 564-581.

ABEL, E. (1984). *Fetal alcohol syndrome and fetal alcohol effects.* New York: Plenum.

ACREDOLO, L. (1978). Development of spatial orientation in infancy. *Developmental Psychology, 14,* 224-234.

ADAMS, R., & PASSMAN, R. (1981). The effects of preparing two-year-olds for brief separations from their mothers. *Child Development, 52,* 1068-1070.

ADELSON, E., & FRAIBERG, S. (1974). Gross motor development in infants blind from birth. *Child Development, 45,* 114-126.

AINSWORTH, M.D.S. (1973). The development of infant-mother attachment. In B. Caldwell & H. Ricciuti (eds.), *Review of child development research* (Vol. 3). Chicago: University of Chicago Press.

AINSWORTH, M.D.S., & BELL, S. (1977). Infant crying and maternal responsiveness: A rejoiner to Gewirtz and Boyd. *Child Development, 48,* 1208-1216.

AINSWORTH, M., BELL, S., & STAYTON, D. (1971). Individual differences in strange situation behavior of one-year-olds. In H. Schaffer (ed.), *The origins of human social relations.* New York: Academic Press.

AINSWORTH, M.D.S., BLEHAR, M.C., WATERS, E., & WALL, S. (1978). *Patterns of attachment.* Hillsdale, N.J.: Erlbaum.

AINSWORTH, M., & WITTIG, B. (1969). Attachment and exploratory behavior of one-year-olds in a strange situation. In B. Foss (ed.), *Determinants of infant behavior IV.* London: Methuen.

ALLIK, J., & VALSINER, J. (1980). Visual development in ontogenesis: Some reevaluations. In H.W. Reese & L.P. Lipsitt (eds.), *Advances in child development and behavior* (vol. 15). New York: Academic Press.

ALPERT, J., & RICHARDSON, M. (1980) Parenting. In L. Poon (ed.), *Aging in the 1980s.* Washington, D.C.: American Psychological Association.

262   *References*

ALS, H., TRONICK, E., LESTER, B., & BRAZELTON, T.B. (1979). Specific neonatal measures: The Brazelton Neonatal Behavioral Assessment Scale. In J.D. Osofsky (ed.), *Handbook of infant development*. New York: John Wiley.

AMERICAN PSYCHIATRIC ASSOCIATION. (1980). *Diagnostic and Statistical Manual* (3rd ed.). Washington, D.C.: APA.

ANISFELD, M. (1984). *Language development from birth to three*. Hillsdale, N.J.: Erlbaum.

ANNIS, L. (1978). *The child before birth*. New York: Cornell University Press.

ANTELL, S., & KEATING, D. (1983). Perception of numerical invariance in neonates. *Child Development, 54,* 695-701.

AREND, L., GOVE, F., & SROUFE, A. (1979). Continuity of individual adaptation from infancy to kindergarten: A predictive study of ego-resiliency and curiosity in preschoolers. *Child Development, 50,* 950-959.

ARONSON, E., & ROSENBLOOM, S. (1971). Space perception in early infancy: Perception within a common auditory-visual space. *Science, 172,* 1161-1163.

ASLIN, R.N., PISONI, D.B., & JUSCZYK, P.W. (1983). Auditory development and speech perception in infancy. In P. Mussen (ed.), *Handbook of child psychology* (Vol. 2). New York: John Wiley.

AZRIN, M., & FOXX, R. (1981). *Toilet-training in less than a day*. New York: Simon & Schuster.

BAHRICK, L. (1980). Infants' perception of properties of objects as specified by amodal information in auditory-visual events. Unpublished doctoral dissertation, Cornell University, Ithaca, N.Y.

BANKS, M. (1980). The development of visual accommodation during early infancy. *Child Development, 51,* 646-666.

BANKS, M., & SALAPATEK, P. (1983). Infant visual perception. In P. Mussen (eds.), *Handbook of child psychology* (Vol. II), *Infancy and developmental psychobiology*. (4th ed.). New York: John Wiley.

BARNES, S., GUTFREUND, M., SATTERLY, D., & WELLS, G. (1983). Characteristics of adult speech which predict children's language development. *Journal of Child Language, 10,* 57-64.

BARNET, A., OLRICH, E., & SHANKS, B. (1974). EEG evoked responses to repetitive stimulation in normal and Downs syndrome infants. *Developmental Medicine and Child Neurology, 5,* 612-619.

BARNETT, R., & BARUCH, G. (1983). Determinants of fathers' participation in family work. *Wellesley College Center for Research on Women Working Papers* (No. 136).

BARRERA, M., & MAURER, D. (1981). Recognition of mother's photographed face by the three-month-old infant. *Child Development, 52,* 714-716.

BARTEN, S., BIRNS, B., & RONCH, J. (1971). Individual differences in the visual pursuit behavior of neonates. *Child Development, 42,* 313-319.

BATES, E., BENIGNI, L., BRETHERTON, I., CAMAIONI, L., & VOLTERRA, V. (1979). *The emergence of symbols: Cognition and communication in infancy*. New York: Academic Press.

BATES, J. (1980). The concept of difficult temperament. *Merrill-Palmer Quarterly, 26,* 299-320.

BATES, J., FREELAND, C., & LOUNSBURY, M. (1979). Measurement of infant difficultness. *Child Development, 50,* 794-803.

BATESON, G., JACKSON, D., HALEY, J., & WEAKLAND, J. (1956). Toward a theory of schizophrenia. *Behavioral Science, 4,* 251-264.

BAYLEY, N. (1935). The development of motor abilities during the first three years. *Monographs of the Society for Research in Child Development, 1.*

BAYLEY, N. (1969). *Manual for the Bayley Scales of Infant Development*. New York: Psychological Corporation.

BECK, A. (1967). *Depression: Clinical, experimental, and theoretical aspects*. New York: Hoeber.

BECKWITH, L. (1972). Relationships between infants' social behavior and their mothers' behavior. *Child Development, 43,* 397-411.

BELL, S., & AINSWORTH, M.D.S. (1972). Infant crying and maternal responsiveness. *Child Development, 43,* 1171-1190.

BELLINGER, D. (1980). Consistency in the pattern of change in mothers' speech: Some discriminant analyses. *Journal of Child Language, 7,* 469-487.

BELSKY, J. (1980). Child maltreatment: An ecological integration. *American Psychologist, 35,* 320-335.
BELSKY, J., ROVINE, M., & TAYLOR, D. (1984). The Pennsylvania Infant and Family Development Project III: The origins of individual differences in infant-mother attachment: Maternal and infant contributions. *Child Development, 55,* 718-728.
BELSKY, J., & STEINBERG, L. (1978). The effects of day care: A critical review. *Child Development, 49,* 929-949.
BENEDICT, H. (1978). Language comprehension in 9-to-15 month old infants. In R. Campbell & P. Smith (eds.), *Recent advances in the psychology of languages: Language development and mother-child interaction.* New York: Plenum.
BENEDICT, H. (1979). Early lexical development: Comprehension and production. *Journal of Child Language, 6,* 183-200.
BENNETT, S. (1971). Infant-caretaker interactions. *Journal of American Academy of Child Psychiatry, 10,* 321-335.
BERENTHAL, B., & FISCHER, K. (1978). Development of self-recognition in the infant. *Developmental Psychology, 14,* 44-50.
BERTONCINI, J., & MEHLER, J. (1981). Syllables as units in infant speech perception. *Infant Behavior and Development, 4,* 247-260.
BHATIA, V., KATIYAR, G., & AGARWAL, K. (1979). Effect of intrauterine deprivation on neuromotor behaviour of the newborn. *Acta Paediatrica Scandinavia, 68,* 561-566.
BIRNHOLE, J., & FARRELL, E. (1984). Ultrasound images of human fetal development. *American Scientist, 72,* 608-612.
BLANCHARD, M., & MAIN, M. (1979). Avoidance of the attachment figure and social-emotional adjustment in daycare infants. *Developmental Psychology, 15,* 445-446.
BLEHAR, M. (1974). Anxious attachment and defensive reactions associated with daycare. *Child Development, 45,* 683-692.
BLEHAR, M., LIEBERMAN, A., & AINSWORTH, M. (1977). Early face-to-face interaction and its relation to later infant-mother attachment. *Child Development, 48,* 182-194.
BLOOM, L. (1970). *Language development: Form and function in emerging grammars.* Cambridge, Mass.: MIT Press.
BLOOM, L., (1973). *One word at a time.* The Hague: Mouton.
BLOOM, L., LIGHTBRONW, P., & HOOD, L. (1975). Structure and variation in child language. *Monographs of the Society for Research in Child Development, 40,* 160.
BLOUNT, B. (1981). The development of language in children. In R. Monroe, R. Monroe, & B. Whiting (eds.), *Handbook of Cross-cultural Psychology.* New York: Garland STPM Press.
BOWER, T.G.R. (1966). The visual world of infants. *Scientific American, 215,* 80-92.
BOWER, T.G.R. (1967). The development of object-permanence: Some studies of existence constancy. *Perception and Psychophysics, 2,* 74-76.
BOWER, T.G.R. (1974). *Development in infancy.* San Francisco: W.H. Freeman and Company Publishers.
BOWER, T.G.R. (1982). *Development in infancy* (2nd ed.). San Francisco: W.H. Freeman and Company Publishers.
BOWER, T.G.R., BROUGHTON, J., & MOORE, M. (1970). Infant responses to approaching objects: An indicator of response to distal variables. *Perception and Psychophysics, 9,* 193-196.
BOWER, T.G.R., & PATERSON, J. (1973). The separation of place, movement and time in the world of the infant. *Journal of Experimental Child Psychology, 15,* 161-168.
BOWER, T.G.R., & WISHART, J. (1972). The effects of motor skill on object permanence. *Cognition, 1,* 28-35.
BOWER, T.G.R., & WISHART, J. (1979). Towards a unitary theory of development. In E. Thoman (ed.), *Origins of the infant's social responsiveness.* Hillsdale, N.J.: Erlbaum.
BOWLBY, J. (1951). *Maternal care and mental health.* WHO Monograph 2. Geneva: World Health Organization.
BOWLBY, J. (1958). The nature of the child's tie to his mother. *International Journal of Psychoanalysis, 39,* 350-373.
BOWLBY, J. (1969). *Attachment and loss* (Vol. 1). New York: Basic Books.
BOWLBY, J. (1977). The making and breaking of affectional bonds. *British Journal of Psychiatry, 130,* 201-210.

BRACKBILL, Y. (1979). Obstetrical medication and infant behavior. In J.D. Osofsky (ed.), *Handbook of infant development.* New York: John Wiley.

BRAINE, M. (1976). Children's first word combinations. *Monographs of the Society for Research in Child Development, 41,* 164.

BRAINERD, C. (1978). *Piaget's theory of intelligence.* Englewood Cliffs, N.J.: Prentice-Hall.

BRANDSTADTER-PALMER, G. (1982). Ontogenetic growth chart. In C. Kopp & J. Krakow (eds.), *The child.* Reading, Mass.: Addison-Wesley.

BRANIGAN, G. (1979). Some reasons why successive single word utterances are not. *Journal of Child Language, 6,* 411-421.

BRAZELTON, T.B. (1961). Psychophysiologic reactions in the neonate: I. The value of observations of the neonate. *Journal of Pediatrics, 58,* 508-512.

BRAZELTON, T.B. (1962). A child-oriented approach to toilet-training. *Pediatrics, 29,* 121-128.

BRAZELTON, T.B. (1972). Implications of infant development among the Mayan Indians of Mexico. *Human Development, 15,* 90-111.

BRAZELTON, T.B. (1973). *Neonatal behavioral assessment scale.* Philadelphia: Lippincott.

BRAZELTON, T.B. (1978). Introduction. In A.J. Sameroff (ed.), Organization and stability of newborn behavior: A commentary on the Brazelton Neonatal Behavior Assessment Scale. *Monographs of the Society for Research in Child Development, 43,* 143.

BRAZELTON, T.B. (1979). Evidence of communication in neonatal behavioral assessment. In M. Bullowa (ed.), *Before speech: The beginning of interpersonal communication.* London: Cambridge University Press.

BRAZELTON, T.B. (1981). Clinical issues of the Brazelton Neonatal Assessment Scale. In M. Coleman (ed.), *Neonatal Neurology.* Baltimore: University Park Press.

BRAZELTON, T.B., KOSLOWSKI, B., & MAIN, M. (1974). The origins of reciprocity: The early mother-infant interaction. In M. Lewis & L. Rosenblum (eds.), *The effect of the infant on its caregiver.* New York: John Wiley.

BREGMAN, E. (1934). An attempt to modify the emotional attitudes of infants by the conditioned response technique. *Journal of Genetic Psychology, 45,* 169-198.

BRETHERTON, I., BATES, E., BENIGNI, L., CAMIONI, L., & VOLTERRA, V. (1979). Relationships between cognition, communication, and quality of attachment. In E. Bates (ed.), *The emergence of symbols: Cognition and communication in infancy.* New York: Academic Press.

BRIDGEMAN, M. (1984). Super babies. *Columbus Dispatch,* Aug. 8.

BRODSKY, P., & BRODSKY, M. (1981). A model integrating risk variables involved in the development of the schizophrenia spectrum. *Journal of Nervous and Mental Disease, 169,* 741-747.

BRODY, L. (1981). Visual short-term cued recall memory in infancy. *Child Development, 52,* 242-250.

BRONFENBRENNER, U. (1977). Toward an experimental ecology of human development. *American Psychologist, 32,* 513-531.

BRONSTEIN, P. (1984). Differences in mothers' and fathers' behaviors toward children: A cross-cultural comparison. *Developmental Psychology, 20,* 995-1003.

BROOKS, J., & LEWIS, M. (1976). Infants' responses to strangers: Midget, adult, and child. *Child Development, 47,* 323-332.

BROOKS, J., & WEINRAUB, M. (1976). A history of infant intelligence testing. In M. Lewis (ed.), *Origins of intelligence,* New York: Plenum.

BROOKS-GUNN, J., & LEWIS, M. (1982). The development of self-knowledge. In C. Kopp & J. Krakow (eds.), *The child: Development in a social context.* Readington, Mass.: Addison-Wesley.

BROWN, R. (1973). *A first language: The early stages.* Cambridge, Mass.: Harvard University Press.

BROWN, R., & HANLON, C. (1970). Derivational complexity and order of acquisition in child speech. In J. Hayes (ed.), *Cognition and the development of language.* New York: John Wiley.

BROUSSARD, E.R., & HARTNER, M.S. (1970). Maternal perception of the neonate as related to development. *Child Psychiatry and Human Development, 1,* 16-25.

BROUSSARD, E.R., & HARTNER, M.S. (1971). Further considerations regarding maternal perceptions of the first born. In J. Hellmuth (ed.), *Exceptional infant* (Vol. 2). New York: Brunner/Mazel.

BRUNER, J. (1970). The growth and structure of skill. In K. Connolly (ed.), *Mechanisms of motor skill development.* London: Academic Press.

BRUNER, J. (1973). Organization of early skilled action. *Child Development, 44,* 1-11.

BRUNER, J. (1983). The acquisition of pragmatic commitments. In R. Golinkoff (ed.), *The transition from prelinguistic to linguistic communication.* Hillsdale, N.J.: Erlbaum.

BRUNER, J., OLIVER, R., & GREENFIELD, P. (1966). *Studies in cognitive growth.* New York: John Wiley.

BUSS, A., & PLOMIN, R. (1975). *A temperament theory of personality development.* New York: John Wiley,

BURGESS, R. (1978). Child abuse: A behavioral analysis. In B. Lakey & A. Kazdin (eds.), *Advances in child clinical psychology.* New York: Plenum Press.

BUTTERWORTH, G. (1977). Object disappearance and error in Piaget's stage IV task. *Journal of Experimental Child Psychology, 23,* 391-401.

BUTTERWORTH, G. (1983). Structure of the mind in human infancy. In L. Lipsitt & C. Rovee-Collier (eds.), *Advances in infancy research* (Vol. 2). Norwood, N.J.: Ablex.

BUTTERWORTH, G., JARRETT, N., & HICKS, L. (1982). Spatio-temporal identity in infancy: Perceptual competence or conceptual deficit? *Developmental Psychology, 18,* 435-449.

CAFFEY, J. (1972). On the theory and practice of shaking infants: Its potential residual effects of permanent brain damage and mental retardation. *American Journal of Diseases of Children, 124,* 161-169.

CAFFEY, J. (1974). The whiplash shaken infant syndrome: Manual shaking by the extremities with whiplash-induced intracranial and intra-ocular bleedings, linked with residual permanent brain damage and mental retardation. *Pediatrics, 54,* 396-403.

CAMPOS, J., BARRETT, K., LAMB, M., GOLDSMITH, H., & STENBERG, C. (1983). Socio-emotional development. In P. Mussen (ed.), *Handbook of child psychology* (4th ed.). (Vol. 2). New York: John Wiley.

CAMPOS, J., HIATT, S., RAMSAY, D., HENDERSON, C., & SVEDIA, M. (1978). The emergence of fear on the visual cliff. In M. Lewis & L. Rosenblum (eds.), *The development of affect.* New York: Plenum.

CAPUTO, D., GOLDSTEIN, K., & TAUB, H. (1979). The development of prematurely born children through middle childhood. In T. Field, A. Sostek, S. Goldberg, & H. Shuman (eds.), *Infants born at risk: Behavior and development.* Jamaica, N.Y.: Spectrum Publ.

CAREY, W.B. (1970). A simplified method for measuring infant temperament. *Journal of Pediatrics, 77,* 188-194.

CAREY, W.B., & MCDEVITT, S. (1978a). Stability and change in individual temperament: Diagnoses from infancy to early childhood. *Journal of the American Academy of Child Psychiatry, 17,* 331-337.

CAREY, W.B., & MCDEVITT, S. (1978b). Revision of the Infant Temperament Questionnaire. *Pediatrics, 61,* 735-739.

CARMICHAEL, L. (1970). Onset and early development of behavior. In P. Mussen (ed.), *Carmichael's Manual of Child Psychology.* New York: John Wiley.

CARON, A., & CARON, R. (1981). Processing of relational information as an index of infant risk. In S. Friedman & M. Sigman (eds.), *Preterm birth and psychological development.* New York: Academic Press.

CARON, A., & CARON, R. (1982). Cognitive development in early infancy. In T. Field, A. Huston, H. Quay, L. Troll, & G. Finley (eds.), *Review of human development.* New York: John Wiley.

CARON, A., CARON, R., & CARLSON, V. (1979). Infant perception of the invariant shape of an object varying in slant. *Child Development, 50,* 716-721.

CARON, R., CARON, A., & MYERS, R. (1982). Abstraction of invariant face expressions in infancy. *Child Development, 53,* 1008-1015.

CARPENTER, G. (1974). Visual regard of moving and stationary faces in early infancy. *Merrill-Palmer Quarterly, 20,* 181-194.

CHAPMAN, R. (1981). Cognitive development and language comprehension in 10- to 21-month-olds. In R. Stark (ed.), *Language behavior in infancy and early childhood.* New York: Elsevier North-Holland.

CHESTER, N. (1979). *Pregnancy and new parenthood: Twin experiences of change.* Presented at the Eastern Psychological Association, Philadelphia.

CHOMSKY, N. (1957). *Syntactic structures.* The Hague: Mouton.

CHOMSKY, N. (1965). *Aspects of the theory of syntax.* Cambridge, Mass.: MIT Press.

CHOMSKY, N. (1975). *Reflections on language.* New York: Pantheon.

CLARK, E. (1973). What's in a word? On the child's acquisition of semantics in his first language. In T. Moore (ed.), *Cognitive development and the acquisition of language.* New York: Academic Press.

CLARK, E. (1978). Strategies for communicating. *Child Development, 49,* 953-959.

CLARK, E. (1983). Meanings and concepts. In P. Mussen (ed.), *Handbook of child psychology* (4th ed.) (Vol. 3). New York: John Wiley.

CLARKE-STEWART, K.A. (1973). Interactions between mothers and their young children: Characteristics and consequences. *Monographs of the Society for Research in Child Development, 38* (153).

CLARKE-STEWART, K.A. (1978). And daddy makes three: The father's impact on mother and young child. *Child Development, 49,* 466-479.

CLARKE-STEWART, K.A., FRIEDMAN, S., & KOCH, J. (1985). *Child Development.* New York: John Wiley.

CLARKE-STEWART, K.A., UMEH, B., SNOW, M., & PEDERSON, J. (1980). Development and prediction of children's sociability from 1 to 2 1/2 years. *Developmental Psychology, 16,* 290-302.

COHEN, L. (1981). Lags in the cognitive competence of prematurely born infants. In S. Friedman & M. Sigman (eds.), *Preterm birth and psychological development,* New York: Academic Press.

COHEN, L., & CAMPOS, J. (1974). Father, mother and stranger as elicitors of attachment behavior in infancy. *Developmental Psychology, 10,* 146-154.

COHEN, L., & CAPUTO, N. (1978). Instructing infants to respond to perceptual categories. Presented at International Conference on Infancy Studies, Providence, Rhode Island.

COHEN, L., DELOACHE, J., & PEARL, R. (1977). An examination of interference effects in infants' memory for faces. *Child Development, 48,* 88-96.

COHEN, L., DELOACHE, J.S., & STRAUSS, M.S. (1979). Infant visual perception. In J.D. Osofsky (ed.), *Handbook of infant development.* New York: John Wiley.

COHEN, L., & GELBER, E. (1975). Infant visual memory. In L. Cohen & P. Salaptek (eds.), *Infant perception: From sensation to cognition.* New York: Academic Press.

COHEN, L., & STRAUSS, M. (1979). Concept acquisition in the human infant. *Child Development, 50,* 419-424.

COHEN, S. (1974). Developmental differences in infants' attentional responses to face-voice incongruity of mother and stranger. *Child Development, 45,* 1155-1158.

COHEN, S., & PARMELEE, A. (1983). Prediction of five-year Stanford-Binet scores in preterm infants. *Child Development, 54,* 1242-1253.

COHN, J., & TRONICK, E. (1982). Communicative rules and the sequential structure of infant behavior during normal and depressed interaction. In E. Tronick (ed.), *The development of human communication and the joint regulation of behavior.* Baltimore, Md.: University Park Press.

CONDON, W. (1979). Neonatal entrainment and enculturation. In M. Bullowa (ed.), *Before speech: The beginning of interpersonal communication.* Cambridge: Cambridge University Press.

CONDON, W.. & SANDER, L. (1974). Neonate movement is synchronized with adult speech: Interactional participation and language acquisition. *Science, 183,* 99-101.

CONNELL, D. (1976). Individual differences in attachment: An investigation into stability, implications, and relationships to structure of early language development. Unpublished doctoral dissertation, Syracuse University, Syracuse, N.Y.

CONNOLLY, K. (1970). Skill development: Problems and plans. In K. Connolly (ed.), *Mechanisms of motor skill development.* London: Academic Press.

CONNOLLY, K. (1980). Motor development and motor disability. In M. Rutter (ed.), *Scientific foundations of developmental psychiatry*. London: William Heinemann Medical Books.

COOK, M., FIELD, J., & GRIFFITHS, K. (1978). The perception of solid form in early infancy. *Child Development, 49*, 866-869.

COOPERSMITH, S. (1967). *The antecedents of self-esteem*. San Francisco: W.H. Freeman and Company Publishers.

CORRIGAN, R. (1978). Language development as related to stage 6 object permanence development. *Journal of Child Language, 5*, 173-189.

CORRIGAN, R. (1979). Cognitive correlates of language: Differential criteria yield differential results. *Child Development, 50*, 617-631.

CORTER, C., ABRAMOVITCH, R., & PEPLER, D. (1983). The role of the mother in sibling interaction. *Child Development, 54*, 1599-1605.

CORTER, C., TREHUB, S., BOUKYDIS, C., FORD, L., CELHOFFER, L., & MINDE, K. (1978). Nurses' judgements of the attractiveness of premature infants. *Infant Behavior and Development, 1*, 373-380.

COWLEY, J., & GRIESEL, R. (1963). The development of second-generation low-protein rats. *Journal of Genetic Psychology, 103*, 233-242.

CRAIK, F., & LOCKHART, R. (1972). Levels of processing: A framework for memory research. *Journal of Verbal Learning and Verbal Behavior, 11*, 671-684.

CRAVIOTO, J., DELICARDIE, E., & BIRCH, H. (1966). Nutrition, growth and neurointegrative development: An experimental and ecologic study. *Pediatrics, 38*, 319-372.

CRNIC, K., GREENBERG, M., RAGOZIN, A., ROBINSON, N., & BASHAM, R. (1983). Effects of stress and social support on mothers and premature and full-term infants. *Child Development, 54*, 209-217.

CROCKENBERG, S. (1981). Infant irritability, mother responsiveness, and social support influences on the security of infant-mother attachment. *Child Development, 52*, 857-865.

CROCKENBERG, S., & SMITH, P. (1982). Antecedents of mother-infant interaction and infant irritability in the first three months of life. *Infant Behavior and Development, 5*, 105-119.

CROSS, T. (1977). Mother's speech adjustments: The contributions of selected child-listener variables. In C. Snow & C. Ferguson (eds.), *Talking to children: Language input and acquisition*. Cambridge: Cambridge University Press.

CROSS, T. (1978). Mothers' speech and its association with rate of linguistic development in young children. In N. Waterson & C. Snow (eds.), *The development of communication*. New York: John Wiley.

DALE, P. (1976). *Language development* (2nd ed.). New York: Holt, Rinehart & Winston.

DALE, P. (1980). Is early pragmatic development measurable? *Journal of Child Language, 7*, 1-12.

DANIELS, D., & PLOMIN, R. (1985). Origins of individual differences in infant shyness. *Developmental Psychology, 21*, 118-121.

DARLEY, J., GLUCKSBERG, S., KAMIN, L., & KINCHLA, A. (1984). *Psychology* (2nd ed.). Englewood Cliffs, N.J.: Prentice-Hall.

DAVIS, A., & WADA, J. (1977). Hemispheric asymmetries in human infants: Spectral analysis of flash and click evoked potentials. *Brain and Language, 4*, 23-31.

DAY, R., & MCKENZIE, B. (1977). Constancies in the perceptual world of the infant. In W. Epstein (ed.), *Stability and constancy in visual perception: Mechanisms and process*. New York: John Wiley.

DAY, R., & MCKENZIE, B. (1981). Infant perception of the invariant size of approaching and receding objects. *Developmental Psychology, 17*, 670-677.

DECASPER, A.J., & FIFER, W.P. (1980). Of human bonding: Newborns prefer their mothers' voices. *Science, 208*, 1174-1176.

DE LAGUNA, G. (1927). *Speech: Its function and development*. Bloomington, Ind.: Indiana University Press.

DELLA CORTE, M., BENEDICT, H., & KLEIN, D. (1983). The relationship of pragmatic dimensions of mothers' speech to the referential-expressive distinction. *Journal of Child Language, 10*, 35-44.

DENNIS, W. (1940). Infant reactions to restraint. *Transactions of the New York Academy of Science, 2,* 202-217.

DENNIS, W., & NAJARIAN, P. (1957). Infant development under environmental handicap. *Psychological Monographs, 71,* 1-13.

DIVITTO, B., & GOLDBERG, S. (1979). The effect of newborn medical status on early parent-infant interaction. In T. Field, A. Sostek, S. Goldberg, & H. Shuman (eds.), *Infants born at risk: Behavior and development.* Jamaica, New York: Spectrum Publ.

DODWELL, P., MUIR, D., & DIFRANCO, D. (1976). Responses of infants to visually presented objects. *Science, 194,* 209-211.

DOMAN, G. (1975). *How to teach your baby to read.* Garden City, N.Y.: Doubleday.

DOMAN, G. (1982). *How to multiply your baby's intelligence.* Garden City, N.Y.: Doubleday.

DORE, J. (1975). A pragmatic description of early language development. *Journal of Psycholinguistic Research, 3,* 343-350.

DOUGLAS, J., & BLOMFIELD, J. (1958). *Children under five.* London: Allen and Unwin.

DUNN, H., MCBURNEY, A., INGRAM, S., & HUNTER, C. (1976). Maternal cigarette smoking during pregnancy and the child's subsequent development: I. Physical growth to the age of 6 1/2 years. *Canadian Journal of Public Health, 67,* 499-505.

DUNN, J. (1983). Sibling relationships in early childhood. *Child Development, 54,* 787-811.

DUNN, J., & KENDRICK, C. (1982a). *Siblings: Love, envy, and understanding.* Cambridge, Mass.: Harvard University Press.

DUNN, J., & KENDRICK, C. (1982b). The speech of two- and three-year-olds to infant sibllings: "Baby talk" and the context of communication. *Journal of Child Language, 9,* 579-595.

DYER, E. (1963). Parenthood as crisis: A restudy. *Marriage and Family Living, 25,* 196-201.

EASTERBROOKS, M., & LAMB, M. (1979). The relationship between quality of infant-mother attachment and infant competence in initial encounters with peers. *Child Development, 50,* 380-387.

EGELAND, B., & FARBER, E. (1984). Infant-mother attachment: Factors related to its development and changes over time. *Child Development, 55,* 753-771.

EGELAND, B., & SROUFE, A. (1981). Attachment and early maltreatment. *Child Development, 52,* 44-52.

EICHORN, D. (1970). Physiological development. In P. Mussen (ed.), *Carmichael's Manual of Child Psychology.* (3rd ed.). New York: John Wiley.

EILERS, R., MORSE, P., GAVIN, W., & OILER, D. (1981). Discrimination of voice onset time in infancy. *Journal of the Acoustical Society of America, 70,* 955-965.

EIMAS, P. (1975). Speech perception in early infancy. In L. Cohen & P. Salapatek (eds.), *Infant perception: From sensation to cognition* (Vol. 2). New York: Academic Press.

EIMAS, P., SIQUELAND, E., JUSCZYK, P., & VIGORITO, J. (1971). Speech perception in infants. *Science, 171,* 303-306.

ELKIND, D. (1981). *The hurried child: Growing up too fast too soon.* Reading, Mass.: Addison-Wesley.

ELLIOT, A. (1981). *Child language.* Cambridge: Cambridge University Press.

ENGELMANN, S., & ENGELMANN, T. (1981). *Give your child a superior mind.* New York: Cornerstone Library.

ERIKSON, E.H. (1959/1980). *Identity through the life-cycle.* New York: W.W. Norton & Co., Inc.

ERIKSON, E.H. (1963). *Childhood and society* (2nd ed.). New York: W.W. Norton & Co., Inc.

ESCALONA, S. (1963). *The roots of individuality: Normal patterns of development in infancy.* Chicago: Aldine.

ETZEL, B., & GEWIRTZ, J. (1967). Experimental modification of caretaker-maintained high-rate operant crying in a 6- and a 20-week-old infant (Infans Tyrannotearus): Extinction of crying with reinforcement of eye contact and smiling. *Journal of Experimental Child Psychology, 5,* 305-317.

EYSENCK, H. (1967). *The biological basis of personality.* Springfield, Ill.: Chas. C Thomas.

FAGAN, J. (1974). Infant recognition memory: The effects of length of familiarization and type of discriminative task. *Child Development, 45,* 351-356.

FAGAN, J. (1977a). An attention model of infant recognition. *Child Development, 48,* 345-359.

FAGAN, J. (1977b). Infant recognition memory: Studies in forgetting. *Child Development, 48,* 68-78.

FAGAN, J. (1982). Infant memory. In T. Field, A. Huston, H. Quay, L. Troll, & G. Finley (eds.), *Review of human development.* New York: John Wiley.

FAGAN, J., & MCGRATH, S. (1981). Infant recognition memory and later intelligence. *Intelligence, 5,* 121-130.

FAGAN, J., MORRONGIELLO, B., ROVEE-COLLIER, C., & GEKOSKI, M. (1984). Expectancies and memory retrieval in three-month-old infants. *Child Development, 55,* 936-943.

FAGAN, J., & SINGER, L. (1983). Infant recognition memory as a measure of intelligence. In L.P. Lipsitt & C.K. Rovee-Collier (eds.), *Advances in infancy research* (Vol. 2). Norwood, N.J.: Ablex.

FANTZ, R. (1961). The origin of form perception. *Scientific American, 204,* 66-72.

FANTZ, R. (1965). Visual perception from birth as shown by pattern selectivity. In H. Whipple (ed.), *New issues in infant development: Annals of the New York Academy of Science, 118,* 793-814.

FANTZ, R., FAGAN, J., & MIRANDA, S. (1975). Early visual selectivity. In L. Cohen & P. Salapatek (eds.), *Infant perception: From sensation to cognition.* New York: Academic Press.

FANTZ, R., & NEVIS, S. (1967). The predictive value of changes in visual preference in early infancy. In J. Hellmuth (ed.), *The exceptional infant* (Vol. 1). Seattle: Special Child Publications.

FARRAN, D., & RAMEY, C. (1977). Infant daycare and attachment behaviors toward mothers and teachers. *Child Development, 48,* 1112-1116.

FEIN, G., JOHNSON, D., KOSSON, N., STORK, L., & WASSERMAN, L. (1975). Sex stereotypes and preferences in the toy choices of 20-month-old boys and girls. *Developmental Psychology, 11,* 527-528.

FEIN, R. (1976). Men's entrance into parenthood. *Family Coordinator, 25,* 341-348.

FELDMAN, S., NASH, S., & ASCHENBRENNER, B. (1983). Antecedents of fathering. *Child Development, 54,* 1628-1636.

FERGUSON, C. (1977). Baby talk as a simplified register. In C. Snow & C. Ferguson (eds.), *Talking to children: Language input and acquisition.* Cambridge: Cambridge University Press.

FIELD, J., MUIR, D., PILON, R., SINCLAIR, M., & DODWELL, P. (1980). Infants' orientation to lateral sounds fom birth to three months. *Child Development, 51,* 295-298.

FIELD, T. (1979a). Differential behavioral and cardiac responses of 3-month-old infants to a mirror and peer. *Infant Behavior and Development, 2,* 179-184.

FIELD, T. (1979b). Infant behaviors directed toward peers and adults in the presence and absence of mother. *Infant Behavior and Development, 2,* 47-54.

FIELD, T. (1982). Social perception and responsivity in early infancy. In T. Field A. Huston, H. Quay, L. Troll, & G. Finley (eds.), *Review of human development.* New York: John Wiley.

FIELD, T., DEMPSEY, J., HALLOCK, N., & SHUMAN, H. (1978). Mothers' assessments of the behavior of their infants. *Infant Behavior and Development, 1,* 156-167.

FIELD, T., & GREENBERG, R. (1982). Temperament ratings by parents and teachers of infants, toddlers, and preschool children. *Child Development, 53,* 160-163.

FIELD, T., & ROOPNARINE, J. (1982). Infant-peer interactions. In T. Field, A. Huston, H. Quay, L. Troll, & G. Finley (eds.), *Review of human development.* New York: John Wiley.

FILLMORE, C. (1968). The case for case. In E. Bach & R. Harms (eds.), *Universals in linguistic theory.* New York: Holt, Rinehart & Winston.

FISCHER, K. (1980). A theory of cognitive development: The control and construction of hierarchies of skills. *Psychological Review, 87,* 477-531.

FISCHER, K., & CORRIGAN, R. (1981). A skill approach to language development. In R. Stark (ed.), *Language behavior in infancy and early childhood.* Amsterdam: Elsevier North-Holland.

FISHER, L., KOKES, R., HARDER, D., & JONES, J. (1980). Child competence and psychiatric risk. *Journal of Nervous and Mental Disease, 168,* 353-355.

FITZGERALD, H., & BRACKBILL, Y. (1976). Classical conditioning in infancy: Development and constraints. *Psychological Bulletin, 83,* 353-376.

FOGEL, A. (1980). Peer vs. mother-directed behavior in one-to-three-month-old infants. *Infant Behavior and Development, 2,* 215-226.

FOX, N. (1977). Attachment of kibbutz infants to mother and metapelet. *Child Development, 48,* 1228-1239.

FREEDMAN, D. (1964). Smiling in blind infants and the issue of innate versus acquired. *Journal of Child Psychology and Psychiatry and Allied Disciplines, 5,* 171-184.

FREEDMAN, D. (1974). *Human infancy: An evolutionary perspective.* Hillsdale, N.J.: Erlbaum.

FREEDMAN, D. (1976). Comments on "From reflexive to instrumental behavior." In L. Lipsitt (ed.), *Developmental psychobiology: The significance of infancy.* Hillsdale, N.J.: Erlbaum.

FREUD, S. (1931/1963). Female sexuality. *Sexuality and the psychology of love.* New York: Collier.

FREUD, S. (1948/1979). Femininity. In J. Williams (ed.), *Readings in the psychology of women.* New York: W.W. Norton & Co., Inc.

FRIEDMAN, S. (1972). Habituation and recovery of visual response in the alert human newborn. *Journal of Experimental Child Psychology, 13,* 339-349.

FRINGS, H., & FRINGS, M. (1964). *Animal communication.* New York: Blaisdell.

FRODI, A., LAMB, M., LEAVITT, L., DONOVAN, W., NEFF, C., & SHERRY, D. (1978). Fathers' and mothers' responses to the faces and cries of normal and premature infants. *Developmental Psychology, 14,* 490-498.

FURROW, D., NELSON, K., & BENEDICT, H. (1979). Mothers' speech to children and syntactic development: Some simple relationships. *Journal of Child Language, 6,* 423-442.

GARDNER, H. (1982). *Developmental Psychology.* Boston: Little, Brown.

GARDNER, J., & GARDNER, H. (1970). A note on selective imitation by a six-week-old infant. *Child Development, 41,* 1209-1213.

GARMEZY, N. (1983). Stressors of childhood. In N. Garmezy & M. Rutter (eds.), *Stress, coping, and development in children.* New York: McGraw-Hill.

GEBER, M. (1958). The psycho-motor development of African children in th first year, and the influence of maternal behavior. *Journal of Social Psychology, 47,* 185-195.

GEBER, M., & DEAN, R. (1957). Gesell tests on African children. *Pediatrics, 20,* 1055-1065.

GEORGE, C., & MAIN, M. (1979). Social interactions of young abused children: Approach, avoidance and aggression. *Child Development, 50,* 306-318.

GESCHWIND, N. (1979). Specializations of the human brain. *Scientific American, 241,* 180-201.

GESELL, A. (1925). *The mental growth of the pre-school child: A psychological outline of normal development from birth to the sixth year, including a system of developmental diagnosis.* New York: Macmillan.

GESELL, A. (1954). The ontogenesis of infant behavior. In L. Carmichael (ed.), *Manual of child psychology* (2nd ed.). New York: John Wiley.

GESELL, A., & ARMATRUDA, C. (1941). *Developmental diagnosis: Normal and abnormal child development.* New York: Hoeber.

GEWIRTZ, J. (1976). The attachment acquisition process as evidenced in the maternal conditioning of cued infant responding (particularly crying). *Human Development, 19,* 143-155.

GEWIRTZ, J., & BOYD, E. (1977). Does maternal responding imply reduced infant crying? A critique of the 1972 Bell and Ainsworth report. *Child Development, 48,* 1200-1207.

GEWIRTZ, J., & STINGLE, K. (1968). Learning of generalized imitation as the basis for identification. *Psychological Review, 75,* 374-397.

GIBSON, E. (1982). The concept of affordances in development: The renascence of functionalism. In W. Collins (ed.), *Minnesota Symposia on Child Psychology* (Vol. 15). Hillsdale, N.J.: Erlbaum.

GIBSON, E., OWSLEY, C., & JOHNSTON, J. (1978). Perception of invariants by five-month-old infants: Differentiation of two types of motion. *Developmental Psychology, 14,* 407-415.

GIBSON, E., OWSLEY, C., WALKER, A., & MEGAW-NYCE, J. (1979). Development of the perception of invariants: Substance and shape. *Perception, 8,* 609-619.

GIBSON, E., & SPELKE, E. (1983). The development of perception. In P. Mussen (ed.), *Handbook of Child Psychology: Cognitive development* (4th ed.) (Vol. 3). New York: John Wiley.

GIBSON, E., & WALK, R. (1960). The "visual cliff." *Scientific American, 202,* 64-71.

GIBSON, E., & WALKER, A. (1982). Intermodal perception of substance. Presented at International Conference on Infant Studies, Austin, Tex.

GIBSON, E., & WALKER, A. (1984). Development of knowledge of visual-tactual affordances of substance. *Child Development, 55,* 453-460.

GIBSON, J. J. (1979). *The ecological approach to visual perception.* Boston: Houghton-Mifflin.

GINSBURG, H., & OPPER, S. (1979). *Piaget's theory of intellectual development* (2nd ed.). Englewood Cliffs, N.J.: Prentice-Hall.

GLEITMAN, L., NEWPORT, E., & GLEITMAN, H. (1984). The current status of the motherese hypothesis. *Journal of Child Language, 11,* 43-80.

GLICK, P. (1977). Updating the life cycle of the family. *Journal of Marriage and the Family, 39,* 5-13.

GOLDBERG, S. (1972). Infant care and growth in urban Zambia. *Human Development, 15,* 77-89.

GOLDBERG, S. (1981). Premature birth: Consequences for the parent-child relationship. In E. Hetherington & R. Parke (eds.), *Contemporary readings in child psychology.* New York: McGraw-Hill.

GOLDBERG, S. (1983). Parent-infant bonding: Another look. *Child Development, 54,* 1355-1382.

GOLDBERG, S., & LEWIS, M. (1969). Play behavior in the year-old infant: Early sex differences. *Child Development, 40,* 21-31.

GOLDIN-MEADOW, S., & FELDMAN, H. (1977). The development of language-like communication without a language model. *Science, 197,* 401-403.

GOLDSMITH, H. (1983). Genetic influences on personality from infancy to adulthood. *Child Development, 54,* 331-355.

GOLINKOFF, R., & AMES, G. (1979). A comparison of fathers' and mothers' speech to their young children. *Child Development, 50,* 28-32.

GOPNIK, A. (1984). The acquisition of (gone) and the development of the object concept. *Journal of Child Language, 11,* 273-292.

GOREN, C. (1975). Form perception, innate form preferences and visually mediated head turning in human newborns. Paper presented at the Society for Research in Child Development, Denver.

GOTTESMAN, I., & SHIELDS, J. (1982). *Schizophrenia: The epigenetic puzzle.* Cambridge: Cambridge University Press.

GOTTEFRIED, A., ROSE, S., & BRIDGER, W. (1977). Cross-modal transfer in human infants. *Child Development, 48,* 118-123.

GOTTS, E. (1972). Newborn walking. *Science, 177,* 1057-1058.

GRATCH, G. (1977). Review of Piagetian infancy research: Object concept development. In W. Overton & J. Gallagher (eds.), *Knowledge and development* (Vol. 1). New York: Plenum.

GRATCH, G., APPEL, K., EVANS, W., LECOMPTE, G., & WRIGHT, N. (1974). Piaget's stage IV object concept error: Evidence of forgetting or object conception? *Child Development, 45,* 71-77.

GRATCH, G., & LANDERS, W. (1971). Stage IV of Piaget's theory of infant's object concepts: A longitudinal study. *Child Development, 42,* 359-372.

GREEN, A. (1978). Psychopathology of abused children. *Journal of the American Academy of Child Psychiatry,* 92-103.

GREEN, J., GUSTAFSON, G., & WEST, M. (1980). Effects of infant development on mother-infant interactions. *Child Development, 51,* 199-207.

GREENBERG, M., & MORRIS, N. (1974). Engrossment: The newborn's impact upon the father. *American Journal of Orthopsychiatry, 44,* 520-531.

GREENBERG, R., & FIELD, T. (1982). Temperament ratings of handicapped infants during classroom, mother, and teacher interactions. *Journal of Pediatric Psychology, 7,* 387-405.

GREENE, J., FOX, N., & LEWIS, M. (1983). The relationship between neonatal characteristics and three-month mother-infant interaction. *Child Development, 54,* 1286-1296.

GREENFIELD, P., & SMITH, J. (1976). *The structure of communication in early language development.* New York: Academic Press.

GROSSMAN, K., THANE, K., & GROSSMAN, K.E. (1981). Maternal tactual contact of the newborn after various postpartum conditions of mother-infant contact. *Developmental Psychology, 17,* 159-169.

GUSTAFSON, G. (1984). Effects of the ability to locomote on infants' social and exploratory behaviors: An experimental study. *Developmental Psychology, 20,* 397-405.

HAAF, R.A. (1974). Complexity and facial resemblance as determinants of response to face-like stimuli by 5-10-week-old infants. *Journal of Experimental Child Psychology, 18,* 480-487.

HAITH, M. (1980). *Rules that babies look by.* Hillsdale, N.J.: Erlbaum.

HAITH, M., BERGMAN, T., & MOORE, M. (1977). Eye contact and face scanning in early infancy. *Science, 198,* 853-855.

HALL, C., & LINDZEY, G. (1970). *Theories of personality* (2nd ed.). New York: John Wiley.

HALLIDAY, M. (1975). *Learning how to mean: Explorations in the development of language.* London: Edward Arnold.

HALLIDAY, M. (1979). One child's protolanguage. In M. Bullowa (ed.), *Before speech: The beginning of interpersonal communication.* London: Cambridge University Press.

HAMILTON, R. (1980). *The Herpes Book.* Los Angeles: Tarcher.

HARDING, C. (1982). The development of the intention to communicate. *Human Development, 25,* 140-151.

HARDING, C. (1983). Setting the stage for language acquisition: Communication development in the first year. In R. Golinkoff (ed.), *The transition from prelinguistic to linguistic communication.* Hillsdale, N.J.: Erlbaum.

HARDING, C., & GOLINKOFF, R. (1979). The origins of intentional vocalizations in prelinguistic infants. *Child Development, 50,* 33-40.

HARDY, J., & MELLITS, B. (1972). Does maternal smoking during pregnancy have a long-term effect on the child? *Lancet, 2,* 1332-1336.

HARDY-BROWN, K., PLOMIN, R., & DEFRIES, J. (1981). Genetic and environmental influences on the rate of communicative development in the first year of life. *Developmental Psychology, 17,* 704-717.

HARLOW, H. (1959). Love in infant monkeys. In *Readings from Scientific American: The nature and nurture of behavior.* San Francisco: W.H. Freeman and Company Publishers.

HARRIMAN, A., & LUKOSIUS, P. (1982). On why Wayne Dennis found Hopi infants retarded in age at onset of walking. *Perceptual and Motor Skills, 55,* 79-86.

HARRIS, P. (1971). Examination and search in infants. *British Journal of Psychology, 65,* 345-349.

HARRIS, P. (1983). Infant cognition. In P. Mussen (ed.), *Handbook of child psychology* (4th ed.) (Vol. 2). New York: John Wiley.

HART, B., ALLEN, E., BUEL, J., HARRIS, F., & WOLF, M. (1964). Effects of social reinforcement on operant crying. *Journal of Experimental Child Psychology, 1,* 145-153.

HARTER, S. (1983). Developmental perspectives on the self-system. In P. Mussen (ed.), *Handbook of child psychology.* (4th ed.) (Vol. 4). New York: John Wiley.

HAVLICEK, V., CHILDIAEVA, R., & CHERNICK, V. (1977). EEG spectrum characteristics of sleep rates in infants of alcoholic mothers. *Neuropaediatrie, 8,* 360-373.

HAY, D., NASH, A., & PEDERSEN, J. (1981). Responses of six month olds to the distress of their peers. *Child Development, 52,* 1071-1075.

HAYES, L., & WATSON, J.S. (1981). Neonatal imitation: Fact or artifact? *Developmental Psychology, 17,* 655-660.

HAYNES, H., WHITE, B., & HELD, R. (1965). Visual accommodation in human infants. *Science, 148,* 528-530.

HEDAHL, K. (1980). Working with families experiencing a cesarian birth. *Pediatric Nursing, 28,* 21-25.

HENNESSY, M., DIXON, S., & SIMON, S. (1984). The development of gait: A study in African children ages one to five. *Children Development, 55,* 844-853.

HETHERINGTON, E., & PARKE, R. (1979). *Child psychology: A contemporary view.* New York: McGraw-Hill.

HIGGINS, J. (1976). Effects of child-rearing by schizophrenic mothers: A follow up. *Journal of Psychiatric Research, 13,* 1-9.

HIRSH-PATEK, K., TREIMAN, R., & SCHNEIDERMAN, M. (1984). Brown and Hanlon revisited: Mothers' sensitivity to ungrammatical forms. *Journal of Child Language, 11,* 81-88.

HOBBS, D. (1965). Parenthood as crisis: A third study. *Journal of Marriage and the Family, 27,* 367-372.

HOBBS, D., & COLE, S. (1976). Transition to parenthood: A decade of replication. *Journal of Marriage and the Family, 38,* 723-731.

HOCK, E. (1980). Working and nonworking mothers and their infants: A comparative study of maternal caregiving characteristics and infant social behavior. *Merrill-Palmer Quarterly, 26,* 79-101.

HOCK, E., COADY, S., & CORDERO, L. (1973). Patterns of attachment to mother of one-year-old infants: A comparative study of full-term infants and prematurely born infants who were hospitalized throughout the neonatal period. Presented at Society for Research in Child Development, Philadelphia.

HOFFMAN-PLOTKIN, D., & TWENTYMAN, C. (1984). A multimodal assessment of behavioral and cognitive deficits in abused and neglected preschoolers. *Child Development, 55,* 794-802.

HOLMES, D., REICH, J., & PASTERNAK, J. (1984). *The development of infants born at risk.* Hillsdale, N.J.: Erlbaum.

HOROWITZ, F., SULLIVAN, J., & LINN, P. (1978). Stability and instability in the newborn infant: The quest for elusive threads. In A. Sameroff (ed.), Organization and stability of newborn behavior: A commentary on the Brazelton Neonatal Behavior Assessment Scale. *Monographs of the Society for Research in Child Development, 43,* 177.

HUBERT, N., WACHS, T., PETERS-MARTIN, P., & GANDOUR, M. (1982). The study of early temperament: Measurement and conceptual issues. *Child Development, 53,* 571-600.

HUMPHREY, T. (1969). Postnatal repetition of human prenatal activity sequences with some suggestions of their neuroanatomical basis. In R.J. Robinson (ed.), *Brain and early behavior: Development in the fetus and infant.* London: Academic Press.

HUSTON, A. (1983). Sex-typing. In P. Mussen (ed.), *Handbook of child psychology* (4th ed.) (Vol. 4). New York: John Wiley.

HUTTENLOCHER, J. (1974). The origins of language comprehension. In R. Solso (ed.), *Theories of cognitive psychology: The Loyola Symposium.* Hillsdale, N.J.: Erlbaum.

INHELDER, B., & PIAGET, J. (1964). *The growth of logic in the child.* New York: W.W. Norton & Co., Inc.

JACOBSON, S. (1979). Matching behavior in the young infant. *Child Development, 50,* 425-430.

JAMES, W. (1890/1963). *Principles of psychology.* New York: Holt, Rinehart & Winston.

JEANS, P., SMITH, M., & STEARNS, G. (1955). Incidence of prematurity in relation to maternal nutrition. *Journal of the American Dietetic Association, 31,* 576-581.

JENSEN, A. (1969). How much can we boost IQ and scholastic achievement? *Harvard Educational Review, 39,* 1-123.

JONES, C. (1981). Children after abuse. In N. Frude (ed.), *Psychological approaches to child abuse.* Totowa, N.J.: Rowman & Littlefield.

JONES-MOLFESE, V. (1977). Responses of neonates to colored stimuli. *Child Development, 48,* 1092-1095.

JUSCZYK, P., PISONI, D., WALLEY, A., & MURRAY, J. (1980). Discrimination of relative onset time of two-component tones by infants. *Journal of the Acoustical Society of America, 67,* 262-270.

JUSCZYK, P., ROSNER, B., CUTTING, J., FOARD, F., & SMITH, L. (1977). Categorical perception of non-speech sounds by two-month-old infants. *Perception & Psychophysics, 21,* 50-54.

KAGAN, J. (1979). Overview: Perspectives on human infancy. In J.D. Osofsky (ed.), *Handbook of infant development.* New York: John Wiley.

KAGAN, J. (1982). The emergence of self. *Journal of Child Psychology and Psychiatry, 23,* 363-381.

KALTENBACK, K., WEINRAUB, M., & FULLARD, W. (1980). Infant wariness toward strangers reconsidered: Infants' and mothers' reactions to unfamiliar persons. *Child Development, 51,* 1197-1202.

KAMIN, L. (1974). *The science and politics of IQ.* Potomac, Md.: Erlbaum.

KARMEL, M. (1959). *Thank you, Dr. Lamaze.* New York: Dolphin.

KAYE, H. (1965). The conditioned Babkin reflex in human newborns. *Psychonomic Science, 2,* 287-288.

KAYE, K. (1978). Discriminating among normal infants by multivariate analysis of Brazelton scores: Lumping and smoothing. In A. Sameroff (ed.), Organization and stability of newborn behavior: A commentary on the Brazelton Neonatal Behavior Assessment Scale. *Monographs of the Society for Research in Child Development, 43,* 177.

KAYE, K. (1979). Thickening thin data: The maternal role in developing communication and language. In M. Bullowa (ed.), *Before speech: The beginning of interpersonal communication.* London: Cambridge University Press.

KAYE, K. (1980). Why we don't talk 'baby talk' to babies. *Journal of Child Language, 7,* 489-507.

KAYE, K. (1982). *The mental and social life of babies.* Chicago: University of Chicago Press.

KELLER, W., HILDEBRANDT, K., & RICHARDS, M. (1981). Effects of extended father-infant contact during the newborn period. Presented at the Society for Research in Child Development, Boston.

KELLMAN, P., & SPELKE, E. (1981). Perception of partly occluded objects: Sensitive to movement and configuration. Presented at the Society for Research in Child Development, Boston.

KEMPE, R., & KEMPE, H. (1978). *Child abuse.* Cambridge, Mass.: Harvard University Press.

KENNELL, J., VOOS, D., & KLAUS, M. (1979). Parent-infant bonding. In J.D. Osofsky (ed.), *Handbook of infant development.* New York: John Wiley.

KLAUS, M., & KENNELL, J. (1976). *Maternal-infant bonding: The impact of early separation or loss on family development.* St. Louis: C. V. Mosby.

KLAUS, M., JERAULD, R., KREGER, N., MCALPINE, W., STEFFA, M., & KENNELL, J. (1972). Maternal attachment: Importance of the first postpartum days. *New England Journal of Medicine, 286,* 460-463.

KOLUCHOVA, J. (1976). Severe deprivation in twins: A case study. In A.M. Clarke & A.D.B. Clarke (eds.), *Early experience: Myth and evidence.* New York: Free Press.

KOPP, C. (1979). Perspectives on infant motor system development. In M. Bornstein & W. Kessen (eds.), *Psychological development from infancy: Image to intention.* Hillsdale, N.J.: Erlbaum.

KOPP, C. (1983). Risk factors in development. In P. Mussen (ed.), *Handbook of child psychology* (4th ed.) (Vol. 2). New York: John Wiley.

KOPP, C., & KRAKOW, J. (1982). *The child.* Reading, Mass.: Addison-Wesley.

KOPP, C., & PARMELEE, A. (1979). Prenatal and perinatal influences on behavior. In J. Osofsky (ed.), *Handbook of infant development.* New York: John Wiley.

KOPP, C., & SHAPERMAN, J. (1973). Cognitive development in the absence of object manipulation during infancy. *Developmental Psychology, 9,* 430.

KORBIN, J. (1981a). "Very few cases": Child abuse and neglect in the People's Republic of China. In J. Korbin (ed.), *Child abuse and neglect: Cross-cultural perspectives.* Berkeley: University of California Press.

KORBIN, J. (1981b). Conclusions. In J. Korbin (ed.), *Child abuse and neglect: Cross-cultural perspectives.* Berkeley: University of California Press.

KORNER, A.F. (1971). Individual differences at birth: Implications for early experiences and later development. *American Journal of Orthopsychiatry, 41,* 608-619.

KORNER, A.F. (1974). Methodological considerations in studying sex differences in the behavioral functioning of newborns. In R.C. Friedman, R.M. Richart, & R.L. Vande Wiele (eds.), *Sex differences in behavior.* New York: John Wiley.

KORNER, A.F. (1979). Conceptual issues in infancy research. In J.D. Osofsky (ed.), *Handbook of infant development.* New York: John Wiley.

KORNER, A.F., ZEANAH, C., LINDEN, J., BERKOWITZ, R., KRAEMER, H., & AGRAS, W. (1985). Relation between neonatal and later activity and temperament. *Child Development, 56,* 38-42.

KOTELCHUCK, M. (1972). *The nature of the child's tie to his father.* Unpublished doctoral dissertation, Harvard University.

KOTELCHUCK, M. (1976). The infant's relationship to the father: Experimental evidence. In M. Lamb (ed.), *The role of the father in child development.* New York: John Wiley.

LAMB, M.E. (1978). The father's role in the infant's social world. In J. Stevens & M. Mathews (eds.), *Mother/child father/child relationships.* Washington, D.C.: National Association for the Education of Young Children.

LAMB, M.E. (1980). The development of parent-infant attachments in the first two years of life. In F. Pedersen (ed.), *The father-infant relationship: Observational studies in the family setting.* New York: Praeger.

LAMB, M.E. (1981). The development of father-infant relationships. In M. Lamb (ed.), *The role of the father in child development* (Rev. ed.). New York: John Wiley.

LAMB, M.E. (1982). Individual differences in infant sociability: Their origins and implications for cognitive development. In H. Reese & L. Lipsitt (eds.), *Advances in child development and behavior.* New York: Academic Press.

LAMB, M.E., FRODI, A., HWANG, C., FRODI, M., & STEINBERG, J. (1982). Mother- and father-infant interaction involving play and holding in traditional and nontraditional Swedish families. *Developmental Psychology, 18,* 215-221.

LAMB, M.E., & HWANG, C. (1982). Maternal attachment and mother-neonate bonding: A critical review. In M.E. Lamb & A. Brown (eds.), *Advances in developmental psychology* (Vol. 2). Hillsdale, N.J.: Erlbaum.

LANGLOIS, J., & STEPHAN, C. (1981). Beauty and the beast: The role of physical attractiveness in the development of peer relations and social behavior. In S. Brehm, S. Kassin, & F. Gibbons (eds.), *Developmental social psychology.* New York: Oxford University Press.

LAWSON, A., & INGLEBY, J. (1974). Daily routines of preschool children: Effects of age, birth order, sex and social class, and developmental correlates. *Psychological Medicine, 4,* 399-415.

LAWSON, K., & RUFF, H. (1984). Infants' visual following: Effects of size and sound. *Developmental Psychology, 20,* 427-434.

LAWSON, K., RUFF, H., MCCARTON-DAUM, C., KURTZBERG, D., & VAUGHN, H. (1984). Auditory-visual responsiveness in full-term and preterm infants. *Developmental Psychology, 20,* 120-127.

LEAVITT, L., BROWN, J., MORSE, P., & GRAHAM, F. (1976). Cardiac orienting and auditory discrimination in 6-week-old infants. *Developmental Psychology, 12,* 514-523.

LEBOYER, F. (1975). *Birth without violence.* New York: Knopf.

LEFKOWITZ, M. (1981). Smoking during pregnancy: Long-term effects on offspring. *Developmental Psychology, 17,* 192-194.

LEIDERMAN, H.P. (1983). Social ecology and childbirth: The newborn nursery as environmental stressor. In N. Garmezy & M. Rutter (eds.), *Stress, coping, and development in children.* New York: McGraw-Hill.

LEIDERMAN, H., & SEASHORE, M. (1975). Mother-infant separation: Some delayed consequences. *Parent-infant interaction.* CIBA Foundation Symposium (Vol. 33). New York: Elsevier North-Holland.

LEIFER, A., LEIDERMAN, P., BARNETT, C., & WILLIAMS, J. (1972). Effects of mother-infant separation on maternal attachment behavior. *Child Development, 43,* 1203-1218.

LEMASTERS, E. (1957). Parenthood as crisis. *Marriage and Family Living, 19,* 352-355.

LESTER, B., HOFFMAN, J., & BRAZELTON, B. (1985). The rhythmic structure of mother-infant interaction in term and preterm infants. *Child Development, 56,* 15-27.

LESTER, B., KOTELCHUCK, M., SPELKE, E., SELLER, M., & KLEIN, R. (1974). Separation protest in Guatemalan infants: Cross-cultural and cognitive findings. *Developmental Psychology, 10,* 79-85.

LEWIS, M., & BROOKS, J. (1974). Self, other, and fear: Infants' reactions to people. In M. Lewis & L. Rosenblum (eds.), *The origins of fear.* New York: John Wiley.

LEWIS, M., & BROOKS-GUNN, J. (1979). *Social cognition and the acquisition of self.* New York: Plenum.

LEWIS, M., & BROOKS-GUNN, J. (1981). Visual attention at three months as a predictor of cognitive functioning at two years of age. *Intelligence, 5,* 131-140.

LIEVEN, E. (1978). Conversation between mothers and young children: Individual differences and their possible implications for the study of language learning. In N. Waterson & C. Snow (eds.), *The development of communication: Social and pragmatic factors in language acquisition.* New York: John Wiley.

LINN, S., REZNICK, S., KAGAN, J., & HANS, S. (1982). Salience of visual patterns in the human infant. *Developmental Psychology, 18,* 651-657.

LIPSITT, L. (1982). Infant learning. In T. Field, A. Huston, H. Quay, L. Troll, & G. Finley (eds.), *Review of human development.* New York: John Wiley.

LIPSITT, L., & KAYE, H. (1964). Conditioned sucking in the human newborn. *Psychonomic Science, 1,* 29-30.

LIPSITT, L., KAYE, H., & BOSACK, T. (1966). Enhancement of neonatal sucking through reinforcement. *Journal of Experimental Child Psychology, 4,* 163-168.

LOCKMAN, J., & ASHMEAD, D. (1983). Asynchronies in the development of mutual behavior. In L. Lipsitt & C. Rovee-Collier (eds.), *Advances in infancy research* (Vol. 2.) Norwood, N.J.: Ablex.

LYNCH, M. (1975). Ill health and child abuse. *Lancet, 2,* 317-319.

MACCOBY, E.E. (1980). *Social development: Psychological growth and the parent-child relationship.* New York: Harcourt Brace Jovanovich.

MACCOBY, E.E. (1983). Social-emotional development and response to stressors. In N. Garmezy & M. Rutter (eds.), *Stress, coping, and development in children.* New York: McGraw-Hill.

MACCOBY, E.E., & JACKLIN, C. (1974). *The psychology of sex differences.* Stanford, Calif.: Stanford University Press.

MACCOBY, E.E., & MARTIN, J. (1983). Socialization in the context of the family: Parent-child interaction. In P. Mussen (ed.), *Handbook of child psychology* (4th ed.) (Vol. 4). New York: John Wiley.

MAHLER, M., PINE, F., & BERGMAN, A. (1975). *The psychological birth of the human infant.* New York: Basic Books.

MAIN, M. (1973). *Exploration, play, and cognitive factors as related to mother-child attachment.* Unpublished doctoral dissertation, Johns Hopkins University, Baltimore, Md.

MAIN, M. (1981). Abusive and rejecting infants. In N. Frude (ed.), *Psychological approaches to child abuse.* Totowa, N.J.: Rowman and Littlefield.

MAIN, M., & WESTON, D. (1981). The quality of the toddler's relationship to mother and father: Related to conflict behavior and the readiness to establish new relationships. *Child Development, 52,* 932-940.

MARATSOS, M. (1983). Some current issues in the study of the acquisition of grammar. In P. Mussen (ed.), *Handbook of child psychology* (4th ed.) (Vol. 4). New York: John Wiley.

MARCUS, J., AUERBACH, J., WILKINSON, L., & BURACK, C. (1981). Infants at risk for schizophrenia. *Archives of General Psychiatry, 38,* 703-713.

MASTERS, J. (1979). Interpreting "imitative" responses in early infancy. *Science, 205,* 215.

MASUR, E., & GLEASON, J. (1980). Parent-child interaction and the acquisition of lexical information during play. *Developmental Psychology, 16,* 404-409.

MATAS, L., AREND, R., & SROUFE, A. (1978). Continuity of adaptation in the second year: The relationship between quality of attachment and later competence. *Child Development, 49,* 547-556.

MATHENY, A., WILSON, R., DOLAN, A., & KRANTZ, J. (1981). Behavioral contrasts in twinships: Stability and patterns of differences in childhood. *Child Development, 52,* 579-588.

MAURER, D., & SALAPATEK, P. (1976). Developmental changes in the scanning of faces by young infants. *Child Development, 47,* 523-527.

MAXWELL, M. (1983). Language acquisition in a deaf child of deaf parents: Speech, sign variations, and print variations. In K.E. Nelson (ed.), *Children's language* (Vol. 4). Hillsdale, N.J.: Erlbaum.

MCCALL, R. (1979). The development of intellectual functioning in infancy and the prediction of later IQ. In J.D. Osofsky (ed.), *Handbook of infant development.* New York: John Wiley.

MCCALL, R., EICHORN, D., & HOGARTY, P. (1977). Transitions in early mental development. *Monographs of the Society for Research in Child Development, 42,* 171.

MCCALL, R., KENNEDY, C., & DODDS, C. (1977). The interfering effect of distracting stimuli on the infant's memory. *Child Development, 48,* 79-87.

MCCALL, R., PARKE, R., & KAVANAUGH, R. (1977). Imitation of live and televised models by children one to three years of age. *Monographs of the Society for Research in Child Development, 42,* 173.

MCCLEARN, G., & DEFRIES, J. (1973). *Introduction to behavioral genetics.* San Francisco: W.H. Freeman and Company Publishers.

MCCUNE-NICOLICH, L. (1981). Toward symbolic functioning: Structure of early pretend games and potential parallels with language. *Child Development, 52,* 785-797.

MCDONALD, L., & PIEN, D. (1982). Mother conversational behavior as a function of interactional intent. *Journal of Child Language, 9,* 337-358.

MCDONNELL, P. (1979). Patterns of eye-hand coordination in the first year of life. *Canadian Journal of Psychology, 33,* 253-267.

MCGRAW, M. (1943). *The neuromuscular maturation of the human infant.* New York: Columbia University Press.

MCGURK, H., & LEWIS, M. (1974). Perception in early infancy: Perception within a common auditory-visual space? *Science, 186,* 649-650.

MCGURK, H., TURNURE, C., & CREIGHTON, S. (1977). Auditory-visual coordination in neonates. *Child Development, 48,* 138-143.

MCNEILL, D. (1970). *The acquisition of language: The study of developmental psycholinguistics.* New York: Harper & Row.

MEAD, G.H. (1934). *Mind, self, and society: From the standpoint of a social behaviorist.* Chicago: University of Chicago Press.

MEDNICK, S., MURA, E., SCHULSINGER, F., & MEDNICK, B. (1971). Perinatal conditions and infant development in children with schizophrenic parents. *Social Biology, 8,* 5103-5113.

MEHLER, J., BERTONCINI, J., BARRIERE, M., & JASSIK-GERSCHENFELD, D. (1978). Infant recognition of mother's voice. *Perception, 7,* 491-497.

MEHRABIAN, A., & WILLIAMS, M. (1971). Piagetian measure of cognitive development for children up to age two. *Journal of Psycholinguistic Research, 1,* 113-124.

MELTZOFF, A. (1985). Immediate and deferred imitation in fourteen- and twenty-four-month-old infants. *Child Development, 56,* 62-72.

MELTZOFF, A., & MOORE, M. (1977). Imitation of facial and manual gestures by human neonates. *Science, 198,* 75-78.

MELTZOFF, A., & MOORE, M. (1983a). The origins of imitation in infancy: Paradigm, phenomena, and theories. In L. Lipsitt & C. Rovee-Collier (eds.), *Advances in infancy research* (Vol. 2). Norwood, N.J.: Ablex.

MELTZOFF, A., & MOORE, M. (1983b). Newborn infants imitate adult facial gestures. *Child Development, 54,* 702-709.

MENDELSON, M., & HAITH, M. (1976). The relation between audition and vision in the human newborn. *Monographs of the Society for Research in Child Development, 41,* 167.

MESSER, D. (1978). The integration of mother's referential speech with joint play. *Child Development, 49,* 781-787.

MIRANDA, S., & FANTZ, R. (1974). Recognition memory in Down's syndrome and normal infants. *Child Development, 45,* 651-660.

MISCHEL, W. (1970). Sex typing and socialization. In P. Mussen (ed.), *Carmichael's manual of child psychology.* (3rd ed.). New York: John Wiley.

MOERK, E. (1980). Relationship between parental input frequencies and children's language acquisition: A reanalysis of Brown's data. *Journal of Child Language, 7,* 229-257.

MOFFITT, A. (1971). Consonant cue perception by twenty- to twenty-four-week-old infants. *Child Development, 42,* 717-731.

MOLFESE, D., FREEMAN, R., & PALERMO, D. (1975). The ontogeny of brain lateralization for speech and non-speech stimuli. *Brain and Language, 2,* 356-368.

MOLFESE, D., & MOLFESE, V. (1979). VOT distinctions in infants: Learned or innate? In H. Whitaker (ed.), *Studies in neurolinguistics* (Vol. 4). New York: Academic Press.

MOLFESE, D., MOLFESE, V., & CARRELL, P. (1982). Early language development. In B. Wolman (ed.), *Handbook of developmental psychology.* Englewood Cliffs, N.J.: Prentice-Hall.

MOLNAR, G. (1978). Analysis of motor disorder in retarded infants and young children. *American Journal of Mental Deficiency, 83,* 213-222.

MONEY, J., & EHRHARDT, A. (1972). *Man & woman, boy & girl.* Baltimore: Johns Hopkins Press.

MORGAN, G., & RICCIUTI, H. (1969). Infants' responses to strangers during the first year. In B. Foss (ed.), *Determinants of infant behavior* (Vol. 4). London: Methuen.

MORSE, P., & COWAN, N. (1982). Infant auditory and speech perception. In T. Field, A. Huston, H. Quay, L. Troll, & G. Finley (eds.), *Review of human development.* New York: John Wiley.

MOSKOWITZ, D., SCHWARZ, J., & CORSINI, D. (1977). Initiating day care at three years of age: Effects on attachment. *Child Development, 48,* 1271-1276.

MOSS, H., & ROBSON, K. (1968). The role of protest behavior in the development of the mother-infant attachment. Presented at the American Psychological Association, San Francisco.

MOSS, S., & HOGG, J. (1983). The development and integration of fine motor sequences in 12- to 18-month-old children: A test of the modular theory of motor skill acquisition. *Genetic Psychology Monographs, 107,* 145-187.

MUIR, D., & FIELD, J. (1979). Newborn infants orient to sounds. *Child Development, 50,* 431-436.

MULLER, A., & ASLIN, R. (1978). Visual tracking as an index of the object concept. *Infant Behavior and Development, 1,* 309-319.

MURPHY, C. (1978). Pointing in the context of a shared activity. *Child Development, 49,* 371-380.

NELSON, C., & HOROWITZ, F. (1983). The perception of facial expressions and stimulus motion by two- and five-month-old infants using holographic stimuli. *Child Development, 54,* 868-877.

NELSON, K. (1973a). Structure and strategy in learning to talk. *Monographs of the Society for Research in Child Development, 38,* 149.

NELSON, K. (1973b). Some evidence for the cognitive primacy of categorization and its functional basis. *Merrill Palmer Quarterly, 19,* 21-39.

NELSON, K. (1974). Concept, word, and sentence: Interrelationships in acquisition and development. *Psychological Review, 81,* 267-285.

NELSON, K. (1981). Individual differences in language development: Implications for development and language. *Developmental Psychology, 17,* 170-187.

NELSON, K., RESCORLA, L., GRUENDEL, J., & BENEDICT, H. (1978). Early lexicons: What do they mean? *Child Development, 49,* 960-968.

NEWPORT, E., GLEITMAN, H., & GLEITMAN, L. (1977). Mother, I'd rather do it myself: Some effects and non-effects of maternal speech style. In C. Snow & C. Ferguson (eds.), *Talking to children: Language input and acquisition.* Cambridge: Cambridge University Press.

OLSEN-FULERO, L., & CONFORTI, J. (1983). Child responsiveness to mother questions of varying type and presentation. *Journal of Child Language, 10,* 495-520.

OLSON, G. (1981). The recognition of specific persons. In M. Lamb & L. Sherrod (eds.), *Infant social cognition.* Hillsdale, N.J.: Erlbaum.

OLSON, G., & SHERMAN, T. (1983). Attention, learning, and memory in infants. In P. Mussen (ed.), *Handbook of child psychology* (4th ed.) (Vol. 2). New York: John Wiley.

OLWEUS, D. (1980). Familial and temperamental determinants of aggressive behavior in adolescent boys: A causal analysis. *Developmental Psychology, 16,* 644-660.

OSOFSKY, H. (1975). Relationships between prenatal medical and nutritional measures, pregnancy outcome, and early infant development in an urban poverty setting. I. The role of nutritional intake. *American Journal of Obstetrics and Gynecology, 123,* 682-690.

OSOFSKY, J.D. (1976). Neonatal characteristics and mother-infant interaction in two observational situations. *Child Development, 47,* 1138-1147.

OSOFSKY, J.D., & CONNORS, K. (1979). Mother-infant interaction: An integrative view of a complex system. In J.D. Osofsky (ed.), *Handbook of infant development.* New York: John Wiley.

OSOFSKY, J.D., & DANZGER, B. (1974). Relationships between neonatal characteristics and mother-infant characteristics. *Developmental Psychology, 10,* 124-130.

OSTER, H. (1981). "Recognition" of emotional expression in infancy? In M. Lamb & L. Sherrod (eds.), *Infant social cognition.* Hillsdale, N.J.: Erlbaum.

OSTER, H., & EWY, R. (1980). Discrimination of sad vs. happy faces by 4 month olds: When is a smile seen as a smile? Unpublished manuscript, University of Pennsylvania.

OVIATT, S. (1980). The emerging ability to comprehend language: An experimental approach. *Child Development, 51,* 97-106.

OVIATT, S. (1982). Inferring what words mean: Early development in infants' comprehension of common object names. *Child Development, 53,* 274-277.

OWEN, M., EASTERBROOKS, M., CHASE-LANSDALE, L., & GOLDBERG, W. (1984). The relation between maternal employment status and the stability of attachments to mother and to father. *Child Development, 55,* 1894-1901.

PAINE, P., & PASQUALI, L. (1982). Effects of intrauterine growth and gestational age upon infants' early psychomotor development in Brazil. *Perceptual and Motor Skills, 55,* 871-880.

PALISIN, H. (1980). The neonatal perception inventory: Failure to replicate. *Child Development, 51,* 737-742.

PALKOVITZ, R. (1982). Fathers' birth attendance, early extended contact, and father-infant interaction at five months postpartum. *Birth: Issues in perinatal care and education. 9,* 173-177.

PALKOVITZ, R. (1985). Fathers' birth attendance, early contact, and extended contact with their newborns: A critical review. *Child Development, 56,* 392-406.

PANNABECKER, M.,, EMDE, R., & AUSTIN, B. (1982). The effect of early extended contact on father-newborn interaction. *Journal of Genetic Psychology, 141,* 7-17.

PARKE, R. (1979). Perspectives on father-infant interaction. In J.D. Osofsky (ed.), *Handbook of infant development.* New York: John Wiley.

PARKE, R., & COLLMER, C. (1975). Child abuse: An interdisciplinary approach. In E. Hetherington (ed.), *Review of child development research* (Vol. 5). Chicago: University of Chicago Press.

PARKE, R., & SAWIN, D., (1980). The family in early infancy: Social interactional and attitudinal analyses. In F. Pedersen (ed.), *The father-infant relationship: Observational studies in the family setting.* New York: Praeger.

PARKE, R., & SAWIN, D. (1981). Father-infant interaction in the newborn period: A re-evaluation of some current myths. In E. Hetherington & R. Parke (eds.), *Contemporary readings in child psychology.* New York: McGraw-Hill. (Originally presented at the American Psychological Association, 1975.)

PARKE, R., & SUOMI, S. (1980). Adult male-infant relationships: Human and non-primate evidence. In K. Immelmann, G. Barlow, M. Main, & L. Petrinovitch (eds.), *Behavioral development: The Bielefeld interdisciplinary project.* New York: Cambridge University Press.

PARMELEE, A., & SIGMAN, M. (1983). Perinatal brain development and behavior. In P. Mussen (ed.), *Handbook of child psychology* (4th ed.) (Vol. 2). New York: John Wiley.

PASSMAN, R. (1976). Arousal reducing properties of attachment objects: Testing the functional limits of the security blanket relative to the mother. *Developmental Psychology, 12,* 468-469.

PASTOR, D.L. (1981). The quality of mother-infant attachment and its relationship to toddlers' initial sociability with peers. *Developmental Psychology, 17,* 326-335.

PAVLOV, I. (1927). *Conditioned reflexes.* New York: Oxford University Press.

PEDERSEN, F., ZASLOW, M., CAIN, R., & ANDERSON, B. (1981). Cesarian childbirth: Psychological implications for mothers and fathers. *Infant Mental Health Journal, 2,* 257-263.

PENFIELD, W., & RASMUSSEN, T. (1950). *The cerebral cortex of man.* New York: Macmillan Co.

PENNINGTON, B., & SMITH, S. (1983). Genetic influences on learning disabilities and speech and language disorders. *Child Development, 54,* 369-387.

PIAGET, J. (1926). *The language and thought of the child.* London: Routledge & Kegan Paul.

PIAGET, J. (1952). *The origins of intelligence in children.* New York: W. W. Norton & Co., Inc.

PIAGET, J. (1954). *The construction of reality in the child.* New York: Basic.

PIAGET, J. (1962). *Play, dreams and imitation in childhood.* New York: W.W. Norton & Co., Inc.

PIAGET, J. (1970). Piaget's theory. In P. Mussen (ed.), *Carmichael's manual of child psychology* (3rd ed.) (Vol. 1). New York: John Wiley.

PIAGET, J., & INHELDER, B. (1969). *The psychology of the child.* New York: Basic Books.

PIAGET, J., & INHELDER, B. (1973). *Memory and intelligence.* New York: Basic Books.

PINKER, S. (1981). On the acquisition of grammatical morphemes. *Journal of Child Language, 8,* 477-484.

PITT, B. (1982). Depression and childbirth. In E. Paykel (ed.), *Handbook of affective disorders.* New York: Guilford Press.

PLOMIN, R. (1983). Developmental behavioral genetics. *Child Development, 54,* 253-259.

PORTNOY, F., & SIMMONS, C. (1978). Day care and attachment. *Child Development, 49,* 239-242.

POWER, T., & PARKE, R. (1980). Play as a context for early learning: Lab and home analyses. In I. Sigel & L. Laosa (eds.), *The family as a learning environment.* New York: Plenum.

PRATHER, P., & SPELKE, E. (1982). Three-month-olds' perception of adjacent and partly occluded objects. Presented at International Conference on Infant Studies, Austin, Tex.

PREVITE, J. (1983). *Human physiology.* New York: McGraw-Hill.

QUERLEU, D., & RENARD, K. (1981). Les perceptions auditives du foetus humain. *Medicine et Hygiene, 39,* 2102-2110.

QUILLIGAN, E. (1980). *Fetal and maternal medicine.* New York: John Wiley.

RADER, N., BAUSANO, M., & RICHARDS, J. (1980). On the nature of the visual-cliff avoidance response in human infants. *Child Development, 51,* 61-68.

RADKE-YARROW, M., ZAHN-WAXLER, C., & CHAPMAN, M. (1983). Children's prosocial dispositions and behavior. In P. Mussen (ed.), *Manual of child psychology* (4th ed.) (Vol. 4). New York: John Wiley.

RAMSAY, D., & CAMPOS, J. (1978). The onset of representation and entry into stage 6 object permanence. *Developmental Psychology, 14,* 79-86.

REIDER, R., BROMAN, S., & ROSENTHAL, D. (1977). The offspring of schizophrenics: II. Perinatal factors and I.Q. *Archives of General Psychiatry, 34,* 780-799.

REZNICK, S., & KAGAN, J. (1983). Category detection in infancy. In L. Lipsitt & C. Rovee-Collier (eds.), *Advances in infancy research* (Vol. 2). Norwood, N.J.: Ablex.

RHEINGOLD, H., & COOK, K. (1975). The contents of boys' and girls' rooms and index of parents' behavior. *Child Development, 46,* 459-463.

RHEINGOLD, H., & ECKERMAN, C. (1970). The infant separates himself from his mother. *Science, 168,* 78-83.

RHEINGOLD, H., GEWIRTZ, J., & ROSS, H. (1959). Social conditioning of vocalizations in the infant. *Journal of Comparative and Physiological Psychology, 52,* 58-73.

RICCIUTI, H. (1965). Object grouping and selective ordering behaviors in infants 12 to 24 months. *Merrill-Palmer Quarterly, 11,* 129-148.

RICCIUTI, H. (1974). Fear and development of social attachments in the first year of life. In M. Lewis & L. Rosenblum (eds.), *The origins of human behavior: Fear.* New York: John Wiley.

RICHARDS, J., & RADER, N. (1981). Crawling-onset age predicts cliff avoidance in infants. *Journal of Experimental Psychology: Human Perception and Performance, 7,* 382-387.

RINGLER, N.M., KENNELL, J.H., JARVELLA, R., NAVOJOSKY, B.J., & KLAUS, M. (1975). Mother to child speech at 2 years: Effect of early postnatal contact. *Behavioral Pediatrics, 86,* 141-144.

RINGLER, N.M., TRAUSE, M., KLAUS, M., & KENNELL, J. (1978). The effects of extra postpartum contact and maternal speech patterns on children's IQs, speech, and language comprehension at five. *Child Development, 49,* 862-865.

ROCISSANO, L., & YATCHMINK, Y. (1983). Language skill and interactive patterns in prematurely born toddlers. *Child Development, 54,* 1229-1241.

RODE, S., CHANG, P., FISCH, R., & SROUFE, A. (1981). Attachment patterns of infants separated at birth. *Developmental Psychology, 17,* 188-191.

RODHOLM, M. (1981). Effects of father-infant postpartum contact on their interaction 3 months after birth. *Early Human Development, 5,* 79-85.

RONDAL, J. (1980). Fathers' and mothers' speech in early language development. *Journal of Child Language, 7,* 353-369.

ROSE, S. (1980). Enhancing visual recognition memory in preterm infants. *Developmental Psychology, 16,* 85-92.

ROSE, S. (1981). Developmental changes in infants' retention of visual stimuli. *Child Development, 52,* 227-233.

ROSE, S., GOTTFRIED, A., MELLOY-CARMINAR, P., & BRIDGER, W. (1982). Familiarity and novelty preferences in infant recognition memory: Implications for information processing. *Developmental Psychology, 18,* 704-713.

ROSENBERG, S. (1975). Individual differences in infant attachment: Relationships to mother, infant, and interaction system variables. (Doctoral dissertation, Bowling Green State University) *Dissertation Abstracts International, 36,* 1930B.

ROSENBLATT, D. (1977). Developmental trends in infant play. In B. Tizard & D. Harvey (eds.), *Biology of play.* London: Heineman.

ROSENBLITH, J. (1979). The Graham/Rosenblith Behavioral Examination for newborns: Prognostic value and procedural issues. In J. Osofsky (ed.), *Handbook of infant development.* New York: John Wiley.

ROSENBLUM, L., & HARLOW, H. (1963). Approach-avoidance conflict in the mother surrogate situation. *Psychological Reports, 12,* 83-85.

ROSENTHAL, R., & JACOBSON, L. (1968). *Pygmalion in the classroom: Teacher expectation and pupils' intellectual development.* New York: Holt, Rinehart & Winston.

ROSETT, H., & SANDER, L. (1979). Effects of maternal drinking on neonatal morphology and state regulation. In J. D. Osofsky (ed.), *Handbook of infant development.* New York: John Wiley.

ROSETT, H., SNYDER, P., SANDER, L., LEE, A., COOK, P., WEINER, L., & GOULD, J. (1979). Effects of maternal drinking on neonate state regulation. *Developmental Medicine and Child Neurology, 21,* 464-473.

ROSS, G. (1980). Concept categorization in 1- to 2-year-olds. *Developmental Psychology, 16,* 391-396.

ROTHBART, M. (1981). Measurement of difficult temperament. *Child Development, 52,* 569-578.

ROTHBART, M.K., & DERRYBERRY, D. (1981). Development of individual differences in temperament. In M. Lamb & A. Brown (eds.), *Advances in developmental psychology* (Vol. 1). Hillsdale, N.J.: Erlbaum.

ROVEE-COLLIER, C., & FAGAN, J. (1981). The retrieval of memory in early infancy. In L. Lipsitt & C. Rovee-Collier (eds.), *Advances in infancy research* (Vol. 1). Norwood, N.J.: Ablex.

ROVEE-COLLIER, C., SULLIVAN, M., ENRIGHT, M., LUCAS, D., & FAGAN, J. (1980). Reactivation of infant memory. *Science, 208,* 1159-1161.

RUBIN, J., PROVENZANO, F., & LURIA, Z. (1974). The eye of the beholder: Parents' views on sex of newborns. *American Journal of Orthopsychiatry, 44,* 512-519.

RUBIN, K., FEIN, G., & VANDENBERG, B. (1983). Play. In P. Mussen (ed.), *Handbook of child psychology* (4th ed.) (Vol. 4). New York: John Wiley.

RUFF, H. (1978). Infant recognition of the invariant form of objects. *Child Development, 49,* 293-306.

RUFF, H. (1980). The development of perception and the recognition of objects. *Child Development, 51,* 981-992.

RUFF, H. (1982a). Role of manipulation in infants' responses to invariant properties of objects. *Developmental Psychology, 18,* 682-691.

RUFF, H. (1982b). Object perception. In T. Field, A. Huston, H. Quay, L. Troll, & G. Finley (eds.), *Review of human development.* New York: John Wiley.

RUFF, H. (1982c). Effect of object movement on infants' detection of object structure. *Developmental Psychology, 18,* 462-472.

RUFF, H., & HALTON, A. (1978). Is there directed reaching in the human neonate? *Developmental Psychology, 14,* 425-426.

RUSSELL, C. (1974). Transition to parenthood: Problems and gratifications. *Journal of Marriage and the Family, 36,* 294-301.

RUSSELL, M.J. (1976). Human olfactory communication. *Nature, 260,* 520-522.

RUTTER, M. (1979). Maternal deprivation, 1972-1978: New findings, new concepts, new approaches. *Child Development, 50,* 283-305.

RUTTER, M. (1983). Stress, coping, and development: Some issues and some questions. In N. Garmezy & M. Rutter (eds.), *Stress, coping, and development in children.* New York: McGraw-Hill.

RUTTER, M., & GARMEZY, N. (1983). Developmental psychopathology. In P. Mussen (ed.), *Handbook of child psychology* (4th ed.) (Vol. 4). New York: John Wiley.

SACHS, J., & DEVIN, J. (1976). Young children's use of age-appropriate speech styles. *Journal of Child Language, 3,* 81-98.

SAGI, A., & HOFFMAN, M. (1976). Empathetic distress in the newborn. *Developmental Psychology, 12,* 175-176.

SALAPATEK, P., BECHTOLD, A., & BUSHNELL, E. (1976). Infant visual acuity as a function of viewing distance. *Child Development, 47,* 860-863.

SALTER, A. (1978). Birth without violence: A medical controversy. *Nursing Research, 27,* 84-88.

SAMEROFF, A. (1975). Early influences on development: Fact or fancy. *Merrill-Palmer Quarterly, 21,* 267-294.

SAMEROFF, A., & CAVANAUGH, P. (1979). Learning in infancy: A developmental perspective. In J. Osofsky (ed.), *Handbook of infant development.* New York: John Wiley.

SAMEROFF, A., & CHANDLER, M. (1975). Reproductive risk and the continuum of caretaking casualty. In F. Horowitz (ed.), *Review of child development research* (Vol. 4). Chicago: University of Chicago Press.

SAMEROFF, A., & SEIFER, R. (1983). Familial risk and child competence. *Child Development, 54,* 1254-1268.

SAMEROFF, A., SEIFER, R., & ZAX, M. (1982). Early development of children at risk for emotional disorders. *Monographs of the Society for Research in Child Development, 47,* 199.

SAYEGH, Y., & DENNIS, W. (1965). The effect of supplementary experiences upon the behavioral development of infants in institutions. *Child Development, 36,* 81-90.

SCARR, S., & MCCARTNEY, K. (1983). How people make their own environments: A theory of genotype → environment effects. *Child Development, 54,* 424-435.

SCARR, S., & WEINBERG, R. (1983). The Minnesota Adoption Studies: Genetic differences and malleability. *Child Development, 54,* 260-267.

SCHACHTER, F., SHORE, E., HODAPP, R., CHALFIN, S., & BUNDY, C. (1978). Do girls talk earlier? Mean length of utterance in toddlers. *Developmental Psychology, 14,* 388-392.

SCHAFFER, H. (1966). The onset of fear of strangers and the incongruity hypothesis. *Journal of Child Psychology and Psychiatry, 7,* 95-106.

SCHAFFER, H., & EMERSON, P. (1964). The development of social attachments in infancy. *Monographs of the Society for Research in Child Development, 29,* 94.

SCHIEFFELIN, B., & OCHS, E. (1983). A cultural perspective on the transition from prelinguistic to linguistic communication. In R. Golinkoff (ed.), *The transition from prelinguistic to linguistic communication.* Hillsdale, N.J.: Erlbaum.

SCHNEIDER-ROSEN, K., & CICCHETTI, D. (1984). The relationship between affect and cognition in maltreated infants: Quality of attachment and the development of visual self-recognition. *Child Development, 55,* 648-658.

SCHUBERTH, R. (1983). The infant's search for objects: Alternatives to Piaget's theory of concept development. In L. Lipsitt & C. Rovee-Collier (eds.), *Advances in infancy research* (Vol. 2). Norwood, N.J.: Ablex.

SCHWARTZ, P. (1983). Length of day-care attendance and attachment behavior in eighteen-month-old infants. *Child Development, 54,* 1073-1078.

SEARS, R., MACCOBY, E., & LEVIN, H. (1957). *Patterns of child rearing.* Evanston, Ill.: Row-Peterson.

SEASHORE, M., LEIFER, A., BARNETT, C., & LEIDERMAN, H. (1973). The effects of denial of mother-infant interaction on maternal self-confidence. *Journal of Personality and Social Psychology, 26,* 369-378.

SELIGMAN, M. (1970). On the generality of the laws of learning. *Psychological Review, 77,* 406-418.

SHAFFER, D. (1980). The development of bladder control. In M. Rutter (ed.), *Scientific foundations of developmental psychology.* London: Heinemann.

SHATZ, M., & GELMAN, R. (1973). The development of communication skills: Modifications in the speech of young children as a function of listener. *Monographs of the Society for Research in Child Development, 38,* 152.

SHERROD, L. (1979). Social cognition in infants: Attention to the human face. *Infant Behavior and Development, 2,* 279-294.

SHERROD, L. (1981). Issues in cognitive-perceptual development: The special case of social stimuli. In M. Lamb & L. Sherrod (eds.), *Infant social cognition.* Hillsdale, N.J.: Erlbaum.

SHIRLEY, M.M. (1933). *The first two years: A study of twenty-five babies.* Minneapolis: University of Minnesota Press.

SIEGEL, L. (1983a). Correction for prematurity and its consequences for the assessment of the very low birth weight infant. *Child Development, 54,* 1176-1188.

SIEGEL, L. (1983b). The prediction of possible learning disabilities in preterm and full-term children. In T. Field & A. Sostek (eds.), *Infants born at risk: Physiological, perceptual, and cognitive processes.* New York: Grune & Stratton.

SIMPKISS, M., & RAIKES, A. (1972). Problems resulting from the excessive use of baby-walkers and baby-bouncers. *Lancet, 1,* 747.

SINCLAIR DE ZWART, H. (1973). Language acquisition and cognitive development. In T. Moore (ed.), *Cognitive development and the acquisition of language.* New York: Academic Press.

SKEELS, H. (1966). Adult status of children with contrasting early life experiences. *Monographs of the Society for Research in Child Development, 31,* 105.

SKINNER, B.F. (1957). *Verbal behavior.* New York: Appleton-Century-Crofts.

SKINNER, B.F. (1974). *About behaviorism.* New York: Knopf.

SLOBIN, D., & WELCH, C. (1973). Elicited imitation as a research tool in developmental psycholinguistics. In C. Ferguson & D. Slobin (eds.), *Studies of child language development.* New York: Holt, Rinehart & Winston.

SMOLAK, L. (1982). Cognitive precursors of receptive vs. expressive language. *Journal of Child Language, 9,* 13-22.

SMOLAK, L., & LEVINE, M. (1984). The effects of differential criteria on the assessment of cognitive-linguistic relationships. *Child Development, 55,* 973-980.

SMOLAK, L., & WEINRAUB, M. (1983). Maternal speech: Strategy or response? *Journal of Child Language, 10,* 369-380.

SNOW, C. (1972). Mothers' speech to children learning language. *Child Development, 43,* 549-565.

SNOW, M., JACKLIN, C., & MACCOBY, E. (1983). Sex-of-child differences in father-child interaction at one year of age. *Child Development, 54,* 227-232.

SNYDER, L., BATES, E., & BRETHERTON, I. (1981). Content and context in early lexical development. *Journal of Child Language, 8,* 565-582.

SORRELLS-JONES, J. (1983). *A comparison of the effects of Leboyer delivery and modern "routine" childbirth in a randomized sample.* Unpublished doctoral dissertation, University of Chicago.

SOSTEK, A., & WYATT, R. (1982). The chemistry of crankiness. *Psychology Today, 15* (Oct.), 120.

SOSTEK, A., SAMEROFF, A., & SOSTEK, A. (1972). Failure of newborns to demonstrate classically conditioned Babkin responses. *Child Development, 43,* 509-519.

SPAN, P. (1984). Can you raise your baby to be a genius? Should you try? *Glamour, 82,* 292-293, 344-346.

SPELKE, E. (1976). Infants' intermodal perception of events. *Cognitive Psychology, 8,* 553-560.

SPELKE, E. (1979). Perceiving bimodally specified events in infancy. *Developmental Psychology, 15,* 626-636.

SPELKE, E., & CORTELYOU, A. (1981). Perceptual aspects of social knowing: Looking and listening in infancy. In M. Lamb & L. Sherrod (eds.), *Infant social cognition.* Hillsdale, N.J.: Erlbaum.

SPELKE, E., & OWSLEY, C. (1979). Intermodal exploration and knowledge in infancy. *Infant Behavior and Development, 2,* 13-27.

SPITZ, R. (1945/1973). Hospitalism: An inquiry into the genesis of psychiatric conditions in early childhood. In L.J. Stone, H. Smith, & L. Murphy (eds.), *The competent infant.* New York: Basic Books.

SPITZ, R. (1946/1973). Hospitalism: A follow-up report. In L. Stone, H. Smith, & L. Murphy (eds.), *The competent infant.* New York: Basic Books.

SPOCK, B.J. (1977). *Baby and child care.* New York: Wallaby.

STECHLER, G., & HALTON, A. (1982). Prenatal influences on human development. In B.

Wolman (ed.), *Handbook of developmental psychology*. Englewood Cliffs, N.J.: Prentice-Hall.

STEPHAN, C., & LANGLOIS, J. (1984). Baby beautiful: Adult attributions of infant competence as a function of infant attractiveness. *Child Development, 55*, 576-586.

STEVENSON, M., & LAMB, M. (1979). Effects of infant sociability and the caretaking environment on infant cognitive performance. *Child Development, 50*, 338-349.

STEWART, R. (1983). Sibling attachment relationships: Child input interactions in the strange situation. *Developmental Psychology, 19*, 192-199.

SULLIVAN, J., & HOROWITZ, F. (1983). Infant intermodal perception and maternal multimodal stimulation: Implications for language development. In L. Lipsitt & C. Rovee-Collier (eds.), *Advances in infancy research* (Vol. 2). Norwood, N.J.: Ablex.

SULLIVAN, M., ROVEE-COLLIER, C., & TYNES, D. (1979). A conditioning analysis of infant long-term memory. *Child Development, 50*, 152-162.

SUPER, C.M. (1981). Behavioral development in infancy. In R.H. Munroe, R.L. Munroe, & B. Whiting (eds.), *Handbook of cross-cultural human development*. New York: Garland STPM Press.

SUTTON-SMITH, B. (1982). Birth order and sibling status effects. In M. Lamb & B. Sutton-Smith (eds.), *Sibling relationships: Their nature and significance across the life-span*. Hillsdale, N.J.: Erlbaum.

SVEDJA, M., CAMPOS, J., & EMDE, R. (1980). Mother-infant "bonding": Failure to generalize. *Child Development, 56*, 775-779.

SVEDJA, M., PANNABECKER, B., & EMDE, R. (1982). Parent-to-infant attachment: A critique of the early "bonding" model. In R. Emde & R. Harmon (eds.), *The development of attachment and affiliative systems*. New York: Plenum.

TANNER, J. (1970). Physical growth. In P. Mussen (ed.), *Carmichael's manual of child psychology* (3rd ed.) (Vol. 1). New York: John Wiley.

TANNER, J. (1978). *Foetus into man: Physical growth from conception to maturity*. London: Open Books.

TENNES, K. (1982). The role of hormones in mother-infant transactions. In R. Emde & R. Harmon (eds.), *The development of attachment and affiliative systems*. New York: Plenum.

THELEN, E. (1981). Rhythmical behavior in infancy: An ethological perspective. *Developmental Psychology, 17*, 237-257.

THELEN, E., & FISHER, D. (1982). Newborn stepping: An explanation for a "disappearing" reflex. *Developmental Psychology, 18*, 760-775.

THELEN, E., & FISHER, D. (1983). From spontaneous to instrumental behavior: Kinematic analysis of movement changes during very early learning. *Child Development, 54*, 129-140.

THOMAN, E., TURNER, A., LEIDERMAN, P.H., & BARNETT, C. (1970). Neonate-mother interaction: Effects of parity on feeding behavior. *Child Development, 41*, 1103-1111.

THOMAS, A. (1982). The study of difficult temperament: A reply to Kagan, Rothbart, and Plomin. *Merrill-Palmer Quarterly, 28*, 313-315.

THOMAS, A., & CHESS, S. (1977). *Temperament and development*. New York: Brunner/Mazel.

THOMAS, A., & CHESS, S. (1980). *The dynamics of psychological development*. New York: Brunner/Mazel.

THOMAS, A., CHESS, S., & BIRCH, H. (1970). The origin of personality. *Scientific American, 223*, 102-109.

THOMPSON, R., & LAMB, M. (1983). Security of attachment and stranger sociability in infancy. *Developmental Psychology, 19*, 184-191.

THOMPSON, R., LAMB, M., & ESTES, D. (1982). Stability of infant-mother attachment and its relationship to changing life circumstances in an unselected middle class sample. *Child Development, 53*, 144-148.

THOMPSON, R., LAMB, M., & ESTES, D. (1983). Harmonizing discordant notes: A reply to Waters. *Child Development, 54*, 521-524.

TIME. (1983). What do babies know? Aug. 15, 52-59.

TIME. (1984). Behavior: Polling for mental health. Oct. 15, 80.

TIMERAS, P. (1972). *Developmental physiology and aging*. New York: Macmillan.

TORGENSEN, A. (1981). Genetic factors in temperamental individuality: A longitudinal study of same-sexed twins from two months to six years of age. *Journal of the American Academy of Child Psychiatry, 20,* 702-711.

TREHUB, S. (1976). The discrimination of foreign speech contrasts by infants and adults. *Child Development, 47,* 446-472.

TREVARTHEN, C. (1979). Communication and cooperation in early infancy. In M. Bullowa (ed.), *Before speech: The beginning of interpersonal communication.* Cambridge: Cambridge University Press.

TREVATHAN, W. (1981). Maternal touch at 1st contact with the newborn infant. *Developmental Psychobiology, 14,* 549-558.

TRONICK, E., & BRAZELTON, T.B. (1975). Clinical uses of the Brazelton Neonatal Behavioral Assessment. In B. Friedlander, G. Sterritt, & G. Kirk (eds.), *Exceptional infant 3: Assessment and intervention.* New York: Brunner/Mazel.

TWITCHELL, T. (1970). Reflex mechanisms and the development of prehension. In K. Connolly (ed.), *Mechanisms of motor skill development.* London: Academic Press.

UNGERER, J., & SIGMAN, M. (1983). Developmental lags in preterm infants from one to three years of age. *Child Development, 54,* 1217-1228.

USDHEW (1979). *Pregnancy and infant health.*

UZGIRIS, I., & HUNT, J. (1975). *Assessment in infancy: Ordinal scales of psychological development.* Urbana-Champaign: University of Illinois Press.

VANDELL, D., WILSON, K., & BUCHANAN, N. (1980). Peer interaction in the first year of life: An examination of its structure, content, and sensitivity to toys. *Child Development, 51,* 481-488.

VAUGHN, B., EGELAND, B., SROUFE, L.A., & WATERS, E. (1979). Individual differences in infant-mother attachment at twelve and eighteen months. *Child Development. 50,* 971-975.

VAUGHN, B., GOVE, F., & EGELAND, B. (1980). The relationship between out-of-home care and the quality of infant-mother attachment in an economically disadvantaged sample. *Child Development. 51,* 1203-1214.

VON HOFSTEN, C. (1982). Eye-hand coordination in the newborn. *Developmental Psychology, 18,* 450-467.

VON HOFSTEN, C. (1983). Foundations for perceptual development. In L. Lipsitt & C. Rovee-Collier (eds.), *Advances in infancy research* (Vol. 2). Norwood, N.J.: Ablex.

VON HOFSTEN, C. (1984). Developmental changes in the organization of prereaching movements. *Developmental Psychology, 20,* 378-388.

WABER, D. (1977). Sex differences in mental abilities, hemispheric lateralization and rate of physical growth at adolescence. *Developmental Psychology, 13,* 29-38.

WADA, J., CLARKE, R., & HAMM, A. (1975). Cerebral hemispheric symmetry in humans. *Archives of Neurology, 32,* 239-246.

WACHTEL, S. (1983). *H-Y antigen and the biology of sex determination.* New York: Grune & Stratton.

WALK, R. (1966). The development of depth perception in animals and human infants. In H. Stevenson (ed.), Concept of development. *Monographs of the Society for Research in Child Development, 31,* 107.

WALKER, E., & EMORY, E. (1983). Infants at risk for psychopathology: Offspring of schizophrenic parents. *Child Development, 54,* 1269-1285.

WALLERSTEIN, J. (1983). Children of divorce: Stress and developmental tasks. In N. Garmezy & M. Rutter (eds.), *Stress, coping, and development in children.* New York: McGraw-Hill.

WATERS, E. (1978). The reliability and stability of individual differences in infant-mother attachment. *Child Development, 49,* 483-494.

WATERS, E. (1983). The stability of individual differences in attachment: Comments on the Thompson, Lamb, and Estes contribution. *Child Development, 54,* 516-520.

WATERS, E., VAUGHN, B., & EGELAND, B. (1980). Individual differences in infant-mother attachment relationships at age one: Antecedents in neonatal behavior in an urban economically disadvantaged sample. *Child Development, 51,* 208-216.

WATERS, E., WIPPMAN, J., & SROUFE, L.A. (1979). Attachment, positive affect, and competence in the peer group: Two studies in construct validation. *Child Development, 50,* 821-829.

WATSON, J. (1928). *Psychological care of infant and child.* New York: W.W. Norton & Co., Inc.

WATSON, J., & RAYNER, R. (1920). Conditioned emotional reactions. *Journal of Experimental Psychology, 3,* 1-14.

WATSON, J., & WATSON, R. (1921). Studies in infant psychology. *Scientific Monitor, 13,* 493-515.

WATSON, J.S. (1966). Perception of object orientation in infants. *Merrill-Palmer Quarterly, 12,* 73-92.

WATSON, J.S. (1979). Perception of contingency as a determinant of social responsiveness. In E. Thoman (ed.), *Origins of the infant's social responsiveness.* Hillsdale, N.J.: Erlbaum.

WEINER, B., & GOODNOW, J. (1970). Motor activity: Effects on memory. *Developmental Psychology, 2,* 448.

WEINRAUB, M. (1978). Fatherhood: The myth of the second-class parent. In J. Stevens & M. Mathews (eds.), *Mother/child father/child relationships.* Washington, D.C.: National Association for the Education of Young Children.

WEINRAUB, M., & LEWIS, M. (1977). The determinants of children's responses to separation. *Monographs of the Society for Research in Child Development, 42,* 172.

WEINRAUB, M., & PUTNEY, E. (1978). The effects of height on infants' social responses to unfamiliar persons. *Child Development, 49,* 598-603.

WEINRAUB, M., & WOLF, B. (1983). Effects of stress and social supports on mother-child interactions in single- and two-parent families. *Child Development, 54,* 1297-1311.

WEISBERG, P. (1963). Social and nonsocial conditioning of infant vocalizations. *Child Development, 34,* 377-388.

WEIZMANN, E., COHEN, L., & PRATT, J. (1971). Novelty, familarity, and the development of infant attention. *Developmental Psychology, 4,* 149-154.

WELLS, G. (1980). Adjustments in adult-child conversation: Some effects of interaction. In H. Gils, W. Robinson, & P. Smith (eds.), *Language: Social psychological perspectives.* Oxford: Pergamon Press.

WENTE, A., & CROCKENBERG, S. (1976). Transition to fatherhood: Pre-natal Lamaze preparation, adjustment difficulty and the adult husband-wife relationship. *Family Coordinator, 25,* 351-357.

WERNER, E., & SMITH, R. (1982). *Vulnerable but invincible: A study of resilient children.* New York: McGraw-Hill.

WERNER, E., BIERMAN, J., & FRENCH, F. (1971). *The children of Kauai: A longitudinal study from the prenatal period to age ten.* Honolulu: University of Hawaii Press.

WERNER, H. (1967). The concept of development from a comparative and organismic point of view. In D. Harris (ed.), *The concept of development.* Minneapolis: University of Minnesota Press.

WERNER, J., & SIQUELAND, E. (1978). Visual recognition memory in the preterm infant. *Infant Behavior and Development, 1,* 79-94.

WEST, M., & RHEINGOLD, H. (1978). Infant stimulation of maternal instruction. *Infant Behavior and Development, 1,* 205-215.

WHITE, B. (1970). Experience and the development of motor mechanisms in infancy. In K. Connolly (ed.), *Mechanisms of motor skill development.* London: Academic Press.

WHITE, B., CASTLE, P., & HELD, R. (1964). Observations on the development of visually directed reaching. *Child Development, 35,* 349-364.

WILLIAMS, J. (1979). *The psychology of women.* New York: W.W. Norton.

WINGERD, J., & SCHOEN, E. (1974). Factors influencing length at birth and height at 5 years. *Pediatrics, 53,* 737-741.

WINICK, M. (1971). Cellular growth during early malnutrition. *Pediatrics, 47,* 969-978.

WINNICOTT, D. (1964). *The child, the family and the outside world.* London: Penguin.

WITELSON, S., & PALLIE, W. (1973). Left hemisphere specialization for language in the newborn: Neuroanatomical evidence of asymmetry. *Brain, 96,* 641-646.

WOLF, D., & GARDNER, H. (1979). Style and sequence in early symbolic play. In N. Smith & M. Franklin (eds.), *Symbolic functioning in childhood.* Hillsdale, N.J.: Erlbaum.

WOLFF, P.H. (1963). Observations on the early development of smiling. In B. Foss (ed.), *Determinants of infant behavior.* II. New York: John Wiley.

WOLFF, P.H. (1966). The causes, controls and organization of behavior in the neonate. *Psychological Issues, 5,* 105.

WOLFF, P.H. (1973). The natural history of crying and other vocalizations in infancy. In L.J. Stone, H.T. Smith, & L.B. Murphy (eds.), *The competent infant.* New York: Basic Books.

YARROW, L.J. (1979). Historical perspectives and future directions in infant development. In J.D. Osofsky (ed.), *Handbook of infant development.* New York: John Wiley.

ZACHRY, W. (1978). Ordinality and interdependence of representation and language development in infancy. *Child Development, 49,* 681-687.

ZAPOROZHETS, A. (1965). The development of perception in the preschool child. In P. Mussen (ed.), European research in cognitive development. *Monographs of the Society for Research in Child Development, 30,* 100.

ZASLOW, M., PEDERSEN, F., KRAMER, E., CAIN, R., SUWALSKY, J., & FIVEL, M. (1981). Depressed mood in new fathers: Interview and behavioral correlates. Presented at the Society for Research in Child Development, Boston.

ZELAZO, P. (1976). From reflexive to instrumental behavior. In L. Lipsitt (ed.), *Developmental psychobiology: The significance of infancy.* Hillsdale, N.J.: Erlbaum.

ZELAZO, P., KEARSLEY, R., & UNGERER, J. (1984). *Learning to speak: A manual for parents.* Hillsdale, N.J.: Erlbaum.

ZELAZO, P., ZELAZO, N., & KOLB, S. (1972). "Walking" in the newborn. *Science, 176,* 314-315.

ZESKIND, P., & LESTER, B. (1978). Acoustic features and auditory perceptions of the cries of newborns with prenatal and perinatal complications. *Child Development, 49,* 580-589.

ZESKIND, P., & RAMEY, C. (1978). Fetal malnutrition: An experimental study of its consequences on infant development in two caregiving environments. *Child Development, 49,* 1155-1162.

Index